RUDE AWAKENINGS

NANZAN STUDIES IN RELIGION AND CULTURE
James W. Heisig, General Editor

Heinrich Dumoulin. *Zen Buddhism: A History. Vol. 1, India and China.* Trans. James Heisig and Paul Knitter (New York: Macmillan, 1988, 1994)

Heinrich Dumoulin. *Zen Buddhism: A History. Vol. 2, Japan.* Trans. James Heisig and Paul Knitter (New York: Macmillan, 1989)

Frederick Franck, ed. *The Buddha Eye: An Anthology of the Kyoto School* (New York: Crossroad, 1982)

Frederick Franck. *To Be Human Against All Odds* (Berkeley: Asian Humanities Press, 1991)

Winston L. King. *Death Was His Kōan: The Samurai-Zen of Suzuki Shōsan* (Berkeley: Asian Humanities Press, 1986)

Paul Mommaers and Jan Van Bragt. *Mysticism Buddhist and Christian: Encounters with Jan van Ruusbroec* (New York: Crossroad, 1995)

Robert E. Morrell. *Early Kamakura Buddhism: A Minority Report* (Berkeley: Asian Humanities Press, 1987)

Nagao Gadjin. *The Foundational Standpoint of Mādhyamika Philosophy.* Trans. John Keenan (New York: SUNY Press, 1989)

Nishida Kitarō. *Intuition and Reflection in Self-Consciousness.* Trans. Valdo Viglielmo et al. (New York: SUNY Press, 1987)

Nishitani Keiji. *Nishida Kitarō* (Berkeley: University of California Press, 1991)

Nishitani Keiji. *Religion and Nothingness.* Trans. Jan Van Bragt (Berkeley: University of California Press, 1985)

Nishitani Keiji. *The Self-Overcoming of Nihilism.* Trans. Graham Parkes and Setsuko Aihara (New York: SUNY Press, 1990)

Paul L. Swanson. *Foundations of T'ien-T'ai Philosophy: The Flowering of the Two-Truths Theory in Chinese Buddhism* (Berkeley: Asian Humanities Press, 1989)

Takeuchi Yoshinori. *The Heart of Buddhism: In Search of the Timeless Spirit of Primitive Buddhism.* Trans. James Heisig (New York: Crossroad, 1983)

Tanabe Hajime. *Philosophy as Metanoetics.* Trans. Takeuchi Yoshinori et al. (Berkeley: University of California Press, 1987)

Taitetsu Unno, ed. *The Religious Philosophy of Nishitani Keiji: Encounter with Emptiness* (Berkeley: Asian Humanities Press, 1990)

Taitetsu Unno and James Heisig, eds. *The Religious Philosophy of Tanabe Hajime: The Metanoetic Imperative* (Berkeley: Asian Humanities Press, 1990)

Hans Waldenfels. *Absolute Nothingness: Foundations for a Buddhist-Christian Dialogue.* Trans. James Heisig (New York: Paulist Press, 1980)

RUDE AWAKENINGS

Zen, the Kyoto School, & the Question of Nationalism

EDITED BY

James W. Heisig & John C. Maraldo

University of Hawai'i Press
HONOLULU

00 99 98 97 96 95   5 4 3 2 1

Library of Congress Cataloging-in-Publication Data

Rude awakenings : Zen, the Kyoto school, & the question of nationalism /
    edited by James W. Heisig, & John C. Maraldo.
        p.   cm. — (Nanzan studies in religion and culture)
    Includes bibliographical references and index.
    ISBN 0–8248–1735–4 — ISBN 0–8248–1746–X (pbk.)
    1. Philosophy, Japanese—20th century. 2. Religion—Philosophy.
    3. Zen Buddhism—Philosophy. 4. Nationalism—Japan. I. Heisig,
    James W., 1944– . II. Maraldo, John C., 1942– . III. Series.
    B5241.R83 1995
    181' . 12—dc20   94–49174
                                                                CIP

Camera-ready copy for this book was prepared by James Heisig

Contents

PART ONE
Questioning Zen

PART TWO
Questioning Nishida

PART THREE
Questioning Modernity

Editors' Introduction

E ACH OF THE ESSAYS in this book examines the relationship between Japanese nationalism and intellectuals in the Kyoto school and the world of Zen. All the contributions were originally presented at a week-long international symposium held in March 1994 outside of Santa Fe, New Mexico, and subsequently revised in preparation for this volume.

The definition of the "Kyoto school" has undergone a change from the time that the name was first introduced in 1931 by Tosaka Jun as a way of branding what he perceived as a rightist tendency in the circle around Nishida Kitarō, Japan's foremost modern philosopher. When the thought of Nishitani Keiji, Tanabe Hajime, Takeuchi Yoshinori, Ueda Shizuteru, Abe Masao, and Nishida himself began to spread in translation through philosophical and religious circles in the West in the 1980s, it rode the wave of the current popularity of Zen thought, whose inspiration was apparent in many of these thinkers. It traveled with little or none of the stigma associated with the fate of Japan's intelligentsia during and after the war. The names of Suzuki Shigetaka, Kōsaka Masaaki, and Kōyama Iwao—all of whom were well known to historians of Japanese nationalism—were left aside as secondary figures, if indeed they were recognized as members of the school at all. Absent the entire problematic of the war years, the phrase "Kyoto school" soon became synonymous with a wide-eyed, open-minded approach to religious philosophy that seemed to answer the need for a serious encounter between East and West as few contemporary systems of thought have.

Among intellectual historians of Japan, particularly those working in the United States, the enthusiastic reception of the Kyoto school religious philosophy in Europe and North America came as something of a surprise. For by and large, the comparative philosophers and theologians who were giving these Japanese thinkers their warm welcome had simply overlooked the political implications of their thought, especially during World War II. Today, the situation has clearly changed.

If there is one single factor we can point to as having brought the political aspect to the fore, it is the case of Martin Heidegger. In the light of new revelations of Heidegger's associations with the German Nazi Party, affections for Heideggerian thought underwent a sea change, and in the process the consciousness of a generation was awakened as perhaps never before to the political practices of supposedly apolitical philosophers and scholars. It was only a matter of time before this rude awakening was transmitted to those attracted to the philosophy of the Kyoto school, not to mention Zen Buddhism.

It was against this backdrop that a group of sixteen scholars (eight Japanese, six from the United States, one Canadian, one Mexican, and one Belgian) gathered to share the results of their research and reflections on the question of nationalism in Zen and the Kyoto school. The present book is a result of the long hours of discussion and debate during the symposium. The essays wind in and out of each other like different colored strings. The four strands that are identified in the table of contents are only one possible way of braiding the concerns into some kind of order.

The first of these strands, "Questioning Zen," has to do with the conflict between Japanese Zen's strong emphasis on transcendence on the one hand, and its actual involvement in secular history on the other, even to the point of vociferous support for militaristic nationalism during the war. *Hirata Seikō* argues that because Zen transcends ethics, it is equally neutral towards participation in war and towards participation in opposition to war. Of itself, Zen is concerned with insight not about how the world is or ought to be run, but only about the nature of the self. *Christopher Ives* presents the counter-position of Ichikawa Hakugen, a postwar Zen activist who insisted that Zen needs to cultivate a moral posture in the secular world. Following Ichikawa's lead, Ives questions the connections between the wartime complicity of Zen leaders and the Zen-inspired philosophy of Nishida.

Kirita Kiyohide's exhaustive research into the writings and letters of D. T. Suzuki leads him to conclude that, short of exposing himself directly to the military authorities, Suzuki did what he could to counter the war effort and its ruling ideology, and that he did so in line with a view of the state that he had held since his earliest writings. *Robert Sharf* undercuts the entire debate about Zen and ethics by claiming that the world-transcending tradition of Japanese Zen which is being questioned is not the historical fact that Suzuki and others have claimed, but a distinctively contemporary construct read back into history.

The second strand, "Questioning Nishida," deals with the patriarch of the Kyoto school, whose writings on the emperor system and Japanese culture were used—or misused—as a philosophical justification of militaristic ideology during the war, and of the search for cultural uniqueness in postwar Japan. *Ueda Shizuteru's* essay revolves around what he calls the "tug-of-war over meaning" between Nishida and the Army for the legitimation of important traditional Japanese concepts. He precedes his argument with a historical analysis of why the problem arose in the first place and follows it with a presentation of Nishida's crowning vision of a pluralistic world order. *Yusa Michiko's* careful study of Nishida's letters and diaries supports Ueda's position by uncovering meanings and intentions that are not always clear in the philosophical writings. These data bring to light a politically active side of Nishida that has yet to receive the full recognition she feels it deserves. *Agustín Jacinto* looks at the final years of Nishida's life, which ended just months before Japan's defeat in the war, and examines the critical notion of "tradition" which underpinned his late thought. He draws a careful distinction between Nishida's support for the mythological Imperial Throne, which belongs to the founding ideal of the nation, and Nishida's view of the actual emperor who belongs to the world of historical fact and moral judgment. The question of whether or to what extent Nishida understood the Imperial Throne as a model for other nations is left open.

A third strand, "Questioning Modernity," considers attempts by Japan's intellectuals to find an alternative to Eurocentric and Western-dominated views of world and nation. The symposium on "Overcoming Modernity" held in 1943 is the focus of an essay by *Minamoto Ryōen*, who examines the background and content of those debates and presents an overview of right-wing and left-wing thinking in Japan at the time. He focuses in particular on the contributions of symposium participants associated with the Kyoto school. *Kevin Doak* argues that Japanese nationalism is best understood as a consequence of competing ideologies in modern Japan. He shows how populist visions of the identity of a people or "ethnic nation" vied with government efforts to define the role of the nation state in the modern world, and how Buddhism lent its voice to the search for national identity. *Andrew Feenberg* draws Nishida into the debate about modernity, and shows how his philosophy attempted to articulate the particular contribution Japanese culture could make to a world increasingly defined by Western science and technology. He contrasts Nishida's vision of an alternative modernity based on Eastern culture with Heidegger's brand of nationalism and disillusionment with technology. Despite the fate that this vision suffered at the hands of Japan's wartime state nationalism, Feenberg suggests that Nishida's insights into cultural pluralism are still of value to us today.

The fourth and final strand in the braid, "Questioning the Kyoto School," brings together a series of inquiries dealing with specific thinkers. *James Heisig* looks at the figure of Tanabe Hajime, whose critics—and indeed whose own philosophy of repentance—have raised questions about his complicity in the war effort. An analysis of the elusive notion of the "logic of the specific" reveals how Tanabe had within his grasp a philosophical idea leading in the very opposite direction of the spirit of nationalism with which he flirted during the war. *Horio Tsutomu* presents a detailed synopsis of the background and contents of the notorious *Chūōkōron* discussions which brought four Kyoto-school thinkers together in 1941 and 1942 for a series of dialogues on subjects directly touching on the military's ideology. In so doing, Horio sharpens many of the questions that history today is asking of the

Kyoto philosophers. Nishitani Keiji, one of the four participants in those discussions, is the focus of an essay by *Mori Tetsuo*, who tries to distance Nishitani's view of the nation and the world from the misunderstandings that have surrounded it.

Jan Van Bragt asks the broader question of whether Kyoto philosophy itself, as seen in Nishitani, Nishida, Tanabe, and in the *Chūōkōron* discussions, is intrinsically nationalistic or only incidentally so. With careful qualification, he comes down on the side of an intrinsic nationalism in their thought. A final essay by *John Maraldo* takes up three figures from among Zen and Kyoto-school thinkers—D. T. Suzuki, Masao Abe, and Nishitani—to consider what is involved in criticizing positions that in their own way were themselves critiques of nationalism. Since critics themselves do not transcend the critical process, responsible critiques of nationalism inevitably make the past into a present, and personal, concern.

No doubt, under conditions of a totalitarian regime like Japan's during the war, the semantic rules are not the same as they are for us today. Even the most abstract philosophical ideas invariably take on the concrete significance of questioning the powers-that-be. At the end of our own labors, the number of questions left unanswered, or only partially answered, is greater than it was at the beginning. The problem of what the Kyoto-school thinkers meant by attributing "subjectivity" to the state, the lack of clarity in the distinction between state nationalism and cultural nationalism, the disparity between the intentions of writers and the effects their writings produce in times of crisis, the relationship between the Kyoto school in the narrow sense and thinkers such as Watsuji Tetsurō and Miki Kiyoshi who were also involved in questions of nationalism—these issues and more remain with us still. In that sense, too, the whole project has been something of a rude awakening.

This book, and the symposium on which it was based, would not have been possible without the generous assistance of the Taniguichi Foundation and the coordinating efforts of Horio Tsutomu and other members of the Kyoto Zen Symposium Committee. Others assisted as well. Sakai Naoki made a substantial contribution to the symposium discussions. The efforts of the translators, Mark Unno and Thomas Kirchner, helped keep the language barrier from interfering with the lively flow of ideas. Tom Schifanella volunteered the cover design for this volume and Mary Jo Maraldo did the calligraphy. To all of them, our thanks. The editors would also like to acknowledge the fellows and staff of the Nanzan Institute for Religion and Culture who assisted in the production of the volume, and to thank Pat Crosby of the University of Hawaii Press for her warm interest and support.

22 September 1994

Contributors

Kevin M. DOAK is Assistant Professor of Modern Japanese History in the Department of History and the Department of East Asian Languages and Cultures at the University of Illinois at Urbana-Champaign. He has authored a volume on *Dreams of Difference: The Japan Romantic School and the Crisis of Modernity*, and is currently doing research on cultural and ethnic nationalism in modern Japan.

Andrew FEENBERG is Professor of Philosophy at San Diego State University. He is the author of *Lukacs, Marx, and the Sources of Critical Theory*, *Critical Theory of Technology*, numerous articles on computer-mediated communications, and the forthcoming *Alternative Modernity* and *Technology and the Politics of Knowledge*. In the area of Japanese philosophy he has published, together with Y. Arisaka, "Experiential Ontology: The Origins of Nishida Philosophy in the Doctrine of Pure Experience."

James W. HEISIG is Director of the Nanzan Institute for Religion and Culture in Nagoya, Japan. He has authored, translated, and edited over twenty books, including *Imago Dei: A Study of C. G. Jung's Psychology of Religion* and *El cuento detrás del cuento: Un ensayo sobre psique y mito*. He is also general editor of a nineteen-volume series of books that includes twelve titles directly related to the thought of the Kyoto school.

HIRATA Seikō 平田精耕 is Head Abbot of Tenryū Temple in Kyoto. Until recently he was also Professor of Buddhism at Hanazono University and director of the Center for the Study of Zen and Culture. He has published commentaries on the *Blue Cliff Record* (碧巌録解説) and the *Heart Sūtra* (槃若経解説), and translated Hisamatsu Shin'ichi's *Oriental Nothingness* into German as *Die Fülle des Nichts*. He maintains an active interest in the revitalization of contemporary Zen Buddhism.

HORIO Tsutomu 堀尾 孟 is Professor of Philosophy at Ōtani University in Kyoto. His published articles include "States of Dependent Transformation Today: The Contemporary Significance of Rinzai's Thought" (「依変の境」と現代—臨済の思想の現代的意義), and "Nishida Kitarō and Suzuki Teitarō" (西田幾多郎と鈴木貞太郎). Currently he is working on the problem of religion and science and on religion and the modernization of Japan.

Christopher IVES is Associate Professor of Religion at the University of Puget Sound. His research focuses on Buddhism in the early Shōwa period (1926–1945) and modern Zen thought in the context of Japanese intellectual history. He is the author of *Zen Awakening and Society* and co-editor with John B. Cobb, Jr., of *The Emptying God*. With Abe Masao he co-translated Nishida Kitarō's *An Inquiry into the Good*.

Agustín JACINTO Zavala is Research Professor and Director of the Center for the Study of Traditions at El Colegio de Michoacán in Zamora, Mexico. His research interests center on Tarascan culture and Japanese philosophy. He has published *Zen y personalidad* and *Mitología y modernización*, as well as numerous studies of Nishida, including *Estado y filosofía* and *Filosofía de la transformación del mundo*.

KIRITA Kiyohide 桐田清秀 is Professor of Education in the Department of Literature at Hanazono University. His research is mainly in the areas of Buddhist ethics and the thought of D. T. Suzuki. His publications include "The Social Thought of the Young D. T. Suzuki" (青年鈴木貞太郎大拙の社会観), "Environmental Bioethics and Buddhism" (環境・生命倫理と仏教), and "The Concept of 'Nature' in D. T. Suzuki."

John C. MARALDO is Professor of Philosophy at the University of North Florida. His areas of interest include comparative philosophy, Japanese philosophy, and Zen Buddhism. In addition to articles in these areas, he has published a study of Schleiermacher, Dilthey, and Heidegger, *Der hermeneutische Zirkel*; a translation and study of Heidegger, *The Piety of Thinking* (in collaboration with James G. Hart); and *Buddhism in the Modern World*, co-edited with Heinrich Dumoulin.

MINAMOTO Ryōen 源 了圓 is Professor Emeritus of Japanese Intellectual History, Tōhoku University, and the author of some 17 books and 100 articles in Japanese, including *Form* (型) and *Studies in the Idea of Practical Learning in the Early Modern Period* (近世初期実学思想の研究). His interests have recently turned to Buddhism and resulted in a book on Rennyo.

MORI Tetsurō 森 哲郎 is Associate Professor at the Institute for World Affairs and Cultures of Kyoto Sangyō University. His publications include "Dreams and Awakening: The Self-Expression of the World," "Nishida's World of Pure Experience" (純粋経験の世界), "Religion in the Philosophy of Nishida" (西田哲学に於ける「宗教」理解), and essays on Zen Buddhism. In addition to continuing research on Nishida, he is presently writing on Schelling's philosophy of mythology and the question of dreams from metaphysical and Zen perspectives.

Robert H. Sharf is Associate Professor of East Asian Religions at McMaster University in Hamilton, Ontario. He has published articles on Ch'an and Zen, and has a book forthcoming on the *Pao-tsang lun*, an eighth-century Chinese apocryphon. His current research focuses on contemporary Hossō Buddhism and *mikkyō* ritual at Kōfuku-ji in Nara, Japan.

Ueda Shizuteru 上田閑照 is Professor Emeritus of Religious Philosophy at Kyoto University and Guest Professor at Hanazono University. His books include *Die Gottesgeburt in der Seele und der Durchbruch zur Gottheit, Reading Nishida Kitarō* (西田幾多郎を読む), and *Experience and Self-Awakening* (経験と自覚), as well as numerous edited volumes on Nishida, the philosophy of religion, and German mysticism.

Jan Van Bragt is Professor of Religion at Nanzan University, Nagoya, Japan, and a Fellow and former Director of the Nanzan Institute for Religion and Culture. He is the translator of Nishitani Keiji's *Religion and Nothingness* and co-author with Paul Mommaers of *Mysticism Buddhism and Christian: Encounters with Jan van Ruusbroec*. He has authored numerous articles on the theology of religions, Buddhist-Christian dialogue, and Pure Land Buddhism.

Yusa Michiko 遊佐道子 is Associate Professor in the Center for East Asian Studies and the Department of Foreign Languages and Literatures at Western Washington University. Her publications include "*Riken no Ken*: Zeami's Theory of Acting and Theatrical Appreciation," several articles on Nishida's philosophy and a textbook on learning Japanese. She is presently writing a biography of Nishida Kitarō.

Abbreviations and Conventions

CK   世界史的立場と日本 [The World-Historical Standpoint and Japan]. Tokyo: Chūōkōron, 1943.

IG   Nishida Kitarō, *An Inquiry into the Good*. Trans. by Abe Masao and Christopher Ives. New Haven: Yale University Press, 1990.

IHC   市川白弦著作集 [Collected Writings of Ichikawa Hakugen]. Kyoto: Hōzōkan, 1993. 4 vols.

KC   近代の超克 [Overcoming Modernity]. Tokyo: Fuzanbō, 1979.

NK   Nishitani Keiji, *Nishida Kitarō*. Trans. by Yamamoto Seisaku and James W. Heisig. Berkeley: University of California Press, 1991.

NKC   西谷啓治著作集 [Selected Works of Nishitani Keiji]. Tokyo: Sōbunsha, 1986–. 14 vols.

NKZ   西田幾多郎全集 [Collected Works of Nishida Kitarō]. Tokyo: Iwanami Shoten, 1978. 19 vols.

PM   Tanabe Hajime, *Philosophy as Metanoetics*. Trans. by Takeuchi Yoshinori. Berkeley: University of California Press, 1986.

RN   Nishitani Keiji, *Religion and Nothingness*. Trans. by Jan Van Bragt. Berkeley: University of California Press, 1982.

RPNK   *The Religious Philosophy of Nishitani Keiji*. Ed. by Taitetsu Unno. Berkeley: Asian Humanities Press, 1990.

RPTH   *The Religious Philosophy of Tanabe Hajime*. Ed. by Taitetsu Unno and James W. Heisig. Berkeley: Asian Humanities Press, 1990.

SDZ   鈴木大拙全集 [Collected Works of Suzuki Daisetsu]. Tokyo: Iwanami Shoten, 1983, 2nd. edition. 32 vols.

THZ   田辺元全集 [Collected Works of Tanabe Hajime]. Tokyo: Chikuma Shobō, 1964. 15 vols.

Japanese names are listed with the family name first, followed by the personal name. Chinese glyphs for names, titles, and technical terms not supplied in the text and notes can be found in the Index.

PART ONE

Questioning Zen

Zen Buddhist Attitudes to War

HIRATA Seikō

I N ORDER FULLY TO UNDERSTAND the standpoint of Zen on the question
of nationalism, one must first consider the Indian Buddhist context out
of which the Zen tradition arose. How were matters of ethnic and
national identity dealt with in the Buddhist sūtras?

ANTIWAR VIEWS IN THE BUDDHIST SŪTRAS

There is a story in the Buddhist sūtras that directly speaks to this question, a
story based on the historical events relating to the destruction of the Śākya
clan—the clan of which Śākyamuni was a member—by King Virudhaka of
Kośala, the powerful country that bordered the Śākya kingdom. These
events, said to have taken place when the Buddha was about fifty years old,
are described in a number of different sūtras.[1] The general outline of the story
as related in the texts is as follows.

Virudhaka, infuriated by a racist insult at the hands of the Śākyas, sent a
large army to destroy Kapilavastu, the capital of the Śākya kingdom. Hearing
of this, the Buddha set himself down under a dead tree in the path of the
army, knowing that Indian custom at the time required an invading army to
give up its attack if it encountered a holy man in the course of its advance.
Coming upon the seated Buddha, King Virudhaka ordered his troops to halt
and asked him, "Why do you sit under this dead tree rather than in the shade
of a living one?" The Buddha replied calmly, "My clan the Śākya is like this
dead tree," alluding to the impending destruction that awaited his people.
At this King Virudhaka, obedient to the ancient custom, ordered his army
back to Kośala.

Still bristling from the insult, Virudhaka invaded a second time, but
found the Buddha seated under the same tree. Once again the King ordered

---

[1] The story can be found in the *Ekottarāgama Sūtra* 増一阿含経巻 26 (T. 2.549, No. 125);
Vai^ūryarāja Sūtra 瑠璃王経 (T. 14.783, No. 513); and *Arthavargīya Sūtra* 義足経 (T. 4.174,
No. 198).

3

a retreat. He invaded a third time, only to have to retreat yet a third time, his way blocked by the holy man. When word reached the Buddha that preparations were under way for yet a fourth invasion, however, he ignored the pleas of his disciples and refused to intervene. As a result the entire Śākya clan was slaughtered and the city of Kapilavastu destroyed.

Śākyamuni was born the crown prince of the Śākya clan, and if events had run their ordinary course would have been king at the time of attack and thus in charge of the country's defense. As it was, he had renounced his claim to worldly authority and taken up the life of a homeless religious mendicant. Realizing that the forces of karma cannot be thwarted by human design, he was convinced that the Śākya people would inevitably be destroyed for having insulted Kośala. Śākyamuni therefore refused in the end to oppose the advancing Kośala army, maintaining an attitude of complete and total non-belligerence, even in the full knowledge that this would mean the extinction of his clansmen and erstwhile subjects.

This story from the sūtras provides a good illustration of the absolute rejection of war in ancient Indian Buddhism. The early Buddhist posture of nonviolence was based not on humanistic ideas about the value of life, but on a religious understanding of the workings of karma. The Buddha's ultimate refusal to act for the sake of clan and country was rooted in his belief that the Buddhist dharma transcends ethnic and national concerns. The message of the story is that Buddhism is free of nationalistic concerns.

The sūtras go on to relate that, in karmic retribution for the destruction of the Śākyas and in accordance with a prophecy made by the Buddha, the people of Kośala were all drowned in a violent rainstorm, the palace was struck by lightning and burned to the ground, and King Virudhaka himself fell into the lowest realm of hell.

ZEN AND THE STATE IN TANG CHINA

Following the transmission of Buddhism from India to China, the body of Hīnayāna and Mahāyāna sūtras was gradually translated into Chinese. A particularly important step in the evolution of Chinese Buddhist thought occurred when Tao-sheng 道生 (355–434) and Seng-chao 僧肇 (378–414), two disciples of the Central Asian translator-monk Kumārajīva (344–413), developed an interpretation of Buddhism based on Taoist and Confucian thought. The work of these monks in many ways laid the foundations for the subsequent development of Chinese Buddhism, one of the most influential products of which was Ch'an (Jap., Zen) Buddhism. Sectarian legend credits the actual founding of Ch'an to the First Patriarch Bodhidharma (470?–543?), who is said to have brought the teachings to China from his native

India, but the tradition can be more accurately seen as a synthesis of Taoist, Confucian, and Buddhist thought.

A brief word is in order about the relation between Zen and Tang China (618–907), the great dynasty during which the Zen tradition developed and flourished. There are many famous encounters between Zen masters and Chinese emperors, including the exchanges between Bodhidharma and Emperor Wu 武, between Nan-yang Hui-chung 南陽慧忠 (d. 775) and Emperor Su-tsung 肅宗 (who regarded Nan-yang so highly that he named him a National Teacher), and between Huang-po Hsi-yün 黃檗希運 (d. 850) and Emperor Tai-tsung 代宗. In content these exchanges deal not with the secular realm and such issues as politics, economics, and the law, but with the Buddhist Dharma as a truth transcending secular concerns. The exchange between Nan-yang Hui-chung and Su-tsung, described in the ninety-ninth case of the *Blue Cliff Record*, is a good example:

> Emperor Su-tsung asked National Teacher Chung, "What is the Ten-Body Controller?"
> The National Teacher said, "Patron, walk on Vairocana's head."
> The emperor said, "I don't understand."
> The National Teacher said, "Don't acknowledge your own pure body of reality."[2]

The *ten bodies* referred to in the expression "Ten-Body Controller" are the ten forms of Buddha bodies. The *Controller* is the particular Buddha body that is able to freely control all the other Buddha bodies. Expressed in terms of the triple-body system of *dharmakāya*, *sambhogakāya*, and *nirmānakāya*, the Controller represents the *dharmakāya*, the most fundamental of the bodies. *Vairocana* and *pure body of reality* are simply other names for the *dharmakāya*. The emperor is asking what the nature of this most fundamental of the Buddha bodies is. Hui-chung replies that only by stepping beyond even this pure, fundamental *dharmakāya* can he ever come to know the true *dharmakāya*.

Behind Su-tsung's question is, no doubt, the belief that ideally the empire should be a manifestation of the Buddha realm, and that he, as its ruler, should be a manifestation of the pure *dharmakāya*. But Hui-chung's answer rejects this view of the Buddha realm. For the Zen person, the concept of the Buddha realm is simply an *upāya*, an expedient device for leading a person to the truth, and nothing more. The true land of the Buddha is a state in which one is unfettered even by ideas like "the Buddha realm." In his response Hui-chung tries to transcend the limitations of the Buddha-land *upāya* and thereby to lead the emperor to an understanding of the true

---

[2] Thomas and J. C. Cleary, *The Blue Cliff Record* (London: Shambhala, 1977), 3:628.

Buddha Dharma. Hui-chung's Zen teaching, according to which the Dharma can manifest itself only when conventional, secular truth has been overcome, eliminates all possibility of seeing the nation as an expression of the Buddha realm.

Hui-chung's standpoint is already present in traditional Indian Buddhism, where the Buddha Dharma is held to be beyond the worldly truths that govern the ruling of nations. But the idea is not an abstraction that itself transcends the things of earth. It is a way of seeing that can be expressed convincingly only by someone like Hui-chung, who spent forty years in seclusion on Mount Pai-ya deepening his practice before reluctantly accepting the emperor's summons to the capital. There were other monks like him, of course—most notably Hui-yüan 慧遠 (334–416), who spent the latter half of his life on Mt. Lu and who espoused the doctrine that monks were not obliged to honor the sovereign—but the majority of the Buddhist clergy lived in quite different circumstances. The harsh reality at the time was that Buddhism could not have survived without the protection and support of the government authorities. This became painfully apparent during the persecution of Buddhism that took place from 843 to 845 under Emperor Wu-tsung 太武 (r. 840–847), during which approximately 40,000 temples were closed, 260,000 monks and nuns returned to lay life, and vast acreages of temple land confiscated and sold. Even in more peaceful times the monks and nuns, while freed of the duty to pay taxes and enlist in the military, remained under the strict control of the Tang government. Even ordination was impossible without express permission from the authorities. For secular reasons such as these, the monastic community was compelled to recognize the rule of the emperor and the authority of the nation. As a result, along with the doctrines that monks were exempted from reverencing the sovereign there emerged a doctrine of the identity of the Buddhist law and the imperial law, and, related to this, the doctrine that truth is identical with *upāya*.

BUDDHIST AND IMPERIAL LAW IN SUNG CHINA

During the Sung dynasty (960–1280) the doctrine of the identity of Buddhist law and the imperial law came to play a more prominent role in Zen Buddhist thought. There was a scriptural basis for this in the apocryphal *Jen wang [hu kuo] pan jo po lo mi [to]ching* 仁王[護國]般若波羅蜜[多]経,[3] according to which the Buddha provides the "secret jewel" of protection for all countries by using his prajñā wisdom to instruct the kings of all nations pre-

---

[3] T. 8.825, No. 245 and 246.

sent and future. The Buddha Dharma, in other words, is the jewel (i.e., the sovereign), while the imperial law is the manifestation (i.e., the subject) of this secret jewel.

As mentioned above, in the time of the Sung dynasty these two aspects came to stand as equals. In the *Ch'an-yüan ching-kuei* 禅苑清規, a Sung text published in 1103 that listed the regulations of the Zen community, one finds the statement, "Contempt for the imperial law and disregard for the monastic community is of no benefit for the operation of the temple." Already at this time we see a clear regulation that not even monks are to slight the law of the land.

During the Southern Sung dynasty the system known as the "Five Mountains and Ten Temples" came into being. In the context of this strong social institutionalization, Sung dynasty Zen developed a new relationship with the state. First, the temples initiated the *chu-sheng* 祝聖 rite, a ceremony held on the first and fifteenth of every month to pray for the health and long life of the emperor. Second, when a new head priest assumed office, a special ritual was held by the temple to pray for the peace of the nation.

Implicit in the introduction of these ceremonies was the view that the state is indeed a manifestation of the Buddha realm and the emperor the embodiment of the pure *dharmakāya* who rules it. In other words, the Buddhist law (religion) and the imperial law (the state) are one. Absent is the earlier doctrine of clerical exemption from reverence for the sovereign. On the contrary, Zen monks began at this time to comment on public ethics, and the Buddhist Dharma came to be thought of as something one could pursue without distancing oneself from the imperial law of the land. This shift of direction was argued in the context of the teaching in the *Vimalakīrti-nirdeśa Sūtra* that enlightenment (*bodhi*) is attained without cutting off delusion.

Zen Master Ta-hui Tsung-kao 大慧宗杲 (1089–1163), who counted a number of government officials among his disciples, openly taught the unity of Buddha law and imperial law. When he was thirty-seven years old the Sung was invaded by the northern Juchen, forcing it to relocate south of the Yangtze and establish a new capital at Lin-an. There was considerable debate at the time over whether armed resistance was the proper course of action or whether it was better to sue for peace. Ta-hui urged a number of the Sung officials to engage in combat with the invading Juchen, even if only for the honor of the dynasty. As it turned out, those arguing for a more conciliatory policy won the day, and they succeeded in having Ta-hui and the officials associated with him exiled to the outlying regions of Heng-chou and Mei-chou. Unruffled by this unhappy turn of events, Ta-hui wrote numerous letters of encouragement to exiled officials, stressing the benefits of adverse circumstances for practicing the Buddha Dharma.

Ta-hui's Zen stands very much in the tradition that sees the Buddhist Dharma as sympathetic to the secular law of the nation. The nonbelligerence of the Buddha as illustrated in the Indian sūtra on the destruction of the Śākya clan is nowhere to be seen. The cornerstone of this identification of Buddhist law and imperial law was the belief that the nation is a manifestation of the Buddha realm. According to this idea of the state, the destruction of the nation is tantamount to the destruction of the Buddha realm, which means that resistance by the state against invasion from a neighboring country is, religiously speaking, fully justified as an act of self-defense.

Views similar to those of Ta-hui were held by the Sung Zen master Wu-hsüeh Tsu-yüan 無学祖元 (1226–1286),[4] who journeyed to Japan in 1279 at the invitation of the Kamakura shogunate. When the Mongol forces launched their second invasion of Japan in 1281, the regent Hōjō Tokimune sought his advice. Wu-hsüeh, who had once given Tokimune a scroll inscribed with the phrase 莫妄想, "Dispel all illusion," advised armed repulsion of the attack. Once again we see a deliberate refusal to oppose a strategy of military defense against an invading army bent on the destruction of what was seen as the "Buddha realm."

Most of the twenty-four lines of Zen succession that were eventually transmitted to Japan were from Sung China. The Rinzai lines in particular attracted the majority of their followers from among the warrior class, a group of people who in those unsettled times had to live constantly faced with the possibility of death on the battlefield. What they sought from the Zen masters, whose practice dealt directly with the question of life and death, was how to prepare themselves for this possibility. What Zen offered to the warriors was a philosophy (or ethic) of life and death. The saying, "Death is the way of the samurai—Seek it out!" aptly expresses the spirit of the *hagakure* warrior. In other words, it was precisely in the law of the sovereign that the law of the Buddha was to be found. The philosophy (or religion) of "transcending life and death" was the samurai's sole support in a feudal society so severe and unforgiving that he might be called on to commit *seppuku* for even a minor slip of protocol. For such persons, with death ever before their eyes, there was no falsehood. Such was the foundation of the warrior ethic.

ZEN IN MODERN JAPAN

In the mid-nineteenth century Japan stepped out of its isolation and took its place in the international community as a modern independent nation. What

---

[4] Jap., Mugaku Sogen, also known as 仏光国師 Bukkō Kokushi. He was the founder of Engaku-ji in Kamakura.

sort of situation did it find itself in at that time? This is a question that historians have examined from many different perspectives, but there is general agreement that in the late-nineteenth and early-twentieth centuries the world was under the sway, both politically and ideologically, of Europe and the United States. Unless one takes this fundamental historical fact into consideration, there is no way to understand the history of modern Japan or the policies adopted by its leaders, which were in large part shaped by the posture of the Western powers towards the rest of the world and in particular towards the East. The progress of the natural sciences had given the nations of the West industrial and military strengths far beyond those of any country in Asia. Western thought and culture also had an enormous impact on the Eastern peoples. Even in my own youth we were educated in the writings of German idealism, in the literature of Goethe, in the economic ideas of Marx, and in theories of Western art and music.

From this position of strength, the Western powers gradually expanded their influence in the East, particularly in China, whose vast expanse of land and rich natural resources made it particularly attractive. The year 1852 marked the visit of Commodore Perry to Uraga and the subsequent opening of Japan. The following decades saw a steady increase of Western control in the East. In 1858, following the suppression of the Indian Mutiny, Great Britain imposed direct Crown government on the Indian subcontinent. In 1863 France forced Cambodia to become a French protectorate; ten years later it took Hanoi and acquired protector status over Vietnam as well. In 1886 all of Burma became a British colony, and in 1887 France colonized the region of Indochina. The Germans, meanwhile, had been expanding their influence in China, where they seized Chiao-chou Bay in Shantung in 1897. The Russians subsequently occupied Port Arthur and Dairen on the Liao-tung Peninsula and secured from China the rights to build the eastern section of the Trans-Siberian Railway across Manchuria to Vladivostok. Around this time England procured a lease on the Kowloon Peninsula opposite Hong Kong.

All of these events took place almost immediately after the Sino-Japanese War of 1894. Set against this background, the Russo-Japanese War of 1904–1905 can be seen as a defensive strategy by Japan to halt the southward advance of the Russian Empire. In any case, following Japan's victory in this conflict, a change occurred in the outlook of the Japanese people. In the negotiated settlement that ended the war, Japan was given southern Sakhalin, control over the Liao-tung Peninsula and the Southern Manchurian Railroad, and protector status over the Korean Peninsula. These gains at the expense of a large European nation brought about a swelling of national pride in Japan, and the idea quickly took root that the country had become one of the world's "first-class nations" (一等国). In the decades ahead, these sentiments would lend their weight to such expansionist moves as the Manchurian

Incident in 1931, the establishment of Manchukuo in 1932, and the invasion of China in 1937. This complex interaction of events on the stage of late-nineteenth- and early-twentieth-century world history led to the formation of the militarist government and ultimately to the outbreak of the Pacific War in 1941.

In hindsight, the historical situation that faced Japan as it stepped out of its long period of seclusion from the rest of the world may be said to have provoked two quite different reactions in the hearts of the Japanese. On the one hand, there was a feeling of indignation at the strategy of the Western powers' aimed at subjugating the countries of the East, and with it a sense that as the leading power of Asia it was incumbent on Japan to stand up to the colonizers. But this sense of an affront to justice is only half of the picture. Along with it went a self-serving attempt on the part of certain Japanese political and economic leaders to jump onto the imperialist bandwagon and carve out a piece of the Asian mainland for themselves. The influence of those who espoused the cause "for peace in the East" was rechanneled to justify the activities of those who held to this latter position, and their view gradually came to central stage in the prewar educational philosophy of Japan.

Hard-line elements in the Imperial Army, meanwhile, pressed ahead with the overseas military operations—the Manchurian and China incidents, for example—that later escalated into the Pacific War. This is not to say that there was no domestic criticism of the trend toward militarism. One example I am personally familiar with was an effort by members of the Kansai area business elite to influence the government by enlisting the aid of my teacher, Seki Seisetsu. In 1936, the year before the outbreak of hostilities with China, some 1,400 troops of the Japanese army stationed in Tokyo attempted a coup d'état (the so-called February 26th Incident). The Kansai business leaders, concerned about the rise of militarism and fearful that Japan might be cut off from the rest of the world, contacted Seisetsu Rōshi with a request that he write to the Minister of the Army, Terauchi Hisaichi, a frequent visitor of the rōshi, and urge him to take what action he could to check the reactionary elements in the officer corps. I know this because it was my father, Hirata Dōzen, who carried the rōshi's letter to Tokyo, which was still under martial law, and delivered it to Terauchi. I can still see him on the day of his departure, tying his straw sandals for the trip to the capital.

Unfortunately, the effort bore no fruit, for whatever reason, and Japan continued its downslide into military rule. Intimidation tactics were employed to assure that no opposition to the military's activities was voiced. Untoward censure of the government soon reached the ears of the authorities and could literally endanger the life of the critic. Viewed from the present, the Pacific War can only be seen as a reckless undertaking that simply reflected the military leaders' ignorance of the international situation. The small handful of internationally-minded intellectuals who did understand the true state of affairs kept silent for reasons of personal safety. It was only with the fall of Okinawa in April 1945 that the Japanese people began their slow but rude awakening to the folly of the war effort. In an effort to bring the war to a speedy conclusion, many military cadets sacrificed their lives in the "special attack" kamikaze squads. The poignant letters these young men left behind bear witness to the hopes for an early peace that spurred them on.

SECULAR FREEDOM AND DESECULARIZED FREEDOM

Having considered the way in which the Indian Buddhist ideal of nonbelligerence was transformed as Buddhism spread west to China and Japan, and after a brief look at some of the developments in world history that led to the Pacific War, we are still left with the question: What positive contribution did Zen and the Zen sect have to make at this time of world crisis? In all honesty, I must admit that it was very meager. The Zen priesthood is made up of individuals, and as in any religion during times of war, there were among them many who appear to have abandoned the ideals of their faith to embrace the narrower ideals of their country. Not a few Zen priests joined hands with State Shinto and its imperialist view of history in order to promote the war. None of the historical arguments brought forth in their defense (for example, the indignation at the West's colonization of the East referred to earlier) can justify their simple failure to speak out on the Buddhist ideal of nonbelligerence, much less their active support of the war effort. As their successors, we have no choice but humbly to accept the criticism their actions have brought upon Zen, and to recognize that the problem was due in part to the ignorance of international affairs among Zen monks at the time.

In the years following the Second World War, Japanese Buddhism was sharply censured by various progressive Japanese intellectuals for its cooperation in the war effort. Zen in particular was the target of the scholar Ichikawa Hakugen, in whose critique I find much of interest. I would mention, for instance, the distinction he draws between "desecularized freedom" (脱俗の自由) and "secular freedom" (世俗の自由).[5] When Zen speaks of freedom, it is usually in the sense of desecularized freedom, as in the famous line in the *Record of Lin-chi*: "Become a master of your circumstances; wherever you stand is the right place" (隨處作主, 立處皆真). This kind of freedom is attained when one is able to accept life just as it is, when one is able to say, like the Sōtō master Ryōkan, "In times of misfortune, misfortune is fine." Such freedom persists even in the midst of suffering.

[5] See IHC 3:60–99.

11

But desecularized freedom is not able to bring about political or social reform. Freedom of the type achieved through the American and French revolutions—freedom from political oppression—is what Ichikawa calls "secular freedom." Desecularized freedom is vertical by nature and secular freedom is horizontal. For Ichikawa, the true freedom of Zen today lies at the point where these vertical and horizontal planes intersect.

I am basically in agreement with Ichikawa here. In fact, he is not the first to point out that the freedom espoused by Zen—and by Buddhism as a whole—is fundamentally *non*ethical (as opposed to *un*ethical) in nature. This was the very position taken by Sung dynasty Confucian scholars in their attacks on Zen. As they saw it, Zen's position that the adept's world of satori can be reached only through a transcendence of dualistic notions of good and evil is one that leaves no grounds for distinguishing the socially beneficial from the socially harmful. Not only is it bereft of social significance, it is also incapable of providing any sort of foundation for social development. Their Zen opponents countered by saying that fixation on the dualistic dimension of good and evil merely promotes delusion and cuts off all possibility of attaining the true peace of satori.

In terms of Ichikawa's formula, the Confucians were in effect saying that the transcendent, vertical plane can never become the social, horizontal plane, no matter how high or how deep it goes, while the Zen side was saying that the horizontal plane can never become the vertical plane, no matter how far or how wide it reaches. As human beings, each of us have both of these dimensions, and therefore there must be a point at which they intersect. The problem, as Ichikawa realized, was how to get there.

A Zen expression sums up our everyday existence this way: "Dreams, illusions, flowers in the sky—why dally to grasp at them?" (夢幻空華, なんぞ把捉を弄せん). The everyday social and historical reality in which we live is in essence "dreams, illusions, flowers in the sky," a tangle of memories, delusions, and desires. Social revolutions and political positions are no exception. When I was a lad, our teachers told us that the war going on in the Pacific was a "just war." Then, when it had all ended, we were told that it had been an "evil war." This simplistic shift of positions was one of the things that made me decide to become a monk. Perhaps this is one of the reasons for my final misgivings with Ichikawa's *ex post facto* critique of Zen's position during the war.

In the 1960s Ichikawa became involved in a somewhat radical movement in Japan against the war in Vietnam.[6] As the protests led to violent clashes with authority, some from the Buddhist world questioned Ichikawa's collab-

---

[6] The movement was called the "Coalition for Peace in Vietnam" (ベトナム平和連合会, popularly abbreviated to ベ平連).

oration in the movement on the grounds that anything that provokes violence is opposed to Buddhism. Ichikawa defended himself by turning the tables on his accusers. If they find his struggles against war in the name of peace so violent and so wrong and so anti-Buddhist, he asked, then why had they not raised a voice in the midst of the violence of the Pacific War? That exchange became the catalyst for Ichikawa's critique of "imperial Zen" and its "moral stumble" during the war.

As I think I have made clear, I do not question the need for such criticism of Zen's past. My problem is rather with the contradictions in Ichikawa's own position, particularly in its embrace of the leftist rhetoric so much in vogue among intellectuals after the war. For example, even if one goes along with his claim that class struggle is justified in the name of social justice, how does this claim hold up in the light of the post-cold-war revelations of gross inequalities and injustices in the former Communist bloc? How much did humanity really gain from the revolution that he had praised so highly, and how much did it lose? Merely to shake the dust of the old position from one's sandals and then to invest all one's moral energies in a new position is not enough. Surely there is *something* to be learned about human nature in all of this. And surely there is a need for a standpoint that tries to learn it. Otherwise, what has the war taught us other than that *we* are right to see that *they* were wrong?

The emphasis that Zen puts on the "suchness" of things in the saying "Willows are green, flowers are red" has been challenged as powerless to change the world. As the critic Maruyama Masao once put it, sometimes green willows need to be made red. There is some truth in this, but it is no longer Zen. When all is said and done, the horizontal world is always and everywhere a samsaric, impermanent world. Only by awakening to the sense in which the transient realm of samsara already *is*, just as it is, the permanent and unchanging realm, does the world that Zen is talking about open up. In terms of Ichikawa's scheme, I would say that the world of Zen is not located at the point where the horizontal and vertical dimensions of human life intersect, but at the point where both dimensions drop out of the picture. This is what Hisamatsu Shin'ichi called "the religion of awakened existence" (覚存の 宗教). From this standpoint willows are, after all, green, and flowers are, after all, red; the form of the mountain is the pure body of the Tathāgata and all the hills, rivers, grasses, and trees have become Buddha. Unless this sense of absolute transcendence is clearly understood, the true significance of the Buddha's ideal of nonbelligerence can never be clear either.

No doubt such a statement will invite the criticism that this standpoint itself needs to be relativized, that its "transcendence" points to an essential limitation in Zen, that so long as Zen stops at the world "just as it is," it effectively cuts itself off from the horizontal plane and forsakes any contribution to the world and its history. If I may "dally to grasp at" a counterposition here, I would say that such complaints do not bother Zen. From such a counterposition, one would have to say that Zen is not so much concerned with deciding issues of right and wrong, of war and peace, as with understanding the self that deals with these questions and makes these decisions. As Dōgen says, "To study the Buddha Way is to study one's self." This concern pervades the history of Buddhism from the time of Śākyamuni's encounter with the forces of Kośala up to the present. Wherever there is a grounding in the vertical dimension, there is Zen. And where it is absent, it does not matter if one is a hawk or dove, a pacifist or militarist—there is no Zen. In the Rinzai tradition, this presence of the vertical dimension has been monitored by means of the kōan, and indeed this is said to be the true meaning of the entire kōan system.

To be sure, these very same claims can also serve as an excuse for settling into a comfortable position impervious to all criticism. In thinking about the relationship between the horizontal and the vertical planes, one can as easily end up absolutizing the vertical as absolutizing their point of intersection. When we see a Zen practicer fall into such a trap, we are reminded how quickly one person's nectar can become another person's poison. I am convinced that the sectarian egoism found in all religious traditions, Zen included, stems from just this kind of "relative absolutism." Naturally, such egoism is not limited to religion; nationalist and ethnic egoisms are cut from the same cloth. This is why Zen rejects the delusion that one becomes an enlightened Buddha merely by "passing the kōans." The Zen practicer needs to come to the point of liberation from the kōans, to the point where Zen is liberated from Zen and where there is no God or Buddha. This I take to be the import of Hisamatsu's "religion of awakened existence" at which the horizontal and vertical pass out of the picture.

It is only at this standpoint of awakened existence that true compassion and prajñā wisdom appear. Stand anywhere else and prajñā wisdom is no more than ordinary discriminating insight; compassion is soon converted into a simple calculation of profit and loss based on ideas of what is right and what is wrong, what the *Vimalakīrti-nirdeśa Sūtra* calls "the compassion of deluded thoughts and feelings." The God-less, Buddha-less standpoint of awakened existence finds a voice in the words, "Willows are green, flowers are red" and "The form of the mountain is the pure body of the Tathāgata and all the hills, rivers, grasses, and trees have become Buddha." It is a standpoint of unbounded wisdom and unbounded compassion.

When Zen, the religion of awakened existence, steps out into the relative world with its vertical and horizontal planes, it must continue to pursue the vertical dimension expressed in kōan training. In the sense in which even Śākyamuni and Bodhidharma are in permanent training, the kōan system represents the framework and essence of Zen. At the same time, this vertical dimension must always find expression in and be transferred to the horizontal dimension. It is a question of how one understands samādhi. Generally samādhi is taken to be a state of passive acceptance of the world or one's situation just as it is. As the term is used in Zen, however, samādhi has also the sense of becoming one with change. To borrow a phrase of Nishida Kitarō, in samādhi the practicer moves from a stance of being created by the world to one of creating the world, albeit in such a way that it neither changes nor hides from view the reality that "Willows are green, flowers are red." Zen adapts itself freely to the spirit of the times. What is called "progress" on the horizontal plane is from the Zen point of view simply change. There are no principles in Zen to improve or develop. So long as Zen is Zen, it is in every age completely open and unhidden. But in samādhi the one who practices Zen has seriously to study the things of the world *as* things of the world. In this respect, the Zen priesthood can be faulted for its ignorance of the international situation at the time of the Pacific War. In view of the results, and in view of the legacy passed down from Śākyamuni, we can only bow our heads and humbly accept our thirty blows.

[TRANSLATED BY THOMAS KIRCHNER]

Ethical Pitfalls in Imperial Zen and Nishida Philosophy

Ichikawa Hakugen's Critique

Christopher IVES

WITH THE EXCEPTION OF Ichikawa Hakugen, virtually no Japanese Buddhist has examined the role of Zen in Japan's Fifteen-Year War (1931–1945). Ichikawa argued that Zen took a submissive stance at the time and that prominent Zen figures helped rationalize, glorify, or even promote Japanese imperialism. A parallel problematic surfaces in wartime writings of layman Nishida Kitarō, who Ichikawa claims "stumbled" ethically no less than Zen had done.[1]

ICHIKAWA'S BACKGROUND

Ichikawa (1902–1986) was born into a Rinzai Zen temple family and spent his entire career as a university student and professor at Hanazono University, from his matriculation in 1921 to his retirement in 1973. In his telling, Ichikawa was a shy child, naturally intimidated and repulsed by the education he received under the imperial educational system and "terrified" of the state and the supreme commander (emperor) who could order his death.[2] With this disposition he found himself increasingly against war and the rhetoric of the *kokutai* (national polity).

Ichikawa's orientation was shaped further by a "positivist" middle-school history teacher and by reading Natsume Sōseki, Turgenev, Dostoevsky, and,

---

[1] Ichikawa set forth his critique of Zen and Nishida primarily in 禅と現代思想 [Zen and contemporary thought] (1967), 仏教者の戦争責任 [Buddhists' responsibility for war] (1971), and 日本ファシズム下の宗教 [Religion under Japanese fascism] (1975). In this paper all quotations of Ichikawa are from these three works, which were republished respectively in volumes 2, 3, and 4 of his *Collected Writings*.

[2] IHC 3:17.

later, Hugo, Tolstoy, Kropotkin, Marx, Engels, and the anarchist Ōsugi Sakae.[3] Gradually, a "humanistic anger toward the evils of society and the state"[4] welled up in him, and his lifelong interest in Buddhism, socialism, and anarchism began to crystallize.

Though his anger did not drive Ichikawa into prewar political activism, he did publish several articles on Buddhism and socialism in the late 1920s and early 1930s, and on several occasions he was interrogated by the Special Higher Police Force (特高) about certain of his writings. During the war he did not publicly recant his socialist stance as many others did, but later he criticized his own failure to oppose Japanese militarism more actively and condemned his passivity as equivalent to recantation (転向).

Through such reflection on his prewar and wartime stance, Ichikawa became more involved in politics, serving on the Kyoto Board of Education in the 1950s and participating in various organizations and movements to address human rights issues in Japan, the security treaty with the United States, and the Vietnam War. In his scholarship Ichikawa examined Buddhist war responsibility, with particular attention to nationalist Zen figures located at the recent end of a fairly continuous history—since the Kamakura period—of close collaboration between Zen institutions and those in political power.

NATIONALIST ZEN

This nationalist trend in modern Zen circles is evident around the time of the Sino-Japanese War (1894–1895), when Suzuki Teitarō (later known in the West as D. T. Suzuki) wrote:

> There is a violent country [China], and insofar as it obstructs our commerce and infringes upon our rights, it directly interrupts the progress of all humankind. In the name of religion, our country refuses to submit itself to this. For this reason, unavoidably we have taken up arms. For the sake of justice and justice alone, we are simply chastising the country that represents injustice, and there is nothing else we seek. This is a religious action.[5]

Zen nationalism found further expression during the Russo-Japanese War (1904–1905) in statements by Shaku Sōen and others, and it attained its most virulent form—what Ichikawa termed "Imperial Way Zen"—during the Fifteen-Year War. In 1934, for example, Iida Tōin declared:

[3] IHC 3:18.

[4] IHC 3:18.

[5] In 新宗教論 [A new treatise on religion], quoted in IHC 4:36.

> Since the distant age of the gods, our country has come into existence equipped naturally with the Great Way of sovereign and subject. The dyad of sovereign and subject is the intrinsic nature of our country, and being unchanging, this nature constitutes righteousness.... It opens no crack for rationally asking "why" to enter.[6]

Continuing along these essentialist lines, Iida later asked,

> If the state were to perish, what would protect the Buddha-Dharma? If the Buddha-Dharma were to perish, upon what would the state be established?...There is no Buddha-Dharma apart from loyalty.... In all corners of the world there is no place where the Imperial Favor does not operate. The voices of pines and bamboo echo "Long may it live!" (*banzai*). The Imperial wind and the Buddha's sun are nondual.[7]

With this attitude toward the state and the imperial system, Iida celebrated Zen connections to militarism in the 1930s: "We should be cognizant of how much power Zen gave to the Way of the Warrior. It is truly a cause for rejoicing that the Zen sect has recently become popular among military men. No matter how much we do *zazen*, if it is not of service in the present events, then it would be better not to do it."[8]

Iida was not alone in urging his compatriots to make Zen "of service" in the "present events" constituting what many Buddhists called a "holy war" (聖戦). Yamazaki Ekishū exclaimed, "In Great Zen Samadhi we become united with the emperor. In each of our actions we live, moment to moment, with the greatest respect [for the emperor]. When we personify [this spirit] in our daily lives, we become masters of every situation in accordance with our sacrificial duty. This is living Zen."[9] Hata Eshō celebrated the attack on Pearl Harbor:

> December 8th is the holy day on which Śākyamuni realized the Way, and [for this reason] it has been a day for commemorating the liberation of humankind. It is exceedingly wonderful that in 1941 we were able to

---

[6] 飯田欓隠 Iida Tōin, 参禅漫録 [Random comments on the practice of Zen] (1934), quoted in IHC 2:30. Iida Tōin (1863–1937) was a prominent Sōtō figure who founded the Shōrinkutsu-dōjō in 1931.

[7] Iida, 槐安国語提唱録 [Zen talks on the *Kaiankokugo*] (1944), quoted in IHC 4:35.

[8] Iida, *Random Comments*, 262; quoted in IHC 2:159. The translation of this quote is adapted from Daizen Brian Victoria's rendering in "Japanese Corporate Zen," *Bulletin of Concerned Asian Scholars*, 12/1 (1980): 64.

[9] 山崎益洲 Yamazaki Ekishū, 敵愾心の興揚と禅 [The promotion of enmity and its relation to Zen], quoted in IHC 4:46. This translation is an adaptation of Victoria's in "Japanese Corporate Zen," 64. Yamazaki Ekishū (1882–1961) served as head priest of Buttsū-ji and head abbot of the consolidated Rinzai Zen sect around the end of the war (1945–1946).

make this very day also into a holy day for eternally commemorating the reconstruction of the world. On this day was handed down to us the Great Imperial Edict declaring war aimed at punishing the arrogant United States and England, and news of the destruction of American forward bases in Hawaii spread quickly throughout the world. We gained a real taste of good fortune, and we must offer thanks—to the four groups of superiors to whom we are indebted—for being able to applaud the freshness of victory in name and reality.[10]

Lest Ichikawa be accused of selectively lifting unrepresentative imperialist statements out of context to construct a straw man named "Imperial Way Zen," a perusal of wartime issues of *Zengaku-kenkyū*, *Daijōzen*, *Daihōrin*, and other Buddhist journals soon reveals that Zen statements such as these were neither rare nor exceptional.

To account for these statements and overall Zen support of Japanese imperialism and militarism, Ichikawa critiqued philosophical, institutional, and historical dimensions of Zen.[11] In his reading, "Zen" emerged at a tumultuous time in Chinese history and, like philosophical Taoism, directed itself toward finding security in the midst of social unrest. As expressed by such Taoist notions as "Because it does not contend, it is never at fault"[12] and the "usefulness of the useless," a prominent religious orientation in East Asia has been to give up resistance to, and then accept and accord with, the actuality around oneself. To promote this "accord with the principles of things as a kind of naturalism,"[13] one restrains from judgmental discrimination and thereby removes oneself from the psychological basis of preferences, struggle, and resulting anguish. Summarizing this Taoistic approach, through which one is said to achieve a kind of harmony with nature and other people, Ichikawa wrote, "If one discards discrimination between affirmation and negation and accords with nature, one can secure one's life."[14]

Ch'an and Zen developed this way of "stabilizing the mind and securing one's life" (安心立命)[15] in the face of social chaos. In their approach, as Ichikawa portrayed it,[16] "By becoming one (成り切る) with actuality, a person

---

[10] In the journal *Dōgen*; quoted in IHC 4:15.

[11] For the sake of focus, this paper will consider only his treatment of the philosophical dimension.

[12] Adapted from D. C. Lau, tr., *Tao Te Ching* (Middlesex, England: Penguin, 1976), 64.

[13] IHC 2:13.

[14] IHC 2:13.

[15] Cf. Dōgen's 永平広録 [The Public Record of Eihei], quoted in IHC 2:9.

[16] Assessment of the historical and philosophical accuracy of Ichikawa's characterization of Taoism and Ch'an/Zen will have to wait for another occasion.

transcends actuality,"[17] in that by relinquishing ego-centeredness and "becoming one" with the situation at hand a person can discover freedom in necessity (必然即自由). The *Record of Lin-chi* conveys this method of finding freedom beyond the dichotomy of relative freedom and necessity with the statements, "Make yourself master of every situation, and wherever you stand is the true [place]"; and "The mind turns in accordance with myriad circumstances, and this turning, in truth, is most profound."[18] In Dōgen's words, "To learn the self is to forget the self; to forget the self is to be confirmed by all things...."[19] And as Shidō Bunan (1603–1676) advised, "While living become like a dead person, then do as you wish." In this liberated freedom, according to D. T. Suzuki, "Zen does not affirm or negate temporal actuality. Actuality has historicity, with which the ultimacy of Zen has no dealings."[20]

Though perhaps existentially liberating for individual Buddhists, this approach to actuality has caused Zen to flounder ethically in socio-political actualities with which it has "become one," especially in the 1930s and early 1940s. For example, reflecting on what might be entailed in the notions of becoming master of one's situation and according with circumstances, Ichikawa problematized the "situation" of which Zen has made people master:

> Is it the situation in which one is placed or participates? Is it a matter of attaining freedom in the sense of becoming master of one's situation by changing in accordance with it? Are we to take the personal initiative to act above and beyond what we are commanded to do, as in "unquestioning compliance with the emperor's directives," rather than resisting or grudgingly obeying "supreme command(s) in the holy war"? In other words, is becoming master of one's situation a matter of living as a faithful and pliant organization man who through self-discipline admonishes himself against civil disobedience?[21]

To Ichikawa, the situations in which Zen has become "master" are the realms of warriors, the military, the anti-communist right-wing, and the industrial sector.[22] Along these lines he concluded that what Zen offers is a stance of accommodation:

[17] IHC 2:129.

[18] Adapted from Ruth Fuller Sasaki, tr., *The Record of Lin-chi* (Kyoto: Institute for Zen Studies, 1975), 17 and 27.

[19] *Genjōkōan* fascicle of the *Shōbōgenzō*.

[20] 禅百題 [One hundred Zen topics], quoted in IHC 4:7.

[21] IHC 2:135.

[22] IHC 2:160.

As indicated in the line [in the *Record of Lin-chi*], "The mind turns in accordance with the myriad circumstances," one creates a way of living that adapts daily to the new historical state of affairs; in the age of the Imperial Way one conducts oneself imperialistically, and in an age of democracy one conducts oneself democratically. Because one does not dwell in any one place, one lives in accordance with all places.[23]

Coupled with the historical cooperation between Zen and those in power (the "state"), this existential orientation opened the door fully for Zen to support modern Japanese imperialism, which is precisely what the tradition did.

Ichikawa suggested that to "become master of one's situation" could have meant to criticize the war publicly, but almost all Zen figures chose to be "masters" of a different sort. To quote Iida Tōin once again, "If one becomes master of every situation, the place where the mind turns is truly profound. Mountains are mountains; the sovereign is the sovereign; waters are waters; subjects are subjects. The great imperial nation of Japan—*banzai, banzai!*"[24] Cognizant of the posture of wartime Zen, Hisamatsu Shin'ichi wrote, as quoted by Ichikawa, "Zen often speaks of 'becoming master of every situation,' but during the war did this not become a situation in which Zen became opportunistic and, rather than becoming a master (主) of circumstances, tended to have its mind snatched by circumstances and thus became a guest (客) of those circumstances?"[25]

To Ichikawa, the ethical stumbling of Zen "masters" also derives from the harmony extolled in much of the discourse about Zen and Japanese culture. Possessing the contemplative wisdom advocated by Zen, "One tends to engage in a way of living that does not fight the pre-existing actuality pressing upon oneself but, on the contrary, accommodates it."[26] Living like the water that takes the shape of whatever vessel into which it is poured, Zen Buddhists run the risk of succumbing to a kind of flexible, shifting submission that lacks the consistency of principles, convictions, and actions necessary for a critical social ethic.[27] More specifically, ideals of harmony, nonresistance, and tolerance found an expression in the twentieth century that at the very least stood in stark tension with Buddhist rhetoric of compassion, of applying "skillful means" to liberate *all* sentient beings:

[23] IHC 3:120.

[24] Iida, *Random Comments*, quoted in IHC 2:139.

[25] 絶対主体道 [The way of absolute subjectivity] (Tokyo: Kōbundō Shobō, 1948), 144–5; quoted in IHC 2:128.

[26] IHC 3:101.

[27] IHC 3:124.

With what has modern Japanese Buddhism harmonized itself? With State Shinto. With state power and authority. With militarism. Accordingly, with war.

To what has modern Japanese Buddhism been nonresistant? To State Shinto. To state power and authority. To militarism. To wars of invasion.

Of what has modern Japanese Buddhism been tolerant? Of those with whom it harmonizes. Of its own responsibility for the war.[28]

Representatives of the Zen tradition have also applauded how the spiritual state of an awakened Zen Buddhist is like a mirror, reflecting what comes before it without discrimination, beyond duality, in an absolute objectivity that does not ask "why?" or wrestle with issues of good and evil. This is often offered to the "West" as a way to overcome the intolerance and conflict criticized by Zen figures as destructive ramifications of dualistic thinking. Ichikawa argues, however, that if such criticism had instead "been directed early on at the intolerance and combative nature of State Shinto and Imperial Way Buddhism, it might have been in time [to stop what happened]."[29] It might have also precluded the court testimony given by Colonel Aizawa Saburō when he was being tried for murdering General Nagata Tetsuzan in 1935: "I was in an absolute sphere, so there was neither affirmation nor negation, neither good nor evil."[30] (Of course, given what Suzuki claimed about Zen ultimacy having no dealings with actuality, perhaps nothing in Aizawa's actions or explanation runs contrary to "Zen.")

ICHIKAWA'S CRITIQUE OF NISHIDA PHILOSOPHY

Parallel to his critique of Zen, Ichikawa also raised questions about the wartime writings of "Kyoto-school philosophy" founder Nishida Kitarō (1870–1945), especially *The Problem of Japanese Culture* (日本文化の問題, 1938), *The Problem of the Raison d'état* (国家理由の問題, 1941), and *The National Polity* (国体, 1944). In these essays late in his career, Nishida applied his philosophical framework to the Japanese imperial system. For example, in a discussion of history he maintained:

The meaning of the formation of the historical world lies in the fact that the creation of heaven and earth is none other than the founding of the nation. For this reason, there is an unbroken lineage through the ages

[28] IHC 2:86–7.

[29] IHC 3:112.

[30] Quoted in IHC 2:166.

that is coeval with heaven and earth.... This is why there emerged the belief that Japan is a divine nation. In imperial edicts we can hear the voice of [the main] *kami* through a *kami* manifest in human form.[31]

Into this divine history Nishida inserted the role of the imperial subject:

> Active intuition is to accord faithfully with the facts of national history that have developed with the myth of the formation of the Japanese nation as their point of origin and main axis, to empty the self and return to oneness with the emperor as the center of the absolute present; it is to act in terms of the national polity as an individual in the historical world, in the manner of "all [is] from the imperial household [and returns] to the imperial household."[32]

This household is the all-encompassing locus of (Nishida's) Japanese existence, for "The imperial household is the absolute present that includes past and future, and we are born in it, work in it, and die in it."[33] This center entails debt and concomitant political duty:

> Our lives are our lives yet are not ours.... Though we may have a meal or a set of clothes, it is not our own.... In our personal lives as well we must not forget the thought of returning to oneness with the emperor and serving the state.[34]

One's ability to serve the state in this way, Nishida argued, has a religious basis, expressed by him in the kind of Zen terms discussed above:

> Religiously awakened people can become "master of every situation" as the self-determination of the absolute present. In all respects these people are active. For each, "the place in which one stands is truth"... From a true religious awakening one can submit to the state.[35]

[31] NKZ 12:409–10; quoted in IHC 3:195. I thank Professor Yusa Michiko for helping me locate this essay.

[32] NKZ 12:409–10; quoted in IHC 4:13–14.

[33] Quoted in IHC 3:194.

[34] NKZ 7:443; quoted in IHC 3:195.

[35] NKZ 11:144; quoted in IHC 3:195. The glorification of submitting to the state appeared in other essays. At one point, for example, Nishida wrote, "Our selves must be national in the sense of always being historical and formative as individuals of the world of the absolute present. True obedience to the nation should be derived from the standpoint of true religious self-awareness. Mere seeking one's own peace of mind is selfish." Nishida Kitarō, "Towards a Philosophy of Religion with the Concept of Pre-established Harmony as a Guide," tr. David A. Dilworth, *The Eastern Buddhist* 3/1 (1970): 45; originally published in 1944 and reprinted in NKZ 11:114–46. Cited by Robert Sharf, "The Zen of Japanese Nationalism," *History of Religions* 33/1 (August 1993): 24.

Nishida thus attributed to Japan a divine history, conceived of the imperial household as the "absolute present" central to that history, and took Japanese existence to be derived from the imperial system and oriented toward selflessly serving it. In Nishida's imperialist statements, made at a time when Japan was engaged in a war based ideologically on the very institutional structures (imperial household, divine nation, imperial edicts), historical claims (imperial lineage, national history), and behaviors (emptying the self, becoming one with the emperor, submitting to the state) that Nishida extolled, Ichikawa discerned philosophical issues similar to what he criticized in Zen.

Parallel to the Zen idea of "becoming one" with what one experiences, in the opening sentence of *An Inquiry into the Good* Nishida wrote: "To experience means to know facts just as they are, to know in accordance with facts by completely relinquishing one's own fabrications."[36] In the course of his writings Nishida's thought developed from this "pure experience" of "facts just as they are" and eventually arrived at consideration of the "historical world." Through this development he attempted to provide a logic and an ontological ground for the initial epistemology of "pure experience" and thereby rid his standpoint of what he called "psychologism." In this process he formulated such notions as the "logic of place," and at times he wrote in a Kegon Buddhist vein about the importance of "See[ing] the universal principle in the particular thing" (事の中に理を見る), with the universal and the particular existing in an "absolutely contradictory self-identity" or in terms of what his friend D. T. Suzuki termed the "logic of *soku-hi* (即非)." Summarizing Nishida's standpoint, Ichikawa wrote that

> actuality, formed in terms of absolutely contradictory self-identity, is the absolute…. The absolutely contradictory self-identity is the formula of the self-expression of the absolute. Logic is not the subjective formula of our thought but the formula of the self-formation of the world. It is not that we think about the world from the self, for we must think about the self from the world. This is "absolute objectivism," in which "the ten thousand things advance and confirm the self." The philosophy that began from "facts just as they are" has arrived at the historical world in which actuality, just as it is, is the absolute (現実即絶対).[37]

From Ichikawa's perspective, this standpoint presents problems when applied to the socio-political realm, as Nishida did when he meshed it with the Japanese imperial system. First, "In 'fact-ism' (事実主義) or 'actuality-ism'

[36] Nishida Kitarō, IG, 3.
[37] IHC 3:193–4.

(現実主義) as the viewpoint of seeing the universal principle in the particular thing, one can discern the nondual structure of 'ought' and 'is'. This 'non-dual' viewpoint, like the viewpoint of [Suzuki's] *soku*, is a contemplative viewpoint."[38] In other words, "This is a matter of seeing the principle at the base of actuality, not of changing the material structure of actuality,"[39] and with such contemplative passivity this approach generally accepts actuality and hence makes no distinction between "is" and "ought" and provides no impetus for social criticism or transformative activism.

Second, in seeing the absolute present and the imperial household as one and locating the universal principle (理) in the particular thing (事) called the imperial household, Nishida helped provide a philosophical foundation for the "holy war" being waged in the name of the emperor.[40] This paralleled the tendency of traditional Zen to accept and even glorify its political actual-ity, whether the Kamakura warrior government or the modern imperialist state.

Third, from the standpoint of what Ichikawa called "actuality-ism," Nishida claimed, "The content of our will(s) is given only by the self-determination of history in actuality."[41] Ichikawa judged this and other facets of Nishida's philosophy as undermining critical ethical freedom, which is based on autonomy and principles that are not shaped "only" by the circum-stances of present actuality, and hence diverges in character from the water that assumes the shape of any vessel into which it is poured. Indeed, the forms the "self-determination of history" took soon after Nishida made his claim about our wills (1934) and prior to his essays on the Japanese state included escalation of the war with China (from 1937), the "national spiritu-al mobilization" of the Japanese (国民精神総動員, 1937), and such Ministry of Education texts as *Fundamentals of the National Polity* (国体の本義, 1937). Ichikawa even declared that Nishida himself was "given content" by his his-torical actuality: "Both Nishida's samurai-style elitism, which was formed in the environment of old families from Japan Sea coastal areas, inclusive of the declining warrior class and bankrupt landowners, and his sensibility, which was formed by life and education under the authoritarianism of the imperial system, determined the historical body called Layman Sunshin [Nishida]."[42] With this socio-historical conditioning, Nishida wrote in his diary about the imperial family, the peerage, senior statesmen, and schoolfellows, but made

[38] IHC 4:107.

[39] IHC 4:107.

[40] IHC 3:210.

[41] IHC 3:121, quoting Nishida's *The Self-Determination of Nothingness* (NKZ 7).

[42] IHC 3:119–20.

virtually no reference to the daily life of ordinary people or such central polit-ical topics of his time as rice riots, elections, debates about "democracy," the formation of socialist and anarchist political parties, antiwar movements, and the Public Order Preservation Law.[43]

Ichikawa called attention to ethical pitfalls not only in Nishida's "actual-ity-ism" but also in his logic of place and the notion of "absolutely contra-dictory self-identity" (as well as in Suzuki's logic of *soku-hi*). Among other things, "absolutely contradictory self-identity" conveys the religious notion that by entering directly into existential insecurity one is liberated from it, such that suffering is liberation even while it remains suffering. Philosophically it expresses the relation between the one and the many, the universal principle and the particular thing. Problems emerge, however, in the socio-political application of this logic. To Ichikawa,

> the logic of *soku-hi*, that is, the logic of the absolutely contradictory self-identity in which non-freedom, just as it is, is freedom, in which [accord-ing to some] 'to become servant of every situation' (to sacrifice the self and serve the public in the holy war) is to 'become master of every situ-ation' (as in Mahāyāna Zen), played the social and political role [of pro-moting the imperial system].[44]

This is a logic of harmony:

> In the place of absolute nothingness, existence and nonexistence, value and anti-value, rationality and irrationality, are identical. More than a logic of confrontation and rejection, this is a logic of magnanimity and harmony. This is [a function of] the non-conflictuality and tolerance of place (場所).[45]

Further, at the social level the logics of place and *soku-hi* hold for all societies and all actualities, just as the sum of the three inner angles of a triangle is always 180 degrees,[46] and hence in and of themselves they provide no basis for critical evaluation of societies or for praxis aimed at transforming a society from what it "is" to what it might or "ought" to be.

With this overall character, Nishida's standpoint offers little philosophical support for critical, autonomous responsibility. Insofar as the will gets its con-tent and "truth" from actuality and "each action is the self-determination of the absolute present such that 'every place one stands is truth' [*Record of Lin-chi*], there emerges no responsibility that can be taken and no thing to take

---

43 IHC 3:201.
44 IHC 3:12.
45 IHC 3:198.
46 IHC 3:198.

responsibility."[47] Of course, this issue goes beyond Nishida, for to the extent Japanese were faithful subjects submitting to imperial decrees during the "holy war," the sense of personal responsibility for the war has been weak.[48] More often than not, Ichikawa claimed, the only responsibility many Japanese Buddhists felt immediately after the war was toward the emperor for their allowing the nation to be defeated. In the final analysis,

> from the standpoint of absolute objectivism, that is, the "fact-ism" of "seeing the principle in the particular thing," while Nishida in one respect negated the fact of the "Greater East Asia Holy War," he ultimately affirmed it and treated it in terms of the logic of "from the imperial household to the imperial household."[49]

Simply put, Nishida's wartime essays served to provide a philosophical basis for the state, the national polity, and the "holy war," and in this way helped "dispel the doubts of students bound for the front and provide a foundation for resignation to death."[50] (Although in many passages Nishida did not specify whether the state and national polity about which he was writing was the actual Japanese state or an ideal state, he at one point wrote that "national polity" was found only in Japan.[51])

For Ichikawa, one of the central problems in the approach of Nishida and Suzuki is the lack of a critical modern self. About Nishida he asserted,

> The doubt and negation that constitute the methodology of philosophy were directed completely inwards, toward the self, and because of this the moment for the maturation of the modern self, which is the subject of the modern critical spirit, was obliterated. As a result of this prior obliteration of the modern self—which could have been expected to doubt, criticize, and resist the absolutism of the imperial system—the central ideology of the Imperial Way settled into an *a priori* position relative to the pure experience underlying the individual self [Nishida], and thus from the start it conditioned that pure experience.[52]

He added:

[47] IHC 3:206.

[48] IHC 3:123.

[49] IHC 2:76.

[50] IHC 2:31.

[51] NKZ 12:410, quoted in IHC 4:108. In his essay on the national polity, Nishida claimed, "Strictly speaking, what is called 'national polity' does not exist outside of our country."

[52] IHC 3:208.

Nishida's emperor worship and authoritarian moral consciousness did not die the Great Death and burn to ashes. One cannot speak of having a cosmopolitan nature when lifting up the Imperial Way. Rather, contrariwise, the Imperial Way was internalized and absolutized through the death of modern intellectuality, took on religious authority, and controlled the private lives of individuals.... To speak of the Imperial Way having a cosmopolitan nature is like speaking of a round triangle....[53]

As conceptualized by Ichikawa, this "modern self" that these Zen-influenced thinkers lacked has the ability to criticize.[54] Though certain Zen figures might condemn this "self" as the locus of attachment, Ichikawa argued that democratic freedom and fundamental human rights were secured through struggles that lasted many years and were sustained through attachment to self and attachment to things.[55] And in one work Ichikawa pondered how absolute, religious freedom, if it had been developed into a critical ethic at the time of the "clarification of the national polity" (国体明徵), "support for the Imperial Way" (皇道翼賛), and the "holy war" might "in the face of the rampancy of parochial, arrogant State Shinto, have dealt it a painful blow of the staff."[56] Whatever the reason, Zen "failed to become like a dead person while alive and, in response to imperial-system fascism, failed to 'refute false doctrines and bring out the truth' (破邪顕正)."[57]

More broadly, in summarizing factors that led prominent Zen figures, Nishida, and Buddhists in general to exhibit passive conformity to or even active support of Japanese imperialism, Ichikawa exclaimed:

In the context of the anti-communist and anti-peace stance seen in the romantically emotional cluster of such concepts as absolute nothingness, [unique] historical actuality, no-self, the identity of contradiction, and "destroying the self to serve the public," many Japanese spread the pollution of their no-self philosophy and extended holy-war egoism throughout Asia.[58]

On a personal note, Ichikawa outlined how this *Zeitgeist* affected him:

Lying deep in my consciousness was the true thought (諦念) that seeing facts "just as they are," accepting actuality "just as it is," and according

[53] IHC 3:208–9.

[54] Consideration of the extent to which Ichikawa held a rather optimistic view of the ethical dimension of the "modern critical self" is beyond the scope of this paper.

[55] IHC 2:63.

[56] IHC 3:50.

[57] IHC 2:187.

[58] IHC 4:47–8.

with the laws of facts and actuality—that is to say, making into one's subjectivity the wisdom that discerns in actuality that necessity is, just as it is, freedom—constituted the path to peace of mind in which one "sees the universal principle in the particular thing." And when I stood in the face of the actuality called the national polity, this thought became a trans-ego foundation for my submissive conformity to the power of that actuality.[59]

Ichikawa's critique of Japanese imperialism is not limited to the above points about Zen and Nishida. Though beyond the scope of this paper, he also attributed the wartime stumbling of Japanese to such factors as the historical interdependency between Japanese Buddhism and those in political power (the "state"); passive interpretations of the doctrine of *karma*; the lack of notions of justice and human rights in Buddhism, partially owing to the doctrine of no-self; the philosophy of debt (恩); Japanese views of the "home" at the level of family and nation and their connection to ancestor worship; and the spirituality of aging and tranquility, which contributes to uncritical passivity in the social arena.

FURTHER ISSUES IN NISHIDA PHILOSOPHY

This paper has outlined Ichikawa's critique of the relationship Zen and Nishida had to Japanese imperialism. Stepping back from and examining this critique, one might argue that we should let bygones be bygones, that the Fifteen-Year War is in the past and should be left there. Given the apparent reluctance of the Zen tradition to look squarely at the issue of war responsibility, however, the possibility of its being "doomed to repeat" past mistakes is not insignificant. And even if one argues that in fact Japanese Zen Buddhists have reflected on and learned from past mistakes, we are still left with the fact that they have rarely spoken publicly about postwar issues related to those of the 1930s and 1940s, such as the Yasukuni Shrine, attacks by rightists, and the human rights problems faced by resident Koreans, *burakumin*, and others. One might contend that this is not the proper domain of Zen, but, as sketched earlier in this essay, prominent Zen figures did take clear political stances earlier in this century and historically Zen has never remained in any unpolitical or apolitical domain. The question, then, is that of how Zen Buddhists will function—inevitably and unavoidably—as political players in history.

Perhaps most challenged by Ichikawa's critique are Zen formulations of compassion. Representatives of the tradition often claim that awakening (*satori*) is necessarily accompanied by wisdom and compassion. Assuming

[59] IHC 2:145.

that support for Japanese imperialism reflects a certain deficiency of the kind of wisdom and compassion Mahāyāna Buddhism advocates, we are left with a dilemma: either Suzuki and the more orthodox Zen figures examined here had not attained awakening (and hence lacked wisdom and compassion), or they *were* awakened and the rhetoric of accompanying wisdom and compassion is just that—rhetoric. (One way around this dilemma is to restrict wisdom and compassion to a narrow religious definition and argue that they do not connote anything ethical, but in their discourse Suzuki and others do portray them as having ethical significance as well.)

Furthermore, given the rather belligerent support for Japanese imperialism shown by persons who functioned as *rōshi* in orthodox monastic Zen and its lineages (unlike Suzuki and Nishida), perhaps Zen should advocate not only killing the buddhas and patriarchs but also turning the sword against one or the other of two sacred cows of Zen: either the notion that awakening is necessarily accompanied by wisdom and compassion; or the notion that lineages include only awakened *rōshi*, who serve as enlightened links in chains of "mind-to-mind transmission" stretching back to the purported founder of the tradition (Bodhidharma) and even to the historical Buddha.[60] That is to say, if one wants to maintain the central claim that all Zen figures with the title of *rōshi* in an orthodox lineage are awakened, one appears compelled to sacrifice the other central claim that awakening is necessarily accompanied by wisdom and compassion (which the ostensibly awakened Zen *rōshi* quoted above appeared to lack). Conversely, if one wants to maintain the central claim that awakening does indeed come equipped with wisdom and compassion, one appears compelled to conclude that those imperialistic Zen *rōshi* were not awakened and hence also compelled to sacrifice the claim that all *rōshi* are awakened.

In short, assuming for the sake of argument that there is such a distinct experience or way of experiencing as awakening, we must conclude either that Zen awakening, though existentially liberating, lacks any fundamental or inherent connection to the realm of ethics, or that there have been *rōshi* who have not realized awakening (despite the usual connotation of their title, or their having received certification (印可証明) or "Dharma-transmission" in a lineage).

Next, any attempt to assess involvement by Nishida in Japanese "nationalism"[61] runs up against several barriers. The first concerns intention: what

[60] Conceptualized in this way, Zen lineages, with their systems of certification and succession, serve as the de facto touchstone for "orthodoxy" and the locus of organization and control in the tradition.

[61] For the sake of convenience, I use the term *nationalism* broadly without attempting to make fine distinctions between *kokka-shugi*, *minzoku-shugi*, and other Japanese expressions that

was Nishida attempting to accomplish through his wartime writings, lectures, and activities, and, more narrowly, what meaning did he ascribe to specific statements and actions? Given the inherent difficulty of reconstructing retrospectively the intention behind statements made over fifty years ago (not to mention the issues of whether authors and actors have intention or motivation that is unambiguously clear to themselves and whether self-representations are accurate or honest), the more manageable question is one of definition: what was the apparent connotation (and denotation) of the terms Nishida employed?

As sketched by Ichikawa, in his later writings on history Nishida marshalled arguments held together by the very terminological warp around which ultranationalists wove their ideology: national polity, imperial household, divine nation, "all the world under one roof," and so forth. Some have claimed that Nishida's definitions of these terms differed from those ascribed by ultranationalists, and that even though Nishida's writings appear to advance arguments nearly indistinguishable from nationalistic propaganda, he participated in the Shinto-based lexicon if not overall discursive space of imperialist and militarist ideologues in order to steer his nation toward the kind of historical creation and co-prosperity sphere he envisioned. At the very least we are left with the need to examine closely the arguments of specific texts while considering their intertextuality (vis-à-vis other works by Nishida and related texts) and their social, political, economic, and historical contexts.[62] Through such careful analysis of Kyoto school wartime texts in all of their complexity and ambiguity we can steer a middle way between the Scylla of obfuscatory apologetics and the Charybdis of accusatory polemics.

A further issue crops up, however, when we shift from texts to their reception. Even if we could somehow reconstruct Nishida's intention and pin down the "exact meaning" of specific terms or texts as a whole, this methodology does not take into account possible effects his discourse had on students, colleagues, general readers, and those in power. Allowing for a distinction between connotative and performative dimensions of texts, and granting that words and texts take on a life of their own (or are adopted into countless interpretive homes) once introduced to an audience of readers, we can consider the possibility that Nishida's discourse had an impact divergent from what he intended. Specifically, his decision to adopt the Shinto terminology brandished by ultranationalists may have actually served to

---

have been rendered *nationalism* in English. Other papers in this volume offer analyses of these expressions.

[62] In this regard, Yusa Michiko's methodology of comparing Nishida's "On Scholarly Methods" with *Fundamental Principles of the National Polity* proves useful as one part of the exegesis necessary for assessing Kyoto-school wartime texts as fairly and accurately as possible.

promote their—not his—overall objectives, in that readers swayed by what he wrote (or awed by his status) and unable to differentiate it from other formulations of the imperial system or Japan's historical role came to be more receptive to those other formulations.

Granting these hermeneutical considerations, analysis of Nishida's formal writings and letters provides evidence supportive of the argument that he was trying to steer his country away from destructive imperialism and hence was not a nationalist in any narrow or belligerent sense. In letters Nishida clearly expressed worries about developments in Japan at that time;[63] he was a consistent advocate of academic freedom;[64] in his wartime writings he occasionally rejected what he termed "invasionism" and imperialist egoism; he was criticized by the army and such rightists as Minoda Muneki for the Western elements in his philosophy, even though—and in part because—he and his Kyoto school colleagues had close connections to Prime Minister Konoe Fumimaro and the navy.

Even acknowledging this evidence and the impossibility of pinning down the actual effects his writings had on his audience, we are still confronted by numerous issues in Nishida's philosophical system, several of which were raised by Ichikawa in his critique. These issues include:

1. a tendency to identify the "is" with the "ought," the particular "fact" with the universal "principle," and the actual with the absolute;
2. an articulation of the state as the source and embodiment of moral value;
3. an affirmation of the myth of Japanese origins and the accompanying pseudo-history of an unbroken lineage of emperors descended from cosmogonic *kami*;
4. an advocacy of submission to the state and fusion with the emperor;
5. a dearth of economic analysis;
6. a bias toward harmony and unity; and
7. an espousal of Japan's taking the lead in Asia at a time when Japan was "taking the lead" through military aggression and colonial rule.

First, Ichikawa's characterization of Nishida's system, as a kind of "actuality-ism" that obfuscates distinctions between what is and what ought to be, seems valid. Similar to statements Ichikawa brought to the fore, in "The National Polity" Nishida explicitly negated reflection in terms of the ought:

---

[63] See M. Yusa, "Nishida and the Question of Japanese Nationalism," *Monumenta Nipponica* 46/2 (Summer 1991): 203–9.

[64] Yusa, "Nishida and the Question of Japanese Nationalism," 204.

Our self is not found in the place where one follows the ought of abstract reason. Human beings are not machines of logic. Nor does mere arbitrariness constitute the self.... Our self is born in terms of a historical body. Without the subject of the ethnic nation (民族) there is no historical formation.... The ethnic nation forms the historical world through the mediation of our selves as the self-formative power of the historical world.[65]

In this same essay Nishida also wrote, "The zenith of Japanese spirit is in 'actuality just as it is, is the absolute'."[66]

Further, as discussed before, Ichikawa reproached Nishida for contending that the imperial household is the absolute present and the fundamental principle upon which Japanese culture and the Japanese state were based. This component of Ichikawa's critique corresponds to points made by other Japanese scholars. Furuta Hikaru argues that

the philosophy of Nishida and the Kyoto school takes a standpoint in which the truly "subjective" way of being relative to actuality is to discover what ought to exist (the *ought*) within what is actual (the *is*) in the state and war and, through uninterrupted practice, to maintain the unity of this *is* and *ought*. This philosophy was welcomed by the intelligentsia at that time, who were in anguish over the gap between the "actuality" of the state's war and the philosophy of the "self," for the one thing able to bridge that gap was that philosophy's logic of "the *ought*, just as it is, is the *is*; the *is*, just as it is, is the *ought*." But insofar as this logic found in the "imperial way" (the political principles of the imperial system) a fundamental principle that could support historical unfolding in terms of "the *is*, just as it is, is the *ought*" and operated on the basis of this great presupposition, it gave precedence not to a functioning in which the *is* was controlled by the *ought* but a functioning in which the *is* was justified by the *ought*.[67]

In conjunction with this facet of his thought, Nishida also argued that the state supplies morality and consequently takes on a religious coloring:

The state is the power that creates value. The true state must, as the subject of historical formation, be the creator of value.... What is called

[65] NKZ 12:398.

[66] NKZ 12:411.

[67] 古田 光 Furuta Hikaru, 十五年戦争下の思想と哲学 [Thought and philosophy of the fifteen-year war], in Furuta Hikaru, 作田啓一 Sakuta Keiichi and 生松敬三 Ikimatsu Keizō, eds., 近代日本社会思想史 [The history of modern Japanese social thought], vol. 2 (Tokyo: Yūhikaku, 1971), 278.

national value is creative value. For this reason it is true moral value. In the background the state possesses something religious.[68]

And again:

...in the history of our nation, which as the self-determination of the absolute present forms history, for the first time was realized the national polity in which the state, just as it is, is morality (国家即道徳).[69]

In conjunction with this articulation of the state in moral terms, Nishida appeared to accept as literally true the divine history—unfolding around an unbroken imperial lineage since the founding of the nation by Jinmu—revered by ultranationalists, even though in passages he used the word "myth" (albeit seemingly in the technical sense of cosmogonic stories about the *kami*). One question demanding an answer here is whether Nishida, whom many have deemed a highly sophisticated, modern thinker with a critical view of history, actually took this "history" at face value.

Even if he did not, Nishida affirmed if not glorified this pseudo-history, as well as both the centrality of the imperial system to Japanese culture and the moral status of the state; and he did so at a time when these highly ideological constructs were being marshalled propagandistically to pursue ends that Nishida seemed nervous about in his personal correspondence. In general, Nishida's thought does not sufficiently resolve the tension between his insistence that the state becomes a genuine state only when it possesses a universality or transcendence (of, among other things, "national egoism") and his parochial championing of Japan's highly particularized national polity and imperial system.

Exacerbating this philosophical problem is Nishida's affirmation of serving the state. As quoted above, he admonished his readers, "we must not forget the thought of returning to oneness with the emperor and serving the state."[70] In "Principles for a New World Order" he affirmed "thought guidance" (albeit while criticizing certain existing forms of it),[71] the notion of gaining one's individual moral mission from the state,[72] and such authoritarian slogans as "the unity of sovereign and subject" and "active support by all subjects."[73] One might question this advocacy of obedience to the state and

[68] NKZ 12:399. Nishida did not clarify the nature of this linkage between moral value and religion in the essay.

[69] NKZ 12:409.

[70] NKZ 7:443; quoted in IHC 3:195.

[71] NKZ 12:431.

[72] NKZ 12:433.

[73] NKZ 12:431.

ask whether Nishida gave sufficient critical attention to the character and policies of the *actual* Japanese state and to the question of whether they were morally acceptable on the basis of autonomous moral principles that transcend that state and its promulgated norms ("morality").

A further issue deserving attention is the dearth of economic analysis in Nishida's thought. Ichikawa criticized Nishida for class bias and a rejection of class struggle as a critical, dialectical "moment" in history while allowing—to a certain, undefined extent—for conflict between mutually negating nations in the world of active creation, of poiesis "from that which is made to that which makes."[74] Interestingly, one of the few economic statements in Nishida's writings is an unqualified affirmation of the factory (as a locus of production in the creation of the historical world) in his wartime essay, "The National Polity." In much nationalist discourse in Japan (and elsewhere) class issues get subsumed and obscured by emphasis on such overarching concepts as the nation state and the national polity (or the Japanese spirit). The use of such categories has led to hackneyed pronouncements about how the Japanese are a homogeneous, harmonious folk (or race), as seen in "The National Polity" where Nishida referred to the Japanese as monoethnic and "blending together" in the imperial system.

One can justifiably argue that this emphasis in Nishida's later thought, even when divergent from and in tension with ultranationalist standpoints, masked socio-economic tensions and contributed indirectly to an expansionist foreign policy by helping foster the sense of unity as an "us" in an antagonistic relationship with a Western "them" (a unity Japanist discourse has claimed was not politically constructed and maintained but present in Japanese society from the beginning because of shared blood, language, and spirit). It is interesting to note here that Marxist critics have argued that, more broadly, capitalists attempted in the early-Shōwa period to divert attention from and mitigate tensions surrounding domestic socio-economic conditions by formulating both an official ideology in terms of a class-blind national polity or Japanese spirit and an expansionist foreign policy. This Marxist analysis, however, overestimates the power that capitalist elites possessed in the 1930s and fails to account for the full and complex range of forces at work in Japanese society at that time.

To Ichikawa and others, the issue of Nishida's handling of economic issues and class conflict is part of a larger problem: Nishida's tendency to downplay conflict (in actuality and in principle) and to move too quickly to an affirmation of harmony. This tendency appeared, for example, in Nishida's sanitized portrayals of Japanese history, as in the assertion, "When we con-

---

[74] Logically, his system allows for mutual negation between individuals, but he granted this virtually no social or political specificity.

sider the history of the emergence of our state, we understand that there was never anything like 'struggle' or 'subjugation' of different races and peoples [in our country], but that the clans, by melting into one united body under the banner of the Heavenly Grandson's clan, came to form the well-rounded body of one people."[75] Based on this and other such statements, Arima Tatsuo contends that

> Nishida...abhorred conflict in any form whatsoever. He had already stated that what characterized Japanese history was the presence of the imperial household and that this presence should be able to overcome the realities of political conflict.[76]

(Paradoxically, despite his overall disavowal of domestic conflict, Nishida accepted its international form: in his New Year's lecture for the emperor in 1941, he explained, "For various peoples to enter this one world means that they enter one and the same environment. Therefore, there necessarily arise mutual struggles and conflicts among peoples, and wars are inevitable."[77])

This tendency to obfuscate distinctions between *is* and *ought* and to downplay conflict prompts the meta-level question of how the metaphysical and religious dimensions so central to much of Kyoto school philosophy play out politically in terms of criticism of concrete actualities or advocacy of specific lines of praxis. That is to say, in making the transition from "pure experience" to the "historical world," was Nishida able to extricate himself from a religious epistemology centered on "pure experience" and a "unifying activity" prior to subject-object duality and give full, critical attention to concrete subjects and objects, their conflicts, and the adjudication—through dualistic principles and non-intuitional, rational thought—of conflicting claims? Or did his starting point of "pure experience," with its somewhat monistic character, prevent him from engaging adequately in such critical analysis, from being able to criticize the *is* insofar as it fell short of an *ought*?

From the perspective of Arima Tatsuo, "The primary sin of a Nishida or a Watsuji was not that their ideal of harmony in the individual might be untenable, but that they confused the realities of politics with personal longings for serenity and harmony."[78] Arima further asserts,

---

[75] NKZ 12:416; quoted by Klaus Kracht, "Nishida Kitarō (1870–1945) as a Philosopher of the State," in Gordon Daniels, ed., *Europe Interprets Japan* (Tenterden, Kent: Paul Norbury Publications, 1984), 202. Kracht argues that Nishida's way of treating contradiction "leads to a theory of permanent reconciliation," to a "dialectic of justification."

[76] Arima Tatsuo, *The Failure of Freedom: A Portrait of Modern Japanese Intellectuals* (Cambridge: Harvard University Press, 1969), 12.

[77] Cited after an unpublished translation by Yusa Michiko.

[78] Arima, *The Failure of Freedom*, 13.

The philosophical category of pure experience, with all its logical embellishments, was used to preach social resignation as a means of achieving individual enlightenment.... When the idea of pure experience is realized within the individual, it encourages a kind of religious submission to reality. This being the ultimate reality, there is no need for the self to remold its social surroundings.[79]

Finally, perhaps equally problematical was Nishida's affirmation of Japan's taking the lead in Asia at a time when Japanese belligerence was being justified in terms of leading Asia out from under Western imperialism. He makes this affirmation in such essays as "The Philosophical Foundation of Communalism" (1939) and "Principles for a New World Order" (1943). For example, in the latter he wrote, "To build the 'one particular world' [of East Asia], there must be one [state] standing at its center, which takes this task upon itself. In East Asia the [leading force] is none other than our country of Japan."[80] This statement takes on an ominous character in light of the last lines of that essay:

It can be said that the solution to the problem of the current world-historical problem is provided by the fundamental principles of our national polity. England and the United States must submit to this, and, moreover, the Axis Powers will come to emulate this.[81]

Although Nishida did warn against certain means of taking the lead, his advocacy of Japan as having a unique role as the leader of Asia put him on a slippery rhetorical slope that in all likelihood served (inadvertently or otherwise) to rationalize actions by the army and other players in militaristic Japanese expansionism.

In conjunction with this issue of Japan's taking the lead, it is worth noting that many Japanese intellectuals, including Kyoto school philosophers, construed the Fifteen-Year War as a war of liberation. Although several hundred years of destructive Western imperialism stood in the background of early-Shōwa historical events, the portrayal of Japanese actions as efforts by a cornered nation—"the one remaining uncolonized nation"—to take the lead and liberate Asia from Western, especially Anglo-Saxon (as portrayed in the *Chūōkōron* discussions in 1941–1942), colonialism flies in the face of several facts: there were such Asian areas as Thailand that were not colonized by Western powers, and Japan itself colonized its Asian neighbors, such as Taiwan from 1895, Korea from 1910, and Manchuria from the 1920s; fur-

[79] Arima, *The Failure of Freedom*, 13–14.
[80] NKZ 12:429; quoted by Kracht, "Nishida Kitarō," 203.
[81] NKZ 12:434.

ther, Japan's non-Anglo-Saxon German and Italian allies had participated in Western imperialism and colonialism in Asia and other parts of the world.

Related to this, when looking at Japan or the Kyoto school and "the war," one must ask "Which war?" Narrow focus only on the "Pacific War" (1941–1945), though promoted by the Occupation's insistence on this terminology, makes it possible to portray Japan as a nation cornered by Western colonialism and blockades that shifted from peace to war in late 1941 to protect itself and liberate Asia. This portrayal diverts attention both from Japan's own aggressive imperialism in the preceding decades (an imperialism perhaps understandable in part as a kind of a mimetic stance towards the very West whose imperialism Japan was ostensibly trying to eradicate in Asia), and from the fact that certain Kyoto-school thinkers apparently accepted Japan's aggression toward China, Korea, and other Asian areas prior to 1941.[82]

Ichikawa's critique of Nishida and the additional discussion above reveal certain patterns. In his essays Nishida did warn against "invasionism" and self-serving imperialism; Nishida was criticized by ultranationalists; and in his correspondence he did express concerns about the direction in which Japan was headed. These data were not presented by Ichikawa, which leaves his critique a bit lacking in nuance. However, though Nishida may not have intended to promote Japanese aggression abroad and authoritarian control at home, and though he may not have had any significant influence on people or events around him (no matter what he might have written, said, or done), his writings at the least validated the main ideological building blocks of militarists at that time: the centrality of and divine history behind a sanctified imperial system; the moral authority of the state; the moral and religious dimensions of submitting to the emperor and the state; and the necessity for Japan to take the lead in Asia. This philosophical validation—though perhaps inadvertent—looms large in comparison with Nishida's personal qualms, his occasional caveats about "invasionism," and the pressure exerted on him by ultranationalists.

Certain Japanese scholars concur with this tentative conclusion that Nishida's writings provided philosophical support for Japan's expansionist nationalism. Furuta Hikaru writes,

> ...during the war the main aspiration common to Nishida and the Kyoto school was to follow along with the movement of the Japanese state while attempting to check as much as possible, from within, the trend toward egoistic imperialism and self-righteous nationalism. To this end he followed the strategy of assenting *in name* to such slogans of the mil-

---

[82] In the *Chūōkōron* discussions Nishitani Keiji spoke of the "opacity" of events in China, and remarked how people "mistakenly" viewed Japanese actions as an imperialist invasion on a par with the imperialism carried out by Europe and the United States.

itary fascists as "national polity," "imperial way," and "all the world under one roof," while transforming their content into concepts of Nishida philosophy and a philosophy of history, and through this tried to redirect the course of the actual state. But, precisely for this reason the philosophy of this school of thought, although drawing a harsh reaction from the army and right-wing thinkers, performed the function of offering a conceptual dialectic that *in terms of content* glorified Japanese imperialistic domination of Asian peoples carried out *on the pretext of* "all the world under one roof." As for the Japanese intelligentsia, this philosophy *in substance* assumed the role of having them, *on the pretext of* the "holy war," participate wholeheartedly in and cooperate with the Pacific War and all of its contradictions. Herein lies the tragedy of the Kyoto school, inclusive of Nishida.[83]

Of course, with regard to the question of Zen, the Kyoto school, and Japanese nationalism, there is much gray and little black or white, as with most ethical and political issues. There was diversity among individuals affiliated with Zen and the Kyoto school, and some of them changed their personal views and stances over time.[84] Clarification of the relationship these Buddhists and intellectuals had to Japanese "nationalism" thus calls for a nuanced approach that takes into account variation in and between the individuals in question. Through such inquiry, one can begin to assess their philosophical views in terms of coherence and consistency and examine linkages between theory and praxis, between philosophical systems and complex political actualities.

---

[83] Furuta, "The Fifteen-Year War," 277.

[84] For example, though beyond the scope of this paper, close examination of the statements in the *Chūōkōron* discussions indicates that Nishitani Keiji, Kōsaka Masaaki, Kōyama Iwao, and Suzuki Shigetaka had a more enthusiastic attitude toward Japanese imperialism than Nishida, and such figures as Tanabe Hajime explicitly changed their standpoint.

Whose Zen?

Zen Nationalism Revisited

Robert H. SHARF

IN THE NINTH CHAPTER OF the *Vimalakīrti-nirdeśa Sūtra* the householder Vimalakīrti asks the great assembly of bodhisattvas to explain how a bodhisattva enters the dharma-gate of nonduality. After listening to numerous bodhisattvas expound on the issue, Mañjuśrī challenges Vimalakīrti to offer his own response. Vimalakīrti, in what is clearly the climax of the scriptural narrative, remains utterly silent. Mañjuśrī, bodhisattva of wisdom, then offers the highest praise for Vimalakīrti's response, calling it "the true entry into the dharma-gate of nonduality."[1]

But this is not the only time we are confronted with silence in this scripture. In chapter seven of the text, in the midst of a *mondō*-like exchange between a goddess and Śāriputra, the goddess asks: "How long has it been since the venerable elder was liberated?" Śāriputra meets the question with silence. When pushed by the goddess, Śāriputra explains that he remained silent because liberation is inexpressible. The goddess then reproaches him: there is no reason to favor silence over speech, she insists, since "words and speech have the nature of liberation."[2]

Why does silence indicate consummate wisdom in the one instance, and confusion in the other? The short answer is that in one case the respondent was Vimalakīrti, an incarnation of highest wisdom, while in the other case it

The paper entitled "The Zen of Japanese Nationalism," which I presented to the symposium on which this volume is based, is to appear in Donald S. Lopez, Jr., ed., *Curators of the Buddha: The Study of Buddhism under Colonialism* (Chicago: University of Chicago Press, 1995). An earlier version appeared in *History of Religions* 33/1 (1993): 1–43. I offer below some further reflections on the topic, stimulated by the often intense exchanges at the symposium.

[1] Kumārajīva trans., T.475: 14.551c.

[2] T.475: 14.548a. *Mondō* (問答) refers to a question-and-answer exchange between master and disciple aimed at testing understanding.

was Śāriputra, a "Hīnayāna" disciple who is depicted as somewhat the fool in this polemical Mahāyāna text.[3] One might call it a matter of credentials.

This issue, trivial as it might at first seem, is not unrelated to a set of Mahāyāna doctrinal formulations that revolve around the "two truths." If there is ultimately no distinction between truth and falsehood, or between liberation and ignorance, how is the *saṃgha* to guarantee the viability of the institutions and teachings that are intended to bring liberation to all beings? How can one transmit the truth when the truth is precisely the realization that there is no "truth" to transmit? The stock Mādhyamika solution to this quandary consists of an appeal to two levels of truth—the contingent and the ultimate. The *contingent* distinction between ignorance and liberation is said to be a "means" (*upāya*) to bring ignorant folk to the realization that *ultimately* there is no distinction between bondage and liberation.

The advocates of Zen subitism (i.e., the "Southern orthodoxy" traditionally traced to Hui-neng) were skeptical of this ploy. How could a teaching that was predicated on a set of false distinctions ever bring one to a realization of the emptiness of all such distinctions? The Zen approach took the form of an uncompromising conceptual emphasis on "emptiness" within an institutional structure that gave pride of place to form. Virtually every facet of life in a Zen monastery was governed by strict rules of ritual decorum; the ritualization of daily life extended to even the most mundane of tasks such as cleaning one's teeth or using the toilet.[4] While the discursive content of the daily prayers and sūtra recitations, the abbot's sermons, and the kōan collections reiterated *ad nauseam* the message that all form is empty, monks were subject to immediate and often harsh punishment for any breach of ritual protocol—a cogent reminder that emptiness was to be found precisely *within* form.

This dialectic between emptiness and form is readily illustrated in the notion of transmission. Zen was, of course, the school that sought to distin-

---

[3] Some might object that while silence was a sublime response to a question concerning nonduality, it was not an appropriate reply to the question posed by the goddess. This is beside the point. Given the characterization of Śāriputra in the text there is little doubt that if he offered silence in response to the question concerning nonduality, his silence would once again indicate "attachment to emptiness," if not simple bafflement.

[4] The rules governing such tasks can be found in Sung dynasty monastic codes such as the 禪苑清規 *Ch'an-yüan ch'ing-kuei*, the 校定清規 *Chiao-ting ch'ing-kuei*, and the 勅修百丈清規 *Ch'ih-hsiu pai-chang ch'ing-kuei*. These early texts served as models for all later Zen codes of conduct; see the discussion in T. Griffith Foulk, "Myth, Ritual, and Monastic Practice in Sung Ch'an Buddhism," in *Religion and Society in T'ang and Sung China*, ed. Patricia Buckley Ebrey and Peter N. Gregory (Honolulu: University of Hawaii Press), 147–208. The earliest extant code, the 入衆日用 *Ju-chung jih-yung* (大日本續藏經 2.16.5) includes detailed instructions on dental hygiene and the use of the toilet.

guish itself from its rivals by its claim to represent an unbroken "mind-to-mind" transmission of the dharma from one authorized master to another. At the same time Zen texts insist that ultimately there is nothing to transmit, rendering transmission the quintessential "empty form." The complex cluster of rites and practices that surrounded the notion of transmission emerged as one of the defining characteristics of the Zen school. Only those who were formally received into the lineage of patriarchs through a ceremony known as "transmission of the dharma" (傳法 *denbō*) or receipt of the "seal of transmission" (印可 *inka*) were accorded the authority to pass on the dharma to others. Once a monk was drafted into the legion of patriarchs his sermons would be dutifully recorded for later study, his portraits produced in numbers to serve as objects of worship, and his bodily remains preserved as sacred relics imbued with miraculous powers.[5] While the patriarch was expected to preside over a number of ceremonial events in which he ritually made manifest his "enlightenment," he had at his disposal a host of conventional rhetorical gestures that served to denote his freedom from social, ritual, and institutional conventions. These gestures were not mere ploys; they were acquired through years of intense monastic study and discipline. Only when a monk had come to embody the full range of Zen ceremonial and rhetorical forms would he be deemed qualified to assume the role of patriarch, effectively rendering him, ex-officio, a living buddha.

The latter point is often misunderstood. According to certain popular conceptions, certification was granted to a disciple only after he could demonstrate that he had attained an authentic experience of awakening or *satori*. While we do find stories in the "recorded sayings collections" (語録 *yü-lu*) that would seem to lend credence to this view, in point of fact certification had little if anything to do with the verification of any specific "religious experience." Rather, it was typically given to those who had spent the requisite years mastering the elaborate scriptural corpus and ritual procedures necessary to perform the duties of abbot. Only after prolonged study under the strict guidance of seasoned monks could one be entrusted to wield the rhetorical sword of emptiness in a manner that upheld, rather than threatened, the long-term viability of the monastic institution. The difference between an authorized master speaking of the "emptiness of form" and a mere student was not so much a difference in their "spiritual experience," or even in their manner of expression, but a difference in the official roles they played within the larger institutional context.

---

[5] See Robert H. Sharf, "The Idolization of Enlightenment: On the Mummification of Ch'an Masters in Medieval China," *History of Religions* 32/1 (1992): 1–31; and T. Griffith Foulk and Robert H. Sharf, "On the Ritual Use of Ch'an Portraiture in Medieval China," *Cahiers d'Extrême-Asie* 7 (1993/94): 149–219.

Modern lay students of Zen might find this concern with credentials and institutional stability a touch troubling; does it not contravene the very spirit of Zen "liberation"? In the popular imagination a master typically manifests his liberation in spontaneous and often antinomian behavior, accompanied by sudden shouts or inscrutable utterances. But we must be careful not to confuse pious mythology with institutional reality. After all, when it comes to "manifesting" or "transmitting" what is supposedly an ineffable dharma, in principle silence is no better than speech, a shout no better than a sūtra, antinomian antics no better than stately ceremony.[6] In fact, traditional Zen monastic training did not countenance spontaneous outbursts, but rather taught forms of speech and action that ritually *denoted* spontaneity and freedom. As in the case of Vimalakīrti and Śāriputra, the denotative force of Zen activity depends largely on how the activity is "framed," i.e., the social role of the protagonist and the ritual context in which his performance takes place. Understandably, the Zen institution exercised considerable caution when it came to authorizing a monk to assume the role of "living buddha."

If the importance of credentials, of institutional sanction, or of traditional authority in Zen comes as a surprise, it may be due in part to the fact that so many of those responsible for popularizing Zen in the twentieth century lacked formal institutional sanction themselves. D. T. Suzuki, Nishitani Keiji, and Abe Masao, to name but a few, all lacked formal transmission in a Zen lineage, and their intellectualized Zen is often held in suspicion by Zen traditionalists. We should be cautious before uncritically accepting their claim that Zen is some sort of nonsectarian spiritual gnosis, for such a claim is clearly self-serving: by insisting that Zen is a way of experiencing the world, rather than a complex form of Buddhist monastic practice, these Japanese intellectuals effectively circumvent the question of their own authority to speak on behalf of Zen. But there is something more pernicious at work here than the attempt of a few "outsiders" to appropriate the authority of the tradition, for in insisting that Zen could be, and indeed should be, distinguished from its monastic "trappings" these writers effectively severed Zen's links to traditional Buddhist soteriological, cosmological, and ethical concerns. Once wrenched from its institutional and ethical context, this free-floating Zen could be used to lend spiritual legitimacy to a host of contemporary social,

---

[6] This dilemma is explored in a number of Zen kōan, such as case 5 of the 無門関 *Wu-men kuan*, Hsiang-yen's "Man up a tree" (T.2005: 48.293c2–4). A man holding onto a branch of a tree by his teeth is asked by a passerby: "Why did Bodhidharma come from the West?" We know, of course, that Bodhidharma went to China to transmit the dharma. But should the man up the tree say so he runs the risk of reifying a "dharma" that could be transmitted. Indeed, to say anything at all will send him plunging to his death. If he remains silent, however, he forsakes the bodhisattva path, abrogating his responsibility to transmit the dharma to all beings.

philosophical, and political movements, from dadaism to Kyoto philosophy, from new-age hedonism to fascism. Thus before reflecting on the question of "Zen and nationalism" we must look carefully at just what sort of Zen we are talking about.

ZEN AS A TWENTIETH-CENTURY CONSTRUCT

The popular "lay" image of Zen, notably the notion that Zen refers not to a specific school of Buddhism but rather to a mystical or spiritual gnosis that transcends sectarian boundaries, is largely a twentieth-century construct. Beginning with the persecution of Buddhism in the early Meiji (廃仏毀釈 *haibutsu kishaku*) Zen apologists have been forced to respond to secular and empiricist critiques of religion in general, and to Japanese nativist critiques of Buddhism as a "foreign funerary cult" in particular. In response, partisans of Zen drew upon Western philosophical and theological strategies in their attempt to adapt their faith to the modern age. As I have discussed this phenomenon in detail elsewhere, I will limit myself here to a brief overview, concentrating not so much on the historical evolution of contemporary Zen rhetoric, but rather on its underlying logical structure.[7] For heuristic purposes I have analyzed this structure in terms of four conceptual stages.

The first stage involves positing a distinction between the "essence" of a religious tradition and its "cultural manifestations." According to this view, while the cultural manifestations of a religion are invariably shaped by social, institutional, and economic contingencies, the essence is an ahistorical truth logically prior to, and thus unsullied by, the cultural forms through which it is made known. Modern scholarship has effectively naturalized this somewhat Platonic distinction between timeless essence and localized manifestation— we tend to forget that the modern version of this distinction is part of a theological enterprise with roots firmly in reformation Europe. This apologetic discourse effectively exonerates religion from crimes committed in its name; the "spiritual essence" of a tradition remains forever untainted by the shortcomings of church or clergy. Thus Japanese Buddhist intellectuals in the Meiji were able to argue that the corruption and degeneracy of the Tokugawa Buddhist establishment in no way impugned the spiritual heart of Buddhism.

Closely associated with the distinction between "pure essence" and "contingent manifestation" is the notion of "pure origins"—the supposition that the original expression of a religious teaching most perfectly reflects its unvarying essence.[8] The founding truth of a religion is, according to this

---

[7] For a historically oriented analysis, see my "The Zen of Japanese Nationalism."

[8] See the discussion in chapter 1 of Bernard Faure's *The Rhetoric of Immediacy: A Cultural Critique of Chan/Zen Buddhism* (Princeton: Princeton University Press, 1991).

view, profoundly compromised and obscured as it becomes institutionalized under the control of a self-serving priesthood. The gradual but virtually inevitable decline of the teachings may, however, be punctuated by periodic revivals in which inspired leaders attempt to reform the institution through a renewed emphasis on the "original teachings."

This notion of spiritual decline is not, of course, new; structurally analogous versions include the biblical genesis narrative, the Buddhist notion of the "decline of the dharma," psychological theories of ego development that view emergence into adulthood as a "descent from grace," and so on. The prevalence and seductiveness of this myth may account in part for the preoccupation among scholars of religion with "origins," despite the fact that the identification of an "origin" is always somewhat arbitrary and therefore suspect. Scholars must be cautious lest the ideological and apologetic dimensions of the "fall narrative" come to compromise their work; historical efforts to reconstruct the life of "the founder," his disciples, and his teachings, for example, often contribute to an academic discourse that tacitly deprecates or disenfranchises later doctrinal or institutional developments.[9] This in turn lends historical credibility to the apologetic distinction drawn between the "essence" of a tradition—the source from which a tradition springs—and the cultural forms through which it is made known.

The second stage in the construction of modern Zen rhetoric consists in identifying the essence as a type of "experience." The heart of Zen thus lies not in its ethical principles, its communal and ritual practices, or its doctrinal teachings, but rather in a private, veridical, often momentary "state of consciousness." I have demonstrated elsewhere that the emphasis on experience in modern Japanese renderings of Zen can be traced directly back to Western writings on religion and psychology, notably the works of William James.[10] In privileging experience the Japanese, like their Western mentors, sought to naturalize the category "religion"—if religious traditions were predicated upon an ineffable, noetic, mystical state of consciousness, then they could not be rejected as mere superstition, infantile wish-fulfillment, or collective hysteria. At the same time, by construing the core of religion in general, and Zen in particular, as a subjective experience, religion was rendered immune to rationalist, positivist, or empiricist critiques. Apologists could then argue that modern scientific rationality was not a viable alternative to religious modes of

---

[9] It is not uncommon, for example, to find the growth of a tradition analyzed under the rubric of "institutionalization," "popularization," "syncretic accommodation," and so on.

[10] See "The Zen of Japanese Nationalism" and "Buddhism and the Rhetoric of Experience," (paper presented at the annual meeting of the American Academy of Religion, San Francisco, November 22, 1992).

understanding; rather, the unchecked rise of "scientism" made the need to plumb the spiritual depths of the "great religions" all the more imperative.

The third stage consists in universalizing the "Zen experience" by denying that Zen is a school or sect of Buddhism per se, or even a "religion." Rather, partisans would insist that the term "Zen" properly understood denotes the universal experiential core of all authentic religious traditions, both Eastern and Western. In short, Zen is truth itself, allowing those with Zen insight to claim a privileged perspective on all the great religious faiths.[11]

The final stage comprises the claim that the universal religious experience of Zen is the ground of Japanese aesthetic and ethical sensibilities. Virtually all of the major Japanese artistic traditions are reinterpreted as expressions of the "Zen experience," rendering Zen the metaphysical ground of Japanese culture itself. Given this exalted spiritual heritage, the Japanese are said to be culturally, if not racially, predisposed toward Zen insight; they have a deeper appreciation of the unity of man and nature, the oneness of life and death, and so on. This is in contradistinction to Western cultures, which are supposedly founded upon philosophical and aesthetic principles—dualism, individualism, materialism, utilitarianism, etc.—that are fundamentally at odds with Zen.

The claim that Zen is the foundation of Japanese culture has the felicitous result of rendering the Japanese spiritual experience both unique and universal at the same time. And it was no coincidence that the notion of Zen as the foundation for Japanese moral, aesthetic, and spiritual superiority emerged full force in the 1930s, just as the Japanese were preparing for imperial expansion in East and Southeast Asia. This use of Zen to provide a rationale for Japanese claims of uniqueness and cultural supremacy is, in brief, what I have called "Zen nationalism."

ZEN AND NATIONALISM

By nationalism I mean an ideology or rhetoric that posits a nation, a state, or an ethnic or racial group, the members of which all participate equally in the glory of their "collective past." The context of modern nationalism is the globalization of forms of knowledge and culture, since national self-consciousness presumes a plurality of "nation states" interacting with one another. Put simply, globalization allows an individual to imagine him or

---

[11] This is clearly the attitude of D. T. Suzuki, Nishitani Keiji, and Abe Masao, for example, each of whom tends to approach interfaith dialogue as an opportunity to expound not only on the meaning of Buddhism and Zen, but on the meaning of Christianity as well.

herself as a member of one geographically, historically, culturally, and/or ethnically distinct "nation" among many.

Globalization is largely coextensive with "Westernization." The spread of modern Western "thought," science, technology, and political and economic systems, coupled with the attendant scourge of industrialization and urbanization, tends to undermine indigenous resources for constructing personal and corporate identity. As traditional allegiances collapse, nationalist alternatives arise, promising to preserve or restore native political, social, and moral norms in the face of the threat of foreign cultural hegemony. Ironically, nationalist discourse cannot escape the ground from which it grew: nationalism is very much the product of modernity and the modernist episteme. That is to say, as nationalist representations of self are inevitably constructed in dialectical tension with the foreign "other," the nationalist promise to restore cultural "purity" is always necessarily empty. Even in the case of so-called ethnic nationalisms, only by coming to see oneself through the eyes of the imagined other does one's own "ethnicity" become self-conscious.

It should now be evident that the issue is not whether Zen is "inherently nationalistic," since the particular notions of "Zen" and "nationalism" invoked here are both very much contemporary constructs.[12] Zen, like any other school of Buddhism, has had a long history of allying itself with state interests, resisting the state only when its own material interests were at stake. Moreover, Zen has had to reinvent itself repeatedly in the face of shifting political, social, and economic circumstances. What is new in the contemporary situation is the global or pluralist context, which presents a tremendous challenge to the survival of *any* religious system.

The Zen of Suzuki and his intellectual cohorts represents one of the more compelling attempts to have one's cake and eat it, too. Despite his romantic streak, Suzuki was very much a modern, insisting that his Zen was fully compatible with rational thought and scientific progress. But at the same time Suzuki, who spent many years in the West, recognized the dangers of Western cultural imperialism (or "Orientalism") entailed in the modernist project. Thus while Suzuki's Zen claimed a privileged perspective that transcended cultural difference, it was at the same time contrived as the antithesis of everything Suzuki found most deplorable about the West.

The *nihonjinron* (日本人論) polemic in Suzuki's work—the grotesque caricatures of "East" versus "West"—is no doubt the most egregiously inane manifestation of his nationalist leanings. We read repeatedly that the "West" is materialistic, the "East" spiritual, that the West is aggressive and imperial-

---

[12] Besides, religion is as good a rubric for the construction of national identity as is race, language, culture, or what have you, none of which are "inherently" nationalistic.

istic, while the East extols nonviolence and harmony, that the West values rationality, the East intuitive wisdom, that the West is dualistic, the East monistic, and that while the West is individualistic, setting man apart from nature, the East is communalistic, viewing man as one with nature.[13] In short, his image of the East in general, and Japan in particular, is little more than a romantic inversion of Japanese negative stereotypes of the West.

The relationship of Japan to the rest of Asia in the writings of the Zen apologists is considerably more complex than the simple antinomy of East and West. Even the staunchest of the Japanese Zen nativists could not ignore the fact that Buddhism was a product of India, and Zen a product of China. Suzuki, himself a capable scholar of Indian and Chinese Buddhism, struggled with this issue, but never relinquished his cultural chauvinism. Thus Suzuki would argue that Japanese "spirituality" is a more developed or refined form of a pan-Asian spiritual ethos, and while this ethos is linked with Buddhism, it was not until Chinese Ch'an met the samurai culture of the Kamakura period that it would attain its consummate form in Japanese Zen. This theory allowed Suzuki to claim that only in Japan was Asian spirituality fully realized.[14]

More to the point was Suzuki's claim (and the claim of many of those who followed) that the Chinese manifestation of this spirituality, i.e., Ch'an Buddhism, died an early death on the continent, and that pure Zen survives today only in Japan. Specifically, we read that Chinese Buddhism ceased to develop after the Sung dynasty—i.e., immediately after Japan assumed the mantle of Zen—and that post-Sung Ch'an is irredeemably tainted by its "syncretism." The Ōbaku (黄檗) school of Zen, a form of Ming Ch'an transplanted to Japan in the seventeenth century, is considered representative of

---

[13] A single example should suffice here. After an extended comparison of a single poem by Tennyson, which Suzuki takes as representative of the "West," and one by Bashō, representative of the "East," Suzuki summarizes his findings as follows: "The Western mind is: analytical, discriminative, differential, inductive, individualistic, intellectual, objective, scientific, generalizing, conceptual, schematic, impersonal, legalistic, organizing, power-wielding, self-assertive, disposed to impose its will upon others, etc. Against these Western traits those of the East can be characterized as follows: synthetic, totalizing, integrative, nondiscriminative, deductive, nonsystematic, nondogmatic, intuitive (rather, affective), nondiscursive, subjective, spiritually individualistic and socially groupminded, etc." (D. T. Suzuki, "Lectures on Zen Buddhism," in *Zen Buddhism and Psychoanalysis* by D. T. Suzuki, Erich Fromm, and Richard De Martino [New York: Grove Press, 1963], 5).

[14] See, for example, the extended treatment in Suzuki's 日本的霊性 (Tokyo: Daitō Shuppansha, 1944; English trans. by Norman Waddell as *Japanese Spirituality* [Tokyo: Japan Society for the Promotion of Science and Japanese Ministry of Education, 1972]); see also my discussion in "The Zen of Japanese Nationalism."

late Chinese Buddhism—it is commonly regarded as a sort of second-rate Zen compromised by its incorporation of Pure Land elements.

In fact, Chinese Buddhism continued to play a dynamic role in China up until the modern period. The oft-repeated allegation that post-Sung Ch'an had become sterile and corrupt is little more than an uncritical rehearsal of the anti-Ōbaku polemics of the Tokugawa period. The sudden appearance of eminent Chinese Ch'an masters in seventeenth-century Japan provoked a defensive and sometimes hostile reaction from Rinzai quarters. The Rinzai monks responded by touting the "purity" of Japanese Rinzai, in contradistinction to the admixture of Zen and Pure Land being propagated by the Chinese émigrés. This was, of course, mere sectarian polemics: Rinzai Zen in Japan had been thoroughly "Japanized" by the Tokugawa period, growing steadily more distant from its Chinese origins. In particular, Japanese religious sectarianism encouraged Rinzai to suppress the "Pure Land" aspects of its practice in order to distance itself from its Jōdoshū and Shinshū rivals. There was, however, no Pure Land "school" in China; Pure Land was a ubiquitous feature of Chinese Buddhism, and Chinese Ch'an included nominally "Pure Land" elements since the "golden age" of the T'ang. In most respects the Ōbaku school more accurately reflected T'ang and Sung Ch'an practice than either the Rinzai or Sōtō sects, and in the end Ōbaku proved to be a pivotal force in stimulating the Tokugawa revival of Zen.[15]

The polemical intent behind the modern Zen nativists' rendering of East Asian Buddhist history, indebted as it was to Tokugawa anti-Chinese polemics, is plain: while the strength of the West might lie in its superior science and technology, the strength of Asia lay in its spirituality. Asians must return to their indigenous spiritual roots in order to recover the resources that would allow them to throw off the yoke of Western imperialism. Since the foundation of Asian spirituality was Zen, and since Zen survived in its "pure" form only in Japan, Japan had the right, and indeed the obligation, to assume the leadership of Asia and guide its disadvantaged brethren into the modern age.

Why, we might ask, would anyone in the West take this view of Zen seriously? To put it simply, the Japanese nativists' discomfort with the seeming triumph of scientific reason, and their yearnings for a spiritual solution to the problems of modernity, mirrored our own. The notion of "pure Zen"—a

---

[15] For a detailed analysis of the anti-Ōbaku polemics in Tokugawa Japan see esp. Helen Baroni, "Buddhism in Early Tokugawa Japan: The Case of Ōbaku Zen and the Monk Tetsugen Dōkō" (Ph.D. dissertation, Columbia University, 1993). For a critique of the notion "Ch'an-Pure Land syncretism" see Robert H. Sharf, "The *Treasure Store Treatise* (*Pao-tsang lun*) and the Sinification of Buddhism in Eighth-Century China" (Ph.D. dissertation, University of Michigan, 1991), chapter 2.

pan-cultural religious experience unsullied by institutional, social, and historical contingencies—would be attractive precisely because it held out the possibility of an alternative to the godless and indifferent anomic universe bequeathed by the Western Enlightenment, yet demanded neither blind faith nor institutional allegiance. This reconstructed Zen offered an intellectually reputable escape from the epistemological anxiety of historicism and pluralism.

But impatience with plurality and uncertainty in the intellectual realm can lead all too readily to impatience with plurality and uncertainty in the realm of politics. It may not be mere coincidence that a surprising number of those who saw Zen as a solution to spiritual anxiety were drawn to authoritarian or totalitarian solutions to social and political unrest. In a similar vein, Hannah Arendt has commented on the "exasperation" we sometimes feel when confronted with the fact that Plato and Heidegger were drawn to "tyrants and Führers." Arendt suggests that this may be more than happenstance; it might in fact attest to a *déformation professionelle*: "For the attraction to the tyrannical can be demonstrated theoretically in many of the great thinkers (Kant is the great exception). And if this tendency is not demonstrable in what they did, that is only because very few of them were prepared to go beyond 'the faculty of wondering at the simple' and to 'accept this wondering as their abode.'"[16] It may well be that the apostles of "pure Zen," accepting wondering as their abode, fell prey to this *déformation professionelle*: they yearned to realize in the world of human affairs the "perfection" they found in their Zen.

The purveyors of Zen insight would like to expurgate this gap between the world of human affairs and the world of Zen through rhetorical fiat. They blithely cite Jōshū's injunction to "wash your bowls,"[17] and insist that true Zen is to be found in the midst of daily activity—in "chopping wood and carrying water." But this seemingly benign exaltation of everyday life is achieved through the leveling gaze of "enlightenment"—the totalizing (non)perspective of "absolute nothingness." (Note that the examples of "daily activities" invariably recall the tranquil existence of a medieval forest monastery, rather than the unrelenting technologized chaos of modern urban life.)

While this intellectualized Zen avers to leave things just as they are, in fact it utterly emasculates the "other," eliminating the possibility for real dialogue or external critique. In the end, Zen's response to plurality is a strategic retreat to "the still point of the turning world," which effaces alterity in

---

[16] Hannah Arendt, "Martin Heidegger at Eighty," in Michael Murray, ed., *Heidegger and Modern Philosophy* (New Haven and London: Yale University Press, 1978), 293–303.

[17] See case 7 of the *Wu-men kuan* (T.2005: 48.293c26–29).

the name of an experientially vibrant but politically ominous "nonduality." I fully concur with Jan Van Bragt's invocation of Emmanuel Lévinas in this regard: "this alleged integration [of self and Other] is cruelty and injustice."[18]

In conclusion I would remind the reader that this Zen is not Zen at all, at least not the Zen practiced by the "masters of old." Those with a monastery to run, disciples to train, gods and emperors to appease, could not, when confronted with difficult moral and political questions, afford to shroud themselves in the cloak of "absolute nothingness." They knew that in order to keep the monastery economically viable the monks had to maintain, at least in public, certain standards of moral conduct and ritual propriety elaborately prescribed in the monastic codes. This does not mean that a medieval Zen abbot would have taken what *we* believe to be the moral high ground on the issue of Japanese imperialist aggression during the first half of the twentieth century. The real question, as I see it, is why we would expect him to.

---

[18] Emmanuel Lévinas, *Totality and Infinity: An Essay on Exteriority,* trans. by A. Lingis (Pittsburgh: Duquesne University Press, 1969), 52; see also the reference at the conclusion of Jan Van Bragt's essay in this volume, page 254.

D. T. Suzuki on Society and the State

KIRITA Kiyohide

B UDDHISM, AS THE OLD ZEN saying has it, spreads toward the east (仏教東漸). D. T. Suzuki (1870–1966) was the first Japanese to spend a significant part of his life working to bring this about, as he traveled eastward from the Japanese islands to the nations of North America and Europe propagating the teachings of Buddhism. He was also a tireless exponent of the Zen and Pure Land traditions at home in Japan.

Suzuki produced an enormous body of writings in the eight decades between his fifteenth year and his death at ninety-five—approximately thirty volumes in English and one hundred volumes in Japanese. However, except for a few biographical works and commentaries by people who knew him personally, very little evaluation of the man or his work has been carried out in Japan. Even the basic materials necessary for serious research on Suzuki are not yet fully available. In the few years I myself have devoted to tracking down his articles in newspapers and journals, I have uncovered literally scores of pieces that were overlooked in the compilation of his *Collected Works*. The records of his unpublished letters and talks are sketchier still.

In this paper I will examine Suzuki's writings, including material that did not find its way into the *Collected Works,* in an attempt to clarify his attitudes towards the state and society. This will, of course, extend to the question of nationalism in Suzuki's thought and to his ideas about Zen, war, the Japanese, and national polity.

YOUTHFUL VIEWS ON THE STATE AND SOCIETY

Suzuki's first book, *A New Theory of Religion,* was published when he was twenty-six years old, just prior to his departure for the United States. In it he discussed his ideas on the relationship between religion and the state. He opens with an exposition of a modern, Enlightenment view of religion:

Religion sees its ultimate purpose as the realization of a cosmic ideal; the state sees as its ultimate purpose the preservation of its own existence.... Religion professes universal brotherhood and enjoins against making any distinction between self and other; the state is based on the principles of loyalty and patriotic sentiment, and exhorts its citizens to independence. Religion never hesitates to question the existence of the state and history; the state always acts on the basis of its own self-centered interests. In this way, religion and the state are incompatible.[1]

He goes on to argue that "the state must constitute a furtherance of social progress. It must, in other words, serve as a means to help humanity bring to realization the purpose of its existence."[2] And again:

Formation of the state is not the purpose of human existence but merely an expedient means, nothing more than a single stage that must be passed by humanity in the course of its development. Humanity exists for the sake of humanity, not for the sake of the state.... In order that the existence of the state does not hinder the realization of the hopes and ideals of religion, that is, of humanity, the state must, I believe, be reformed when necessary.[3]

Thus in Suzuki's view the state does not exist as an end in itself but merely as an instrument, a means to promote human interests. It is a view predicated upon the existence of a modern civil society, and might best be characterized as a libertarian *Nachtwächterstaat*. At the same time, he was aware that the idea did not reflect the actual condition of a state in which "loyalty and patriotism are the basic principles" and which "sees its final purpose in the preservation of its own existence." Against this conflict of the ideal and the actual, Suzuki proposes that the role of religion is "first of all to try to support the state and to abide by the history and sentiments of its people" in order to "work for the progress and development of the nation."[4]

Thus, while realizing that religion and the state differ in principle and are incompatible in many respects, he strikes a compromise relationship that keeps their respective roles separate but clearly places the state under the guidance of religion:

The interests of religion and the state do not conflict but rather aid and support each other in a quest for wholeness.... The problem is easily resolved if one thinks of religion as an entity with the state as its body,

[1] 新宗教論 (1896), SDZ 23:134.
[2] SDZ 23:137.
[3] SDZ 23:136.
[4] SDZ 23:137.

and of the state as something developing with religion as its spirit. In other words, religion and the state form a unity; if every action and movement of the state takes on a religious character and if every word and action of religion takes on a state character, then whatever is done for the sake of the state is done for religion, and whatever is done for the sake of religion is done for the state.[5]

All of this does not quite offset the impact of his initial statement that religion ought "first of all to try to support the state," which seems to lead to an acceptance of state supremacy. His rather "Zen-like" approach to religion and his abstract notion of the way nations operate seem far too unrealistic. These criticisms, though not entirely on the mark, have some truth to them and deserve closer attention.

Suzuki was much clearer in his views on the state and society following his move to the United States in the late 1890s. His position was basically critical of the current Japanese governmental structure (including the role of the imperial family) and of those who supported it: the Meiji political and bureaucratic establishment, the ultranationalists, and the various proponents of Japanism. We find his views on the imperial family expressed, for example, in magazine articles critical of the ultranationalists, whom he characterized as follows:

They say, "Obey the rescripts on the Imperial Restoration," "Study the *Imperial Rescript on Education*," "Display a nation-building spirit," "Honor the ancestors of the country." All of this is fine. But while these people on the one hand proclaim reason as their supreme sword and shield and talk on and on about the results of nineteenth-century historical research, on the other hand they manipulate the weaknesses of the Japanese people, embracing the imperial family and the imperial rescripts and attempting to imbue them with a religious significance. The hypocrisy of it all is quite overwhelming....

Let us stop pretending that the Japanese are a great people merely because their imperial family has continued unbroken for the past 2,500 years.[6]

In his personal correspondence Suzuki expressed his feelings even more frankly.

I believe that it contributes nothing to progress if the imperial family dreams on about its former transcendence and mystery, and if the people

[5] SDZ 23:139.

[6] 旅のつれづれ [Random thoughts while traveling] , 六合雑誌 20 (25 June 1898): 70–2. Full references are given only to those of Suzuki's writings not included in the *Collected Works*.

view its statements as august beyond compare. Whenever anything untoward happens the government attempts to hide behind such attitudes and to seal the mouths of the people. What is more, the road to free thought is cut off and the people must obey without hesitation those who exalt the imperial family and take refuge behind the imperial proclamations. What an unfortunate situation. [In the margin: *You must never make these words public. I must wait for the right time*].... What a shame how people stand in awe of things like the *Imperial Rescript on Education*. I had better not say too much. And what do you think?[7]

Such opinions were expressed on several occasions in letters to his close friend Yamamoto Ryōkichi. The earliest such statement was in 1888 when Suzuki was eighteen years old:

The emperor's birthday celebration the other day was a huge affair. Why is it necessary to make such a fuss? The people involved are a frivolous bunch. I think the whole thing is completely unnecessary. What about you?[8]

This statement may be read as a kind of frustrated "cry in the wilderness" by a gifted young man stuck in the remote countryside of the Noto Peninsula, but it more or less reflects Suzuki's attitude toward the imperial family until at least the end of the Meiji period. He saw the existence of the imperial family as not only violating the equality of the people but also as providing the ultranationalists with a pretext both for their Japanist mystique and their dangerous, backward-looking traditionalism, as well as for their attempts to stifle the freedom of speech and thought. Suzuki therefore regarded the imperial family as a hindrance to the modernization of the country and to the realization of his ideal of a state and society unified under the guidance of religion.

This naturally raises the question of how Suzuki envisaged the workings of the state. We want to ask, for example, what he means when he says that the state "must...serve as a means to help humanity bring to realization the purpose of its existence." In fact, Suzuki takes up the question of society in a number of his writings, including many of his contributions to the journals *Rikugō zasshi* (六合雑誌, *Universum*) and *Shin Bukkyō* (新仏教, *New Buddhism*) while he was in America. His idea, briefly put, was that "the ideal society provide a structure within which individuals can cultivate their respective strengths as they want." He explains this in further detail:

[7] Letter no. 48, 14 June 1898, 鈴木大拙未公開書簡 [Unpublished letters of D. T. Suzuki], ed. by Zen Bunka Kenkyūjo (Kyoto: Zen Bunka Kenkyūjo, 1989). Not in SDZ.

[8] Letter No. 7 (13 November 1888), *Unpublished Letters*.

The greatest possible motivation we can have for organizing our society is the chance to develop our natural abilities freely and apply them toward the advance of society as a whole. For this to come about, all individuals must be provided with equal opportunities and circumstances. The most important factor here is to reduce to an absolute minimum the gap between rich and poor. If the obstacles of food, shelter, and clothing were removed and people were free to cultivate their innate talents and moral nature, to devote themselves entirely to the advance of society as a whole, the progress of culture would be truly amazing.[9]

Suzuki kept his distance from the socialists, but he did acknowledge the views of contemporaries sympathetic with this way of thinking. "Recently I have been studying socialism," he wrote, "and I am in sympathy with ideas like social justice and equality of opportunity. Present society (particularly as it is in Japan) must be reformed from the ground up."[10] In the opening paragraph of the article in which the remarks cited above appears, he expressed approval of socialism:

It is said that the government has forbidden the formation of the Social Democratic Party. I deeply regret the Japanese government's irresponsibility and lack of farsightedness, and its inattentiveness to social progress and human happiness.

Suzuki studied socialist thought in the pages of journals like *Universum*, even as he saw all about him the problems that youthful, vigorous America was facing in its capitalist society. Already by this time his social consciousness as an independent Buddhist reformer had developed enough for him to write:

When we look for reasons for the plight of the impoverished in today's society, we see that their poverty is due not so much to any fault of their own as to the defects of the social system and the maldistribution of wealth.... One can hardly expect impoverished people in such difficult circumstances to be satisfied with spiritual comfort bereft of any material aid.... My earnest desire is that Buddhists do not remain satisfied with personal peace and enlightenment but take it upon themselves to help society.[11]

---

[9] 社会民主的党の結党禁止につきて(社会主義の宗教的基礎) [On the prohibition of the formation of the Social Democratic Party: The religious foundations of socialism], 六合雑誌 249 (15 September 1901): 45.

[10] Letter No. 50 (6 January 1901), *Unpublished Letters*.

[11] SDZ 28:422–3.

FROM THE RETURN TO JAPAN AND UNTIL THE END OF THE WAR

In 1909 Suzuki, then thirty-eight and having spent the last twelve years in the United States and Europe, returned to Japan and took up employment at the Gakushū-in Tokyo. The Gakushū-in was a special boarding school attended by the sons and daughters of the very royalty and nobility that Suzuki had earlier criticized. He was eager to fulfill his duties as an English teacher and housemaster. His life as a teacher under the leadership of Nogi Maresuke, a typical career soldier of the "loyalty-and-patriotism" school, and a representative of the "good old" Meiji era, must have been rather awkward.[12] Suzuki's own philosophy of education was based on respect for the individual and aimed at nurturing independence and spontaneity. For him, the twentieth century was an age of world-historical significance that could only require serious change in society. Even in Japan

> it is impossible to say what will become of the aristocratic class. The day may come when it is no longer necessary to maintain the privileged class in order to preserve the nation. I do not think it desirable to have a system where a wall of privilege exists between the imperial family and the common people, separating the two. There should be only the imperial family and the common people. Perhaps the day will come when this becomes a reality.

Turning his remarks directly to the students, Suzuki exhorted them to develop their natural abilities and not to rely on privileges of birth or inheritance:

> Most of you are children of the nobility. You form a special class in Japan and receive privileged treatment from the imperial family. You must remember that wherever special favor is shown, special responsibility is also demanded....
>
> Natural ability means not claiming for your own that which does not belong to you and not entrusting yourself to good fortune. It is, in a sense, individualism. The only way to develop your natural abilities is to make full use of your independence and freedom....[13]

And again elsewhere:

> Individualism is not selfishness; it means to become one's own master. From the standpoint of ethics, this is something lacking in young

---

[12] Nogi Maresuke committed ritual suicide on 13 September 1912, following the death of Emperor Meiji on 30 July 1912. The incident evoked great public interest. Arguing that it was not up to others to judge Nogi's actions, Suzuki distanced himself from the incident, writing that "those who imitate him are fools. Each person should act on their own." SDZ 17:50–2.

[13] SDZ 28:224, 226.

people today. Of course, individualism has dangers as well, but one should not disregard its merits. As for me, I will cling to its merits.[14]

Suzuki wrote nine essays for the *Hojinkai zasshi* (輔仁會雑誌), a publication of the Gakushū-in, under the personal name of Teitarō, not Daisetsu. In these essays he stressed again and again the importance of an "enterprising spirit" and "self-reliance" based on autonomy, independence, and freedom.[15] Many of his pupils attest that as housemaster and as English teacher Suzuki treated everyone, students and faculty members alike, without favor, sharing his inimitable personality and exerting a strong influence on all around him.[16]

Suzuki's writings from the end of the Meiji era through the Taishō era appeared chiefly in the two monthlies *Shin Bukkyō* and *Zendō* (禅道, *Zen Way*), but also in the *Hojinkai zasshi* and the Buddhist newspaper *Chūgai nippō* (中外日報). *Shin Bukkyō* was a Pure Land Buddhist journal promoting the reform of Meiji Buddhism. From its inception in 1900 until its termination in 1915, it ran some sixty articles by Suzuki, mainly pieces of social commentary. *Zendō* was a Zen monthly that Suzuki served as editor-in-chief. He published some fifty articles on Zen in its pages, beginning with the monthly's first issue in August 1910. One notes a clear difference in his approach to the two publications. In the articles for *Shin Bukkyō*, Suzuki makes little reference to Buddhism but focuses rather on a comparison of Eastern and Western civilization, culture, and society, as well as religion, morality, customs, and manners. Allusions to the state are not as frequent as in writings composed when he was living in the United States. With the demise of *Shin Bukkyō*, Suzuki's social commentary decreased and the bulk of his lectures and essays, apart from those of his publications that appeared in the various scholarly journals of Ōtani University, appeared in *Shindō* (信道, *The Way of Belief*), a popular magazine published under Pure Land Buddhist auspices. His contributions to *Shindō* dealt with Zen and Pure Land Buddhism, and included some social commentary. Other articles on Zen appeared occasionally in *Daijōzen* (大乗禅, *Mahāyāna Zen*), a monthly founded in 1924, the year

---

[14] SDZ 28:44.

[15] SDZ 28:44, 47, etc. The name of the journal literally means *Journal of the Society for the Promotion of Humanness*, the two characters for this final phrase (輔仁) being an allusion to the closing words of the twelfth book of the *Analects* of Confucius.

[16] 松方三郎 Matsukata Saburō, 学習院時代の鈴木先生 [Dr. Suzuki's Gakushū-in period], in 鈴木大拙の人と学問 [Suzuki Daisetsu, the man and his scholarship] (Tokyo: Shunjūsha, 1961), 63–74. 犬養 健 Inukai Takeru, 鈴木大拙居士——その絶対的他力論について [Layman Suzuki Daisetsu's theory of absolute Other-power], in *Suzuki Daisetsu, The Man and His Scholarship*, 75–85. 日高第四郎 Hidaka Daishirō, 乃木大将と鈴木大拙先生の印象及び思い出 [Memories and impressions of General Nogi and Suzuki Daisetsu] in 鈴木大拙——人と思想 [Suzuki Daisetsu: The man and his thought] (Tokyo: Iwanami Shoten, 1971), 279–88.

after *Zendō* ceased publication, and in *Shōbōrin* (正法論, *The True Wheel of the Dharma*).

During his twelve years at the Gakushū-in, in addition to numerous essays on Zen and social problems, he also wrote pieces for the edification of his students with titles such as "A Missive to the Children of the Noble and Wealthy" and "On Poverty." The same dedication he had shown there he took with him to Ōtani University, where he taught from 1921 until after the end of the Pacific War.[17]

From the early years of the Shōwa period (1925–1989), Suzuki became interested in the *Laṅkāvatāra Sūtra* and subsequently in the *Platform Sūtra*, the Tun-huang manuscripts, the writings of Zen masters Lin-chi and Bankei, and Pure Land Buddhism. The period beginning from shortly after his transfer to Ōtani University in 1921 until the end of the war in 1945 was the time in Suzuki's long life when he concentrated the most on the study of Buddhism. It was also the period in which he established his reputation as a scholar. During this time he published several works in English including the three volumes of *Essays in Zen Buddhism* (1927–1934), *Studies in the Laṅkāvatāra Sūtra* (1930), which became the core of his doctoral dissertation, and *Zen Buddhism and Its Influence on Japanese Culture* (1938). Among his publications in Japanese were his major works on Zen Buddhism such as *The Records of Shen-hui Discovered at Tun-huang* (1932), *Sanskrit-Chinese Index to the Laṅkāvatāra Sūtra* (1934), *The Unborn Zen of Bankei* (1940), *Studies in the History of Zen Thought: I* (1943), *Zen Thought* (1943), and such representative writings on Pure Land Buddhism as *Detachment* (1939), *Treatise on the Logic of Pure Land Thought* (1942), and *The Fact of Religious Experience* (1943).

During the war years his only non-Buddhist writings were on the subject of Japanese culture, among them a volume later translated into English as *Japanese Spirituality*,[18] and his essays on the Japanese people. *Japanese Spirituality* is an attempt to find a unique Japanese spirituality in Buddhism, especially its Pure Land and True Pure Land sects. Suzuki's writings on the Japanese people discuss their special characteristics in comparison with western Europeans, the Japanese understanding of history, and the Japanese view of death. Although these writings deal specifically with Japan, his intention was not only to encourage his fellow Japanese during the devastating years of the war, but also to discover and demonstrate a Buddhist spirituality that could be appreciated by all humanity. In none of his essays does he praise the superiority of the Japanese people. The following passage is typical of his style:

[17] See SDZ 17:80–99; 19:307–76; 28:359–61; 29:50–65, etc.

[18] SDZ 8:1–223. English translation by Norman Waddell, *Japanese Spirituality* (Tokyo: Ministry of Education, 1972).

The Japanese are highly sentimental and lacking in logic, have difficulty in forming an independent judgment on the right and wrong of things, are only concerned about being ridiculed by others, and are reluctant to enter into unknown and unexplored areas, and if they should dare to do so, they do it recklessly and without any plans made in advance.[19]

Suzuki further claims that this sentimentality lay behind the "human torpedoes" and "kamikaze squadrons," but at once questions how the sacrifice of human life in an attempt to make up for the shortage of mechanical equipment and the inadequacy of scientific technology could ever be considered a noble cause.[20] This was also a criticism of the military establishment.

Such statements are products of the times in which they were made, a period when a narrow-minded, self-righteous "Japanese spirit" centered on Hirata Shinto (平田神道) was being propagated throughout the country. I would add that Suzuki's essays on the culture and people of Japan represent his personal criticism of and resistance to the understanding of the Japanese spirit circulating at the time. The year after the publication of *Japanese Spirituality*, just prior to the end of the war, he prepared a lecture on "A Japanese Spiritual Awakening" (日本的霊性的自覚) to be delivered at Ōtani University, a draft of which still exists. In it he explains the term *spirituality* and presents a critique of the idea of *Japanese spirit*:

The term *Japanese spirit* used by our colleagues nowadays includes elements of special political characteristics, patriotic zeal, historical reminiscing, moral self-respect, and peculiarities of aesthetic appreciation. In addition, the term also emphasizes an exclusive narrow-mindedness and the conservative characteristics of an insular, anti-cosmopolitan people.... This is because our conception of Japan has become so subjective that it has psychologically, logically, philosophically, and historically distorted our way of thinking. Once begun, the distortion grows without bounds, turning into something grotesque.[21]

The military establishment and State Shinto were not alone in championing this *yamato-damashii* (大和魂) or spirit of Japanese uniqueness. Many Zen Buddhists expressed similar views. For example, during this period one of the journals Suzuki contributed to frequently, *Daijōzen*, fairly bristled with pro-militarist articles. In issues filled with essays proclaiming "Victory in the Holy War!" and bearing such titles as "Death is the Last Battle," "Certain Victory for Kamikaze and Torpedoes," and "The Noble Sacrifice of a

[19] SDZ 21:179.
[20] SDZ 21:194.
[21] SDZ 9:150–203; citation on 156.

Hundred Million," Suzuki continued with contributions on subjects like "Zen and Culture."[22]

A further indication of his posture during the war years is his work for the Buddhist newspaper *Chūgai nippō*. Between 1941 and the end of the war in 1945 Suzuki contributed two regular articles and 191 short installments for a column entitled "Zen." Virtually none of these pieces contain any reference made to the current political and war situation.[23] Instead, they simply introduce the lives and recorded sayings of the masters or explain the outlook of Zen. He did, however, occasionally lapse into lines like the following:

> Some people think that to die recklessly is Zen. But Zen and death are not the same thing. *Makujikikōzen* (驀直向前) does not mean to sit in the grip of the hand of death. It is deplorable to think of Zen as a purification rite. The Zen understanding of human life is based on Mahāyāna Buddhism. Zen without this is not Zen. It isn't anything at all…. To regard the foolhardy and senseless sacrifice of one's life as Zen is a mish-mash idea. Zen absolutely never teaches one to throw one's life away.[24]

Passages such as these make plain Suzuki's resistance to movements trying to associate Zen with war and death. They are also a clear criticism of Shinto. The circumstances at the time he was writing may be gathered from the words of the *Chūgai nippō*'s president, who commented in his "Editor's Diary" column that

> Daisetsu Suzuki's light-hearted, childlike nature is itself the everyday expression of Zen, yet within his eloquent words one finds statements— almost digressions—that to the ordinary way of thinking can be seen as quite dangerous.[25]

Suzuki, who had lived in the United States for over ten years, was well aware of its strength and foresaw the defeat of Japan. He was also aware of the ideological vacuity of the Shinto concepts of national polity and the government's pronouncements on the Greater East Asia Coprosperity Sphere. He had never been a government official and in general remained a lone wolf where connections with large organizations was concerned. He was a private citizen with no links to the military establishment. When the war broke out, he was over seventy years of age. He lived alone and in relative independence.

---

[22] 大乗禅 21/7 (1 July 1944), et alibi.

[23] See SDZ 15:157–425.

[24] SDZ 15:222.

[25] 中外日報 (30 November 1943).

Under these circumstances Suzuki, in addition to his work on Zen and Shin Buddhism, appears to have devoted considerable thought to the question of what could be done to help rebuild Japan after the fighting was over. Many of his activities at this time—his writing of *Japanese Spirituality* and "The Global Mission of Mahāyāna," his lecturing, his collecting of volumes for the Matsugaoka Library—were directed towards protecting and later disseminating the "jewel of Japan," Zen. Under the limits of the strict censorship in force at the time, he had to restrict his critical remarks about militarism and "the national polity" to a few letters written to close friends.[26] Only an occasional touch of irony appeared in his writings, as in the following:

> There is a swarm of people all around eager to commit suicide with the past, to embrace what is Japanese, no matter how limited geographically it is, and defend it to the last.... We must go beyond such limited terms as "Greater East Asia" and find more expansive terms like *tenjō tenge* (天上天下, heaven and earth).[27]

However, he did not take a firm stance against the war or write essays criticizing the military or Shinto nationalists head-on. What is clear, in any case, is the fact that he disliked the reckless manner, self-righteousness, and parochialism of the military and its idea of "national polity," and that he did not go along with the mood of the times.

THE YEARS AFTER THE WAR

Following the end of the war Suzuki turned his thoughts to the creation of what he called a "spiritual Japan." In the three-year period immediately after Japan's surrender he wrote numerous articles on this topic as well as over ten books: *A Japanese Spiritual Awakening, The Building of a Spiritual Japan, Self-reliance, The Spiritualizing of Japan, Religion and the Modern Person, Religion and Culture, To the Young,* and *East and West.* All of these works described the construction of a new Japan based on the principles of Buddhist spirituality, and all of them rejected the wartime notions of national polity, the Japanese spirit, State Shinto, military dictatorship, and military support by the Buddhists.

[26] For example, in a letter dated 17 March 1945, he wrote, "Without people, without things, without tools, without machines, and even without any ideas, nothing at all can be done; and then with the helplessness of the authorities and the ignorance of the army and civil servants, the situation is hopeless" (SDZ 31:343). On 6 July 1945 he wrote, "Those responsible for the ruin of Japan are the intolerant *kokugakusha* [nativists], the Shintoists. It is a shame that everything has been dominated by them" (31:358). See also SDZ 31:295, 348, 350, etc.

[27] SDZ 29:58.

The basis of Suzuki's criticism of the old order and the construction of the new Japan was the "spirituality" principle. In one of his essays he summarized in three points what he called "the fundamental concepts for building a new Japan" that were to link "spirituality" with the nation state. First, and above all, Japan must think independently. But this independent thinking, secondly, must have a cosmopolitan character. Finally, Japan's actions must be based on humanitarianism.[28]

Granted that there were strict controls over information during the war years, many Japanese swallowed the pronouncements of the military hook, line, and sinker. In this way a narrow-minded Hirata State Shinto came to be set up that professed Japan as the progenitor of all nations, the imperial dynasty as the ruler of all nations, and Shinto as the religion of the world. Suzuki considered the Japanese narrow-mindedness and lack of independence to be a defect of the race, and found it natural that the old Japan should have collapsed. He believed that a new spirituality was needed to construct a new Japan. The three points of this spirituality may be considered Suzuki's basic position on society, the state, and the world. During this period of his life he constantly stressed the notions of independent thinking and cosmopolitanism,[29] notions that we find expressed already from his youth and through the years of the war.

In the postwar period, as international relations came to be dominated by the tensions between the United States and the Soviet Union, Suzuki went beyond his criticism of Japanese national supremacy and militarism to consider ways to counter what might be called "nation-centeredness." While voices of doom were predicting the outbreak of World War Three, Suzuki was moved to face the question of the inevitability of war.[30] While recognizing that warfare was probably an inevitable part of human history, his proposal for limiting it to the greatest possible extent was to suppress all ideologies that give absolute authority to the state. These include state nationalism (国家主権), state supremacy (国家至上権), and the idea of national polity (国体観念). His opposition to such concepts was based, first, on his conviction that all such nationalistic sentiments have at their root a belief in the supremacy of force, the belief that "might makes right." "As long as force is used to suppress force," Suzuki comments, "we will never be without war." Second, he believed that all forms of totalitarianism—in particular Communism and Nazism—deprive people of their freedom, autonomy, and dignity and hinder their spiritual awakening. Though it may only have been an

[28] SDZ 21:162–68.
[29] SDZ 30:31–8, 50–7, 395–402, etc.; 21:96–106.
[30] SDZ 9:401–22.

idea never destined to be realized, Suzuki envisaged a world that would be rooted in "spiritual awakening" and a "world government" that would relativize the state.

Another facet of Suzuki's political and cultural thought—idealistic as always, but based on a sound knowledge of political realities—comes to light several years after the war. In October 1952 the journal *Sekai* (世界, *The World*) conducted a survey on rearmament published in a special issue devoted to "The General Election: Opinions, Criticisms, Hopes." It was a time when the situation in Japan was vastly different from what it had been immediately after the war, principally because of the outbreak of the Korean War in 1950, the signing of the San Francisco Peace Treaty in 1951, and the end of the Occupation in 1952. Suzuki's response to the questionnaire shows a tone somewhat different from many of his earlier pronouncements but gives a good indication of the viewpoint he held from that point on:

> I consider rearmament unavoidable.... If we do not at this time undertake some form of armament, Japan as a country will cease to exist. Even if one is not particularly bothered by that thought, it would be an enormous tragedy for human existence as a whole if our culture were to disappear, a culture that has been represented, maintained, and developed by our people.... In order to protect Japan's distinctive cultural expressions, the Japanese, as human beings who need bodies to exist, must have concrete means to defend themselves. Rearmament is therefore a necessity for the Japan of today. There are some who say that, trapped as we are between the two great powers of the United States and the Soviet Union, we should remain neutral. But such people are completely blind to the present situation. Faced with the alternative of being annexed by the Soviets or occupied by the American army, we should opt for the United States, which stands for freedom, rather than become victims of Soviet Communist and imperialist tactics.... Do we really have any choice between a country that lets the end justify the means and one that professes freedom, respects the law, and keeps faith with the world. Geography dictates that Japan must make a decision now.[31]

Interestingly, the large majority of intellectuals who responded to *Sekai*'s survey opposed the idea of rearmament. Suzuki's position was by far the minority one. I cannot bring myself to accept the idea that without arming itself Japan will cease to exist as a country. But at the same time, I have only respect for his view that culture (Zen Buddhist culture in particular) is superior to nation and that without a nation the preservation and development of

[31] SDZ 30:540–1.

culture is exceedingly difficult. I admire also the level-headedness of his appraisal of global political realities.

Suzuki was first and foremost a realist. Not only did he maintain a balanced perception of events in the world around him, he also refused to let himself be swayed by the demands of competing ideologies and "isms." As each new situation presented itself, he reevaluated the circumstances and reached an independent decision based on how he perceived the facts. (Might this not be the working of what he called "no mind"?) We see this, for example, in the no-nonsense approach he took toward the San Francisco Peace Treaty. There was much opposition to this agreement from the Japanese intelligentsia, who protested against it on the grounds that it was not comprehensive enough, that it contravened the principles of Japan's postwar constitution, that it made no provision for popular consensus, that it ignored China, and so forth.[32] Suzuki was not ignorant of these arguments nor of the various principles and ideologies involved, but he did not make his decisions on the basis of them. His "position that is not a position," if we may call it that, was rooted in his own spirituality which took its stand on "Great Mercy and Great Compassion" (大慈大悲).

QUESTIONING SUZUKI'S VIEWS OF SOCIETY AND THE STATE

Religion and the State

In his 1948 work "State and Religion" Suzuki commented that "religion, viewed from what might be called the standpoint of the absolute, is not concerned with matters of the state."[33] This ties in with his view that "in Zen experience itself there is no democracy, nor is there imperialism or hegemonism."[34] Zen—and as Suzuki saw it, religion in its true sense—"is concerned with the absolute individual self," and "has nothing to do with the state." Hence "the world of spiritual awareness is at peace regardless of what political system it is under." In contrast, "The individual as conceived by the state is not a religious entity but rather a political or ethical one."[35] This view in turn ties in with Suzuki's recognition that war is the inevitable destiny of mankind on the one hand, and his tireless quest for ways to avert it on the other. Suzuki constantly emphasized that the basis of life must be in the religious self (i.e., in spirituality), but that human beings are also political and ethical beings that exist within a certain historical and social context.

---

[32] SDZ 30:530–1.

[33] SDZ 9:287.

[34] 禅と民主主義 [Zen and democracy], 大乗禅 23/No. 1 (1 May 1946): 8.

[35] SDZ 9:287.

These views are fundamentally in line with those expressed by the young Suzuki in *A New Theory of Religion*: everything depends on whether the self is taken as a religious entity or as a political and ethical entity. In other words, it is a matter of the conflict and tension between religion and the state, and hence of the conflict and tension present in an individual as a religious and as a historicosocial entity. The young Suzuki wrote, as we remarked earlier, that if the state is not to obstruct the realization of the hopes and ideals of humanity, it must "be reformed when necessary." A half-century later, he writes as if that time of necessity had arrived:

> The role of the leaders who form the government is not so much to actively implement policies, but rather to supervise affairs as unobtrusively as possible. That is, government should cast such a pale shadow that one begins to wonder whether it even exists at all.... For that reason, the state as an organization propped up by scientific concepts and harboring imperialistic ideas and fanatical ideology is not compatible with human life. At some time or another it must face a fatal crisis.[36]

From his youth and throughout his life Suzuki never regarded the state as absolute and never placed the state above the individual. In his view, the only possible absolute was "the awakening of spirituality." Suzuki's views in this regard are crystal clear. His assertions of "non-citizenship" and "non-nationality" were condemned by right-wingers who complained, "Has Suzuki ever thought of the debt he owes to his country, let alone to the emperor?"[37] In the last year of his life, Suzuki once remarked at a symposium that "I believe that anarchism is best."[38] He was of course fully aware that anarchism was not feasible and he knew that there was no escape from "being a political and moral individual," but perhaps there is a sense in which we may take his words as a sincere prayer for humanity. In any case, during the years just before and after the end of the war, Suzuki considered "spiritualization" to be the only possible way to reconstruct Japan. Because the period right after the war was a time of fundamental change of the state system, he pursued with increased vigor his youthful ideal "to make every action and movement of the state religious."

[36] SDZ 8:339.

[37] 島田 享 Shimada Tōru, 禅学彷徨記 [Meanderings in Zen studies] (Tokyo: Keisō Shobō, 1993), 138, 150.

[38] アメリカの不安 [Unrest in America], 心 5/10 (1 October 1952): 27. See also the comment reported at a colloquium in 鈴木大拙坐談集第二巻, 東洋と西洋 [Suzuki Daisetsu colloquium II: East and West] (Tokyo: Yomiuri Shinbunsha, 1971), 29. See also 無題放談 [Random discussions], 大法論 26/3 (1 March 1959): 113, for a statement in the same vein. Not included in the *Collected Works*, but later printed in 鈴木大拙坐談集第一巻, 人間の智恵 [Suzuki Daisetsu colloquium I: Human wisdom] (Tokyo: Yomiuri Shinbunsha, 1971).

Furthermore, Suzuki saw the life of the human person as caught up in contradiction. As an individual, a human being must be a religious entity, and at the same time as the citizen of a country, a historical and political entity. For him religion is based on compassion and the state on physical force. The problem of how to reconcile these two fundamentally incompatible stand-points is a cross we must all bear throughout life. We have no choice but to live with conflict, despite the tragedy that invariably follows in its wake. Human desire is unbounded; it brings progress and leads to destruction. The human being is constantly being pulled in two directions and lives in con-stant conflict and tension. This idea is essentially the same as, and in fact orig-inates in, the fundamental Buddhist view that the passions, just as they are, are wisdom and enlightenment (煩悩即菩提). Here we also find Suzuki's view of human life:

> Instead of saying, "It isn't possible so we shouldn't try," we should say, "It isn't possible so we should do it," because this is what being human is all about. It is what in Buddhism we call "pursuit" (欣求).[39]

In this contradictory state of human existence, in full awareness of the impos-sibility of realization, Suzuki continued to make efforts. This is his act of "Great Mercy," his "bodhisattva path."

Zen Experience and Zen Thought

Suzuki was the first Zen Buddhist deliberately to distinguish between Zen experience and Zen thought, and to recognize the importance of the latter:

> It is true that Zen transcends thought. However, this does not mean that Zen ignores thought. Zen experience can be articulated only after it has been formulated in thought. When this articulation is not present,... Zen ceases to be Zen.[40]

For Suzuki, even though there is no direct, immediate connection between Zen experience and thought, Zen experience must *become* thought. He elab-orates elsewhere on this relationship:

> Strictly speaking, Zen has no philosophy of its own. Its teaching is con-centrated on an intuitive experience, and the intellectual content of this experience can be supplied by a system of thought not necessarily Buddhistic. If the masters find it more expedient for some reason, they may build up their own philosophical structure not always in accordance with the traditional interpretation. Zen Buddhists are sometimes

[39] "Unrest in America," 27.
[40] "Zen and Democracy," 9.

Confucianists, sometimes Taoists, or sometimes even Shintoists; Zen experience can also be explained by Western philosophy.[41]

Suzuki continues in the same vein in another place, writing that "there is no reason why Zen must be considered only from the viewpoint of Buddhism."[42] This raises the question of the relationship between Zen and Buddhism, and the relationship between the ultimate experience of Zen and other religions. For Suzuki, this ultimate experience is the same in all religions as it is for Zen, whatever name one chooses to give it. In the passage just cited, however, his only point was that Zen itself is not directly bound to thought.

Nevertheless, Suzuki insisted that the ultimate fact of experience be "expressed in thought":

> Buddhists must not fall behind in taking notice of current trends in the world today.... Buddhists who think their duty done when they have learned the simple traditional thought and practice, can be considered the greatest enemies of Zen, the snake in its bosom.... Thought is absolutely necessary.[43]

This call for the necessity of thought in Buddhism is a constantly recurring theme of Suzuki's. He was convinced that Shinto's self-righteousness and narrow-mindedness prevented it from expressing itself in thought, even though he had occasion to observe many Buddhists who had drawn close to and ingratiated themselves with Shinto. Suzuki's statements during the war period reflect his fear that unless Zen found new ideas in which to express itself, not only would it be of no use to contemporary society, it would also compromise itself with the currents of the times and would in the end have a negative effect on the course of history. He further argued from the results of his own study of Zen that those Buddhists whose names have come down to us in posterity achieved a thought that was suited to the conditions and society of their day, as in the case of Rinzai"s "Person" and Bankei's idea of the "Unborn." Suzuki also prided himself on the fact that he was the first person in Zen to attempt a history of Zen thought.

But what is thought? The Japanese term *shisō* (思想) ordinarily combines three elements: a knowledge of present conditions, an understanding of the way things ought to be, and a means to realize the way things ought to be. In

---

[41] SDZ 11:85–6. See *Zen and Japanese Culture* (Princeton: Princeton University Press, 1993), 44–5.

[42] SDZ 18:12. Note that the *Collected Works* contains a misprint that gives the direct opposite meaning. Instead of what is said in the original essay, "there is *no* reason why," the text has "there is *every* reason why."

[43] SDZ 29:452.

other words, thought always includes a recognition of the values of contemporary society but must have lasting, not merely ephemeral, significance. Although Zen experience or *satori*, the experience of ultimate reality, is an intuitive experience that transcends history and society and can only be understood by another when it is made conscious and expressed, Zen experience itself is value-neutral. It is without plan or continuity. How then are Zen experience and thought connected? In Suzuki's own case, there was no avoiding the question, since thought meant for him Zen thought. How exactly does "Zen experience" become "Zen thought"?

If Zen thought is not born immediately of Zen experience, what makes it "Zen"? As Suzuki explains it, Zen thought is always particular to the individual who has it. There is no Zen thought in general. It is always and ever the expression of a specific, definite process of ratiocination. When this process takes place in a Zen Buddhist, it can be called Zen thought. This of course raises the question, How does one decide who is a Zen Buddhist? The conventional wisdom in Japan has it that Zen Buddhists include the masters (beginning with Bodhidharma), persons who propagate Zen, and lay Buddhists such as Suzuki. But if we define Zen thought as no more than what happens when a Zen Buddhist thinks, then the term seems superfluous. If this term is to mean anything, surely there must be a more important connection between Zen and thought, and surely this connection must possess certain defining characteristics. Does this mean that Zen and thought necessarily entail one another? Zen people in general may try to deny that any such entailment exists and that there is anything definitively characteristic about "Zen thought." Yet Suzuki insists that there *is* such a thing as Zen thought—that indeed there must be. Therein lies his new Zen thought.

It is said that Zen Buddhism "does not rely on words and letters; it is a separate tradition outside the teachings." It has no fixed body of doctrine because the basis of Zen is experience, which is prior to doctrine. Zen experience always finds new modes of expressing itself, depending on the time and social circumstances in which it takes place, just as its teaching is continually growing and developing through the lives and thinking of individual Zen Buddhists. Though it professes not to rely on words and letters, it has produced a vast body of literature. As long as Zen is propagated and remains in existence, it must find such expression. Suzuki's "Zen thought" is one example of this.

The question of the relationship between Zen experience and Zen thought is not incidental to the relationship between religion and society. Suzuki's idea is that Zen *transcends* thought and morality but does not *ignore* them. Zen experience as such is independent of time and place, but as it takes place in human beings who live at a particular time and in a particular society, from the very moment it seeks expression it relies on language, praxis, and so forth. That is, it takes on a worldly meaning. This leads to two important questions. First, to what extent is the individual aware of the meaning this expression has in the world? Second, how wide and how deep is the individual's awareness of the time and society in which he or she lives? These are not questions of non-discriminating wisdom (*prajñā*) but of discriminating knowledge (*vijñāna*) that involves the intelligence and education of the person who has had the Zen experience. Zen consciousness and Zen thought differ according to one's learning and intellect.

For Suzuki, spirituality entails a thoroughgoing Great Mercy (大悲), Great Compassion (大慈), Vow (誓願), and "boundless and inexhaustible aspiration" (無辺無尽の悲願).[44] Zen experience for him is precisely the "awakening" of this spirituality at its very source. In this sense, it may be considered the fountainhead of Mahāyāna Buddhism. His idea of "Zen thought" consists in the identification of Zen experience with the awakening to spirituality and stresses the realization of Great Mercy and Great Compassion. For him, "Zen experience" that lacks this awakening to spirituality, Great Mercy, and Great Compassion is not Zen experience at all. This is why a living Zen thought is needed today.

In this connection, he criticized Zen Buddhists who put too much stress on the kōan and also those who valued enlightenment (上求菩提, 往相) over the salvation of sentient beings here below (下化衆生, 環相). In other words, Suzuki felt that in the contemporary world of Zen too much emphasis was being laid on "Zen experience" to the neglect of the saving acts of mercy (衆生済度). In the Four Universal Vows of a Bodhisattva, the vow to save all sentient beings without exception (衆生無辺誓願度) precedes the vow to extinguish all the defiled passions (煩悩無尽誓願断).[45] This is also part of the "Zen thought" of Suzuki, who understood Zen Buddhism as Mahāyāna.

As shown in the *Oxherding Pictures*, the third stage, finding the ox, still leaves seven stages to go. Traditionally, the ascetical practice following the attainment of *satori* (聖胎長養) was considered much more important than the ascetical practice undertaken to attain *satori* in the first place. The fact that it is so demanding shows just how difficult it is to understand the times and society one lives in and how difficult it is to transform Zen experience into Zen thought. In any case, Zen experience by itself is not enough. "Unless one's will and feelings have become Zen, the experience is not genuine." Even after awakening, "effort is required...until Zen and the personality function

---

[44] SDZ 9:165.

[45] See 「煩悩・宗教・近代文明」談話会, [Defiled passions, religion, and modern civilization], 知と行 3/10 (1 October 1948): 1–23. Later reprinted in 鈴木大拙坐談集第三巻, 現代人と宗教 [Suzuki Daisetsu colloquium III: Religion and people today] (Tokyo: Yomiuri Shinbunsha, 1972), 257–97.

in unison."[46] (In fact, Śākyamuni and Maitreya are said to be doing ascetical practice still.) By continuous practice throughout one's life and the renewal of *satori* over and over, one deepens Zen experience, and this in turn gives shape to a creative discriminating insight independent of how much or how broad one's previous insight had been. This is the way in which doctrine comes to life and Zen thought takes form.

Zen and War

Even though Zen experience is said to transcend all thought, the claim has been made that Zen thought and Zen consciousness have played a particular role in promoting warfare, even within Buddhism. In an essay published in 1914, Suzuki wrote:

> Someone asked a Zen practicer his opinion on the present war. The practicer answered, "I have no particular opinion, and in particular I have no opinion as a Zen practicer." ...Zen practicers have no set view with regard to war—at least I as an individual have no set views.[47]

This may be, but during both the Sino-Japanese War and the Pacific War, Zen was very popular. It is also true that Zen gained popularity in tandem with the development of the warrior class during the Kamakura period. In his book *Zen and Japanese Culture* Suzuki admits that Zen gave ethical and philosophical support to the warrior class insofar as it taught that in the face of any circumstance one should be prepared to risk one's life without hesitation: "Ethically, because Zen teaches that once one has decided on a certain course, one should not look back; philosophically, because it treats both life and death with impartiality."[48] The context of these remarks was the warrior class in Japanese history, not the military in the modern state, but it seems a short and logical step to substitute *soldier* for *samurai* and thus apply Zen's spiritual composure and its transcendence of life and death to the present world as well.

The emphasis on the here-and-now in Zen thought breaks the ties between before and after. It breaks with all value judgments and distinctions between good and evil. Recognizing this here-and-now and stressing it as "non-thought" is also part of Zen thought. The distinction is important, as is the fact that during the war this idea in effect encouraged soldiers to push on and do battle without a thought, totally unconcerned with the historical and social circumstances. The emphasis on the here-and-now is related to the Zen

[46] SDZ 17:237.

[47] SDZ 28:547.

[48] *Zen and Japanese Culture*, 61; SDZ 11:34.

idea that "wherever you stand is the right place" (立處皆真) and the ideal of "becoming a master of one's circumstances" (隨處作主). By discouraging one from pausing to think rationally, such teaching blinds one to the realities of history and society. Any situation whatsoever, any setting can become "true," so that one can even murder enthusiastically. Such Zen ideas of the here-and-now are particularly efficacious in time of war, as not a few Zen Buddhists recognized during the Second World War, lending the arm of Zen to the war effort.

For his part, Suzuki never stressed this kind of thinking. As noted above, he stated emphatically that "Zen absolutely never teaches one to throw one's life away." His idea of what constituted Zen thought is altogether different. In *Zen and Japanese Culture*, which was written in 1938 just prior to the outbreak of the World War, he does note the connection between Zen and samurai culture, which may lead the modern reader to assume that he had the modern soldier in mind, but this was not the case. His intention was to show that since Zen experience itself is value-neutral, it can be adapted to various times and societies. The here-and-now is the key to Zen experience, but one must be wary of emphasizing it without qualification.

Zen and Suzuki's View of the Japanese People

Leaving for the United States of America at the age of twenty-six and encountering a totally different civilization and culture in his ten years of life there, Suzuki was forced to compare Japanese and American culture and civilization and to rethink his own identity in the process. This led him to some remarkably accurate observations on the merits and demerits of America in the early, formative stages of a capitalist society upheld by modern scientific technology. He turned a similar eye on his homeland and wrote a considerable body of social commentary. During his life in the United States, Suzuki had to rethink and reintegrate his own identity, and this brought him to a heightened realization that an indispensable element of his identity was the fact that he was not American but Japanese, not Christian but Buddhist. That he should have loved his homeland and been concerned for its welfare is hardly to be wondered at. Still, as we noted above, throughout his life he never absolutized his country or made it his primary concern. He was not a nationalist or national supremacist. He remained a religious person who sought to base his life on his own religious experience or "spirituality," a believer in the universality of the spiritual dimension who was both a cosmopolie and an individualist.

Whether one accepts Suzuki's idea of spirituality depends greatly on how that spirituality is expressed in the concrete. *Spirituality* (靈性) was not a term of his own coinage, but it appears already in his first essay "The Land of

Spiritual Peace and Enlightenment."[49] In his later writings, expressions like "spiritual awakening" and "Japanese spirituality" became important elements in his discussion of Zen thought. Was Suzuki ever able to formulate a satisfactory explanation of what he meant by the word? For all his talk about the universality of spirituality, are his arguments really convincing? Time and again he stressed the importance of explaining Buddhism in rational, European languages, and he himself wrote over thirty volumes in English in an attempt to do so. A familiar refrain in his writings is that insofar as one seeks to explain in words, then one's words must be based on reason and be rationally convincing. Otherwise, the explanations will lack universality. In principle, therefore, he believed that what cannot be rationally explained to a non-Japanese, cannot be explained to a Japanese either. Suzuki spent his life in the pursuit of trying to express the inexpressible. If he was not able to explain Zen Buddhism completely, it is because it is a task that must always be left incomplete and handed on to posterity.

The problem of explaining Zen rationally is the problem of our attitude to matters we cannot convince ourselves of rationally. Do we simply admit that certain things exist without a rational explanation, or do we refuse to allow that possibility and simply deny them from the start? Suzuki once made a remark to the effect that Americans could not understand Zen. And when asked whether anyone in the United States understood Zen, he replied with a flat, "No."[50] Some have read this exchange and concluded that Suzuki was convinced that Americans cannot understand Zen, that Zen is something superior and special that only Japanese can appreciate. They further read into his comments the belief that the Japanese people themselves are somehow special and superior. Nothing could be further from the truth in Suzuki's case, and only a complete disregard for context can yield such conclusions. Interest in Zen in the Western world has a very short history, and the lack of understanding only demonstrates the difficulty of Buddhism's advance eastward. As Suzuki himself clearly stated, "It is not something that can be accomplished in one or two years, or ten or twenty. It may take fifty or a hundred years, but there is no cause for worry."[51]

---

[49] 安心立命の地 [The land of spiritual peace and enlightenment], 宗教 26 (5 December 1893), and 28 (5 February 1894).

[50] アメリカの禅を語る [A dialogue on Zen in America], 禅文化 14 (1 February 1959): 28.

[51] "A Dialogue on Zen in America," 22. The dialogue deals with the general difficulty of the spread of Buddhism eastwards and mentions several points in particular, among them the understanding of Zen in the United States up to 1950, and "beat-Zen" or Zen as a passing fashion. Problems on the part of the Japanese who were trying to propagate Zen included the failure to fully appreciate cultural differences, the narrow outlook of the Zen masters, and especially the lack of "intellectual integrity" (知的節操) and "moral pride"(道徳的矜持).

It took centuries for Buddhism to spread from India to China and centuries more to spread from China to Japan. In the course of its history Buddhism took on specifically Chinese and specifically Japanese forms. If Buddhism is to spread through the Western world, it is obvious that it will take time, and also that it will take forms quite different from those of Japanese Buddhism. D. T. Suzuki was a pioneer in introducing and propagating Buddhism, especially Zen Buddhism, to the world of the West. For this, at the very least, history will remember him.

[TRANSLATED BY RICHARD SZIPPL & THOMAS KIRCHNER]

PART TWO

Questioning Nishida

Nishida, Nationalism, and the War in Question

UEDA Shizuteru

I N THE BACKGROUND OF ALL discussion about the Kyoto school and nationalism lies the problem of the war that ended in 1945 with Japan's unconditional surrender. Since the two are so inextricably bound together, I would like to begin with some general reflections on that war as a basis for framing the more specific question of nationalism.

THE WAR IN QUESTION

The naming of the war—World War II, the Fifteen-Year War, the Pacific War—depends in part on how one views its historical context. But one thing is clear: the defeat that Japan suffered at its end marked a turning point in Japan's history. The modern period that began in 1853 when Commodore Matthew C. Perry, commander of the East Asia squadron of the American Navy, first sailed his Black Ships into Edo Bay off Uraga, was over. This relationship with the outside world, which had lasted for nearly a century, came to an abrupt halt on 2 September 1945, in the very inlet (now known as "Tokyo Bay") that had received the Black Ships. As Japanese officials boarded the USS Missouri to sign the document of surrender to the Allied Powers, it is said that the flag of Perry's squadron was hoisted on its mast.

For Japan, the appearance of Perry's ships off Uraga was a bolt from the blue, an event in Japan's history comparable only to the threat of the Mongol invasion in the thirteenth century. Only fifteen years elapsed between Perry's arrival and the Meiji Restoration in 1868; yet so great was the shock Japan experienced at the sight of Perry's Black Ships that this short span of time saw the total collapse of the Tokugawa feudal system that had been stable for some 260 years, a duration nearly unparalleled in world history. For the West (Europe and America), however, the opening of Japan was but one more stage in the implementation of a grand design, a single step in the centuries-old march towards global colonialist expansion.

The gradual push to the south of Tsarist Russia, beyond the steppes of Siberia and on to the Pacific Ocean, and the landing of several Russian expeditions on the northernmost islands had already alarmed Japan from the end of the eighteenth century. Just prior to Perry's arrival, Western powers had initiated the subjugation of China by military force in the Opium Wars (1840–1842), eventually reducing the country to a virtual colony in the Treaty of Nanking. The sense of impending danger had already spread to Japan by the time Perry showed up. But now the threat of gunboat diplomacy was striking at the very heart of Japan. In the wake of Perry's fleet, the onslaught of the West continued unabated. In 1856, English and French allied forces invaded northern China and in 1860 occupied Beijing. The Treaty of Nanking gave England possession of Hong Kong in the form of a 99-year lease, and delivered the maritime provinces to Russia as a reward for having mediated the alliance between the Chinese and Anglo-French. The semi-colonial status of China was sealed. Still the Western march did not come to a halt. In 1863 British war ships bombarded Kagoshima and in 1864 the combined forces of England, France, America, and the Netherlands occupied Shimonoseki.

As the van of Western expansionism approached the shores of the distant islands of Japan, it seemed as if the grand scheme of global expansion was coming to its final stage. The fall of the Tokugawa regime and the birth of the Meiji political system took place as a direct result of this challenge from the West. Such change was unprecedented in Japan's history. The radical shift from aristocracy to rule by a warrior class at the end of the Heian period, as well as the emergence of the Tokugawa feudal system, had both been *internal* transitions. Now, for the first time, changes were being made under the pressure of tense relations with the outside world. It was under such circumstances that modern Japan was born.

With the Meiji Restoration, Japan opened up to the world and stepped on to the stage of world history. The play was already in progress and the very survival of the nation and its people depended on the role Japan would take. Nearly all the countries of Asia had, with varying degrees of intervention, been made colonies or semicolonies of Western countries, and for the foreseeable future would remain so. Having escaped colonization, it took Japan nearly two decades of all-out effort at a national level to have the inequitable treaties imposed on it amended, and that only in part. (It would take another two decades to have them revoked entirely.)

The fact is, the only hope of survival for non-Western nations, caught up in the plans of Western expansion and face-to-face with the Western powers, was to forge a new "national consciousness" and make themselves as powerful as the nations of the West. At the time there was no question of any Western power withdrawing out of respect for any non-Western culture. The idea of a plurality of cultures and value-systems would not even reach the level of nominal recognition at the political level, let alone at the level of practical policies, until a century later. In the interim world history would have to witness a good many tragedies.

Behind the global expansion of the West lay "Western civilization" in the broad sense of the term. In the main, this meant military power backed by modern industry. The first problem that faced Japan, newly arrived on the set of world history, was how to secure a place for itself while it shared in the processes of others. The Meiji regime caught the urgency of this demand in the motto, "Enrich the Country, Strengthen the Military" (富国強兵). Japan succeeded in its task in a relatively short time.

But for a non-Western country, the acquisition of such power in so short a time could only come at the price of a rupture whose social, cultural, and spiritual effects were bound to be traumatic. In Japan this problem erupted in the form of a dispute over "Westernization" in the early years of the Meiji era. Rival factions led by Ōkubo Toshimichi, an advocate of Europeanization, and Saigō Takamori, a champion of the samurai ethos, went so far as to take up arms against one other. In the end, the samurai rebels were defeated by the imperial conscript forces equipped with its Western weapons.

These two problems, fortifying the country and establishing Japan's place in the world on the one hand, and striking a balance between Western-style modernization and Japanese tradition on the other, were of course interrelated, but as the direction of the "nation" began to take shape, they tended to develop separately. The latter problem was complicated by the fact that the strife between traditional culture on the one hand and modernization through imitation of the West on the other was symptomatic of a larger possibility being played out in the soul of Japan: a new synthesis of Western and Eastern (Japanese) culture that would extend beyond the frontiers of Japan. Such a synthesis would be an immense task and require centuries to complete. Nishida's intellectual engagement in history is mainly related to this latter problem. Meantime, the imbalance created by this rapid outward development and increasing retrocession of the internal conflicts over culture and tradition only worsened as time went on. The war in question grew directly out of developments related to the former problem. The strength Japan acquired originally in order to insure independence from Western powers did not stop there. In order to gain recognition as a power equal to the countries of the West, Japan began to act imperialistically towards Korea, China, and others of its Asian neighbors.

The turning point came with the Russo-Japanese war waged over Manchuria. It pitted a Tsarist Russia that had already obtained a lease on Port Arthur and Dairen against a Japan that perceived the Russian advances as a threat to its own lifeline. In the larger context of history, the war involved three elements. First was the matter of Japan's self-preservation and self-affirmation as a nation in the face of the Russian threat. Second, it occurred in the midst of a race among Western nations to defend and expand their own imperialist "rights and interests" in East Asia. This connection is clear from the Anglo-Japanese treaty signed in 1902 as a joint effort to counteract the Russian "drive southwards," and also from the support England and America gave to Japan during the war. Third, the Russo-Japanese war was part of the wider struggle of East Asian countries for independence from Western rule. Indeed, Japan's victory served to raise national consciousness among the peoples of India, China, and even Turkey, and to strengthen their resolve against Western colonization.[1]

Victory in the Russo-Japanese War brought Japan, in 1911, a complete revision of the inequitable treaties. For the first time it was recognized, in formal treaty, as an independent nation. Far from tempering its pursuit of equality with the Western powers, this only prompted Japan to exercise its imperialistic tendencies still further. Through rights obtained in Manchuria at the expense of Tsarist Russia, it began quasi-colonialist incursions in North China and, in 1910, annexed Korea as a colony in what it euphemistically referred to as "the merger of Japan and Korea." At the very time when the West was completing its partition of Africa into colonies and semicolonies, Japan stepped into the ranks of imperialist world powers, thereby aggravating tensions among those Western nations that had already secured a foothold in East Asia.

From the time of the Russo-Japanese War, there was a marked ambivalence to Japan's self-affirmation. In relation to the countries of Asia, Japan was behaving like another invading power. To the Western colonizers, it was an obstacle to their plan of world hegemony. The ambivalence was not lost on other Asian nations. China's Sun Yat-sen, for example, acknowledged it in a speech entitled "Great Asia Spirit," which he delivered in Kobe in October 1924, a year before his death. He first spoke of Japan's posture against the West:

> Thirty years ago there was not a single fully independent nation in our Asian continent…. But, when Asia reached the nadir of its weakness, there came a turning point; and that turning point is the starting point of Asia's resurgence…. Where do I situate that starting point? I see it in Japan…. The day, thirty years ago, when Japan rejected the unequal treaties with foreign countries, was the day of resurgence of all our coun-

---

[1] For historical details of the period, see the chapter entitled "An Historical Investigation of the National Interests of Japan," in 鈴木成高 Suzuki Shigetaka, 世界史における日本 [Japan in world history] (Tokyo: Sōbunsha, 1990).

tries of Asia. At that moment Japan became the first independent nation in Asia.

But then his tone changes:

> You, the Japanese nation, possess the essence of the kingly way (王道) of Asia but have already set a foot on the dominating way (覇道) of America and the West. Before the tribunal of world culture, you, the Japanese nation, will have to make a serious choice whether from now on to become an agent of the Western dominating way or a bulwark of the Eastern kingly way.[2]

Sun Yat-sen's words reflect the concern of other Asian countries concerning the direction the Japanese nation would take after the Russo-Japanese War.

These two currents in Japan's policy flowed together, responding at each turn to the international political situation. The continuation of these trends led to the war in question—the war that started with China, spread out to involve England and America, and finally formed one of the arenas of World War II, drawing the greater part of East and South Asia in with it.

Within Japan, the attitude towards the last war underwent a complete turnabout. During the actual fighting, the idea of opposition to Western hegemony was stressed and the goal of state policy was presented idealistically as a "New Order" for East Asia and the world at large. Talk of Japanese expansionism and invasions was kept out of the picture. After the war, it was customary to define it as a unilateral war of aggression by a militaristic Japan, brushing aside talk of putting a halt to Western expansionism. Both views distort historical reality and historical praxis, each of them inspired by historical moods and special interests, whether it be the "holy war" or the pro-Soviet "peace movement." Those who see the war exclusively in terms of Japan's aggressions tended to side with Soviet Russia in the post-war conflict between the two superpowers, Russia being the "peace power" and America the "war power." (In its first stages, the movement to ban the atomic bomb even referred to Soviet atomic bombs as "forces for peace.") Such posturing only served to heighten already existing tensions.

Others, meantime, came to take a clear and balanced view of both sides. Takeuchi Yoshimi, for example, who had lived through the travails, advocates the idea of "Asia as a method." In a later critical commentary on the "Overcoming Modernity" symposium held during the war,[3] Takeuchi speaks of the "twofold structure of the Pacific War" as "a war of conquest and a war

[2] Cited in 桶谷秀昭 Oketani Hideaki, 昭和精神史 [An intellectual history of the Shōwa period] (Tokyo: Bungei Shunjūsha, 1992), 58-9.

[3] See the essay by Minamoto Ryōen in this collection, pages 197–229.

against imperialism." He traces the duplicity back to the policies of the Meiji nation, which imposed unequal treaties on Korea and China even as it worked to reverse the unequal treaties that had been imposed on Japan itself. Takeuchi asserts further that this duplicity was perpetrated without being clearly recognized as such. During the Pacific War, "the two sides fused together so firmly that it was impossible at the time to pry one loose from the another." For Takeuchi, this amounts to an "aporia of history."[4] In an explanatory introduction to the symposium, Matsumoto Ken'ichi makes a similar observation:

> [The war] had a double character: Asia and Japan's resistance to the advanced imperialist powers, and Japan's aggression and imperialism. When the war broke out, Takeuchi tried to shift the character of the war away from the latter and towards the former. He tried to do in theory what Ozaki Hotsumi endeavored to do in politics. Of course, both ventures ended in failure.[5]

Neither aspect can be reduced to the other. It took them both to bring the war about, and both to bring it to an end. But history did not end there. Taking the war in tow, world history entered an age of new international tensions, the "cold war" between the two superpowers of America and the Soviet Union. Meanwhile, any number of secondary, vicarious wars brought new devastation and abominations. Looking at the last war in question from where we stand today, it is both unfair and unhistorical to see Japan's role as the only tarnish on the El Dorado of world history.

The war in question *was* a war of aggression against the countries of East Asia. For us Japanese to equivocate on this point is morally unacceptable. At the same time, to stop there is to land ourselves in a historical naiveté that can only distort our view of today's world. The fact is, a powerful faction within the Japanese army actively promoted aggressive military action. But it is not the case that the war, viewed as a collective effort that includes the ideals of the people, was a simple act of aggression and no more. Phrases bandied around at the time such as "the liberation of Asia" and "new world order" were not mere slogans aimed at camouflaging unjustified incursions into foreign lands. They were slogans, to be sure, but the reason they were believable to so many Japanese (and to so many other Asians as well, as we see in Sun Yat-sen's words) was that they touched on something very real in conditions at the time.

One need hardly mention the fact that virtually all the Asian countries that achieved independence after the war, were colonies or semicolonies of

[4] KC, 324, 306.
[5] KC, viii–ix.

82

Western powers during the war. Historically speaking, the Second World War marked the end of the age of colonization. Such developments in postwar Asia cannot, of course, be credited to Japan. Still, they did not take place in isolation from the war.[6] Giving that side of the story its due consideration does not require pronouncing a general absolution on aggressive components of the war. Responsibility for our past demands that Japan take a long, hard look at the aggressions and bear the burden that is ours. However severe the moral judgments that history passes, historical events are not decided by morality alone. This is the pessimistic wisdom of history. Japan was punished by history, but history took Japan's place and went on to run its course in Asia.

In his book *The One Pacific War and Another*, Shinobu Seizaburō represents one attempt to take this broader perspective I am suggesting. He treats the relevant history without playing down the aggressive side or exonerating Japan for the war it waged. Shinobu bases his position on the work of the Filipino historians Renato and Leticia Constantino, a husband and wife whose thesis Shinobu summarizes as follows:

> The ordinary interpretation of Japan's role in the war sees Japan exclusively as the villain and disregards any positive historical effects that may have resulted from its crimes. The effect is to whitewash the other imperialist countries. Paradoxical as it may sound, the Japanese invasions in Southeast Asia broke the back of European colonialism, and stimulated the colonized nations to rethink their status.[7]

Shinobu makes no attempt to excuse Japan of its misdeeds. All sorts of domestic and international elements come into the picture, and some of them may be important in understanding why Japan turned aggressive toward its neighboring countries in East Asia and how this eventually led to the Pacific War. But in the final analysis, Shinobu argues, the war should not have taken place; much effort should have been expended to resolve the problems by peaceful means. He rejects the idea that the war was inevitable. By the same standard, there is some question whether America's attitude to Japan was the right one, but even this does not change the fact: Japan was responsible for beginning the war and it owes a debt to the world. As a Japanese, I can only say that there was no excuse for what happened, and I believe that many feel as I do.

---

[6] For example, in Burma, one group in the Japanese military lent its support during the war to the local Freedom Fighters. In 1981, the independent Burmese government honored seven Japanese soldiers of that group with the country's highest Medal of Honor. See 信夫清三郎 Shinobu Seizaburō, 「太平洋戦争」と「もうひとつの太平洋戦争」 [The one Pacific war and another] (Tokyo: Keisō Shobō, 1988), 176.

[7] See note 6 above. The summary appears on page 3.

It is not enough to say that there was "no excuse for what happened." To be sure, there is much in history that eludes the measure of morality, but this does not absolve us of our historical responsibility. The gap between ethics and historical knowledge remains, and with it the "historical aporia" this has left us with. In the half century since the end of the war, other wars have broken out. What are the causes, what the conditions, and what is to be done to eliminate them? These questions represent no less a task for us today than coming to terms with the past. In August 1945, the "war in question" ended in the defeat—the utter defeat—of Japan. And rightly so.

I offer these general reflections as a prelude to the main subject of this essay: the question of Nishida's involvement in the war. I am aware that much more needs to be said, both of conditions at home in Japan and on the international scene, but I defer to more detailed historical studies.[8]

NISHIDA AND THE WAR

In considering the relationship of Nishida to the war, we not only need to take into account the criticisms that have been leveled at him, but also to paint as full and objective a picture as we can from the relevant facts and documents at our disposal. In this latter regard, the first thing to note is that the nineteen volumes of Nishida's *Complete Works* and the numerous other written sources related to his life contain very few statements of his about the war. We must accordingly be doubly careful to insure that what he did say is presented in proper context.

The Problem of Japanese Culture

We may begin with Nishida's general views on the historical developments of the time, particularly as they are outlined in his oft-criticized 1940 book, *The Problem of Japanese Culture*.[9] In it we find a short phrase that serves both as a declaration of principle and a warning to "Japan facing the world":

> In my view, the main thing we must be careful to avoid is making Japan into a subject (主体).... To take a position as one subject vis-à-vis other subjects, and thereby to negate the others or try to reduce them to oneself, is nothing other than imperialism.[10]

---

[8] I can recommend, for example, 中村隆英 Nakamura Takafusa, 昭和史 [A history of the Shōwa period, vol. 1, 1926–1945] (Tokyo: Tōyō Keizai Shinpōsha, 1993), and the previously cited work of Oketani Hideaki, *An Intellectual History of the Shōwa Period*.

[9] NKZ 12:275–383. The original was published in 1940 by Iwanami Shoten of Tokyo.

[10] NKZ 12:344, 349.

These words, written in the thick of the China War and two years before the outbreak of hostilities with England and America, are an unambiguous public criticism directed at what he perceived as a real danger that circumstances were forcing on Japan at the time. *In his opinion* the nation must not think of itself as a *subject* because this would be tantamount to *imperialism*. The words are as clear as the noonday sun, and nothing in the context can leave room for misunderstanding. It is hard to see how later critics can have overlooked them or misrepresented their intent.

Takeuchi Yoshirō, whether deliberately or inadvertently, misreads the term *subject* to refer to the Western imperialistic attitude and then has Nishida saying that this was *not* a danger for Japan. This enables him to conclude that Nishida was both sanctioning Japan's imperialistic wars of aggression and "glorifying the meaning of waging the war."[11] This is typical of the criticisms aimed at Nishida who was in fact warning of the very dangers he is being accused of precipitating. Oketani Hideaki, meantime, gives great weight to *The Problem of Japanese Culture* as "focused directly on Japan's situation at the time." Oketani stresses its call for a "self-negation of modern Japan" which lay behind "his warning against the idea of becoming a subject":

> He was not talking about Japanese culture as a historical reality but about the *idea* of Japanese culture.... Nishida's logical system did not fit with the image of the world contained in the idea of Japanese culture that the new political order required. On the contrary, it cut a path that turned its back on that image of the world as a "way of domination."[12]

I believe Oketani's is the only possible reading of the passage.

The Outbreak of the War in Question

The tensions that would eventually culminate in the Greater East Asia (Pacific) War were rapidly growing and Nishida began to feel more and more apprehensive about the direction things were taking.[13] When war finally did break out, Nishida fell into a deep depression. One of his disciples, Aihara Shinsaku, recalls Nishida's feelings on 8 December 1941, the day the Japanese Navy attacked Pearl Harbor. Nishida was hospitalized at the time with a rheumatic condition. Aihara, learning of what had just transpired, picked up copies of several newspapers bearing the ominous headlines and went to visit him:

[11] 竹内芳郎 Takeuchi Yoshirō, 戦後日本哲学の条件 [The state of philosophy in postwar Japan], 思想 (March 1987): 150.

[12] *An Intellectual History of the Shōwa Period*, 390, 393.

[13] See his letters No. 1541 and 1575, NKZ 19:149, 162.

Sure enough, Nishida had not yet heard the day's big news. I will never forget the expression on his face when I told him what was in the articles prominently displayed in the special editions of the newspapers. It was a face filled with grave concern and anxiety over the terrible force that had been let loose. There was nothing in him of the excitement over a great victory that most people felt. At that moment, his whole body had become one mass of sadness.... After being released from the hospital, Nishida had to spend some time in bed. As Japan chalked up one victory after another and euphoria spread among the public at large, his mood seemed only to deepen in the opposite direction. On great occasions like the fall of Singapore, everyone in the school was obliged to take part in the celebration, whether they wanted to or not. When we visited Nishida at such times, he invariably expressed his deep apprehension and depression, all the more impressive for its contrast with the prevalent mood among the people at large.[14]

Thirty-five years earlier, during the Russo-Japanese war, Nishida is said to have fallen into a similar depression, refusing to be mesmerized by the mood of the moment, concerning himself rather with the course of history over the long run. On 5 January 1905, as the fall of Port Arthur was being celebrated in Japan, Nishida, who was thirty-five years old at the time and living in Kanazawa, wrote in his diary of the "frivolity" of the festivities.[15] He had spent the entire day, morning to night, in zazen, contemplating the victims of the war and the "long, hard road" that lay ahead. Far from serving as an escape from reality, zazen gave him the composure he needed to put events in a larger perspective. Little did he know how long or how hard that road would be, stretching from the China War to the Pacific War, and eventually to the life-and-death struggle of a World War that would end in the fall of modern Japan. But contrary to what his critics are fond of intimating, he was not blind to historical reality.

Nishida was born immediately after the Meiji Restoration and lived to see the rapid changes that took place in Japan in its attempt to face the world as a modern state through the Meiji, Taishō, and Shōwa periods. He was alert to historical events and had no little insight into the direction that history was taking. As early as March of 1937 we read in one of his letters:

[14] 相原信作 Aihara Shinsaku, 先生によって予見せられた日本民族の運命 [The lot of the Japanese as foreseen by Nishida], in 西田寸心先生片影 [A profile of Nishida "Sunshin"] (Kyoto: Reimei Shobō, 1949), 42–3.

[15] The passage, which can be found in NKZ 17:130, is reproduced in the contribution of Yusa Michiko to this collection. See below, page 122 and note 48.

Contrary to what certain people are saying, the world of the future is not going to settle into a pattern of nationalisms, each country by its isolated self. The world will have no rest until it finds a way to global coopera-tion.[16]

The actual course that Japan took, however, led down a winding path, in a direction different from the one ethat Nishida had envisioned.

Principles for a New World Order

In May 1943, some eighteen months after the outbreak of the Pacific War, the leaders of the Army approached Nishida to write his ideas about Japan's role in East Asia. As the military situation grew more serious, an East Asia Conference was being convened to clarify the idea of the "Greater East Asia Co-Prosperity Sphere." Nishida disliked the Army clique, whom he saw as the real driving force behind the war effort, but he decided to comply with their request because it had to do with questioning the underlying *principles* that were steering Japan through a time of historical crisis; and perhaps also because it would give him the rare opportunity of directly criticizing the Army.[17]

The outline of Nishida's presentation is preserved in two different texts bearing the same title, "Principles for a New World Order."[18] Although not composed on his own initiative, it represents one of the few statements Nishida made about the war and shows Nishida's view of history in direct and concrete relation to the world-historical situation at the time. "In each age the world has a particular task," Nishida begins, "and it moves from age to age in the quest to fulfill those tasks." If the eighteenth century was the age of the self-awakening of the individual and the nineteenth century the age of the self-awakening of nation-states, the twentieth century, in his view, is that age in which the plurality of nations undergoes a world-awakening to

---

[16] No. 1078, NKZ 18:589–90.

[17] 田辺寿利 Tanabe Juri, a young man on familiar terms with Nishida and involved in the episode, explains that "Nishida's arrival at such a decision, despite his intense dislike of the Army, shows that he considered the question a matter of gravest importance for the state." See 晩年の西田幾多郎先生と日本の運命 [Nishida Kitarō's late period and the fate of Japan] (Unoke: Memorial Society for Nishida Kitarō, 1962).

[18] 世界新秩序の原理, NKZ 12:426–31. Another version, somewhat different in style and wording, can be found at the beginning of the booklet cited in note 17. A critical examination of the texts makes it difficult to ascertain how much of the text was actually written by Nishida himself. I have chosen to use this text because the expressions related to the East Asia Co-Prosperity Sphere basically correspond to Nishida's ideas on the matter, and because this is the text cited by those of Nishida's critics who want to argue that he was an "ideologue of imperial-ism."

a single, world-historical world. Each nation must open up to the world as the age of imperialist colonialism draws to a close, and this requires first that each nation open itself up to the particular sphere into which geographic conditions and cultural traditions have placed it (not unlike what is going on today in the move for a united Europe). It is out of the mutually reinforcing relationships of these particular worlds, Nishida felt, that a global world can become a reality. This was his basic *principle* for a *new world order*. We may summarize the basic ideas common to both versions of the text as follows, using Nishida's own words as far as possible:

> A peace that embraces all of humankind is possible only if all nations and peoples, awakened to their common world-historical mission, first form particular worlds or "co-prosperity spheres," in line with existing geographical and cultural bonds; and further if, through the mutual cooperation of these different co-prosperity spheres, a world in the true sense of the word, a *global* world, comes into being. To make such a global world a reality by setting up co-prosperity spheres that can cooperate among each other is the world-historical task that has fallen to the present age.... The historical task of the peoples of East Asia here is to build an East Asia Co-Prosperity Sphere...and by means of it, to help make the global world a reality.
>
> Peoples and nations that formerly lacked adequate means to connect with each other due to geographic limitations, have been brought into a common world space through scientific progress and the improvement of communications. But today that world has been cast into a violent struggle in which gigantic states compete with each other in that world space. There is only one way to put an end to this, and that is for each state to become aware of its world-historical mission, and to contribute to the formation of a single global world by transcending itself while remaining true to itself. This is what I mean by referring to the present as the age of the world-awareness of peoples and states. The particular task of the peoples of East Asia as we stand at this new frontier of the history of humanity, the realization of a global world, is to establish an East Asia Co-Prosperity Sphere.

As the above résumé makes clear, Nishida takes the idea of a "Greater East Asia Co-Prosperity Sphere" that was being propagated at the time and puts it in a larger context of a plurality of co-prosperity spheres. The fact that he does not himself adopt the almost sacrosanct formula "*Greater* East Asia Co-Prosperity Sphere" is not without significance. For him, "East Asia" was merely one particular geographical division and "co-prosperity sphere" no more than the single form of a plural reality.

Nishida's idea of co-prosperity spheres is based on the idea of a plurality of "particular worlds" (特殊的世界) in his philosophy of history. Particular worlds mediate between individual peoples or states on the one hand and the global world on the other. (In mentioning peoples as well as nations, Nishida frequently means to single out peoples subjected to colonial rule by other nations, and thus to hint at their potential for independence.) He assigns a central role to "particular worlds" in bringing a peaceful, new world order because he feared that without the mediation of concrete unities based on regional and cultural traditions, multinational institutions by themselves—for example, international federations—would end becoming no more than new arenas for new clashes of interests among the great powers. Accordingly, he calls on individual peoples and nations, which he envisions as joining to form particular worlds that then unite to form a single global world, "to transcend themselves *while remaining true to themselves*." This later qualification re-iterates his continued respect for the historical life of specific people with specific cultural traditions. The enjoinder to "transcend themselves and the particular historical conditions out of which they developed," on the other hand, implies a limit to the political sovereignty of individual nations by themselves.[19]

The pivotal role that Nishida assigns to particular worlds in his principles for a new and peaceful world order was not without its own foundation in history. The experience of World War I had convinced him world peace was impossible at the two extremes of self-determined, isolated individual countries and peoples on the one hand, and large world organizations on the other. World organizations (like today's United Nations) are, of course, nec-essary, but Nishida's point was that they need the infrastructure of relations among particular worlds small enough in scale to retain a concrete communal character. Only in this careful interplay of particular worlds and the global world can we understand the difference between Nishida's East Asia co-pros-perity sphere and the "Greater East Asia Co-Prosperity Sphere" in whose name the war was being waged.

The title of his proposal, "Principles for a New World Order," is delib-erate. The *New World Order* suggests an old order that is passing away, namely the order shaped by global expansion and world domination on the part of Western countries. The historical reasons for why the countries of the West were able to attain world hegemony do not, he insisted, suffice to justi-fy the perpetuation of that hegemony. If a new order is to come about, it will require full consciousness of that fact—as self-evident as this may sound to us

[19] Nishida originally suggested that the foundation for the unity of the human race would lie in a cultural synthesis. In *The Problem of Japanese Culture*, he writes: "Without achieving a cul-tural synthesis, we cannot really speak of a unity among human beings" (NKZ 12:375).

in 1994, it was far from self-evident half a century ago—and also an awareness of the task that history has given non-Western nations and peoples,
namely to come up with an alternative.

Moreover, by focusing his proposal on the *Principles* for a new world
order, Nishida implies that the standpoint from which a new order is created
must take care not to become imperialistic itself. This same point comes out
clearly in the pages of *The Problem of Japanese Culture*. It is reiterated in a
conversation between Nishida and leaders of the Army as reported in a
memorial lecture by Tanabe Juri (who was present on the occasion as a go-
between). At one point Nishida is said to have thundered back at one of the
officers in unmistakable terms:

> What are you saying? It sounds like imperialism to me! You call it a "Co-
> Prosperity Sphere," but how can it be co-prosperity if it doesn't meet the
> needs of all the peoples involved? If it means giving our side the right to
> make all the decisions and tell the other side to "Do this and don't do
> that," it is a simple coercion sphere, not a co-prosperity sphere.[20]

Still, it seems clear that Nishida's ideas on global awareness were lost on
the leaders of the Army, and this left him more discouraged than ever. We
read in his letters at the time statements like these:

> I get more and more disgusted at what I read in the papers. My ideas are
> not being understood at all. Nothing seems to get through. The expres-
> sions I used are not important; what matters are the basic principles
> behind them.

> I am truly saddened at the thought that our country is getting to the
> point that we old bookworms in our studies have dreaded from the start.

> I have already given up all hope.[21]

The Tug-of-War over Meaning

That the global or "world" character of Nishida's thought came under heavy
attack by proponents of a narrow Japanism (日本中心主義) and ideologues of
the "Japanese spirit" who held sway over public opinion is hardly surprising.[22]
The text and the wider context of "Principles for a New World Order" represented a clear critique of the Japanists and an unmistakable warning to the

---

[20] *Nishida Kitarō's Late Period and the Fate of Japan*, 27.

[21] Letters No. 1783, 1784, 1951 (July 1944), and 1986 (September 1944). Like D. T.
Suzuki, Nishida had foreseen the defeat of Japan from quite early on.

[22] As Nishida confided in a letter at the time, "Of late even the likes of me have become the
target of attacks by these narrow Japanists." Letter No. 1791, NKZ 19:247.

90

Army. By twisting the phrase "Greater East Asian Prosperity Sphere" to his own purposes, Nishida set up a kind of "war over words" with the Army and the Japanists. In the tense atmosphere of a war in progress, Nishida's tug-of-war for the meaning of words could not but be taken as a criticism of the war effort in general. The powers-that-be were quick enough to realize this and hence redoubled their attacks on him. A passing comment by Shimomura Toratarō illuminates the situation:

> After the war, it [Nishida's text] became the brunt of simplistic criticisms. We must not forget, however, that at the time nobody was able to propose a theory against the fanatical idea of national polity (国体論). We should rather be impressed by Nishida's courage and fervor.[23]

THE "IMPERIAL WAY"

Nishida's engagement in the war of words was not restricted to his 1943 redefinition of the co-prosperity sphere. It applied also to the term *Imperial Way* (皇道) and the much-touted *Japanese spirit* (日本精神).[24] In each case, it will not escape the attentive reader that Nishida is not promoting these slogans. He is no more a theoretician of the Imperial Way and the Japanese spirit than he was of the Greater East Asia Co-Prosperity Sphere. Quite the contrary, at a time when many were bandying these ideas around mindlessly, Nishida seemed to be saying: if these words are to be used, then let them be used in a clearly defined sense. On his own, he would have no reason to use these terms. But as they were already on everybody's lips, he tried to give them an acceptable content. His phrasing makes his intentions clear enough in passages where he writes "that would turn Imperial Way into a way of domination," or "that is not the Japanese spirit."

The Problem of Japanese Culture and "Principles for a New World Order," together with the other material appended to volume 12 of the *Collected Works*, must not be read as Nishida's own program but as critical writings in a deliberate "tug-of-war" over meaning. To borrow a phrase from Nakajima Kenzō's, "Even today, if one reads the texts in that light, it is easy to see what Nishida was doing."[25] I have the impression that those of

---

[23] Cited from the afterword to the addenda of the volume in Nishida's *Collected Works* that contains the text of "Principles for a New World Order," NKZ 12:470.

[24] We find this as early as 1940 in *The Problem of Japanese Culture.*

[25] 中島健蔵 Nakajima Kenzō, 昭和時代 [The Shōwa period] (Tokyo: Iwanami Shoten, 1957), 115; see 112–15 and 125 for more on Nishida. Nakajima also examines a text that is often mistaken by critics for a document of Nishida's "Japanese spirit" ideology, namely, the "Opinion Paper" that Nishida sent to the first general meeting of the Committee for the Renewal of Education and Scholarship set up by the Ministry of Education, of which Nishida was a member. Nakajima shows how, given the context of the time, its tone is critical of that ideology.

Nishida's critics who fail to sense here "the agony of an awakened mind" are still reading in the dark.

One further aspect of this semantic struggle needs mentioning in connection with *The Problem of Japanese Culture*. Although first published in 1940, the book is actually an expansion on a series of "Monday Lectures" that Nishida delivered at Kyoto Imperial University in the spring of 1938 and that were printed soon after as a tract with the same title.[26] We thus have at our disposal two texts, which I will refer to as the *lectures* text and the *book* text. The latter incorporates the former but is more than three times as long and is also rather different in content. The differences I will examine here were introduced in the two-year interval between their respective publications.

Both editions of *The Problem of Japanese Culture* appended the text of separate talks on "Scholarly Method" delivered in Tokyo in 1937. Clearly Nishida himself felt that the contents of the Tokyo talks were central to his treatment of Japanese culture. The lecture text opens with a remark on the Tokyo talks:

> I entitled the talk "Scholarly Method" in order to stress the importance of methodology and to make clear my firm conviction that it be given due respect in future discussions about Japanese culture. The reader may feel, as in fact I do myself, that this is too obvious to mention. I wish it were so, but I think we find ourselves in a time when it needs repeating. Nowadays things that are clear enough without being said have to be spoken.[27]

This simple statement makes it clear that Nishida wanted his voice to be heard as a critique of the times. As the rest of the contents of the lectures show, the focus of his critique was the fashionable idea of "Japanese spirit."

The book text and lectures text both preserve this basic thrust, but they differ widely on two counts. First, in the book Nishida added a great deal of material that clarifies his original intention to distance himself from the ideology of the "Japanese spirit." Three of the book's eight chapters (2, 3, and 4—in all, 45 pages or nearly half of the whole) were new. The preface explains: "In these chapters I have stated the main premises that guide my thinking in treating problems like those that occupy me in this book." In them Nishida summarizes ideas recently developed in his *Philosophical Essays*, especially in his essay on "Theory and Life." The expressions *Japan*, *Japanese spirit*, and *Japanese culture* do not appear in these pages. While this may seem to destroy the balance of the book, it serves Nishida with a chance to make it clear that his own basic interest lay on a different level.

[26] The text based on the 1938 lectures appears in NKZ 14:381–417.

[27] NKZ 14:389.

The second difference between the two versions of the text has to do with the attention given to the term *Imperial Way*. In the lecture text, the term does not occur at all, except obliquely in one reference to the "imperial family." "Scholarly Method" uses the term once, in a phrase that reads: "...the Imperial Way must be seen as global [世界的, open up to the world]." In the book text, however, *Imperial Way* appears often and conspicuously throughout the second half. But his aim is not to champion the idea but to engage it in the "semantic struggle." The years during which he wrote the book text, 1938 to 1940, were a time when the ideologues of Imperial Way had succeeded in swaying public opinion as never before. Chapter 5 introduces the term precisely in order to give Nishida the chance to distance himself from those with whom it is associated:

> A confrontation is being proclaimed in our country between totalism and individualism.... Those who try to think from the standpoint of our country itself speak of the Imperial Way.[28]

The context makes it clear that he is not trying to present Imperial Way an an ideal, but to warn against its inherent danger of making Japan into a subject, "which would make the Imperial Way no more than a way of domination; it would turn the Imperial Way into an imperialism."[29] The "true meaning" of the term, he goes on to say, is disclosed only from a global standpoint: "it must contribute to the world."

As mentioned earlier, the three middle chapters of the book were Nishida's way of drawing the questions back to a more basic, philosophical level. In fact, after completing *The Problem of Japanese Culture,* he published a series of philosophical essays in rapid succession that proved to be a great drain on his energies. In 1940 he wrote a piece inspired by Kierkegaard, "Prolegomena to a Practical Philosophy," and another on "Poiesis and Praxis." In 1941, he composed "Artistic Creation as an Act of Shaping History." And so he continued his philosophical labors proper through to the last two essays written in 1945, the year he died: "The Philosophical Foundation of Mathematics" and his swan song, "The Logic of Place and a Religious Worldview."

THE EMPEROR AND THE IMPERIAL FAMILY

Another point of contention for Nishida's postwar critics was the view of the "imperial family" presented in *The Problem of Japanese Culture.*" By and large those who lodge the complaints are "anti-emperor" to begin with and dis-

[28] NKZ 12:334–5.
[29] NKZ 12:341.

posed to hold Emperor Shōwa responsible for his role in the war. Simply put, the facts at our disposal do not support the conclusion that the emperor encouraged the war effort. Already in 1936, in what has come to be known as the 2-26 (26 February) Incident, it was the emperor himself who decided to hold the leaders of the attempted military coup subject to the charge of mutiny. It can also be demonstrated that the emperor was extremely wary about entering into war with the West. Nor is the case any stronger for those who shift the focus away from the emperor personally to the "emperor system" as such. If anything, the presence of the emperor was seen by warmongering elements in the military as an obstacle to be overcome in the pursuit of their goals. There is every reason to believe that without him, things would have been much easier for them.

Nishida himself was sympathetic to the imperial family. That is a fact. He was born into the very age that saw Japan become a modern state with the emperor as a symbol of the new experiment in national unification. This very symbolic presence was instrumental in drawing the curtain on the rule of a warrior class that had lasted for several centuries and in helping inaugurate a nation that might take its place in the world. As a "Meiji youth" Nishida grew up watching the newborn state take its first stumbling steps.

The important point to note here is that Nishida's cordial sentiments toward the emperor are *not* directly related to the meaning he attaches to the *idea* of the emperor in his philosophy. Far from advocating the emperor-ideology of the champions of the "Japanese spirit" during the war, Nishida had early premonitions that the alliance of the "reactionary caucus of intellectuals" with the imperial family is "something extremely dangerous."[30] Not surprisingly, the Japanists criticized him for "a philosophy not in line with the empire of Japan."[31]

Critics of Nishida's stance towards the emperor almost invariably point to his phrase, "The imperial family is a self-identity of contradictories, a being of non-being (無の有)."[32] This is taken of proof that he held the emperor (or the imperial family) to be absolute, and from there it is but a short leap to conclude that he was a collaborator in the war. Only a look at the actual context of these remarks can resolve the question.

To begin with, Nishida never refers to the imperial family as an "*absolute self-identity of contradictories*" but only as a simple "self-identity of contradictories." The two expressions are carefully distinguished in *The Problem of Japanese Culture*, and the non-absolute formulation—as indeed the expres-

[30] Letter No. 758 (1932), NKZ 18:464.
[31] See his introduction to 伝統 [Tradition], NKZ 11:189.
[32] NKZ 12:336

sion "a being of non-being"[33]—is used in other contexts as well. An examination of the text clearly shows that when Nishida uses the term in reference to the imperial family he is describing it *without absolutizing* it. In contrast, the "*absolute* self-identity of contradictiories" is reserved for such things as "Buddha-life" or the original "Self."[34]

WAR AND STRUGGLE

Nishida's cautious use of the word *war* in *The Problem of Japanese Culture* also deserves attention. Note the following, where the term is clearly spoken of as an evil to be overcome:

> When one nation possesses enormous power, peace may be preserved for a while. But this peace is made possible only by the enslavement of other peoples. Not only does this lead to human decadence, it is impossible to keep hold on such power forever. As other peoples rise up in strength against it, it has no choice but to fall into the miseries of war. And this can end up in the destruction of human culture.[35]

On the other hand, the term *struggle* (闘争) is used occasionally to refer to something of positive significance:

---

[33] For example, Nishida writes, "Buddhism is a radical pursuit of the Self and thinks of the Self as something that is being yet non-being" (NKZ 12:364).

[34] The *absolute* expression is used most frequently in the first three chapters of *The Problem of Japanese Culture*, where Nishida is summarizing his philosophical position, and only occasionally in chapters 5 and later. Thus the philosophical context for his allusions to "the world of the absolute self-identity of contradictories" is clearly his idea that "the point at which we become historically creative in shifting from the position of what has been made to that of maker brings us into touch with the absolute self-identity of absolute contradictories" (NKZ 12:316).

The *simple* expression also occurs in the three philosophical chapters, as for instance when he claims that "the world of matter is a self-identity of the contradictories space and time," or "the laws of physics represent the form in which the world moves in the manner of a self-identity of contradictories" (12:294). Later he applies the simple expression, again with no reference to the imperial family, to "heaven and earth" (12:347), "subject and environment" in Greek culture, (12:354), and the transition from one age to another (12:378). In none of these cases is the qualifier *absolute* used.

After chapter five, we still find him using the absolute expression. For example, he refers to the world of matter as "the self-determination of a world as a self-identity of contradictories." But he reverts to the absolute formula in explaining the famous formula from Hua-yen Buddhist philosophy, "the unobstructed interpenetration of things" (事事無碍), as reality determining reality itself. Or again, in a Zen reference, he claims that "[The place of the self] must be the Buddha-life of which Dōgen speaks and which itself is an absolute self-identity of contradictories" (12:369).

[35] NKZ 12:373.

Struggle is always present in history as the pain accompanying the development of a new world. The progress of history is tragic. That is where new humans have to be born.... In today's world, too, this is where a new mode of being human has to come to birth.[36]

In passages such as these Nishida scrupulously avoids the term "World *War*" and speaks rather of a "World *Struggle*." I believe that he does this in order not to give the impression of approving of war in history. For Nishida, war was something that ought not to be; and where it existed, a tragedy. People that have passed through the gates of tragedy need to be reborn, creatively. If not, human culture may come to an end.

Conclusions on Nishida and the War

I conclude from the foregoing that criticisms depicting Nishida as a nationalist, a promoter of the "Japanese spirit," a supporter of the war, an ideologue of the Greater East Asia War, an absolutizer of the emperor, and so forth cannot be substantiated either in Nishida's own writings or in their actual historical context. Rather, precisely because these labels could *not* be applied to him, Nishida was misunderstood by the military and attacked by the ideologues of the "Japanese spirit."

This being so, the real question is then how to explain this critique of Nishida as a historical phenomenon. As a group his accusers do not seem to have gone to the trouble of reading the entire text of *The Problem of Japanese Culture*, looking at its historical context, or paying attention to Nishida's own interests as outlined in the philosophical essays he wrote during this period. During the war, Nishida was attacked as an anti-nationalist "globalist" by nationalists who promoted the "Japanese spirit." After the war, left-wing ideologists, radical Marxists, and their followers spearheaded the attack against him as a nationalistic ideologue of the "Japanese spirit." That Nishida's philosophy should have been subjected to the affliction of so much misunderstanding during the war and afterwards is a historical phenomenon of some moment. No doubt, each side did so in order to justify its own position, a justification on whose final verdict history will one day speak. At present in Europe and the United States, half a century after the end of the war, the shades of these criticisms rise up again. Quite apart from the attempt of philosophers, theologians, and scholars of religion to engage in a positive dialogue with thinkers like Nishida and Nishitani, a countercurrent seems bent on washing Nishida out of the picture as a nationalistic theoretician of "Japanese culture" and a promoter of the war. It is a phenomenon, I repeat, whose meaning eludes me.

[36] NKZ 12:334.

Throughout his life, in everything that happened to him and everything that he did, Nishida remained the philosopher. Even while under attack by the nationalists and actual warmongers in the Army, and in a condition of "utter starvation," Nishida wrote one philosophical essay after the other, all the way up to his death in June 1945. As he wrote in a letter, "I want to do as much as possible of the work that only I can do, and leave it to posterity."[37] Two months after Nishida's death, modern Japan collapsed in a defeat that he had long foreseen.

Nishida lost his "tug-of-war over meaning." The turn of events obliges us to acknowledge that his plan ended in failure. We cannot but acknowledge his failure in the context of his time. But matters did not end there. After the war criticisms of Nishida resumed with no less vehemence, but from a different quarter. Instead of being accused of obstructing the war effort he was accused of having promoted it. This makes his failure seem all the greater.

History often has a way of absorbing the destinies of individuals into its own currents, and I believe that this is what happened to Nishida's war of words with the Army. This does not mean that Nishida's thought as such suffered a failure. Among those who judge him guilty of collaboration in the war there is considerable difference of opinion about his philosophy. Some argue from his complicity in the war that there is no point to looking any further into his philosophy, that it should simply be rejected as is. Others find the grounds for his participation in the war in his philosophy itself, that his complicity points to an intrinsic flaw in his thought. Finally, there are those who claim that certain weak points in his philosophy led Nishida, unknowingly, into complicity with the war. In each case, the assumption is that Nishida conspired with the war effort and that this is somehow due to the nature of his philosophy. The assumption of complicity, as I have tried to show, lacks foundation either in fact or in the written word. If any of those positions are to be pursued, this assumption has first to establish itself as a conclusion based on evidence.

Criticism of Nishida's philosophy as such, including the social dimension, is another question altogether. Moreover, the question of the significance of Nishida's ideas at the time and of what meaning they may have for us today who have survived the defeat of the "war of words" he waged in different circumstances, are matters that merit treatment in their own right. Here again, however, we must take care not to isolate our questions from the factual and textual evidence discussed above.

In the foregoing I have put the primary accent on Nishida's published writings, but the material found in his letters and diaries is important for a

---

[37] See letters 2126 and 2128 (NKZ 19:390–1), and NKZ 17:702.

balanced picture. I would like to close this treatment of Nishida and the war by citing a few short passages from letters he wrote near the end of his life.

> As to the present situation of our country, ...unfortunately things have come to just where we thought they would. I think the fundamental mistake was entrusting the self-confidence of the people in the hands of military power.[38]

> Tokutomi says people did not show the same energy in the present war that they did in the Sino-Japanese and Russo-Japanese wars—in other words, that they did not march to the beat of his drum. But the people are more advanced in their thinking than leaders like Tokutomi were.[39]

> The Jews laid the foundations for development into a world religion during the years of the Babylonian captivity. This is how a truly spiritual people should be. A nation that associates its self-confidence with military might perishes when the military power does.[40]

> Hitler, too, has come a miserable end. The proverb has it that, "whatever you can get away with is justified," but when all is said and done, this is not the case. Many people today are saying that power-worshipping totalitarianism is the direction to go, but I find such an idea thoroughly old-fashioned and outdated. The direction we need to take is one that reverses the move towards totalitarianism, namely a new globalism. Whether we admit it or not, the world is already going that way.[41]

The terms *world* and *global* are pivotal here, both in Nishida's philosophy as a whole and in his understanding of the historical situation of the time.

Nishida's letters show that he followed the course of the war closely, month after month, aware of what was happening and with the foresight to realize that it would end in the defeat of Japan. This spurred him all the more to direct his thinking beyond the problem of "modern Japan" to consider the place of Japan as a "culture" or "historical body" in the wider world. "Must we not turn our efforts in the direction of discovering what is global in the culture of our country and at rebuilding Japan on that basis?" he asked in

---

[38] Letter No. 2147 (14 March 1945), NKZ 19:401–2.

[39] NKZ 17:708 (10 May 1945). 徳富蘇峰 Tokutomi Sohō, a prominent nationalist, was arrested as a Class A war criminal after the war and banned from public office through the years of the Occupation.

[40] Letter No. 2194, NKZ 19:426.

[41] Letter No. 2195 (11 May 1945), to D. T. Suzuki, NKZ 19:426. The original proverb reads 無理が通れば道理が引っ込む.

one of his last letters.[42] It is to that "problem of culture" that we turn our attention in the next section.

NISHIDA AND THE PROBLEM OF CULTURE

Nishida's ideas on the encounter among cultures in a global community represent, I believe, a concrete answer to the question of what meaning his philosophy can still have for us today. From the time of "the war in question" on, intercommunication among the different cultures of the world has become one of humanity's most pressing concerns. Each culture has something special about it that pervades everything from religion to social behavior, and it is those very differences of thinking, acting, and living that continue to cause frictions and even lead to war. Nishida's *The Problem of Japanese Culture* and his 1937 lecture on "Scholarly Method" are an attempt to address this very problematic.

To begin with, the choice of the word *problem* in the title of his book makes it clear that his concern is not with analyzing Japanese culture as such but in clarifying what is at stake in its encounter with the cultures of the west: "The problem of [Japanese] culture today is what attitude to take towards world culture." In stating the question this way, Nishida sets himself up in critical opposition to the current ideological currents proclaiming the virtues of the "Japanese spirit":

> Current conventions think in terms of digesting Western culture with a Japanese spirit, a kind of twist on the old saying "Japanese soul, Chinese learning" (和魂漢才). In other words, the idea is that there is something called "Japanese spirit" and...that it is up to us to package a synthesis of foreign culture around the core of this spirit.... I find this an extremely shallow and unprofitable approach.[43]

Nishida continues this unmistakable criticism of the "shallowness" of the ideology of the "Japanese spirit" with remarks like the following:

> One of the fashionable superficialities going around today is the talk of a "Japanese science." The adjective *Japanese* adds nothing.... People that talk about the Japanese spirit today tend to boast of the particularity of Japanese culture. But...now that the *world* has become a reality, we cannot relate to it as a mere particularity. That particularity must take on an international historical character.

[42] No. 2181 (12 April 1945), NKZ 19:417–18.
[43] NKZ 14:399–400.

Japan is in the world, and therefore reverence for our particularity alone, for things Japanese, is not enough. True culture does not lie there.... Japanese culture must acquire a global character.[44]

These are strong words, and indeed the text as a whole is the bold expression of someone who continued his whole life to fight for a way of thinking that would open the initial encounter of East and West out into the wider world. This single word *world* runs like a leitmotif throughout the pages of *The Problem of Japanese Culture*. At a time when everything having to do with the wider "world" was suspect—so much so that Nishida even noted ironically that the word itself had all but become taboo[45]—such an insistence on fitting the particularity of Japan into a global context represents a strong critique of the spirit of the times.[46]

The assumption is, of course, that Japan must continue to learn from Western culture. That is what Nishida himself had done already from his youth. For him the learning process went hand-in-hand with a critical reflection on his own culture. He often repeats the claim that Japanese (and Eastern) culture "has no theory." (His frequent interchange of the terms *Japanese* and *Eastern* indicates that he considered the two together vis-à-vis Western culture and saw Japanese culture always in relation to its background in the East.) What he means is that it lacked a theory *with scholarly form*. The following passages illustrate the point:

[Culture] should not be dogmatic. It must be formed conceptually by strict scholarly methods. It must have theory.... It must contain self-criticism. For a spirit to become scholarly means that it should be objectively recognizable to people.[47]

I am of the opinion that the serious study of basic theory in our country is still weak in every branch of learning.[48]

A living spirit must possess theory.[49]

The choice of the word *spirit* in the last remark belongs to the "tug-of-war over meaning" dealt with earlier. Fully aware of the associations his readers

[44] NKZ 14:402, 397.

[45] NKZ 14:396.

[46] See his letter No. 1665: "To study our national history, one must first study Western history. What is wrong with national history today is that one studies only national history" (NKZ 19:195).

[47] NKZ 12:387.

[48] NKZ 12:393.

[49] NKZ 12:389.

would make with "Japanese spirit," he deliberately gave the word a meaning different from that of the rightists at the time. He is saying in effect: if you must talk about a "Japanese *spirit*," then you should realize what this word *spirit* implies. Once this transposition has been made, Nishida himself was not averse to taking over the term *Japanese spirit* for his own critical purposes. As Nakajima Kenzō reminds us, in the "mood of the times," such an "audacious critique" was "not hinted at so much as clearly written between the lines." He offers the following paraphrase of Nishida's critique of the "Japanese spirit":

> Its advocates pretend to be unifying the intellectual world of our country for the present and the future by means of the Japanese spirit. But this Japanese spirit is not even a mode of thought. It is unreasonable to expect it to unify anything.... Even from where we stand today, Nishida's intentions are clear if read in this light.[50]

Nishida's idea is that by learning from Western culture the spirit of giving scholarly form to theory, Japanese culture will be able to overcome itself and step out into the world. But learning theory means first of all learning the methods that shape theory. This is what he means when he tells his fellow Japanese, "We need new theory."[51]

For the East to step out into the world entails realities that fall outside the pale of the theoretical concerns of the West. Theory may have originated in the West, but the East presents the challenge of new elements to be incorporated into theory. I am reminded here of the oft-cited remarks of Nishida:

> [Might we not say that] at the bottom of Eastern culture lies something like "seeing the form of the formless" or "hearing the voice of the voiceless"?... I would like to give that claim philosophical footings.[52]

As highly as he valued Japanese and Eastern culture, Nishida took a stance that straddled East and West:

> I resonate with the depth and dignity of Eastern culture, but I cannot bring myself to forego my fondness for the wealth of Western culture that has meant such a great development of free humanness. My appreciation for things Eastern, like the paintings of Sesshū and Chinese verse, is not dimmed by the fact that the oil paintings of Rembrandt and the poetry of Goethe move me as they do.[53]

[50] Nakajima, *The Shōwa Period*, 115.
[51] NKZ 12:391.
[52] NKZ 4:6.
[53] NKZ 18:398.

In speaking of a *new* theory for Japan, Nishida was therefore concerned that its global embrace include not only Western culture, the birthplace of theory, but also the traditions of the East. Indeed, the very fact that the East had not developed theoretical form gave it a distinct character and value.

The position of learning from the other through self-negation that Nishida took, the standpoint in the *between* (間) of intercultural space, was one that he saw as a common vocation for all humanity "now that the world has become a reality." The *reality* of that world as the locus for both self and other, generates the demand for theory shaped by cultures East and West:

> It is not a question of Eastern culture negating Western culture or vice-versa, nor of subsuming one into the other. It is a probing deeper than we have gone so far until both are bathed in a new light.[54]

This seems to me to offer a new principle in terms of which to think. It also broadens the task of culture into something eternal that arches over the history and the present moment. (By now, the encounter of North and South also has become an explicit part of the task.) This concern with forming a new theory, spanning East and West, out of a deeper foundation is one that occupied Nishida to the end of his life. Only weeks before he died, he wrote Kōsaka Masaaki asking him to send a copy of John Dewey's *Essays in Experimental Logic*, anxious as ever for any scrap of insight that would broaden the base of this intercultural *between*.

The "something fundamentally different"[55] about Eastern cultures that Nishida spoke of was more apparent at first to those outside of the West, since it was these latter who were forced to adapt to Western culture for their own survival. The division this created within the soul of those raised in Eastern cultures made the heterogeneity painfully evident. The coming to birth of a global world was experienced by those in non-Western cultures as a dividedness in their own inner selves. To talk of unifying cultures East and West meant healing a dividedness in their own existence brought about by a world that had already become a reality. At the very time that this pain was intensifying among non-Western cultures, culture in the West tended to look on them as "outsiders," low-level civilizations, or exotic curiosities. The recognition of non-Western cultures as "other cultures" with which to relate is a relatively recent phenomenon, perhaps as recent as the latter half of the twentieth century.

The "problem of Japanese culture" as Nishida saw it is therefore clearly a problem for the entire world today. His answer, a new unity based on a deeper foundation, has to heal not only the rift between cultures but also the rift in

---

[54] NKZ 12:391.

[55] NKZ 14:405.

the self that this "being-in-the-one-world" originates. What brought Nishida clarity of insight in this regard was his contact with the problem of "Zen and Western philosophy."

As is well known, for a period of nearly ten years, beginning in his twenties, Nishida gave himself heart and soul to the practice of Zen meditation. At the time, as his diaries and letters attest, he was also devouring the classics of Western philosophy, from the ancient Greeks up to contemporary authors. In his own person the global world had become a reality and a painful split: on the one hand, a philosophy that originated in the West as a science of reflection, and even a high-flown reflection on reflection; on the other, the Eastern praxis of Zen, which implied an overcoming of reflection, a knowing of "non-knowing." The split was too deep and too broad to think of subsuming one into the other. But neither would Nishida forsake one for the other. Only the awareness that this was the world in which he had been "located" enabled him to accept the world-split in his very person as a task to be overcome. It was as if he had given himself over to two worlds whose otherness split him down the middle but whose unity was already in the making. The split was itself his gateway to the "deeper foundations" of unity. Unlike *nihonjinron* (日本人論) theories of Japanese uniqueness, or even of comparative culture and thought, being bandied about at the time, Nishida's intellectual efforts were rooted in his own self, and it was out of this self that all his philosophical works sprung.[56]

In a sense, Nishida represents the first encounter of the history of Zen and the history of Western philosophy. He himself saw a precedent in the art historian, Alois Riegl (1858–1905).[57] In Western aesthetical theory, "classical" Greek art had become the standard of beauty, but Riegl argued that this approach did not serve to explain other artistic traditions, such as the geometrical art of Egypt. This led him (with others like Jane Harrison, Konrad Fiedler, and Robert W. Worringer) to propose the idea of an absolute aesthetic impulse at the root of all artistic endeavor, which he described as a "formative will" that branches out in two directions: the impulse toward "em-pathy" (*Einfühlung*) and the drive toward "ab-straction" (*Abstraktion*).[58] This enabled Riegl to recognize a form of beauty in Egyptian art distinct from that of Greek art but no less rooted in the aesthetic impulse.

[56] For a fuller description of these questions, see my 経験と自覚 [Experience and self-awareness] (Tokyo: Iwanami Shoten, 1994), chapter 3, "Zen and Philosophy."

[57] The directly relevant passages can be found in NKZ, 12:390–1 and 14:403–5. Nishida treats Riegl's thought in detail in 歴史的形成作用としての芸術創作 [Artistic creation as a history-making activity], NKZ 10:177–265.

[58] Nishida "translates" these ideas in his own way: "one is the joy of personalizing nature and finding the human in nature; the other is the direction of negation of the human that bestows order on the non-human, in other words, the direction of religious deliverance" (NKZ 12:390).

103

Nishida found himself in deep sympathy with Riegl's idea:

According to Riegl—and I consider this an important idea—in comparing things our thinking must not begin from their perfected forms, but from the process by which they formed.[59]

Riegl proposed his theory in connection with art forms, but I wish to extend this to philosophy and religion.... Just as Riegl brought to light a deeper and wider concept by his study of different aesthetic traditions,... I believe we can uncover the essence of human culture itself [in its true depth and scope].[60]

Nothing here contains the slightest trace of the ideology of the "Japanese spirit" or the idea of the "superiority of Japanese culture." Nishida's ruling idea was that a true encounter between different things leads to "something deeper." We see this in the idea of an *Urkultur* (原文化) that he proposed as a way to flesh out his notion of a "deeper foundation."[61] Coined in analogy with Goethe's idea of an "original plant," the hypothesis of an "original culture" helped him to understand different cultures as transformation of one and the same original. The suggestion is not that we seek some primordial culture existing in a distant past by following the transformations of culture through history back to their source. Nishida's *Urkultur* looks rather to the future, as a project to be undertaken by a plurality of particular cultures in encounter, learning each to understand itself as a specific form of a common culture, "complementing and being complemented by other cultures in order to form a world culture and give shape to a complete humanity."[62]

In relativizing one's own culture, one comes at the same time to recognize it as something that is non-relative, particular, and unique. This explains how Nishida is able to incorporate the obvious particularities of Eastern culture without submitting to their ideological agenda of the right. Far from impeding contact with other relative cultures, the origin of relativity in a common root puts it on a solider basis. Thus he is able to speak of Eastern culture as "fundamentally different" from Western culture and yet of "entering deeply into the foundations of Western culture." And within this interrelationship of different cultures a new world culture is taking shape, making the "original culture" projected into the future a reality of the present.

I find these ideas a seedbed of suggestiveness for us today, fifty years after Nishida's death, in an age highly conscious of cultural plurality. He envi-

[59] NKZ 14:403.
[60] NKZ 12:391.
[61] NKZ 12:377-8; 14:405.
[62] NKZ 12:405.

sioned a new possibility, different from cultural imperialism or the simple "clash of civilizations," in which something absolute would work creatively to bring about a new reality, a new form of relationship among cultures in which the relativization of each culture would include a self-negation enabling it to relate to every other relative culture (or what Nishida called the transition from that which makes to what which is made). The "absolute" he spoke of was not some preestablished reality but rather something that functions in the form of a "place" at which one unique relative works together with another, giving rise to the creation of a new reality.

Nishida took part in the ongoing encounter among cultures East and West by stepping for a moment out of his own Eastern tradition in order to experiment in himself with a new relationship between East and West and to propose that new relationship as the meaning of Eastern culture for the world as a whole.[63] The "problem" of Japanese culture, as he saw it, consisted at present in responding to this historical challenge:

> From the deepest recesses of Eastern culture, we [must] discover a new way of seeing and thinking, and thus throw new light on world history.[64]

> Only what comes from the inner core of Japan can stand as world culture.[65]

Nishida harbored no illusions about the difficulty of bringing about such an "enormous enterprise." Unlike the "shallow, simple-minded" ideologues of the "Japanese spirit," he devoted himself for decades to constructing a philosophical vision open to the wider world. Well did he understand that encounter of cultures East and West was an undertaking on the scale of the encounter of Christianity with Greek thought that inspired Western history for centuries. The point bears repeating only because it is so important:

---

[63] Nishida's own existential engagement in this idea reverberates in his philosophical reflections on the aspect of "self-awareness" in the *I-Thou* relationship. Simply put, his idea is that having encountered the other and returned to oneself, one no longer describes oneself by negating the other, but reaches the awareness that both self and other are "located" together. At that moment, one ceases to think of the *I* as a fixed substance and realizes it as a unique perspective from which to describe a given context (場所), or perhaps better, to allow that context to mirror itself. In this way the continuity of self-identity is broken through. "At the bottom of the *I* there stands a *Thou*, and at the bottom of the *Thou* the *I*" (NKZ 6:381). Or viewed from the standpoint of the self as subject, the co-location of self and other is a relationship wherein "in not being the I, I am I." This break in continuity of self-identity is the prototype of Nishida's idea of the "self-identity of contradictories. Inasmuch as it can take place only insofar as the *I* is open to a context in which *I* and *Thou* are co-located, he refers to it as a "self-identity of place."

[64] NKZ 12:390.

[65] NKZ 14:402.

[Eastern culture and Western culture] are divided, but in their foundation they are joined together and complement each other. Without discovering that deeper foundation, a world culture in which cultures East and West can unite is unthinkable.... In the same way that Riegl revolutionized our way of looking at art by returning to the foundations, so, too, must we see things anew from their foundations.[66]

Nishida set great store on the unique specificity of the Japanese cultural heritage as set against the backdrop of the cultural heritage of the East. At the same time, his guiding concern was one that opened him to the wider world: What can Japanese culture contribute to the formation of a new world culture and how can it go about making that contribution? There is no question of putting Nishida in the camp of the nationalists or cultural supremacists of the time. His thought grew out of the cradle of the encounter of East and West and can serve us still as a means to advance that dialogue further.

[TRANSLATED BY JAN VAN BRAGT]

---

[66] NKZ 14:406–7.

Nishida and Totalitarianism

A Philosopher's Resistance

Yusa Michiko

J UST HOW IT WAS THAT NISHIDA KITARŌ and others in the so-called Kyoto
school first came to be branded "nationalists," and why that label should
have persisted into the present in certain academic circles, is not clear. A
careful study of Nishida's activities and philosophical writings presents a picture that is far from anything we normally associate with the word *nationalism*.[1] What emerges is rather a thinker who resisted fanatic nationalism and
struggled against the attempts of the pre-1945 military government to
impose its program of "thought control" on Japan's intellectual community.[2]
Nishida's systematic philosophy was far too universal in scope to submit to
the petty racial egoism, cultural chauvinism, and pseudo-religious belief in
the superiority of the Japanese people that was the hallmark of the nationalism—or rather ultranationalism—prevalent at the time. At the height of the
Pacific War, Nishida incurred the open censure of ruling right-wing factions
for his "Westernized" conviction that individual freedom and creativity must
not be sacrificed to national interests. He died on 7 June 1945, just months
before Japan's final defeat, after which the mood among the intelligentsia
shifted to a more progressive stance. A few years later the new leftist intellectuals, taking aim at everything that seemed politically reactionary, began to
criticize Nishida for having acknowledged the historical significance and the

The author wishes to acknowledge that the research for this paper was made possible by a
grant from the Japan Foundation.

---

[1] See my "Nishida and the Question of Nationalism," *Monumenta Nipponica* 46/2 (1991):
203–9.

[2] Nishida's interest in the political situation of his time is indicated by the number of letters
on this subject. Of the 2,717 letters included in the *Collected Works*, about 350 (13%) contain
references to the current politics; of the 1,845 letters written between 1935 and the time of his
death in 1945, 320 (17%) contain such references. Letters are referred to here by number and by
volume and page number in the *Collected Works*.

role of the imperial family, conveniently overlooking his broader perspective. In their eyes, the emperor system had been the willing vehicle for colonial expansion and military aggressions, and the idea of supporting the imperial household was enough to bring the thought of Nishida and others in the Kyoto school under suspicion of fascist ideology. To understand these charges and to assess their validity, it is not enough to patch together quotations here and there from Nishida's philosophical writings, diaries, and copious correspondence. We need first to have a look at the general political, historical, and intellectual scene in pre-1945 Japan.

NISHIDA'S BASIC POLITICAL STANCE

In an important sense, the basic ingredients of Nishida's political stance were already present from his youth. Born in 1870, he grew up breathing the liberal democratic air of the early Meiji period. But like many of his boyhood friends, he came to feel that something had been lost in the rapid turn away from traditional Japanese customs. He joined with Yamamoto Ryōkichi, Fujioka Sakutarō, Suzuki Daisetsu, and Matsumoto Bunzaburō to form a literary circle known as the "Gasonkai."[3] On 11 February 1889, the day the Meiji Constitution was promulgated, they posed in front of a camera with a banner that read "We Stand Free at the Top of Heaven," a sign of their defiant hope for a new nation emancipated from the unfair trade treaties that Japan had been subjected to (and which were in fact rescinded four years later).

From early on, too, Nishida took a position against the government bureaucrats who were carry-overs from the old feudal system and formed an oligarchy or *hanbatsu* (藩閥) system. It was not so much that he opposed the system as that his own loyalties lay rather with the former Kaga fiefdom, whose rulers he saw as representing the kind of open-minded liberalism that Japan needed. As an act of resistance against the government's attempt in 1886 to centralize education, Nishida and Yamamoto dropped out of school, a decision that was not without consequences for their futures. Behind this resistance lay a firm belief in the legitimacy of the constitutional state and in the efficacy of parliamentary government, political parties, and honesty in civil service. Throughout his life he was to maintain an active interest in developments on the political scene.

---

[3] Translated literally, Gasonkai 我尊会 means "Respect-the-Individual Society." In writing for this group, Nishida assumed the pen name Pegasus 有翼. By the time the *Gasonkai* was formed, Suzuki had already dropped out of school because of financial problems at home. The boyhood friendship among Nishida, Yamamoto, and Suzuki was to last throughout their lives.

Against a backdrop painted in such bold strokes, Nishida's reverence for the emperor and his attachment to the emperor system can only seem inconsistent, but his understanding of the historical landscape was far more nuanced. In 1898 D. T. Suzuki expressed opposition to the movement to sacralize the imperial family as a distortion of an important symbol. Again in 1961, as an old man, he spoke of how his generation had been "kindly disposed" to the emperor but of how the military had abused that affection for their own purposes.[4] The same could surely be said of Nishida. Although he never seems seriously to have questioned the validity of the Meiji constitutional monarchy, neither did he at any time slip into blind worship of the emperor. His grandson and biographer, Ueda Hisashi, recalls Nishida's opposition to the indoctrination of the youth in State Shinto:

> Grandfather used to tell us that the emperor was an ordinary human being whom we should feel sorry for because he had been deprived of his freedom. This confused us, since what we were being taught in junior high school was strongly colored by the official military ideology. When we went to Kyoto, grandfather would take us out for walks, but we could not understand why he would not pause when we passed a shrine but would walk by without making the customary bow. Even though we had been instructed at school to make obeisance to the shrines, he told us that the "sacred object" of the shrine was only a stone or piece of paper.[5]

Nishida approved of a cultural role for the imperial family, but he considered the Japanese polity (国体 *kokutai*) to have its roots elsewhere: in the nobility of human reality as such. A letter to Yamamoto dated 26 December 1918 contains the earliest record we have of his views in this regard:

> I would like to see the imperial family play the role of a patron of culture. "Revere the Emperor" may have been a viable slogan at the time of the Restoration, but the imperial family today is no longer a symbol of opposition to the Shogunate. It is something for all of Japan.
>
> Nowadays one hears a lot of clamor about the national polity, but no one bothers to recognize that *the Japanese kokutai is grounded in humanity*. They are content with their dogma of the unbroken line [of imperial succession]. For me, this "unbroken line" is rather a symbol of great mercy, altruism, and partnership.[6]

[4] Suzuki Daisetsu, 私の履歴書 [My curriculum vitae], SDZ 30:591.

[5] 上田 久 Ueda Hisashi, 祖父西田幾多郎 [Grandfather, Nishida Kitarō] (Tokyo: Nansōsha, 1983), 48–9.

[6] No. 239, NKZ 18:206–7, emphasis added. A year earlier, in 1917, Nishida wrote an article "On Things Japanese" expressing dissatisfaction with the trend of exclusivist Japanism.

In short, Suzuki and Nishida's generation felt free to accept on their own terms the ideology of the emperor system that the 1890 *Imperial Rescript on Education* was trying to implant. For them the emperor was a regent who ruled subject to the constitutional structures of a modern nation. The doctrine of imperial divinity that would appear in later years was altogether foreign. It is hardly surprising that right-wing elements in the military would use the emperor to develop and spread its ideology of aggressive nationalism. Around 1935 the idea of the emperor as a living deity or *kami* became official doctrine. No less than the late Emperor Shōwa himself is said to have remarked of this:

> It was Honjō or Usami who called me *kami*. I told them that my body is made the same as any other human being, that I did not qualify as a *kami*, and that to use that name for me was nothing but trouble.[7]

When tempers among young military officers boiled over into an attempted coup on 26 February 1936, Nishida was incensed. He at once saw through the hypocrisy of the military factions who, hiding behind the slogan "Absolute Reverence for the Emperor," murdered government leaders and ministers trusted by the emperor without the least compunction:

> This is an atrocity neither God nor the people can forgive. It reminds one of the French Revolution.... What they are doing is destroying our country.... It is time for the Japanese people to stand up. The future of the country looks grim if we do not take firm action at once.[8]

The coup was suppressed quickly by government forces and its leaders executed at the express wish of the emperor.

Nishida was always concerned about the well-being of the imperial family. He felt it his duty to accede to the request for a New Year's lecture to Emperor Hirohito in 1941. He chose as his subject "The Philosophy of History,"[9] apparently the first time that one of these lectures had dealt with philosophy. Nishida knew only too well that this was to be his first and last opportunity to speak his mind on the current world situation directly to the emperor. In hindsight he felt that his lecture might have been too abstruse.[10] In it he argued that the philosophy of history presents a notion of the world fundamentally different from that of the natural sciences. What distinguishes

---

[7] 昭和天皇独白録 [Recollections of Emperor Shōwa], recorded by 寺崎英成 Terasaki Hidenari (Tokyo: Bungei Shunjū, 1991), 30–1.

[8] Letter to Hori Koretaka, Nos. 1005 (27 February 1936) and 1009, NKZ 18:561, 563.

[9] NKZ 12:267–72.

[10] Letter to Tomonaga Sanjūrō 朝永三十郎, No. 1534 (25 January 1941), NKZ 19:146.

the historical world from the biological[11] is that the former depends on the human spirit shaping the course of events.

Conflict, Nishida goes on to say, arises out of the interaction of divergent ethnic groups, but so does the resolution of conflict. In that sense, war is by implication inevitable but not an end in itself. The vision he proposes is of a pluralistic community of nations within which each nation is able to maintain its own identity,[12] the leadership falling to those countries with the most highly developed global orientation to history.

In this context, the ideal country is one where individual rights are not violated and where each individual contributes creatively to the life of the whole. Here Nishida adds a note of protest against current military policies: "Any totalitarian system that negates outright the role of the individual is an anachronism." He concludes his lecture by expressing his faith in the continually regenerative vitality of history, whose central symbol in Japan is the imperial family, and his hope that a new era was dawning with a new and more active international role for Japan to play.

NISHIDA AND THE FIRST WAVES OF TOTALITARIANISM

Nishida was especially critical of the direction taken by the Ministry of Education, whose decisions directly affected the lives of students and professors alike. In this regard he was openly skeptical of the educational-reform package of 1918 whose aim was to strengthen Japanese national power in the years following World War I.[13] In the years to come his skepticism would only have cause to deepen. Toward the end of the 1910s and in the early 1920s, liberal thinkers found a common platform in what has since come to be known as "Taishō Democracy." To counter the influence of these ideas, reactionary forces began to organize themselves inside the academic community and out.[14] The power struggle between the two factions had already consoli-

[11] Emperor Shōwa was known for his work in marine biology.

[12] The former director of the Center for Statistics of the Ministry of Education, Hayashi Chikio 林 知己夫, analyzes statistical data to argue that some change is visible among contemporary Japanese. In the past people classified themselves either as nationalist or internationalist, but recent data indicates a tendency toward a stance of "asserting Japanese self-identity in international society" (朝日新聞 [Asahi News], 13 January 1994). Japanese consciousness appears to be headed in the direction Nishida favored.

[13] See his letter to Yamamoto No. 239 (26 December 1918), NKZ 18:206–7.

[14] For further details on this, see 山田宗睦 Yamada Munemutsu, 昭和の精神史 [An intellectual history of the Shōwa period] (Kyoto: Jinbun Shoin, 1970). Yamada points out that there were two opposing intellectual camps at the University of Tokyo during the Taishō period: a liberal one headed by Yoshino Sakuzō 吉野作造 and Minobe Tatsukichi 美濃部達吉, and an ultranationalistic one headed by Uesugi Shinkichi 上杉慎吉.

dated as early as in 1920. In 1925 the government launched an all-out policy of thought control with the introduction of the Peace Preservation Law,
whose initial overt aim was to suppress communist movements. In April 1929
a nationwide offensive against the Communist Party was inaugurated with
the arrest of 339 of its members. By the following year the number had risen
to 1,500.[15] In September of 1929 the Ministry of Education initiated its own
nationwide program of thought control, and in the process began to revoke
the civil rights of dissidents. The invasion of Manchuria by the occupying
Japanese forces in September 1931 set the country off on a "Fifteen-Year
War" that meant an escalation of aggressive military campaigns abroad and an
instilling of ultranationalistic sentiments at home.

In 1926 Nishida felt that his philosophical vision was finally coming
together. He retired from his teaching position at the University of Kyoto in
1928 under the mandatory retirement rule with the intention of spending his
days in the leisure of philosophical contemplation. His plan was short-lived.
Within four years he felt himself called to take up the challenge of educating
the younger generation. The immediate occasion was the government's
establishment of a Center for National Spiritual Culture on 23 August 1932.
The Center was divided into three sections to deal respectively with research,
with the "reeducation" of students who had fallen prey to Marxist or socialist ideas, and with the ongoing training of teachers in methods for ideological resistance. Nishida was quick to respond to this latest and crudest turn to
the right of the Ministry of Education:

> What the Ministry of Education is passing off in the name of "spiritual
> culture" is not right. From now, so long as my strength does not fail me,
> I intend to write as much as I can. I want to gather bright young stu-
> dents around me and engage them in debate and discussion, to train
> them how to think. In this way I will be satisfied that I have done my
> part if I can accomplish something on the intellectual and academic
> level.[16]

The year 1932 was filled with ominous events. The "May 15th Incident"
claimed the life of Prime Minister Inukai. On 29 June the Department of
Police set up a formal system of thought police known as the Superior Special
Police Force. With branches across the country, the thought police succeed-
ed in creating a cloud of suspicion around the freedom of expression.
Meantime, government bureaucrats, spurred on by the ultranationalists,

[15] Information taken from 岩波雄二郎 Iwanami Yūjirō, 岩波書店五十年 [Fifty years of the
Iwanami Bookstore] (Tokyo: Iwanami, 1964), 61–9.

[16] No. 758 (8 November 1932), NKZ 18:465. The term I have rendered here as *spiritual
culture* is 精神文化.

began to monitor the circulation of ideas more closely and to meddle aggressively in the traditional freedoms of academia. The Takikawa Incident of 1933 at the University of Kyoto, and the Minobe Incident of 1935 belong to this turn of events.

Regarding the former,[17] Nishida responded only halfheartedly, apparently feeling that "the university should not be closed for the sake of one Takikawa."[18] Iwanami Shigeo, the founder and president of the Iwanami Bookstore, was upset by the reactions of Japan's leading intellectuals, including Nishida. In retrospect, Iwanami's instincts were right. If the intellectuals and the academic community had concentrated their efforts and taken a stance against the government, subsequent academic disasters may well have been averted. But the dike was cracked and the trickle of ultranationalist and right-wing accusations soon broadened into a steady stream that carried away more and more of the academic community with it.

The Minobe Incident, in which a certain right-wing group attacked a liberal reading of the Meiji Constitution,[19] dealt a decisive blow to academic freedom. The fanaticism behind the ousting of Minobe Tatsukichi was aggravated by the opportunistic maneuvering of the Seiyū Party, a majority opposition party, to overthrow the cabinet of the ruling government. At the instigation of Suzuki Kisaburō, president of the Seiyū Party, the Diet passed a resolution demanding that the government "clarify the national polity." This turned out to be the beginning of the end of party politics in pre-1945 Japan. On this occasion Nishida was less guarded in his criticism. He was

[17] The Takikawa Incident is also known as the Kyoto University Incident (京大事件). Takikawa Yukitoki 滝川幸辰 (1891–1962), professor of law at the University of Kyoto, maintained that society has a duty to seek out the causes of a crime before taking retaliation against the criminal, and that it is unfair to punish only the wife in cases of adultery. Minoda Muneki 蓑田胸喜 of the Genri Nipponsha attacked this theory as "red." The Minister of Education, Hatoyama Ichirō 鳩山一郎, took up this issue, and on 10 May demanded of President Konishi of the University of Kyoto that Takikawa either resign or take a leave of absence. On May 26, at a faculty meeting of the Department of Law, it was unanimously decided that the entire law faculty would resign en masse if the Ministry of Education did not rescind its demand.

[18] Cited by Abe Yoshishige 安倍能成 in 岩波茂雄伝 [A biography of Iwanami Shigeo] (Tokyo: Iwanami, 1957), 348.

[19] Minobe Tatsukichi (1873–1948), professor of constitutional law at the University of Tokyo, had already as early as 1912 proposed a theory of the emperor as "an organ of the state" (天皇機関説), which meant that the emperor's legal powers were defined by the constitution. See Tsunoda Ryūsaku et al., eds., *Sources of Japanese Tradition* (New York: Columbia University Press, 1971), 746–7, and 宮沢俊義 Miyazawa Toshiyoshi, 天皇機関説事件 [The "imperial organ theory" incident] (Tokyo: Yūhikaku, 1970), 2 vols.

Minobe's interpretation of the Meiji Constitution was generally accepted among leading scholars, judges, and close assistants to the emperor. Apparently, Emperor Shōwa himself was for the "imperial organ theory," and regretted what happened to Minobe.

113

visibly angered at the badly-timed tactics of the Seiyū Party, which had only its own interests at heart and was endangering the principles of the parliamentary system itself by inviting further military interference. The Minobe Incident seems to have led Nishida to rethink the role of law and the meaning of the state, resulting in his 1941 essay on "The Problem of the *Raison d'état*."

Nishida against the Japanists

In March 1937, riding comfortably in the wake of the Minobe Incident and the parliamentary resolution to "clarify the national polity," the Ministry of Education published a tract called *Fundamentals of the National Polity* (国体の本義), which became the textbook of the *kokutai*-cult[20] and ultranationalism. With it the government sought to maximize "ideological uniformity" among the people of Japan.[21]

Nishida was well aware of what was happening and did not hesitate to apply the label "fascist" to these events. A letter to Hidaka Daishirō, dated 13 October 1935, advises the younger generation to stay their resistance and bide their time:

> As you know, we've fallen into a period of fascism. If one thinks deeply and selflessly about the future of our country, one will not lash out against the present situation but will bear with it, making efforts where one may to return it gradually to its normal state.[22]

A series of clashes between the government and the academic world—of which the Takikawa Incident and the Minobe Incident were only the best known—prompted the Ministry of Education in late 1935 to establish a Committee for the Renewal of Education and Scholarship. The purpose of the committee was to implement the "clarification of the national polity" in education by reexamining Japan's "indigestion from Western culture," actively promoting the distinctively Japanese learning, and returning to the spirit of the *Imperial Rescript on Education*.[23] Simply put, the committee's task was to turn back the clock on current education and antique the whole

[20] William Woodard, *The Allied Occupation of Japan 1945–1952 and Japanese Religions*, (Leiden: E. J. Brill, 1972), proposes this term "for Japan's emperor-state-centered cult of ultranationalism and militarism" (11).

[21] Tsunoda, *Sources of Japanese Tradition*, 785. This short work sold more than 2 million copies. It was "designed to set the ideological course for the Japanese people. Study groups were formed to discuss its content, school teachers were given special commentaries, and a determined effort was made to reach ideological uniformity by guarding against deviation."

[22] No. 963, NKZ 18:544–5.

[23] 石川 謙 Ishikawa Ken et al., eds., 教学刷新評議会総会議事録 [Minutes of the Secretariat for the Renewal of Education and Scholarship], in 近代日本教育制度史料 [Sources for recent educational systems in Japan] (Tokyo: Kōdansha, 1957), 14:255–7.

114

with a thick varnish of nationalist spirit. Nishida was asked to serve on the committee, an appointment that he found loathsome in the extreme. He knew that the conclusions were foregone, and that his own views, critical of the Ministry of Education as they were, would not be welcome. The thought of being associated with the likes of Kihira Tadayoshi,[24] an influential member of the Center for National Spiritual Culture, and other advocates of an exclusive Japanism[25] was further cause for concern. (Actually, Kihira had been a former editor of Nishida and was instrumental in bringing out *A Study of the Good* in 1911, but the two gradually drifted apart as Nishida strengthened his liberal convictions and Kihira turned more and more ultranationalistic.)

In a letter dated 9 February 1938 to Yamamoto, Nishida complained of school superintendents from the Ministry of Education "going around Japan attacking him":

> The word seems to have got around that when some officials from the Academic Department visited me last year, I severely criticized the policy of the Center for National Spiritual Culture and its attitude. It appears that quite a few of them have turned hostile towards me.[26]

Though somewhat encouraged by the fact that the Committee for the Renewal of Education and Scholarship included two former colleagues, Watsuji Tetsurō and Tanabe Hajime, he doubted the usefulness of his own presence, as he wrote to Watsuji:

> The presence of you and Tanabe-kun at the meetings will be a reinforcement, but how can we make our views heard in such company? It is clear from the outset that our efforts will be in vain—especially mine. I am getting old and I think the best contribution I can make to the country is to complete my work and not waste even a moment.[27]

Nishida did, however, attend the first meeting, which was convened on 5 December 1935. That was quite enough to convince him to skip the rest. In January of the following year he wrote to Yamamoto that he had found the committee a "truly biased group" and that he worried for the future of Japan with such a group of people at the helm. Kihira seems to have recommended

---

[24] Kihira Tadayoshi 紀平正美 (1874–1949) was known for his interpretation of Hegel. He adhered to nationalism, and with the advent of totalitarianism began to advocate Japanism. The existence of some 1,200 letters addressed to him by the leading intellectuals of his time has just been made known (朝日新聞 [Asahi News], 20 October 1993). The letters themselves will not be made public for some time, since, in the judgment of Kihira's grandson, they may compromise certain persons still living.

[25] No. 971 to Yamamoto, NKZ 18:547–8.

[26] No. 1193, NKZ 19:9–10.

[27] No. 978 (1 December 1935), NKZ 18:551.

dropping Darwin's theory of evolution from the classroom, which Nishida found a bad joke. But rather than retire from the committee in silence, he decided to prepare a written opinion for the January 15th meeting. It was read at the meeting by Konishi Shigenao, former President of the University of Kyoto, despite the efforts of the chairman, Matsuda Genji, Minister of Education, to suppress it.[28] The communique is a good summary of Nishida's basic position on education and research vis-à-vis the aims of the committee. I cite it in full:

> In order to "unify the world of thought of the present and the Japan of the future by means of the Japanese spirit," we need to conduct scholarly research into the history of Japan and things Japanese and to clarify their essence objectively. If the humanities[29] are to be applied, they need first to be approached from the ground up, to be studied carefully and well understood. A spirit that rests only on the past and lacks a future is no longer living. Clear and superior ideas do not survive in isolation from other ideas, but by nature serve to unify them. This is the only way to unify Japanese thinking, the only way for Japan to become one of the centers of world culture. The fact is, however, that when it comes to basic research, Japanese scholarship is still in its infancy. Even in the area of physics, where we are most advanced, we have yet to produce a Dirac or a Heisenberg. In the humanities things are still worse.
>
> Without laying a solid foundation for scholarship in Japan, we have no more hope of diverting the radical infiltration of foreign ideas than the Yellow River has of becoming clear blue. To be sure, this is no easy matter, but no one with great expectations for Japan can afford to ignore it. To succeed, we need not only to give first-rate scholars the freedom to engage in basic research in their various disciplines, but also actively to train such scholars. Concretely, I think these questions deserve the attention of a special committee, but in the meantime offer two suggestions of my own: that we increase the number of full scholarships for students who have proved their academic excellence, and that we establish positions for professors who can engage full-time in research.[30]

As soon as Nishida's communique had been read to the committee, Tanabe and Watsuji spoke up in support. As Nishida expected would happen, their voices were a cry in the wilderness.

[28] For an account and minutes of the proceedings, see Ishikawa, "Minutes," 363.

[29] The term used here, 精神科学, appears to be a Japanese translation of the German term *Geisteswissenschaften*.

[30] Cited in Ishikawa, "Minutes," 363–4.

NISHIDA AND TOTALITARIANISM

Things were not yet as bad as they would get, however. Nishida seems to have felt free to express his defiance at a public meeting held on 9 October 1937 in Hibiya Park, Tokyo, to mark a conference on philosophy sponsored by the Society for the Promotion of Science. Nishida felt that the event was a sham. As soon as he had completed his talk on "Scholarly Method"[31] he walked off the stage. In his talk, he pleaded for academic freedom in the face of the rising tide of ultranationalism and fanatic Japanism. Nishida argued that Japan's task was "to create a new world culture, strengthened by an Eastern heritage that has nurtured us for millennia." This can only happen if the "Japanese spirit" becomes "scholarly and rational through and through." He criticized as superficial the distinctions the Japanists made between the morality of the East and the natural sciences of the West. Genuine intellectual growth into a world culture that will serve humanity at large does not think in such clichés but seeks to understand ideas from all quarters. Throughout his remarks, criticisms of current government policy are clear.

Simply put, what Nishida sought was a marriage of Western learning and Japanese scholarly discipline, not an irrational divorce of the two. Such a cross-cultural marriage, a living union of partnership and love, would enable Japanese academics to discover a deeper standpoint from which to carry out their work.

Nishida against Totalitarianism

The forces of irrationality came to dominate the political scene with almost sinister dispatch. As the social milieu grew more and more tense, concerned intellectuals responded by enlivening the debate on humanism. In an interview with Miki Kiyoshi in September 1936, Nishida observed:

> The reason we talk about humanism so much today is that we are driven to it. The humanism of the Renaissance signaled a return to the human away from the religious control and authority of the middle ages. This laid the foundations for later culture. This movement has come to a dead end today, as we see in the counterdemand for greater control of society. In both fascism and Marxism, the question of control is central. And as the control gains strength, social freedom recedes further and further from the grasp of the individual. Faced with this turn of events, the question of humanism arises once again.[32]

---

[31] NKZ 12.385–94. The intent of his talk, which was later printed by the Ministry of Education, is clearer when read as a criticism of the *Fundamentals of the National Polity* .

[32] "The Contemporary Significance of Humanism—An Interview with Dr. Nishida Kitarō," NKZ, 17.492–504. The quotation can be found on pages 492–3.

Nishida rejected totalitarian attempts to suppress individual freedom, and in their place proposed what he called a "new humanism." Near the end of the Pacific War, Nishida felt that his views had been vindicated by the course of history.[33] He wrote to D. T. Suzuki on 11 May 1945:

> Many people today are saying that power-worshipping totalitarianism is the direction to go, but I find such an idea thoroughly old-fashioned and outdated. The direction we need to take is one that reverses the move towards totalitarianism, namely a new globalism. Whether we admit it or not, the world is already going that way.[34]

Nishida and his circle never once let go of the conviction that totalitarianism was a dishonor to the country that embraced it.

Nishida's Support of Liberal Groups

Nishida kept up a constant and active support for the group of progressive-minded young graduates of Gakushū-in who had come to study at the University of Kyoto. Among them were Harada Kumao, Kido Kōichi, and Konoe Fumimaro, commonly known as the "court group" since they were aristocracy and worked closely with the emperor and played a prominent role in Japanese politics. Konoe, who was appointed prime minister in June 1937, regarded Nishida as one of his mentors. Saionji Kimmochi, the last of the elder statesmen, treated Konoe, Kido, and Harada as his "three treasures," and counted on Konoe as the only hope to bridle the military and avert war. As it turned out, it was during Konoe's administration that the military campaign began, with the invasion of China in August of 1937. Konoe never forgave himself for having condoned the invasion, but the fatal step had been made and there was no turning back.

Nishida tried for a time to convince Konoe to take measures to counter the narrow, dogmatic government policies of recent years. He wrote to the prime minister on this point in September 1937, and later met with him privately, only to discover that Konoe lacked the courage to make the decisions that needed to be made. When Kido took over as Minister of Education in October, Nishida immediately went to see him. Kido left the impression that his hands were tied in the present situation, that the current of events had grown too strong to swim against. Nevertheless, Nishida accepted Kido's offer to serve as a counselor to the Ministry in order to "do something for the young people" whom "present policies of the Ministry of Education put at a disadvantage."[35]

[33] See his letter of 1 May 1945 to Tomonaga Sanjūrō.
[34] No. 2195, NKZ 19:426–7.
[35] Letter to Watsuji, No. 1302 (19 November 1937), NKZ 19:54–5.

Nishida took it upon himself to be the gadfly in the Ministry of Education for the following eight months. To give one example, on the question of ethnicity and nationalism he wrote in a letter to Kido:

> The idea that "each country of the world needs to awaken to its ethnic and nationalistic identity" seems at first blush to deny the "world" and to encourage each ethnic group to close in on itself. But in historical actuality, it means that each country has no choice but to stand on its own two feet as one part of the wider world. The term *world* was once no more than an abstract idea, but now it has become real. That the Japanese nationalists of today have not understood this I find an abomination.[36]

Gotō Ryūnosuke, a former high-school classmate of Konoe's, was convinced that Konoe would one day become prime minister. Seeing the need, "as a friend of Konoe, to study the political situation at home and abroad," he set up an office in 1933, which later developed into the Shōwa Study Group. The group attracted liberal thinkers from various walks of life, all of them eager to cooperate in the stance against the fascist military powers-that-be. Like Nishida, Gotō opposed the policies of the Ministry of Education. He felt the need to train a younger generation that could think on its own, make its own decisions, and steer Japan prudently into the coming age of global interaction. To this end he set up a private school in September 1938, the Shōwa Juku, and invited Nishida to be on the board of advisers. Nishida gave nominal consent and spoke to the students on at least one occasion.

Around this time, Miki Kiyoshi, a progressive "leftist" thinker who had studied philosophy under Nishida Kitarō, Hatano Seiichi, and Tanabe Hajime, joined the Shōwa Study Group and soon became one of its most zealous members. Although the group had many devoted and active members, it disbanded in November of 1940 when Gotō was asked to take a central role in the newly organized Taisei Yokusan-kai 大政翼賛会, a national non-governmental organization. The following year the Shōwa Juku was also dissolved, when Ozaki Hotsumi, one of the active directors, was arrested on charges of espionage.

NISHIDA AND THE SWELLING TIDE OF NATIONALISM

One of the most pernicious shelters for ultranationalist thinkers was formed in 1925 under the name Genri Nipponsha 原理日本社, the Japan Principle Society. Its founding purpose was to "denounce democracy and Marxism,

---

[36] Contained in 木戸幸一関係文書 [Writings related to the diaries of Kido Kōichi], edited by the Association for the Study of the Diaries of Kido Kōichi (Tokyo: Tokyo University Press, 1983), 540–1.

both of which go against the spirit of the Japanese national polity."[37] Apart
from Nishida, those who were singled out for attack by this group included
Ichiki Kitokurō, Minobe Tatsukichi, Miyazawa Toshiyoshi, Sasaki Sōichi,
Kawakami Eijirō, Yanaihara Tadao, Nanbara Shigeru, Iwanami Shigeo, Tsuda
Sōkichi, Amano Teiyū, Abe Yoshishige, Hisamatsu Shin'ichi, Miki Kiyoshi,
Tanabe Hajime, Kōyama Iwao, Kōsaka Masaaki, and Watsuji Tetsurō. These
figures were regarded as liberal, pro-democracy, and pro-individualism, and
thus "dangerous," in the eyes of the ultranationalists.

One of the leading figures in the Japan Principle Society, Minoda
Muneki, first reacted against the popularity of Nishida's philosophy in 1927.[38]
Within a decade his criticisms had turned into an all-out attack against a
"dangerous" thinker who posed a "threat to the ultranationalists' agenda."
By then ultranationalists in general had begun to interfere openly with free
speech. Under their influence the Ministry of Education denounced liberal
democracy thought as a form of "individualism" that put egoism ahead of
national pride. Such amateurish, deliberate distortions became commonplace.

In a lecture delivered in 1938 Nishida drew laughter with the remark
that things had gotten so far out of hand that "it has even become a crime
nowadays to use the word *world*."[39] He felt it important to avoid precipitous
confrontation if there was to be any hope for the restoration of sanity and
rationality. Accordingly, he advised young scholars like Kōsaka Masaaki to
take care not to become a target of the ultranationalists.[40] For his own part,
he found the attacks of Minoda irritating and ignorant. He wrote to a former
student, Mutai Risaku, that he would do his best "not to become a target of
those mad dogs."[41]

But the nightmare continued to become reality. In February 1940 the
Minoda camp turned its sights on Tsuda Sōkichi, a scholar of ancient
Japanese history, and succeeded in bringing him and his publisher, Iwanami
Shigeo, to trial. Nishida's own *Problem of Japanese Culture* was published the

[37] 原理日本社研究綱領 [Study-plan of the Japan Principle Society], 原理日本 [The Japan principle] 19/2 (1943): 1–3.

[38] 西田博士の認識論を評す [Critique of Dr. Nishida's epistemology], *The Japan Principle*, 7–14. Minoda accused Nishida's thought of being "static," of "not having gone beyond the realm of idealistic metaphysics," and of "lacking the power to guide the new era." He found it "sad that such a philosophical system should be considered representative of modern Japanese philosophy," and attributed Nishida's popularity to ideas he shared with "that despicable Marxist ideology."

[39] NKZ 14:396.

[40] No. 1240 (25 June 1938), NKZ 19:28–9.

[41] No. 1243 (4 July 1938), NKZ 19:30. See also his letter to Takizawa Katsumi 滝沢克巳, No. 1248 (11 July 1938), NKZ 19:33.

following month by Iwanami Bookstore,[42] but its attenuated language saved it from a similar fate. In it he tried to argue for a non-Eurocentric perspective from which to view contemporary world culture and to consider the role that Japan has to play. Given the power of the ultranationalists to mobilize the thought police, Nishida had to be more careful than usual and complained of the harassment of the ultranationalists.[43] Later he would compare the mood of the times to the burning of books during the Qin period in China.

Nishida on War

On a humanistic level, Nishida of course deplored the suffering and devastation that always accompany armed warfare. But intellectually he recognized the role that conflict has had to play in the unfolding of history:

> The more the world becomes unified as a total environment, the more "horizontal" relationships give way to "vertical" ones. The struggle between one subjectivity and another cannot be avoided. History is the story of racial struggles.[44]

Nishida did not question the legitimacy of the Russo-Japanese War of 1904–1905, the first war to mobilize the Japanese people as a nation. But it was this war that brought him face to face with the absurdity of armed conflict, for it cost him the lives of a dear friend and of his own younger brother. Nishida's way of dealing with the shock was to take up his pen and compose moving tributes to the two loved ones. These pieces, published in local newspapers, tried to justify the deaths by appealing to the governmental propaganda that "if the power of our country is extended to East Asia as a result of this war, and if the bodies of the fallen become the foundation of a new empire,"[45] then somehow they have not died in vain. But his heart was far from the official explanation. He was devastated and fell into a deep depression from which he did not emerge until a year later.[46]

On 2 January 1905, when the news of the fall of Port Arthur reached Japan, Nishida wrote in his diary that he, too, "could not help feeling the euphoria."[47] But he was deep into Zen practice at the time and the clarity of

[42] The work sold 40,000 copies right after its publication, attesting to the popular demand for Nishida's work. It is contained in volume 12 of Nishida's *Collected Works*.

[43] See his letters to Yamamoto, No. 1434 (30 March 1940), NKZ 19:109–10, and No. 1574 to Yamamoto (8 May 1941), NKZ 19:161–2.

[44] NKZ 12:375.

[45] NKZ 13:170.

[46] See his letter to Yamamoto of 8 March 1905, No. 47, NKZ 18:66.

[47] NKZ 17:129.

insight this brought him seems to have kept him from sharing in the victory celebrations. His diary reads:

> This afternoon I sat in meditation. At noon there was a rally in the park to celebrate the fall of Port Arthur. I could hear people shouting "Banzai!" They are going to have a lantern procession this evening to celebrate the occasion. How fickle the heart to give itself to such foolish festivities! People don't think about the many lives that were sacrificed and about the fact that the war has still a long way to go before it ends.[48]

His mixed emotions reached beyond the popular reaction to the political arena as well. As a Japanese, Nishida was pleased with the final victory, but he was also noticeably irritated by the settlement Japan's statesmen had secured. At the same time, his diaries speak of the need for a "self-reform" that goes beyond the political arena:

> The most courageous act is to conquer oneself. There is no greater enterprise than self-reform and self-improvement. It surpasses the control of Manchuria. The Way and scholarship—these are my enterprise.[49]

The next armed conflict to engage the entire nation of Japan was the Pacific War of 1941–1945. Nishida had already been concerned about the escalation of the war in China when Navy Captain Takagi Sōkichi, who was in charge of a "think tank" made up of able-minded persons, approached him for a philosophical perspective that he might use to give direction to the Navy. For some time already the Army and Navy had been at loggerheads for control of Japanese military policy. Nishida complied, hoping that in some way his ideas might help influence the course of events. The association between the Kyoto school and the Navy may be said to have begun with a meeting that Harada Kumao arranged on 18 February 1939. Nishida spoke about the Japanese spirit, the pressures being brought to bear on state universities, and political negotiations with China.[50] Takagi called on Nishida at his home in Kamakura in September 1939, and it was probably on this occasion that he asked Nishida's collaboration. Nishida recommended Kōyama Iwao, a former student teaching at the University of Kyoto, as someone who could take part in the efforts of the Navy.[51] This is how the Kyoto school members came to collaborate with the Navy's think tank.

---

[48] NKZ 17:130.

[49] NKZ 17:134.

[50] 高木惣吉 Takagi Sōkichi, 高木惣吉日記 [The diaries of Takagi Sōkichi] (Tokyo: Mainichi Shinbunsha, 1985), 14.

[51] 花沢秀文 Hanazawa Hidefumi, 高山岩男の思想と行動の研究 [The ideas and activities of Kōyama Iwao], 岡山県立邑久高等学校研究紀要, 13 (1987): 6.

Nishida saw Takagi only twice in 1943. In 1944, when the Ministry of Education's "Thought Inquisition" (思想審議会) had begun to scrutinize Nishida's writings as "unpatriotic," Takagi was able to intervene on his behalf. The final report of the committee found Nishida and his fellow Kyoto philosophers innocent of the charges.[52]

Despite the efforts made by the more level-headed among the nation's statesmen and intellectuals, and despite the emperor's own resistance to go to war, movements within the military to launch war against the United States had gained too much momentum to stop. As mentioned, Nishida was critical of the Japanese military campaign in China. He was also worried about his son Sotohiko, who was in Tsitsihar (Qiqihaer) at the time. But in any case, Nishida was opposed to the Pacific War and predicted that Japan would eventually be defeated. It was an open secret among top statesmen, Navy officers, and a handful of intellectuals, that Japan lacked sufficient oil reserves to carry on a campaign against the United States for any longer than six months, a year at best. On 18 October Tōjō Hideki was appointed prime minister and within two months Japan had declared war against the United States. This gave the warmongers the chance they had been waiting for to test their strength. Nishida learned of the declaration of war in the Kyoto Prefecture Hospital, where he had been admitted shortly before for treatment of acute rheumatism.

Nishida on the New World Order

In March of 1943, Nishida was visited by Yatsugi Kazuo, a member of the Center for National Strategy. This meeting led to his meeting with military officials. There are conflicting reports as to why Nishida agreed to do so. Furuta Hikaru, who has tried to sort out the facts, concludes that Yatsugi was told by Kanai Shōji of rumors that Nishida was under the secret surveillance of the military police and might be arrested. Kanai's aim, as an admirer of Nishida, was to prevent this from happening. He thus arranged for Yatsugi to visit Nishida under the pretext of asking him to write his views regarding the Japanese situation in East Asia, and possibly to draft a blueprint of the proclamation of the Greater East Asia Co-Prosperity Sphere that the Tōjō government might use for a Greater East Asia Meeting scheduled to be held in November of that year.[53]

[52] 黒田秀俊 Kuroda Hidetoshi, 昭和言論史への証言 [A testimony on the history of freedom of expression in the Shōwa period] (Tokyo: Kōbundō, 1966), 55–6. On this problem, Nishida wrote to Kōsaka Masaaki on 28 July 1944 (No. 1967, NKZ 9:317–8).

[53] 古田 光 Furuta Hikaru, 「世界新秩序の原理」事件考 [Thoughts on the "Principles for a new world order" incident], supplements to NKZ 14 and 19.

123

Although Nishida's first reaction at the visit was one of anger, after he had time to think the matter over he acceded to the request, perhaps reckoning that it would not be an altogether bad thing if some of his ideas could seep into the military. At the meeting, which was held on 19 May, Nishida criticized the position of the government for exploiting the countries of southern and eastern Asia. Yatsugi told Nishida of the rumor that the secret police might try to arrest him. Those present promised not to let such a thing happen. Yatsugi recalls: "I was relieved. It seemed the professor was also relieved. But he only nodded slightly with no word of thanks, without even so much as a 'I wish you well.' I was impressed."[54]

In the following week, Nishida was asked to write up the gist of his comments that evening. Troublesome as it was, he complied with a paper entitled "Principles for a New World Order," which was submitted on 28 May. It turned out to be too difficult for the military officials to understand, and was returned with a request that it be rewritten. This only infuriated Nishida all the more. Tanabe Juri, a sociologist specializing in French thought who had served as the go-between for these negotiations, undertook the rewriting himself. He finished the work in a few days—"simplifying" the original, as he said, "so that it would make sense to the military officials." The edited version was then passed on to Yatsugi, who had it mimeographed and copies passed on to the prime minister, ministers and vice-ministers of the Army and Navy, the minister of foreign affairs, and to a few others.[55]

It is hardly surprising that the edited text lacked the subtlety of the original. A few days later, Tanabe brought twenty copies of the mimeographed pamphlet to Nishida, who sent copies to Hori and Watsuji for comment. He did not seem to object strongly to the editorial work. His concern was rather, as he wrote to Hori, that its basic ideas might influence a speech that Tōjō was preparing on the topic: "I am not very certain as to how much impact all of this will have on the speech scheduled for tomorrow,… but I tried to bring out the dimension of universality present in the Japanese spirit."[56] As it turned out, Nishida was "disappointed" to read Tōjō's speech in the newspaper and see that virtually nothing of his vision had found its way into it.[57]

[54] 矢次一夫 Yatsugi Kazuo, 昭和動乱私史 [A personal account of the disturbances of the Shōwa period] (Tokyo: Keizai Ōraisha, 1973), 2:381.

[55] 田辺寿利 Tanabe Juri, 晩年の西田幾多郎と日本の運命 [Nishida Kitarō's late period and the fate of Japan] (Unoke: Memorial Society for Nishida Kitarō, 1962), 29–31.

[56] No. 1780 (14 June 1943), NKZ 19:243.

[57] The remark appears in a letter to Watsuji of 23 June, No. 1784, NKZ 19:245. Nishida reworked his talk on his own and the final version is contained in NKZ 12:426–34. For the background of this piece, see my "Fashion and Aletheia: Philosophical Integrity and Wartime Thought Control," 比較思想研究 16 (1989): 281–94.

The last essay Nishida wrote on current affairs was published in 1944 under the title "The State and National Polity." He had not intended to publish it, but since its existence was already known to those in the government, he thought it better to express himself openly than to provoke further suspicion.[58]

Nishida on Japan's Spiritual Reawakening

Nishida sensed the end of the war was near as the year 1945 rolled around. He wrote to D. T. Suzuki that he took heart in the example of the Israelites who survived the Babylon captivity by strengthening their spirituality. Convinced that "a people who identifies its pride with arms is destroyed by arms,"[59] he believed that the Japanese people would be able to lift themselves up out of defeat only if they could continue to believe in themselves. A letter to Hisamatsu Shin'ichi dated 12 April 1945 reiterates the point:

> The war situation is getting worse at such a quick tempo. This is the autumn of Japan, which may lose its very existence as a country.... We have to make a renewed effort in the intellectual arena by putting the notion of national polity on a more spiritually elevated plane, instead of identifying national confidence with military might alone and identifying the national polity with the military.... Even if the worst happens, if the people have a deep faith in the lofty spiritual national polity, we will certainly rise again and there will come a time when we can make great progress.[60]

Less than a month later, on 7 June, Nishida died of nephritis. He did not live to see the end of the war.

EVALUATION

As we remarked earlier, Nishida's 1917 essay "On Things Japanese" argued for the universal dimension of Japanese culture—that the Japanese tradition can be understood and appreciated by those of other traditions, and vice-versa. The position seems to have strengthened as time went on. Sometime around 1937 Nishida began to respond concretely to the social, political, and historical issues of the day, turning a philosophical eye to such specific questions as the imperial family, national polity, and the state. In this connection

[58] See, for instance, No. 2057 to 沢潟久敬 Omodaka Hisayuki (5 December 1944), and No. 2058 to 木村素衛 Kimura Motomori (6 December 1944), NKZ 19:356–7.

[59] No. 2194 (11 May 1945) NKZ 19:426.

[60] No. 2181, NKZ 19:417–8.

he tried to redefine expressions created by the ultranationalists or used as slogans by the militarists: "the Japanese spirit, "the participation of all," "the essence of national polity," "all the world under one roof," "the way of the emperor," and "holy war."

One has to wonder why Nishida would venture out into such an open minefield, and this in turn raises the possibility that his thought was in fact inherently nationalistic. On the basis of the argument laid out in the foregoing pages and the background material amassed in its preparation, I can only conclude that Nishida's aim was to present an alternative to the nationalism of his day. As a philosopher he sought to give different, more reflective meaning to words and ideas that had been expropriated by the right. Let it suffice to single out a few representative passages from his writings where it should be clear that Nishida was trying, in his own way, to relieve the tensions that ultranationalistic elements had built up in the Japanese people and to promote clear thinking about the future of the country. I organize my remarks around some of the key words indicated above.

"All the world under one roof" 八紘一宇

We may begin with the slogan, *hakkō ichiu* (or *hakkō iu*), "all the world under one roof." The term had become so much a catchphrase of the nationalists that the mere fact of using it at all seems to place Nishida in their camp. What Nishida is about, however, is closer to what Ueda Shizuteru has called the "semantic struggle" of pitting his philosophical vision against the irrational forces of ultranationalism. In *The Problem of Japanese Culture*, for instance, he argued that as an island country Japan had developed in relative isolation from the rest of the world for thousands of years. It had become a world unto itself. But that world has ceased to exist. Japan is no longer a string of secluded islands lying in the eastern seas. It is "in" a larger world and must open up itself to that world. It cannot afford to become a subjectivistic power unto itself. "To make Japan 'subjective' is in effect to turn the 'Way of the emperor' into a form of hegemony and imperialism."[61]

Nishida recognized that there was no single power that ruled Japan from one epoch to the next.[62] The controls shifted hands with the passage of time, even though the imperial family was always present in the background as a kind of axis around which history unfolded itself. Throughout most of Japan's history, its emperors did not come to the political fore, but their pres-

---

[61] NKZ 12:341. Nishida used the word 主体的 *subjective* in a negative sense here.

[62] Examples of "the subjective" in Japanese history, according to Nishida, include the Soga clan, the Fujiwara Family, the Taira Family, the Minamoto Family, the Hōjō Family, the Ashikaga Family, and the Tokugawa Family (NKZ 12:335–6.).

ence was always felt.[63] Nishida finds this visible kind of ongoing presence amidst the changes of history significant and reckons it a kind of "principle of the self-formation of the contradictory self-identical world itself." What Japan has to bring to the international community is a heritage of continuity symbolized in the way of the emperor, which is "the true meaning of the phrase, *hakkō ichiu*."[64]

Nishida was, of course, well aware of the current connotations of the phrase *hakkō ichiu*. He knew that it had been taken over as a slogan to rally support for a grand union of the countries of eastern Asia. He tried to rehabilitate the term by making it serve a broader philosophical and political perspective. Lest his intentions be mistaken, he seasoned his comments with direct and harsh criticisms of current military policies. The military, for its part, was in no position to reject Nishida's appropriation of their vocabulary, since they themselves had insisted all along that their true aim was "the liberation of Asian countries from European and American colonialists," and their "motivation was not one of imperialism." At the same time, in his accusations of "hegemony" and "expansionism," "ethnocentric egoism," and "imperialism" Nishida made no attempt to disguise his ire at the activities of the militarists.[65]

In an addendum to his article, originally entitled "The State and the National Polity," Nishida used the phrase *hakkō iu* in speaking of the historical foundation of Japan as a country through reference to episodes from the *Kojiki* and *Nihongi*. In his view, this radical historicity of Japan is a defining characteristic of its national character or *kokutai*:

> It is only in virtue of the fact that the Japanese national polity, as the creative modality of the formation of the historical world, contains a principle of the formation of the world that a principle of the formation of an East Asian world can emerge from it. This is how we need to think about *hakkō iu*.[66]

In "Principles for a New World Order," Nishida locates the true significance of *hakkō iu* in the global interaction of ethnic-nations, each seeking to secure its own independence in order to contribute to the formation of world history. "This is what Japan's ideal of *hakkō iu* must be," he concludes. In short, the ideal of "bringing everything under one roof" is not a nationalist slogan for Nishida, but the expression of a principle aimed at realizing a global unity

[63] In this sense, Nishida describes the imperial family as a "being of non-being" (無の有), NKZ 12:336), as an "absolute present" (340), and as "the alpha and omega" (409).

[64] NKZ 12:341.

[65] See 12:349, 399, 404, 410, 432–3.

[66] NKZ 12:"419.

of independent countries. And this principle is already present in the unfolding of Japanese history.[67]

East Asian Union

Nishida treated the related slogans of "creating a Greater East Asia Co-Prosperity Sphere" and "Japan as the leader of East Asia" in similar fashion. In *The Problem of Japanese Culture* he argued that there are things in the culture of Japan that can be "exported" to the West with pride. To illustrate his point, he quotes Bruno Taut's praise of the simple beauty of the buildings of the Ise Shrine. He takes the occasion to reiterate his view that the age of isolationism is over for Japan, that it has now become a world power in the Rankean sense of the term. Thus the most pressing issue for Japan is how to maintain its traditional past and at the same time open itself to the rest of the world:

> Japanese culture exhibits its flexibility in the manner of [Dōgen's] "dropping off of body-mind, body-mind dropped off." This means that Japan is not one subjectivity standing over against others, but rather that it embraces other subjectivities *as a world*. It means building a single world at one with concrete reality in a contradictory self-identical way. This is where I see the mission of Japan in building up East Asia. If it is merely one subjectivity pitted against others, seeking either to negate the others or to assimilate them, it is nothing more than imperialism. That is not what the Japanese spirit is about.[68]

It is not clear from the above just how Japan is to embrace other subjectivities constructively. Nishida is more forthright about Japan's role of leadership in his "Principles for a New World Order." Noting the oppression that Asian countries have suffered under the siege of Western colonial powers, he argues that the time has come for each country to be awakened to its own mission in the world, and that to this end a regional unity of the countries of eastern Asia will enable them to assert their independence and fulfill that historical role in the new emerging order of things. This is how he understood the "principle of the constitution of an East Asia co-prosperity sphere." It means Asian countries combining strengths to uphold ideals different from those of European and American countries, and thus to become actors rather than mere victims in the making of world history:

> For a regional world to take shape, it is necessary for one country to assume a central position and shoulder the responsibility. In East Asia,

---

[67] NKZ 12:428.
[68] NKZ 12:430.

Japan is the only country for this. In the same way that the victory of Greeks against the Persians determined the course of the culture of Europe all the way up to the present, the outcome of the Greater East Asia War taking place today will in retrospect be seen to have given a certain direction to world history.[69]

What does Nishida mean by singling out Japan as the only country able to bear the burden of central leadership among the countries of eastern Asia? Given his tough criticisms of the activities of Japan's military as exploitation and imperialism, as well as his wish that Japan not become a "power in control" of Asia, it is hard to interpret his words as meaning that he supported a cultural dominance backed up by military might. It is more logical to read these lines as a call for Japan to return to the humaneness and morality of its original national spirit, to lay down its arms and only then to presume to guide its Asian neighbors into a new era. One may dismiss the idea as romantic. One may even argue that in some sense Nishida is paying lip service to the ideals of ultranationalism by giving Japan a privileged position in the scheme of things. Or yet again, one may read it as a plea for the restoration of humanity to politics and the restoration of a Japanese spirit that had gone astray.

As with not a little of Nishida's writing, the variety of interpretations is due not only to the ambivalence of the text but to the presuppositions that the reader brings to it. From our present position, we may wish for Nishida to have been clearer. At the time, he seems to have been testing the limits of free expression with that very same ambiguity.

Kokutai 国体

Nishida's most problematic remarks on *kokutai* or national polity[70] are to be found in his essay on "The State and National Polity." Here, too, he seems to be arguing on two levels, the general and particular. Speaking first in general terms, Nishida reasons that "the national polity is the personality of state," which means that every state has its national polity. For Nishida, the state emerges from ethnic groups that have evolved beyond the level of a biological race to the self-awareness of unity as a world. In other words, ethnic groups have to transcend their ethnic identity in order to become a state. The state, meantime, becomes a moral and rational entity to the extent that it mirrors the world within itself. At the same time, when the state is based on an

[69] NKZ 12:429.

[70] Woodard, *The Allied Occupation of Japan*, 11, notes that this word can be translated "national entity," "national structure," "fundamental character of the nation," or more commonly "national polity."

exclusive ethnocentrism, it becomes imperialistic and expansionist, and ceases to be a state in the true sense of the word. In this sense, "nationalism" for Nishida means a racial egoism that does *not* belong to the state.[71]

If national polity is to provide a model for moral action, it must do so in the light of "absolute reality." The best means to do so, Nishida argued, is to keep in touch with the country's historical unfolding. "It is at this radically historic dimension of our existence that we encounter the divine, and it is there that we ground our attempts to be rational."[72]

Turning to the particular level, Nishida goes so far as to conclude that "in the highest sense of the term, no other country has what we call *kokutai*." Later he adds:

> The Japanese *kokutai* captures the essence of the idea of *kokutai* as that which makes up the historical world; what the Japanese people think of when they hear the word has no counterpart in any foreign language.[73]

This is a strong claim, certainly much stronger than Nishida tried to substantiate by sustained historical or philosophical argument. To read it in the weak sense that only in Japan does one find a "Japanese" *kokutai* is conciliatory but hardly fair to the context. We have no choice but to read his words as a statement of his personal conviction that the historical bonds between the national polity and the imperial family as found in Japan is somehow normative for the notion of "national polity" itself. Since this brings us as close as we come in Nishida to a nationalistic ideology, it bears pausing for a moment to consider his intentions.

In contrast to the popular views being advocated by the ultranationalists that the essence of the Japanese *kokutai* is its "family-like" feature, Nishida emphasizes the historical founding of Japan by imperial decree. The shift of emphasis away from current social structures to past fact opens the way to a truly religious dimension. His aim is not to sacralize present strategies but to desacralize them by locating the sacred in a larger landscape. This larger landscape is what he understands by *kokutai*.[74] However Nishida might have developed this initial intuition in its general and particular aspects, it is clear that he consistently opposed the identification of *kokutai* with military strength and insisted that the true roots of national polity lie deep in our common humanity.

[71] NKZ 12:403–4.
[72] NKZ 12:408.
[73] NKZ 12:410, 415.
[74] NKZ 12:417–9.

To the end Nishida left no doubt of his dissent against Japan's expansionist policies in Asia. His vision of Japan as part of the world community was one with his love for his country, and it was out of this vision and this love that he called for a reawakening of conscience, rationality, and above all spiritual depth. His concern for the future of Japan was not a matter of abstract philosophical categories but of living realities of very concrete consequence. When he locked horns with nationalistic ideologues, he did so in the language of the day. Rather than invent a new vocabulary that would rise above the fray, he took up the jargon and slogans of the day and sought to redeem them from their petty provincialism by opening them up to a more universal perspective. Whether and to what extent he succeeded may not be as important for us today as the fact that he tried to sound a note of conscience and rationality amidst the tumultuous fanaticism all around him. In such circumstances, any attempt to address the immediate political issues of Japan philosophically was bound to invite misunderstanding, particularly for later generations left with only written texts to go by. Had he never left the realms of pure philosophy, our task as interpreters might have been easier. Easier, but somehow less than real.

The Return of the Past

Tradition and the Political Microcosm in the Later Nishida

Agustín JACINTO Z.

T HE HISTORY OF JAPAN, like the history of the world, proceeds from present to present, from reality to reality, from epoch to epoch, from form to form. In this process, things that are formed become things that themselves give form. The transformative power that keeps history moving as an ever-recurring origin of the new from the old is tradition, and at the center of this process sits the Imperial Throne of Japan (皇室). Such were the conclusions that Nishida Kitarō reached during the years 1930 to 1945, the final period of his philosophy, and it is in the light of them, I believe, that we must consider his general view of Japan as a nation-state and his vision of a new, global world order.

For Nishida, the emperor system was a microcosm within a wider historical macrocosm. Its central role in the course of events, he argued, is due to a unique, almost rhythmical pattern in Japan's political history whereby different forms of government alternated with the Imperial Throne as the moving force of tradition. For Nishida, this periodic ebb and tide of the *subjective* force of governmental structures and the *transcendent* force of the Imperial Throne reached its climax in the Meiji Restoration—in his scheme, we would do better to call it the Meiji Renewal—when "it took visible form as an authoritative constitution."[1]

In such a scheme, political history is not only the stage on which alternating forces of tradition play their roles, but is itself a story in the making, or in Nishida's terms, an ongoing transformation of that which has been made into that which in its turn makes. He describes the special character of this transformation as "a return-in-renewal" (復古即維新).[2] The Imperial Throne is axial because it is "eternally present" in the course of events:

[1] NKZ 12:336.

[2] NKZ 12:272.

The return of the past in our nation has always had the character of a renewal. It has never been a mere return to the past but always a step forward as the self-determination of the eternal present.[3]

From these introductory remarks it should be obvious that without a clear idea of what Nishida meant by "tradition" there is no understanding his views on the nation and the emperor system. What may not be equally obvious at first, though I trust will become so the further we proceed, is that Nishida did not work out his ideas merely in response to the political events of his time, but was ever bent on seeing things against the broader horizon that philosophical reflection opened up to him. In this sense, his political views, no matter how immediate, are always coded in the universal language of his philosophy. It is in this sense, too, that we must read the connection that took shape in his thinking from 1935 on between the idea of tradition and its source in the Imperial Throne. To make this connection as explicit as possible, I will begin with an account of the development of Nishida's notion of tradition as best we can reconstruct it from his later writings. In the second place, I will consider how he relates tradition to the "mode of production" of the historical world. Next, I will focus on how he sees the idea of tradition at work in the political history of Japan in general and its relation to the Imperial Throne in particular. It is in this third section that the question of Nishida's "nationalism" will come into sharpest relief. In a fourth and concluding section, I will try to lay out the logic of Nishida's advance from this understanding of tradition to his vision of a global world larger than the world of Japan.

THE IDEA OF TRADITION

Nishida's interest in the idea of tradition seems to have been stimulated both by his reading and by ongoing discussions with students and colleagues. He held Watsuji's book *The Idea of Reverence for the Emperor and its Tradition* (尊皇思想とその伝統) in high esteem and even referred to its author as "the Japanese Fustel de Coulanges."[4] He was also most certainly familiar with Miki Kiyoshi's "On Tradition (伝統論),"[5] and in fact during the war held a colloquium with Miki on Japanese culture in which the question of tradition was alluded to. We will have occasion to return to this colloquium later in the concluding section of this essay.

---

[3] NKZ 12:136.

[4] Nishida's comment appears in Letter No. 1871, dated 7 January 1944.

[5] 三木清全集 [Collected works of Miki Kiyoshi] (Tokyo: Iwanami, 1967), 14:307–17.

For his part, Nishida had attempted a more critical, philosophical reading of the themes dealt with in *Fundamentals of the National Polity*, a work issued in May of 1937 by the Japanese Ministry of Education. In place of the clichés about Japan's "historical mission" in Asia, Nishida proposed that "the fundamental meaning of our national polity lies in the creation of the historical world."[6] In arguing his case he touched on the ideas of tradition and the myth of the founding of the nation (肇国). This latter idea bears looking at more closely, as Nishida gives it attention in other writings of his at the time.

In a number of essays, Nishida sees *mythos* as the origin of tradition, both logically and chronologically. Taking his lead from social thinkers of his day, he understands myth as a "form of social production" or more generally as "the fundamental principle in the construction of a world." For example, alluding to Malinowski's *Myth in Primitive Psychology*, Nishida calls myth "a living reality that governs the human world." And from Jane Harrison he came to see that myth is grounded in ritual, which in turn grows out of the *dromenon*, the emotionally charged activity of the group, and dramatizes a common hope. Extrapolating from these theories of primitive societies, Nishida concludes that tradition itself has from its very beginnings "the character of ethnic religion."[7]

Naturally, the question about Japan is always just beneath the surface of Nishida's speculations, and perhaps to some extent guided his conclusions. In any case, he is disposed to trace Japan's emotional roots as well as the roots of the national polity in myth:

> Our national polity begins in the myth of the founding of the nation, and though it has undergone numerous social changes, it continues right up to the present to grow out of those mythical foundations.... The fundamental meaning of our national polity is the creation of a historical world.

> History begins with the appearance of things like myth and legend, which, though they look like so much superstition, carry deep within them something capable of developing into tradition.[8]

The writings of Friedrich Karl von Savigny (1779–1861), especially *Vom Beruf unserer Zeit*, also worked on Nishida as he tried to forge his notion of tradition, as did T. S. Eliot's "Tradition and Individual Talent," with which

---

[6] NKZ 10:334.

[7] See NKZ 9:133, 185; 10:69, 182, 185, 200; 11:190; 13:187, 194. Harrison showed that the word for ritual, *dromenon*, derived from the same root as the word *drama* (literally "things done"), namely the Greek *drao*, "to do."

[8] See NKZ 10:334; 14:382–3.

he felt a strong affinity. Indeed, he adopts Eliot's own language in speaking of tradition as "the feeling of history," as a force and a creative will that "resurrects our ancestors in the flesh and blood of the present."[9]

Eliot's characterization of tradition as a "catalyst" that brings the past and the present together also seems to be at work in Nishida's rather more ponderous formulation of tradition as the "constitutive principle of historical reality" and as "the self-determination of the eternal present." His idea is that the haphazard of things that make up the historical world need a principle of organization and unification in order to function as history rather than as a mere string of coincidences. This principle is tradition. And where tradition is weak or absent, things fall apart. For Nishida this is what had happened in present history with the dissolution of the bond between insight and feeling. The restoration of tradition therefore requires—and here again he cites Eliot—a recovery of poetic creation, without which there is no culture.[10]

Not surprisingly, Nishida's idea of tradition as the social construction of reality gives a place of special prominence to knowledge. In fact, he even goes so far as to suggest that "genuine *perception* is only possible from within tradition, for each and every thing is *something historical*." The artistic creativity of revitalizing tradition, therefore, means learning to see things anew. The eye that sees, half unconsciously, the outer things of the world, and the eye that sees in artistic intuition or in moral responsibility are not the same. Learning to "see things" anew is not merely a matter of a post-Cartesian consciousness aware of other consciousnesses, but entails construction of a "kind of public *topos*." What the phenomonologists call *Sachen* only goes part way because it stops short at psychological description. It has forgotten the *Tat* in *Tatsache*."[11] For Nishida, only a sense of tradition as a place (場所) in which we are located can restore our contact with the facts that make up the historical world.

As the mention of the moral dimension already suggests, Nishida's insistence on seeing is not divorced from the realm of doing. In terms of tradition, this means not only that tradition brings past and present into contact and thus makes it possible for the world to create itself as a history, but also that the activity of individuals can be seen as a manifestation of tradition at work. Only by engaging the perception, insight, and activity of individuals within a society does tradition fulfil its formative role.[12]

[9] See NKZ 10:224; 12:35; 13:120.
[10] See NKZ 8:194, 212; 12:378–9; 14:379, 381, 383–5.
[11] See NKZ 7:347, 359–60, 364; 14:379.
[12] See NKZ 11:192; 14:380.

With this, all the ingredients for a comprehensive definition of tradition are assembled, but one looks in vain for anything like it in Nishida's own texts. He prefers to work on a few short formulas, turning them over and over in his mind until he has exhausted their implications or until they open up into other formulas. Without that fuller, descriptive context, his claim that tradition is "the constitutive principle of the historical world" or a "force" that forms the historical world and is itself reformed in the process, seems hopelessly abstract.[13] In a sense Nishida's refusal to settle on a single definition of tradition seems to reflect his conviction that tradition is itself an energy in search of form, a principle of transmuting and being transmuted in time, not a collection of items from the past preserved into the present. This brings us to the philosophical framework within which Nishida located the creative forces of history.

THE MODE OF PRODUCTION OF HISTORY

That Nishida explained the formation of the historical world in terms of his logic of place is hardly surprising, since one of the reasons that drove him to this concrete, dialectical, and practical logic was the attempt to explain in formal terms the self-expressive and self-formative nature of the production of historical reality.[14] Here, however, I will restrict myself to the relationship between tradition and the making of history.

To begin with, Nishida's idea of historical reality as a "self-formative" production is offered as a direct alternative to Hegelian and Marxist interpretations of history. For Nishida the dialectic of history—the relationship between past, present, and future—functions in the manner of an identity of contradictories, that is, as a mutual and manifold opposition that is at the same time an identity. This identity of the opposing forces of time *is* the historical world.[15] Like Ranke, Nishida sees this identity constellated in the present as charged with an infinite past and pregnant with an infinite future. In his words, it is the "eternal present."

Nishida adapts the familiar logical pattern of thesis, antithesis, and synthesis to detail his understanding of this dialectic. The past, "insofar as it is something determined and given," may be called the *thesis*. Standing in *antithesis* to the past are "countless negations, countless futures" possible in the unbounded expanse of time that opens up the world of unrealized possibilities. Though the two stand opposed in terms of formal logic, true contra-

[13] See NKZ 11:189; 14:384.
[14] NKZ 8:551.
[15] NKZ 9:163.

diction is not generated between them so long as the past remains given and the future remains possible. This is what Nishida means when he claims that absolute contradiction can only be present in a world that moves on its own from form to form, "from that which has been made into that which in its turn makes." And by the same token, the sublation of the contradictions into a higher *synthesis* is only possible as a relationship between these absolute contradictories.[16]

As synthesis, then, the present is the self-identity of everything given in the past and the manifold of negations that move the past into the future. When Nishida refers to the synthesis as an "identity," he does not have in mind a mere harmonizing of opposite energies, but the creation of something new, a "new world." In this sense, identity neither eliminates nor alleviates opposition, but integrates the opposing elements in the service of something greater. Indeed, the stronger the opposition, he insists, the more sublime the new creation that it gives rise to. To be born into the historical world is therefore to "bear on one's shoulders an infinite task," namely the formation and transformation of our times. To carry out this task requires that we see ourselves as part of the process. To understand it is to see that our very understanding is part of the process. It is in this context that Nishida appeals to his notion of "active intuition" as an event in which the world discloses itself to our insight and in that very act of self-awareness is itself determined; in other words, an event in which the opposition between maker and the made is transmuted into a new, creative identity.[17]

More concretely, Nishida refers to the formative events of history as diverse "modes of production" or "historical specificities" that he at once identifies as the various societies that make up the human world. This order of proceeding from the production of history in general to human society in particular accents his view that society is by its very nature a form of *poiesis*.[18] It also allows him to reiterate his conviction that societies begin in ritual action and myth:

> Without the social element, there is no movement from the made to the making: there is no *poiesis*....Without veneration of the ancestors, the social element cannot come into being.[19]

In short, we see two elements coming together here. First, each society is seen as specific to its own historical epoch. And second, each historically

[16] NKZ 9:115, 163.

[17] NKZ 9:163–5, 180.

[18] NKZ 9:163, 166–7.

[19] The citations linked together here are from NKZ 12:418 and 9:154. See also 12:409.

specific society is but one instance of the ongoing mode of production of the historical world. When Nishida claims that society is always tied to tradition, he means it in both senses.

Taking a step closer to the concrete, Nishida observes that society requires the contradiction (thesis-antithesis) and integration (synthesis) of the bodily historical self and the natural environment. In making this claim, he notes that the idea of a mutual dependency between individuals and the environment is a distinctive feature of the modern world that developed in response to an inflated anthropocentric subjectivism. Specifically, the predominance of industrial modes of production and the ascendancy of the capitalist society bred a form of individualism that naturally crystallized in the form of "class struggles." This, together with the imperialistic, nationalistic self-understanding of the economically dominant societies, was the origin of numerous conflicts among nations. For Nishida, this whole inflated anthropocentrism was a relic of the past whose time was over.[20]

Taking up a distinction that F. Tönnes had introduced more than half a century before, Nishida argued that if a society is to contribute to the advance of understanding—that is, if it is to be truly a "self-perception of the historical world"—then it must be both a *Gemeinschaft* (community) and a *Gesellschaft* (society). Only a social order that enhances the creative *poiesis* of the subject as a member of a community can meet that demand. Once again, we see him applying his dialectic of opposites. On the one hand, individual subjects must think and act as members of a larger community. On the other, each subject must learn to see the things of the world fresh, as if for the first time, as only he or she can. Only a society where individuals can straddle these conflicting standpoints is capable of achieving the higher synthesis of a global world.

In order to actually move towards the production of a global world, history needs to be moved by two opposing dynamics at once: linear and circular. The first, the linear dynamic of history, Nishida identifies as the immanent pole. It is the chronological or "this-worldly" aspect of the world's mode of production whose basis is matter and whose dominant force is the law of physical necessity. By itself, the linear advance of time propelled by the drive to fulfill needs as they arise marks only a passage from one satisfaction to the next—or in Nishida's language, "from what has been made to what has been made." One cannot speak here of *historical* necessity proper—or the passage from "the determined to the determining."[21] Only when the complementary circular dynamic, which Nishida refers to as the transcendent pole, comes into the picture is it possible to speak of a positive, formative influence on

[20] NKZ 10:276, 337; 9:61, 64; 12:427.
[21] NKZ 9:177; 10:302, 356; 11:238, 250, 260.

138

history from without. The "transcendence" of this dynamic (which Nishida occasionally refers to as "space" to distinguish it from the "time" of the linear dynamic), therefore, constitutes the ground for freedom from physical necessity at the same time as it opens up the possibility of awakening to larger historical needs.[22]

As chronological, the linear dynamic of history-in-the-making is irreversible. Like the clock, it cannot turn back for so much as a single moment.[23] At the same time, as it progresses from one stage to the next, the discontinuities in the linear process disclose a stable, circular continuum beneath the flow of time. It is what Nishida calls a "continuity of discontinuities."[24]

In any case, the combined effect of this twofold dynamic of the immanent and the transcendent, of the discontinuous and the continuous, of time and space, characterizes both historical development in general as well as the development of the individuals that make it up. In other words, the "identity" of these two contradictory histories, that of the individual subject and that of the world, requires the collaboration of conflicting orientations to the temporal process. Time can never simply be identified with the products of history (the made) nor with the producer (the maker). Something more is needed to combine the two dynamics of time, and that something more is tradition.[25]

The requirements that tradition has to fulfill are clear from the fuller descriptions Nishida gives of the historical process, which we cannot go into here. Suffice it to say that he is determined to show tradition as both logically and historically necessary, lest it be taken for a mere *deus ex machina* summoned on stage to solve an otherwise unsolvable riddle. For him, the production of the world is unthinkable except as the self-expression of historical reality itself, and equally unthinkable without an ongoing process of self-negation.[26] History by nature is always and irrevocably both has-been and not-yet. Anything that slackens the tension between these two central ingredients of historical necessity cannot properly be called a mode of production of the world. At the same time, activity that is simply absorbed without remainder into that tension cannot account for the ongoing transmutation of the past into the future. What is needed is an Eternal Now, an absolute present that sets the ongoing metamorphosis of specific historical realities against a worldwide horizon.[27]

[22] NKZ 11:184.

[23] NKZ 10:392, 528, 550; 11:324.

[24] NKZ 8:518, 547, 580; 10:24.

[25] NKZ 8:270, 477, 516, 519; 9:12.

[26] NKZ 9:16, 24, 42, 95, 126, 148.

[27] NKZ 9:140; 10:337.

This, then, is what Nishida asks the idea of tradition to do as a synthesizing force that transmutes what has been formed into what forms. At this point he takes a critical step in the light of his own concerns with the Japanese situation. Consistent with his view that societies grow out of a ritual-mythical substratum, Nishida asks of tradition that it also somehow make manifest the ethnos or specific nature of a people.

The term *ethnos* normally suggests a group with a common racial or cultural basis, but Nishida's view of the way historical reality is produced requires a kind of collective subject in which the social and individual demands of living in the concrete historical world can be brought together. "As individual items in the world, the self of each of us...is not born into the world accidentally but traditionally, that is to say socially, in an historically specific way." That is to say, our subjective "self" is itself a particular historical reality in which we participate, something already made that we inherit in order to make it over. Accordingly, insofar as tradition expresses an ethnos with a subjective dimension, it may be called the point at which the self comes to life. He continues:

> To say a tradition is living is to say that it is a kind of feeling of the temporal and the eternal, what T. S. Eliot calls the feeling of history. Our self is born in the "active intuition" wherein historical tradition is the self-determination of the absolute present.[28]

As indicated earlier, Nishida saw active intuition not as a mere contemplation of the facts of history but as a productive participation in the creation of the historical world. In it seeing and making work together as one: seeing-in-making, making-in-seeing. But precisely because active intuition engages the individual so radically in the processes of history, it needs a firm foothold in the world, the kind of foothold that only an ethnos or people can provide:

> To say that tradition is living must also imply that the self, as that part of the historical world capable of seeing itself, is also shaped by tradition at the same time as it shapes the world...in active intuition.[29]

For Nishida, then, the historical world is produced over and over as each age takes up the task that tradition has set it. In our times, that task is to forge a global world, but without the perspective of tradition there is no way to recognize that fact, let alone begin to carry it out. This is what Nishida means by insisting that tradition is a necessary condition for the self to engage in its distinctive activity of seeing-in-making, active intuition.

[28] NKZ 10:293–4.
[29] NKZ 11:190.

THE IMPERIAL THRONE AS PROTOTYPE OF THE NATIONAL POLITY

Nishida's philosophical notions of tradition, the historical production of the world, and the task of the epoch all take on a more problematic character when forced into the ideological clothing of the wartime Japan. His reactions to this process are a matter of some debate, but a careful examination of his texts, diaries, and letters, as well as other written materials, paints a fairly consistent picture of his position regarding the key ingredient in that ideology: the national polity or *kokutai* (国体) of Japan.

Nishida seems always to have read Japan's political history through the lens of his idea of tradition as we have just presented it. Thus in his attempts to reevaluate the ideology of the militarist government, we see him returning to the myth of the Founding of the Nation of Japan (建国). A good illustration of this is an essay published in 1944 in which Nishida took cause with Maki Kenji's *Theory of the National Polity of Japan*.[30] Maki had argued that if the Emperor were viewed as a *paterfamilias*, this would give more latitude in interpreting the meaning of *kokutai*. As Nishida saw it, Maki's argument came down to five points:

1. The Imperial Throne was held in reverence by various primitive clans (氏) in Japan's history, among them the Nakatomi, Fujiwara, Taira, and Minamoto clans.
2. This reverence implied a recognition of the Throne as a Sacred Family.
3. The "harmonious formation" of Japan as a single people—a primitive predecessor of the *kokutai*—did not come about through warfare but by way of the idea of divine descent of the people.
4. In ancient times, the government, or "national-familial subject," was formed through the unification of the various clans and the subsequent subordination of other clans and peoples to them.
5. The fundamental character of this *kokutai* is that of a "familial state" that served as a prototype for developments in later ages.[31]

On the whole, Nishida's outline is rather faithful to Maki's position, though Maki also recognizes the value given to the oracle of Amaterasu-ō-mi-kami and to the myth of the Founding of the Nation. The difference is that Maki did not find this an adequate foundation, from a sociohistorical

---

[30] Maki Kenji 牧 謙二 (1892-1989) was a specialist in the history of Japanese political thought and institutions. His book 日本国体の理論 appeared in 1944 *after* Nishida had already completed his own text for the September issue of 哲学研究 [Philosophical studies]. Nishida added the reference to the work just prior to the publication of his essay. See his letter to Omodaka Hisayuki, No. 2990 (10 December 1944). Maki's position is developed on pages 250-7.

[31] NKZ 12:416–7.

perspective, for the *kokutai* and therefore had recourse to the position of the emperor and the imperial family.

Nishida did not completely dismiss the historical accuracy of Maki's account, but set it aside as a matter for experts to decide. At the same time he acknowledged how well it expresses "the internal unity of our unparalleled *kokutai*." Nevertheless, he disagreed with Maki on each point, arguing that they are one-sided in stressing only the "immanent" dimension of the *kokutai* and ignoring the "transcendent" dimension, which for Nishida was all-important.

He outlines his own contrasting position in four points:

1. The origins of the *kokutai* lie in the Founding of the Nation (肇国).
2. The *kokutai* emerges against the background of the myth of the Beginning of Heaven and Earth (天地開闢).
3. The *kokutai* further relies on an oracle (神勅) of the gods revealing to Amaterasu-ō-mi-kami that her descendants (the Imperial Throne) would rule the earth.
4. Accordingly, the Imperial Throne is a dimension different from the Sacred Family that the different clans, according to Maki, recognized.[32]

Clearly Nishida's idea of adding a "transcendent" dimension of a *kokutai* centered on the Imperial Throne amounts to the introduction of myth as a counterbalance to historical fact. In other words, for the *kokutai* to constitute a historical world *in the full sense of the word,* the Founding of the Nation must in some sense be synonymous with the "Beginning of heaven and earth." Without a grounding in myth, the politics, law, economy, and other elements that make a historical society a self-formative process cannot be understood. Without the dimension of the religious, the familiar aspect of the *kokutai* lacks a solid foundation.[33]

Nishida's approach complicates the prototype of Maki, but it also has direct implication for his reinterpretation of the ideology of the militarist government. On the one hand, he accepts the central, mediating position of the Imperial Throne as "a single lineage reaching across millennia and coeval with heaven and earth," and recognizes it as the symbolic origin of the idea of Japan as the "land of the Gods." But he resists the idea that the imperial family or any specific social, historical, and political constellation of power for that matter can assume this status. In this sense, his insistence on the Imperial Throne as the proper locus of the prototypical *kokutai* brings myth and history together in such a way that neither can absorb the other. In his language,

[32] NKZ 12:416-8.
[33] NKZ 12:340, 409, 419, 426; 11:188.

only a prototype that is a self-identity of such absolute contradictories can bear the weight of serving a nation as an ideal.

It is therefore misleading in Nishida's case to render the term *kōshitsu* (皇室) in English as "Imperial Household," since he clearly rejected the idea of the emperor as a mere *paterfamilias*. The emperor's mythical, religious quality as a divine epiphany god (現神) is rather better associated with the Throne than with a particular individual or group of individuals.[34] This is the sense in which he sees the emperor system as a microcosm that mediates a wider historical macrocosm, perhaps even *the* historical macrocosm.

In terms of his developed philosophy, Nishida linked the Imperial Throne to tradition by seeing the former as the spatio-temporal "place" (場所) at which the historical world of the *kokutai* is founded:

> As a self-determination of the absolute present, the Imperial Throne is the center from which everything originates and develops.... All material things belongs to the public domain, ...to the world of the Imperial Throne.... That everything originates from the Imperial Throne and to it returns is the quintessence of our country."[35]

Nishida's choice of words is deliberate. *All* material things belong to the throne, and this means that even within the microcosm of the emperor system itself, the Throne transcends the Sacred Family. Thus, to see the Imperial Throne as the alpha and omega of history, as an absolute reality, is to elevate it not only as the transcendent foundation of the nation but also as the foundation of the imperial blood that is merely its "self-expression" in history. Even though he speaks of the history-making activity of the people as based on the "mystique of blood," he is careful to stress the transcendence of the throne over blood ties in the imperial family. Only in this way does the *kokutai*, the people with their emperor, attain the "absolute character of a historical world."[36]

We are now in a position to appreciate how Nishida understood the relationship between tradition and state sovereignty. In the main, it has the following four aspects.

First, sovereignty comes about through the self-negation of the state. This does not entail that state as such disappear, or even that it turn into a kind of "relative nothingness." Rather, a society that has attained to statehood must, if it is to shape a larger, global world, engage in self-negation.

Second, concrete self-negation entails a return to its origins. This renders a state more rational and its individuals more moral.

[34] NKZ 12:409, 419.

[35] Quotations combined from 12:346, 409, 417.

[36] NKZ 11:334, 336; 12:418, 433–4. See also NKZ 8:537–8.

Third, a return to the origins entails a recovery of the tradition of the prototypical *kokutai*. In this regard, Nishida writes:

> In the history of our country, there was always a return to the Imperial Throne, a return of the past. This has never meant a return to the systems and culture of antiquity but has involved taking a step ahead in the direction of a new world.[37]

This return of the past is, properly speaking, a return of the origins to the present. Nishida cites the *Kujihongigengi* (舊事本紀玄義): "Do not say that antiquity returns. The age of the Gods is now."[38] For Nishida, all of Japanese history can be read as a "return-in-renewal, a renewal-in-return."[39] The circle is complete: renewal means returning to the past, and returning to the past means renewal. This is the sense in which tradition, with the Imperial Throne at its center, entrusts the present with the task of creating a global world.

Nishida invoked this formula in December 1941 in a special lecture delivered to the emperor. His talk ends with these words:

> There have been times when a certain total power has been the center, but always we have returned to the founding spirit of our nation and set out in the direction of a new age with the Imperial Throne at the center. I have said that history always proceeds with the present—which includes in itself the past and the future—at the center. In the case of our country, it is the Imperial Throne that has always signified this present. Therefore, to return to the spirit of the Foundation of Our Nation does not simply mean a return to antiquity, but rather always an advance into a new age. I believe that the return of the past (復古) always signifies a renewal (維新).[40]

So far the link between tradition and sovereignty has focused on the role of tradition in Nishida's later philosophy. We may now turn to a consideration of his ideal of building a global community in history.

FROM TRADITION TO A GLOBAL WORLD

Towards the end of his life Nishida came under the influence of the nineteenth-century historian Leopold von Ranke, both through his own readings and through the interpretations of Suzuki Shigetaka. We may single out a

[37] NKZ 12:337.
[38] NKZ 12:409.
[39] NKZ 12:418. See also note 2.
[40] NKZ: 12:271–2.

144

number of ideas sympathetic to Nishida's later philosophical thinking, most of which have already appeared in one form or another in the previous pages:

1. Each epoch is immediate to God.
2. The historical present is charged with an infinite past and is pregnant with an infinite future.
3. The state that becomes a real spiritual entity, a world power, is the fountainhead of eternal cultural values.
4. Each individual event is unique and at the same time can only be understood in the context of a universal history.
5. The writing of history is always and everywhere universal history.
6. Each epoch is characterized by its own historical tendency.

For Nishida, the task of the philosopher is to "delve deep into the heart of the world" and therein to "apprehend its historical task."[41] For Nishida, as noted earlier, this task—or in Ranke's terms, this historical tendency—lay in the construction of a global world. In reaching this conclusion Nishida relied not only on his own considerable powers of intuition, but also on a studied understanding of contemporary world history. The key models in terms of which Nishida thought of history, as his contemporary Miyajima Hajime observed, were historical action, *poiesis*, and production.[42] The impact of Marxism is not, of course, to be discounted. Nishida supplemented his own reading with discussions held with leading thinkers, in particular with Miki Kiyoshi and Tosaka Jun. This ongoing dialogue with disciples and intellectuals sympathetic to his philosophy served him as a refinery for old ideas and a sounding board for new ones. The idea that world history is headed in the direction of a global world was one such new idea. A brief consideration of the intellectual atmosphere in which this idea took shape may help us face the charge of militarism that has been leveled at Nishida for his ideas of world history.

Although most historians agree that Nishida's political thought was woven warp and woof into the general fabric of his philosophy, virtually no one would claim that Nishida was in any sense a rabid militarist or even an imperialist. Where he comes in for criticism is that his arguments in favor of a global world remain in the abstract, without any particular directives, and therefore that overlaps between his language and that of the militarist ideologues easily provoke the charge that he was lending their cause his tacit support.

To face these criticisms, we need to ask what limitations Nishida placed, if any, on the new world order he was calling for. This needs to be supplemented by further research on why he chose the socio-political terminology

[41] NKZ 11:442.

[42] 宮島 肇 Miyajima Hajime 民族と歴史哲学 [Race and the philosophy of history] (Tokyo: Baifūkan, 1943), 160–2.

he did at the height of the war, on what his motives were for major meetings (there were eight or nine of them, by my count) with political figures during the war, on his own lobbying activities during the three cabinets of Prime Minister Konoe, and on his ongoing dialogue with other Kyoto philosophers of differing viewpoints. Here I shall only consider this final point, and that only insofar as it helps us to clarify the question of Nishida's concrete vision of a global world.

Nishida's Ongoing Dialogue

Nishida's dialogues with Kyoto thinkers was not something new to the war years (1930–1945), though they did intensify during that period. Already during his years as a teacher (he retired from active teaching in 1928) he had been in the habit of gathering the better students around him and encouraging them to write on matters of common interest and to develop their own positions. Nishida elicited the views of disciples and colleagues on a wide range of subjects and incorporated their ideas into his own writings, refining them as he went along. Perhaps the first of these brainstorming sessions to become "public" was the Monday lecture series that Nishida began at the suggestion of Amano Teiyū. Nishida's inaugural lecture was followed by Kōyama Iwao's address on "A Morphology of Cultures," Tanabe Hajime's on "Historical Reality," and others.[43]

Nishida's ongoing dialogue reached beyond this, to include a number of more formal colloquia, such as that held with Miki Kiyoshi on Japanese culture and contemporary humanism.[44] In this latter Nishida presented his own version of "objective humanism," which stressed the creativity of the individual in the creation of world history. Indirectly, Nishida's dialogue with Kyoto intellectuals also stands in the background of the much-debated *Chūōkōron* roundtable discussions held during the war by four of his disciples. It also extends to Nishida's considerable correspondence, which represent important public documents for understanding the direction of the "Kyoto school" during these years.

To give the main gist of these years of dialogue, let alone to assess their significance, is a formidable task. Even to speak only of those exchanges that relate to the problem of tradition and nationalism would take us far beyond the scope of this essay. I mention only the better-known examples. The discussion of the "historical specificity" in the previous pages, for example, clearly owes a debt to Tanabe's "logic of the species." Similarly, his idea of

[43] See 天野貞祐 Amano Teiyū, 学生に與ふる書 [Books for students] (Tokyo: Iwanami Shoten, 1939).

[44] ヒューマニズムの現代的意義 [The contemporary meaning of humanism], in *Collected Works of Miki Kiyoshi* 17:492–504.

I-Thou-He relationships within society takes on greater significance when seen in the context of Tosaka Jun's criticism of the I-Thou relation. Or again, his work on cultural morphology needs to be set in the context of Kōyama's original contribution on the topic.

As mentioned earlier, Nishida's notion of tradition was influenced by the writings of Watsuji and by Miki's essay on tradition, as was his view of world and state by Nishitani Keiji's *View of the World, View of the Nation* and by Yamanouchi Tokuryū's *The Polis-Style Shaping of the Human*. Nishida's position on the relationship between the state and the community of believers, and the relationship between the state and the Pure Land can only be appreciated in the light of D. T. Suzuki's *Treatise on Pure Land Thought*. His philosophy of history, as noted earlier, owes much to Suzuki Shigetaka's work on Ranke, as his interest in myth does to the work of Mutai Risaku. His idea of a "people" (民族) needs to be contrasted with Kōsaka Masaaki's *Philosophy of the People* to be fully appreciated. And the list goes on.[45]

When we read Nishida's portrait of "the new person in a global world," it is therefore important that we do not approach the text as the private musings of a retired professor locked in a monologue with himself, but rather as a philosophical vision forged out of an ongoing conversation with his peers and students. Nishida's ideal was for a new kind of individual in a new age and a new culture. The world had already begun the concrete process of becoming one, and the *kokutai* of Japan—like any state aware of its historical mission—was being called to hasten the birth of a global world.[46] He saw this constructive task as the responsibility of the people, imbued with the Japanese spirit and guided by "imperial morality."

The New Global World: Limits and Requirements

This brings us back to the question of the boundaries—cultural, moral, political, and so forth—within which this new global world was to be built up. For a new vision of the world to spread horizontally across cultures and nations, Nishida was convinced that the *kokutai* would have to play a mediating role, and that the mediation would begin with an act of absolute self-negation. In particular, it would have to renounce imperialism and colonialism (both of which only subjectivize Japan, and therefore impede its ability to mediate an objective order), as well as the force of arms and military strategy.[47] Furthermore, the *kokutai* must take care not to destroy regional

---

[45] I have treated some of this in my *Filosofía de la transformación del mundo* (Zamora, Michoacán: El Colegio de Michoacán, 1989), 257–406.

[46] NKZ 11:460; 12:285, 374, 427.

[47] See NKZ 12:338, 341, 349, 373.

traditions or to make unilateral policies regarding other peoples and states.[48] These were not restricted to Nishida's correspondence or expressed only in private. He did not hesitate to state them publicly when the occasion presented itself.

On the positive side, Nishida laid out several requirements for making the global world a reality. They include, as already indicated, the condition that it be something accomplished by the people; that the creative contribution of the individual within the state be encouraged as an essential ingredient in a creative world; and that the variety of regional traditions be protected and actively promoted.[49] In order for the full creativity of history to be unleashed, a plurality of peoples, each with its own traditions, would have to be given due recognition.[50] In this process, the Imperial Throne would stand at the center, but with the proviso that the *kokutai* be defined in terms of a self-negation, and that this self-negation be extended to include a plurality of other *kokutai* or states no less conscious of their own historical mission.[51] This idea of a multiplicity of *kokutai*, according to Matsumoto Masao, was one that Nishida entertained in the final years of his life.[52]

Many more questions remain concerning the meaning of tradition in Nishida's thought. Principal among them are his view of Japan and his view of Japan's role in the construction of the coming global world order. Granted his attachment to the Imperial Throne as the principal motivating force of the Japanese microcosm, it is not at all clear how far he expected the imperially-founded tradition of the country to serve as *the* defining tradition for all of culture, not just in the political arena. And in summoning the historical and the mythological, the immanent and the transcendent, to join hands in explaining the formation of the prototypical *kokutai*, it is not clear how far he meant to extend the role of the Imperial Throne beyond the frontiers of his own country into the Greater East Asia Co-Prosperity Sphere and into the wider world of nations that were to make up the new global world. Immensely important as these questions are, I cannot deal with them here.[53]

[48] See 晩年の西田幾多郎先生と日本の運命 [Nishida Kitarō's late period and the fate of Japan], (Unoke: Memorial Society for Nishida Kitarō, 1962), 19ff.

[49] NKZ 12:432.

[50] NKZ 10:333; 12:378–9.

[51] NKZ 12:409, 417; 10:335.

[52] See 松本正夫 Matsumoto Masao, 西田先生との最後の出会い [A final encounter with Dr. Nishida], in 下村寅太郎 Shimomura Toratarō, ed., 西田幾多郎—同時代の記録 [Nishida Kitarō: A record of his contemporaries] (Tokyo: Iwanami Shoten, 1972), 230. I thank Professor Ueda Shizuteru for drawing my attention to this essay.

[53] See my *Filosofía de la transformación del mundo* for further details on thse questions.

PART THREE

Questioning Modernity

The Problem of Modernity in
the Philosophy of Nishida

Andrew FEENBERG

> "What we call the study of the East today has meant only taking
> the East as an object of study. As yet a profound reflection about the
> Eastern way of thinking, in order to evolve a new method of think-
> ing, has not been undertaken."
>
> —Nishida Kitarō, "The Problem of Japanese Culture."

I N THE 1930S AND EARLY 1940S, Japanese philosophy reflected the political
climate by becoming increasingly nationalistic and authoritarian. With a
few honorable exceptions, the major thinkers, such as Kuki Shūzō,
Tanabe Hajime, and Watsuji Tetsurō, defended Japanese imperialism.[1]
Nishida's ambiguous stance was particularly significant since he was the first
Japanese philosopher able not only to understand the major trends of
Western thought, but also to employ the Western heritage to elaborate an
original philosophy of his own. He is generally considered the founder of
modern Japanese philosophy.

The association between philosophy and nationalist politics was not forgotten after the War and sometimes caused the one to be rejected with the
other, especially on the Left. But philosophers' enthusiasm for government
policy varied widely and Nishida was by no means the worst. As we will see
below, his nationalism was primarily cultural, not military, and he was critical
of racist and totalitarian interpretations of official policy. Nevertheless, his
inner doubts about the War do not appear to have affected his theoretical

The author would like to take this opportunity to acknowledge his gratitude to Arisaka Yōko, Peter
Dale, and Kazashi Nobuo for their advice and help. Needless to say, they bear no responsibility for the
final results.

[1] For the imperialist background to Japanese thought before the War, see Peter Dale, *The
Myth of Japanese Uniqueness* (New York: St. Martin's Press, 1986).

conception until quite late, and his ideas were turned to account by thinkers far more enthusiastic about imperialism than he was.[2] So far as I can tell, he continued to hope until near the end that Japan would emerge from the War as the center of an original politico-cultural sphere. One of his chief political essays of the late 1930s summarized his cultural ambitions for Japan as follows:

> Up to now Westerners thought that their culture was superior to all others, and that human culture advances toward their own form. Other peoples, such as Easterners, are behind and if they advance, they too will acquire the same form. There are even some Japanese who think like this. But...I believe there is something fundamentally different about the East. They [East and West] must complement each other and...achieve the eventual realization of a complete humanity. It is the task of Japanese culture to find such a principle.[3]

Although there is much in this position that is still of interest, it gradually became so mixed up with the fate of Japanese imperialism that today it is difficult to extract its lasting significance from the circumstances of its formulation. The aim of this essay is to explain Nishida's views, and so far as possible to identify his contribution to debates on culture that are far from resolved even to this day.

Recently there has been a revival of interest in a key intellectual event of the War that sheds some light on Nishida's position. In 1942 the theme of cultural originality inspired several seminars, the most famous of which was titled "Overcoming [European] Modernity" (近代の超克).[4] The meeting represented a wide range of views, some irrationalist and anti-Western, others more moderate in their claims for Japanese culture. A number of Nishida's followers were present, including Nishitani Keiji who argued that Japanese culture is an original and authentic spiritual dispensation, comparable with the Western heritage in its ability to support a modern civilization. He thus

---

[2] For an example of Nishida's doubts, see his letter to Harada of June 1942, NKZ 19:199–200.

[3] *The Problem of Japanese Culture*, NKZ 14:404–5. Unless otherwise noted, all translations from the Japanese are by Arisaka Yōko.

[4] The "Overcoming Modernity" seminar papers were published in 文学界 [Literary world], July 1942, and issued as a book the following year by Sōgensha of Tokyo. The participants included, among others, several writers, a famous literary critic (小林秀雄 Kobayashi Hideo) and three of Nishida's students (Shimomura Toratarō, Suzuki Shigetaka, and Nishitani Keiji). For contemporary Japanese evaluations, see 廣松 渉 Hiromatsu Wataru, 浅田 彰 Asada Akira, 市川 浩 Ichikawa Hiroshi, and 柄谷行人 Karatani Kōjin, 「近代の超克」と西田哲学 ["Overcoming modernity and Nishida's philosophy], 季刊思潮 4 (1989); and Hiromatsu Wataru, 「近代の超克」論 [Theories on "Overcoming modernity"] (Tokyo: Kōdansha, 1990).

rejected the claim of European civilization to define modernity for the entire human race. As Harootunian notes, "The problem was to find a way to conceptualize a modernity that was made in Japan, not in the West."[5]

Also in 1942 *Chūōkōron* published several roundtable discussions of Nishida's students on "The World-Historical Standpoint and Japan."[6] These discussions reflect Nishida's simultaneous defense of traditional Japanese culture *and* affirmation of modern scientific-technical civilization. This is a pattern familiar from German reactionary modernism, which, as Jeffrey Herf explains, succeeded after World War I in reconceptualizing science and technology as dimensions of a specifically German cultural heritage, and thus salvaged them from the traditional romantic critique of materialist civilization in the West.[7] However, in Nishida's own writings the pattern remains abstract, unrelated to the Nietzschean and nihilist themes of his German contemporaries, and compatible with a variety of different political positions that were in fact explored by his students.

His students' comments in *Chūōkōron* concretize this pattern in terms of the ideas of Ernst Jünger and other German reactionaries. They celebrate the fusion of *moralische Energie* and modern technology that characterizes wartime Japan. Rather than worrying about the justification of the War, the participants express enthusiasm for the moral and aesthetic dimension of total mobilization. They see the struggle in China as a contest of cultures in which Japan will forcibly liberate Asia from the West. In their defense, it might be said that the participants were endorsing an imaginary war, but this is the common mode of engagement in real warfare in an age of ideology. It is fair to say that in these conversations, militarist nationalism acquired a paradoxically anti-imperialist aura from Nishida's philosophy of culture.

The idea of "overcoming modernity" foreshadows strangely the later attempts of other non-European intellectuals in the anticolonialist movement to declare their spiritual independence from the European sources of their modernity. Today it is cited with increasing frequency as a precedent for the remarkable flowering of theories of Japanese exceptionalism (*nihonjinron*, 日本人論) in the 1960s and 1970s. The *nihonjinron* owe a subterranean debt

[5] H. D. Harootunian, "Visible Discourses/Invisible Ideologies," in Masao Miyoshi and H. D. Harootunian, eds. *Postmodernism and Japan* (Durham: Duke University Press, 1989). See also Najita Tetsuo and H. D. Harootunian, "Japanese Revolt Against the West," in P. Duus, ed., *The Cambridge History of Japan* (Cambridge: Cambridge University Press, 1988), vol. 6.

[6] Participants were Kōsaka Masaaki, Kōyama Iwao, Suzuki Shigetaka, and Nishitani Keiji. For these meetings see Sakai Naoki, "Modernity and Its Critique: The Problem of Universalism and Particularism," in *Postmodernism and Japan*, 105ff.

[7] Jeffrey Herf, *Reactionary Modernism: Technology, Culture, and Politics in Weimar and the Third Reich* (Cambridge: Cambridge University Press, 1984).

to these predecessors, but much of interest in the earlier formulations has been lost along with the more embarrassing traces of nationalism.

It is important to distinguish Nishida's rather complex dialectical universalism from the particularism of these various expressions of cultural nationalism. Writing before World War II, Nishida was one of many thinkers who attempted a positive philosophical expression of Japan's contribution to a world culture he experienced as still in the making. Optimistically, he believed that "a point of union between Eastern and Western culture can be sought in Japan."[8] And he argued, against all forms of isolationism, "To become global, Eastern culture must not stop at its own specificity but rather it must shed a new light on Western culture and a new world culture must be created."[9]

In this context, Western culture means, of course, the specific forms of rationality associated with modern science and technology; the cultural synthesis at which Nishida aimed involved investing these with new meaning derived from the Eastern tradition. But for the *nihonjinron* written after the War, the historical possibilities have been foreclosed. The highest expression of Japanese culture is now the production of difference, particularity, in those regions of life still untouched by scientific-technical rationality. Thus what was originally put forward as a hypothesis about the formation of modern world culture, in which Japan would be Europe's equal and assimilate its science and technology, is today expressed in terms of the ethnically unique deviation of Japan from universal European models. That less ambitious project has less sweeping implications.[10]

Despite the obvious questions that can be raised about the culturalist enterprise of the *nihonjinron*, they bring into focus the inadequacy of theories that uncritically identify modernization with Westernization. This aspect of his philosophy is quite contemporary, and has brought about a "return" to Nishida on the part of some Japanese intellectuals who have found anticipations of a Japanese "post-modernity" in his thought, while others worry about the renewal of nationalism this return appears to imply.[11]

[8] Nishida Kitarō, "The Problem of Japanese Culture," in W. T. de Bary, ed., *Sources of Japanese Tradition* (New York: Columbia University Press, 1958), 2:365.

[9] NKZ 14:407.

[10] As Sakai Naoki writes, "Contrary to what has been advertised by both sides, universalism and particularism reinforce and supplement each other; they are never in real conflict; they need each other and have to seek to form a symmetrical, mutually supporting relationship by every means in order to avoid a dialogic encounter which would necessarily jeopardize their reputedly secure and harmonized monologic worlds" ("Modernity and Its Critique," 105).

[11] For an accessible example of these new approaches, see Nakamura Yūjirō's interesting article, "Nishida: Le Premier Philosophe Original au Japon," *Critique* 39 (1983): 428-9. For the major survey of Nishida and his school in a Western language, see Ōhashi Ryōsuke, *Die Philosophie der Kyoto-Schule: Texte und Einführung* (Freiburg: Karl Albers Verlag, 1990).

EXPERIENCE AND SCIENCE

Like other literate non-Western peoples, the Japanese were easily able to understand scientific-technical rationality and the material advantages it gave the West. The contradiction between that form of rationality and their own cultural tradition troubled them deeply. Should they resist modernity altogether and remain loyal to their past? Would they, on the contrary, have to abandon their way of life to acquire the technical means of resistance to the West? Or could they adopt science and technology for practical purposes such as defense while retaining their traditional spiritual values?[12]

Each of these questions implies a naive exteriority, in the first case, of a nation to its history and the encounters that irreversibly mark its destiny; in the second, of a people to its culture, which cannot be dropped like an old glove; and in the third, of a spiritual tradition to the material life of society. Nishida rejected all these illusory solutions and argued instead that Japan could forge a specifically Japanese modernity out of a synthesis of Eastern and Western elements. He hoped to accommodate modernity to Japanese tradition not by rejecting Western science but by encompassing it in a concept of experience that grew naturally out of his culture.

Nishida understood modernity on fairly standard modern terms as the emergence of rational inquiry in opposition to doctrine-bound traditions and prejudices. Since Western thought advanced through rigorous attention to facts, any similar Japanese characteristics would constitute an indigenous potential for modernization. Accordingly, Nishida believed that the Japanese orientation toward "the true facts of things"—experience in its pure state—was proto-modern even before the encounter with the West.[13]

But Nishida's understanding of experience was radically different from the prevailing Western view. As Arisaka Yōko has argued, the Japanese idea of experience is neither empiricist nor romantic.[14] Empiricism eliminates the "secondary qualities" of the object and abstracts purified conceptual entities such as "sense data" or "brute facts" from the immediate content of experience, while romanticism calls for a return from conceptual activity to pure immediacy. But for the Japanese, experience is a paradoxical return to a kind of *cultural* immediate. It involves refining the web of associations to a univer-

---

[12] The latter position characterized forward-looking thinking in the nineteenth century in China under the slogan, *Chung-hsueh wei-t'i, hsi-hsueh wei-yung* (中学爲體, 西学爲用 "Chinese learning for fundamental principles, Western learning for practical applications"); but that balance was never achieved. For this earlier experience see Ssu-yu Teng and John K. Fairbanks, *China's Response to the West* (Cambridge: Harvard University Press, 1954), part 3.

[13] "The Problem of Japanese Culture," 352.

[14] Arisaka Yōko, "Haiku, Nishida, and Heidegger: Toward a New Metaphysics of Experience" (1993 manuscript).

sally shared remainder. Haiku, for example, are often said to be concerned with the experience of nature. But in fact they articulate the natural world poetically in all its rich emotional and historical associations without distinguishing a purely material content from the contributions of culture and the subject.

This concept of experience is incompatible with Western naturalism. It makes sense to consider nature, abstracted from culture and history, as the foundation of experience only if the object can be conceived outside of any connection to a subject. Nishida claimed, on the contrary, that not nature but experience is the ontological basis of reality. In his account, the original "pure" experience is "as yet neither subject nor object" and in it "knowledge and its object are one."[15] Undifferentiated into subject and object, it does not consist in material things, but neither is it individual and psychological. Experience in this sense forms a shared realm of intersubjective meanings. It is exterior and culturally specific, "a kind of public field," not inward and universal like the idea of experience in the West.[16] Yet like the latter, it retains a unique foundational pathos in the context of an absolute historicism such as Nishida was eventually to elaborate.[17]

Nishida's fame dates from the publication in 1911 of his first book, *An Inquiry into the Good.* It was in this remarkable book that he proposed his concept of an all-embracing field of experience. Nishida's later writings suggest that this concept and its various successors in his thought express a peculiarly Japanese approach, not in any exclusive sense, but simply as products of the natural sequence of development of Japanese culture. He believed that Japanese philosophy was destined to raise this feature of Japanese culture to universality much as the natural sciences had universalized Western culture.

In what did this universalization consist? In fact, in the presentation of Japanese ideas in Western dress. This becomes clear from the first page of Nishida's maiden effort, for he begins by appropriating William James's concept of "pure experience" to explain his own idea. But despite this similar starting point, real differences divide Nishida and James. For example, while pure experience for James was simply an explanatory category, in Nishida it also sometimes appears to signify a version of Buddhist "no-mind," a particular way of relating to experience. Here pure experience risks regressing to a special psychological attitude, a kind of secular enlightenment.[18]

[15] NKZ 1:1.

[16] Nishida Kitarō, *Fundamental Problems of Philosophy,* trans. by D. Dilworth (Tokyo: Sophia University Press, 1970), 186.

[17] NKZ 14:410.

[18] Andrew Feenberg and Arisaka Yōko, "Experiential Ontology: The Origins of the Nishida Philosophy in the Doctrine of Pure Experience," *International Philosophical Quarterly* 30/2 (1990): 183–5.

Although Nishida's borrowings from James call into question the authenticity of his notion of a specifically Japanese culture of experience, his procedure is less absurd than it seems. For Nishida, James represented a quasi-universal logic of modernity with which Japanese philosophy would have to come to terms in its break with traditional Eastern modes of discourse. Yet the goal was not indiscriminate Westernization. It was precisely James's critique of Western metaphysics that made his thought a suitable vehicle for modernizing Japanese philosophy. As Whitehead remarked, James did not so much continue the Western philosophical tradition as introduce a sharp break in its continuity comparable with the Cartesian revolution in scope and significance: he "clears the stage of the old paraphernalia" in harmony with profound transformations taking place throughout European culture.[19] Nishida believed that these innovations opened the doors to a broader international participation in modernity. In the early 20th century, James was not a bad place to look for access to this emerging world culture.

The oxymoron, "quasi-universal," is thus appropriate in describing Nishida's evaluation of contemporary Western philosophy. While he recognized its cultural limitations, he nevertheless rejected the idea of an external critique of modernity from the standpoint of a construct of a supposedly Eastern alternative. Instead he chose to plunge into Western philosophy in the confidence that the originality of his peculiarly Japanese insight would shine through. As Shimomura explains, he took "Western philosophy as a mediation to be used in challenging Western philosophy itself."[20]

Nishida's confidence was not misplaced, but the operation in which he was engaged was far more difficult than he imagined in 1911. For over thirty years he was occupied in the construction of one after another version of his system, none of which ever satisfied him. In any case, his choice enabled him to steer a new course between both imitative Westernization and Eastern exoticism.[21]

[19] Alfred North Whitehead, *Science in the Modern World* (New York: Macmillan, 1925), 205.

[20] Shimomura Toratarō, "The Modernisation of Japan, with Special Reference to Philosophy," *Philosophical Studies of Japan* 7 (1966): 16.

[21] This aspect of his achievement is lost, however, in much recent scholarship. Because Nishida attempted to reformulate a putatively Japanese worldview in the language of Western philosophy, students of his thought often read it as an elaborately encoded version of traditional Mahāyāna metaphysics. See Robert Carter, *The Nothingness Beyond God: An Introduction to the Philosophy of Nishida Kitarō* (New York: Paragon House, 1989). While decoding Nishida's writings in Eastern terms can be useful, unfortunately this approach has also contributed to the widespread impression that Nishida was an anti-modern, traditionalist thinker; but in fact, like most of his generation, he evaluated modern science and civilization positively on the whole (a view, be it said, that is not incompatible with a sympathy for Buddhism).

In Nishida's later work, his already cultural concept of experience became the basis for a historicist ontology. He argued that insofar as the knowing subject is a human individual, it is not only a knower but also an actor, related not only to things but also to history. If one sees knowing as more than a contemplative encounter of a cogito with truth, but also as a practical social activity, then it is plausible to ask what else this activity entails besides pure knowledge. In question is not merely the validity of theory nor the goal of the activity it orients, but even more its place in a lifeform. Nishida called this his "fundamental idea":

> Ordinarily, we think of the material world, the biological world, and the historical world as being separate. But in my view the historical world is the most concrete, and the material and biological worlds are abstractions. Thus, if we grasp the historical world, we grasp reality itself.[22]

Today such formulations resonate with the notion that the universality of Reason is an illusion. Following Foucault, feminist theory, and constructivist sociology of knowledge, a case can be made that our science is really only one "ethnoscience" among others.[23] However, in his historical situation, Nishida could not simply call for a full-scale return to ethnoscientific traditions without surrendering to reactionary obscurantism.[24] Nativist ideas of "Japanese science" (日本科学) seemed to him an excuse to resist the sincere confrontation with the cultural achievements of the West required by the globalizing process of modernity. Instead of proposing a return to an ethnically rooted "local knowledge," Nishida attempted to put science in its "place" in a historical framework that reflected the values of his culture. Science was to be given a new meaning in this context, not merely employed to secure material wealth and national independence. Such ideas were widely accessible to Japanese writers and intellectuals, caught in the midst of a mod-

---

[22] NKZ 14:408.

[23] Sandra Harding, "Is Science Multicultural? Challenges, Resources, Opportunities, Uncertainties," in T. Goldberg, ed., *Multiculturalism: A Reader* (London: Basil Blackwell, 1994).

[24] A Western reader who wants to understand the liberating impact of modern science in Japan (as opposed to the fear of its military technology) should look at Sugita Genpaku's famous book, *Dawn of Western Science in Japan*, trans. by R. Matsumoto and E. Kiyooka (Tokyo: Hokuseido Press, 1969). Sugita recounts his experience (in 1771!) examining the dissected body of an executed criminal while comparing Chinese and Dutch anatomy books. All that he had been taught as a doctor was suddenly overthrown, and he devoted the rest of his life to translating the Dutch book in which he had found the truth his eyes confirmed. Naturally, this does not exclude a later recovery of a different level of meaning from Chinese anatomy once it is no longer taken literally as an image of bodily organs.

ernizing movement they lived simultaneously as a response to both the Universal (scientific truth) and the Particular (Western power).

Nishida sought the principle of an absolute historicism in the underlying assumptions of Eastern culture. However, in turning to these Eastern sources, he believed himself to be advancing forward rather than backward in accordance with the tendencies of modern science. This apparent paradox makes sense if we share Nishida's view of the revolutionary character of modern science along lines already anticipated less self-consciously in his earlier appropriation of James. He believed that recent physics and mathematics had already broken with the West's own most parochial limitations, such as Christian transcendentalism and the substantialism inherited from the Greeks. But these traditional views hung on in the historical sciences, where they would inevitably be overcome as other cultures appropriated modernity.

Eastern thought was uniquely qualified to contribute to this revolution in historical understanding. Like Greek thought it defined reality in this-worldly terms, but it lacked the substantialist prejudice of the Greeks. Through its intervention, the historical world was to be swept up in the same sort of whirlwind as nature; not Aristotelian "things" or Cartesian "cogitos," not even Newtonian "laws," but tumultuous processes of conflictual structuration operate over the abyss of nothingness. To Nishida, Japanese modernity promised just such an up-to-date vision.

DIALECTICS OF PLACE

Under Hegel's influence, Nishida's argument for this approach took the form of a dialectical system. As a good Hegelian, he believed that "the truth is the whole." Isolated parts are "abstract moments" of the "concrete universal," i.e., the totality to which they belong. His system began with the abstract parts and worked toward the reconstruction of the whole by continually shifting the point of view to broaden the context of explanation, moving from abstractions to the lifeforms that animate them. This method yielded a dialectical progression of levels of knowledge, reflection, action, and experience, each of which represented a more or less abstract dimension of the concrete totality of experience; that totality itself was conceptualized, however, in a more Heideggerian than Hegelian style as the absolute activity of presence.[25] At this highest level, Nishida located something he called the "place of

[25] That this similiarity is no accident is argued in Graham Parkes, "Heidegger and Japanese Thought: How Much Did He Know, and When Did He Know It?", in C. Macann, ed., *Heidegger: Critical Assessments* (New York: Routledge, 1992).

absolute nothingness," a philosophical concept derived from his earlier concept of pure experience and retaining its Buddhist allusion.

Here, schematically presented, are the four basic levels of Nishida's dialectic:[26]

1. Judgement, or knowledge of nature: the known abstracted from the knower.

2. Self-consciousness, or the psychological self of knowledge and action: the knower/doer abstracted from culture.

3. The world of meaning or values as ground of action: the self considered in its cultural significance.

4. "Absolute nothingness": experience as a field of immediate subject-object unity underlying culture, action, and knowledge, and making them possible as objectifications of this prior unity.

Nishida called each level a *basho* (場所, "place" or "field"). Within the various *basho*, he distinguished between an objective and a subjective aspect. What is subjective at one level appears as objective at the next level, and vice versa. For example, the subjective side of the level of judgement is the "field of predicates," the universal concepts employed in describing things. To these predicates corresponds the specific objectivity of the Aristotelian thing of which they are predicated. But what is this thing? Its individuality is inconceivable from the standpoint of a judgement that works exclusively with universals.

Only an individual can relate to an individual. An adequate approach to the thing known requires us to go beyond the horizon of logical predication to identify a knowing thing, a subject that knows. This transition marks the passage to self-consciousness, the next level of the dialectic. The objective side of the dialectic of predicates—the thing—is now thematized as the knowing subject which transcends its predicates through embracing them on the field of knowledge. The predicates which first inhered in the thing now inhere in the consciousness that knows them. We have in a sense moved from Aristotle to Kant.

But the dialectical progression continues. As we saw in the last section, the knowing subject is more than a knower; it is a human being necessarily situated in a cultural world. "'Knowing' itself," Nishida wrote, "is already a social and historical event."[27] Paradoxically, although knowing is a culturally

---

[26] The originator of this sort of systematic interpretation of Nishida is 高山岩男 Kōyama Iwao, 西田哲学 [Nishida philosophy] (Tokyo: Iwanami Shoten, 1935). See also Abe Masao, "Nishida's Philosophy of 'Place'," *International Philosophical Quarterly* 28/4 (1988).

[27] *Fundamental Problems of Philosophy*, 96.

situated activity, culture appears arbitrary to it. Mere facts cannot determine the values that move the person to action, nor discriminate between the good and the bad, the beautiful and the ugly. This is the function of culture, which can only be explained by a theory of the will in its relation to meanings. At that level consciousness appears to be determined by moral and aesthetic values which embrace it and provide the wider context for its actions. The subject—consciousness—becomes object in the framework of the cultural system of which it is a manifestation or "self-determination." This notion refers us not to a scientific theory of culture, but to a cultural theory of action.

At each level, Nishida's dialectic moves toward greater concreteness, away from abstract knowledge toward "existence," toward an experience so familiar we constantly overlook it in our attempts to categorize and explain. That experience is the immediate unity of subject and object in action. In most Western thought this unity is regarded as the effacement of consciousness in mere reflex. Philosophy, as a form of knowledge, quite naturally considers the objects of knowledge to be the primary reality. But for Nishida, the reverse is true: the engagement of the actor with the environment is more fundamental than cognition. Knowledge must dethrone itself and learn to see through the eyes of action.

That vision is not thoughtless, but the concept of self-consciousness is inadequate to represent it. This is another reason why Nishida's cultural theory moves beyond the stage of self-consciousness to a unifying intuition that is neither a knowing nor a doing as we usually conceive them, but the knowledge implicit in action itself. At that level, we find ourselves again in the world of pure experience, in which meaning and being are joined in cultural immediacy prior to the abstract distinction of fact and value, situation and will.

This "action-intuition" (行為的直観) is similar to Heidegger's concept of "circumspection" (*Umsicht*) in that it, too, aims to liberate the subject-object relation from the limitations of rationalistic models. That means, among other things, overcoming a voluntaristic view of action as mere implementation of preconceived plans in pursuit of subjective ends. And like Heidegger, Nishida rejected the privilege of knowledge over the culturally defined world of action in which it finds its roots, and instead asserted the relative priority of culture over knowledge.

However, Nishida believed that Heidegger's approach was insufficiently dynamic. He claimed that "Even though Heidegger's idea of existence is historical, it is without movement or action."[28] Here Nishida is at least partially unfair. Heidegger undoubtedly attained the standpoint of action, but it is true that he concerned himself only with the circumspective understanding of things as objects of practice and failed to grasp the self-constitution of the

---

[28] *Fundamental Problems of Philosophy*, 40.

human subject in interaction with the Other. Nishida's philosophy, unlike Heidegger's, focused on the objectivity of the acting subject, its essential situatedness in a "place" (*basho*) out of which it must act and in which it is acted on and shaped.

This focus points beyond hermeneutics toward dialectics. But here, too, Nishida was unsatisfied with Western formulations. He believed that Hegel, while developing all the basic categories of dialectics, had remained stubbornly at the level of self-consciousness:

> Hegel sought reason behind reality rather than seeking reality beyond reason. In this his dialectical method was subjective and fell into mere formalism in trying to understand concrete reality....We should not understand reality through logical formulas. Rather, reason must be interpreted historically as one aspect of our lives. Instead of understanding Hegel's logic in terms of its developmental process, it should be understood as an abstraction from concrete life as the self-determination of nothingness.[29]

In sum, Nishida introduced action-intuition into Hegel's dialectic and reconceptualized it from the standpoint of practice, while introducing dialectics into the hermeneutics of historical practice he had found in Dilthey and Heidegger. As he put it elsewhere: "In the true historical world, the world of true objectivity, the approach to things and the approach to the Thou have become one."[30]

The concept of history that emerges from this unusual synthesis is a kind of anticipation of systems theory summed up in the notion of a process in which the "formed" becomes the "forming." Nishida deconstructed history into various circular processes of self-production and self-transformation. The subjects whose actions create history are themselves historical products. Values are at once objective historical givens and dynamic principles of action. So understood, history cannot be reduced to a concatenation of stable nature-like things, because it is composed ultimately of actions. Knowledge of the natural scientific sort cannot comprehend this historical world, which must be grasped instead by dialectics.[31]

So far in this exposition of his system I have emphasized the relationship between Nishida and the Western thinkers who influenced him and through

---

[29] NKZ 12:80.

[30] *Fundamental Problems of Philosophy*, 95 (translation modified).

[31] *Fundamental Problems of Philosophy*, 216ff. For a different reading of Nishida's conception of history (and the only other one I have found in English), see Huh Woo-Sung, "The Philosophy of History in the 'Later' Nishida: A Philosophic Turn," *Philosophy East and West* 40/3 (1990).

whom his ideas become comprehensible. However, as with James, here too Nishida's thought cannot be reduced to its Western sources because the Eastern tradition to some extent shaped his use of them. This is especially apparent in the final stage of Nishida's dialectic. This stage, the "place of absolute nothingness," is not some sort of mystical intuition, but it is indeed difficult to understand without reference to Buddhism.[32] It was here that Nishida most clearly attempted to validate his notion of a unique contribution of the East to modern culture. I can only sketch an approach to this difficult concept, taking off from the historical and cultural problems that are my principal concern.

There is a dimension of Nishida's view of history that transcends mere theory of practice toward existential realization. In Nishida, actors necessarily posit an environment against which they must assert themselves to live, yet as they express their life they objectify themselves in the struggle and become the environment of each other. This is the "identity of opposites": "Action means negation of the other, and means the will to make the other [an expression of] oneself. It means that the Self wants to be the world. But it also means, on the other hand, that the Self denies itself and becomes a part of the world."[33] "Acting," in sum, "is essentially 'being acted'."[34]

The Leibnizian image of a community of monads each reflecting the world in itself suggested a model of this dialectic of self and other.

Each existential monad originates itself by expressing itself; and yet it expresses itself by negating itself and expressing the world. The monads are thus co-originating, and form the world through their mutual negation. The monads are the world's own perspectives; they form the world interexpressively through their own mutual negation and affirmation. Conversely, the concrete matrix of historical actuality that exists and moves through itself enfolds these monadic perspectives within itself.[35]

The objectivity of history thus arises from the mutual perceptions of the individuals engaged within it. Put another way, its objectivity is simply the necessarily reciprocal relations of these actions because actor and object have become perspectives on each other rather than distinct species.

---

[32] Although he does not cite Nishida in this connection, Nishitani's interpretation of *śūnyatā* in *Religion and Nothingness* could almost be a commentary on the Buddhist background to Nishida's concept of absolute nothingness. For further explanation, see also his *Nishida Kitarō*.

[33] *Intelligibility and the Philosophy of Nothingness,* trans. by R. Schinzinger (Honolulu: East-West Center Press, 1958), 171.

[34] *Intelligibility and the Philosophy of Nothingness,* 186.

[35] *Last Writings: Nothingness and the Religious Worldview,* trans. by D. Dilworth (Honolulu: University of Hawaii Press, 1987), 58.

The inner realization of this truth is the existential discovery of the "field" (*basho*) on which self and other deploy their identity and difference. When the self identifies concretely with that field, it "discovers the self-transforming matrix of history in its own bottomless depths."[36] That field is a scene of struggle understood in traditional Buddhist rather than Western individualist terms: one plays one's role without reserve but also with an immediate sense of the system formed by one's interactions with other individuals. The more one identifies with the system as a whole, the more one is properly in one's own place within it, and vice versa. This peculiar double structure of action, operating as an ontological postulate, provides an original image of the concrete totality as the "place of nothingness."

Nishida's conclusion is profoundly paradoxical. He founded an absolute historicism that encompassed modern science in an account of experience derived from the Eastern tradition. That account is itself modern in the sense that it responds to the thoroughgoing epistemological atheism that underlies twentieth-century science and philosophy. Yet in demonstrating that history is the ultimate reality, Nishida brought back the science question from a different angle. As I will argue in the next section, his own Eastern logic forbade a nativist regression. Scientific knowledge, as the culture and action of the West, cannot be dismissed, but must be encountered authentically in the struggle for modernity. The dialectical system was intended to engage Japan in that struggle.

In sum, Nishida grasped the cultural connections that threaten scientific self-certainty and the social reciprocities that undermine subjective autonomy, and yet affirm science and subjectivity. He refused the transcendence of culture in knowledge without adopting a comforting relativism that would at least allow disengagement from the hegemony of Western science. Nishida seems to have been determined to leave himself no resting place. This ambivalence is related to Japan's difficult place in the system of world culture.

CULTURAL SELF-AFFIRMATION

Nishida's philosophy of culture attempted to vindicate the self-assertion of Japan as an Asian nation against European world hegemony. The new order emerging from the War would restore Japan's historic "world mission," lost so long as "Asian nations were suppressed by European imperialism and viewed from a colonial standpoint."[37]

---

[36] *Last Writings*, 84.
[37] NKZ 12:429.

All modern cultures, including the Japanese, are equal, according to Nishida, in the sense that each has a contribution to make to an emerging world culture.[38] There can be no single universal replacement for national culture, for "when they lose their specificity they cease to be cultures"; but the uniqueness of each culture does not authorize "a merely abstract advance in an individual direction." "A true world culture will be formed only by various cultures preserving their own respective viewpoints, but simultaneously developing themselves through global mediation."[39] All modern cultures must participate in a fruitful intermingling and mutual contamination. World culture consists in a field of dialogue and conflict rather than a specific substantive way of life, comparable to the existing cultures.

> Each people stands on its own historical ground and has its own world mission, and that is how each nation possesses a historical life. When I say that each nation must realize itself while transcending itself and creating a world culture, I mean that each nation must realize itself through its own particular culture. It is in this way that particular cultures emerge from the foundation of history and constitute a world culture. In such a world each national culture expresses its own unique historical life and, at the same time, through their world-historical missions they all unite to form one world.[40]

This dialectic of world culture is consistent with Nishida's conception of action. The Eastern engagement with the West embraced a deeper collaboration under the surface conflict; it was to be a productive transformation of modernity with global consequences.

Because modern cultures all share science, they now subsist generally in the "truth" and can no longer be described as mere errors or divagations. But what then explains their multiplicity? Nishida's historicist ontology promised a "multicultural" bridge between national particularity and rational universality. The categories of the various stages of his dialectic can each be employed to describe the unique emphasis of a cultural type. Cultures consist in horizons of thought and action, paradigms or "archetypes," in which one or another category is unilaterally absolutized.[41] National struggles manifest conflicts between the diverse conceptual frameworks of social ontology at the level of whole peoples and their ways of life. In sum, ontological and cultural categories are mutually translatable. Presumably, cultures communicate and

---

[38] NKZ 12:267–8.

[39] *Fundamental Problems of Philosophy*, 254.

[40] NKZ 12:428.

[41] "The Problem of Japanese Culture," 353–4.

complete each other through the processes of exchange and discussion in which ontological visions are elaborated.

This view certainly owed something to Hegel's *Phenomenology*, although Nishida refused the final synthesis at which Hegel was traditionally said to aim. In this regard, Nishida was actually closer to contemporary Hegel scholarship, which argues that the ultimate *Begriff* does not resolve contradictions metaphysically in a substantive totality but embraces them methodologically, maintaining the opposition between its terms. Such anti-metaphysical readings of Hegel respond to skeptical and neo-Kantian currents in contemporary thought.[42]

Nishida's reasons for rejecting synthesis were quite different: his emphasis on action excluded a purely conceptual resolution of the contradictions. This would explain why his writings do not offer third terms but rather endlessly alternating emphases among the fragmented field of historical and cultural contradictions and their corresponding action positions in the world system.

Alongside this affirmation of multiplicity, Nishida defended the apparently contrary notion that Japanese culture has a global character. Since modern culture is scientific in character, Japan's global mission cannot be merely religious or aesthetic as is sometimes supposed, but must include a unique intellectual content, a "logic," with the sort of universal value attributed to other achievements of modern thought.[43] This logic was Japan's culturally specific appropriation of modernity in terms of the "identity of contradictions" as described in the previous section.

This is the same logic that underlay Japan's long history of flexibility and assimilation of alien influences. In ancient times, Japan absorbed Chinese culture, and so today will it assimilate Western culture, serving thereby as a global point of junction.[44] According to Nishida, the "formlessness" or "emptiness" of Japanese culture enables it to harbor unresolved contradictions in itself. This formlessness reflects at the historico-cultural level the philosophical notions of pure experience and absolute nothingness. Here these apparently abstruse philosophical categories turn out to signify a unique cultural identity and role.

It is difficult to be sure what Nishida thought of the function of philosophy in modern life, but it seems to serve as a cultural crossroads, an essential point of translation and communication in an era characterized by intensifying interactions between peoples. Nishida saw his own thought as the prod-

[42] Robert Pippin, *Modernism as a Philosophical Problem* (Cambridge, Mass.: Basil Blackwell, 1991), 66–79.

[43] "The Problem of Japanese Culture," 363.

[44] NKZ 14:417.

uct of the confrontation of cultures in the new era of world culture. It did not offer a final synthesis but a language in terms of which the philosopher can be at home in a multiplicity of forms of thought. Nishida's ambition was not to resolve these contradictions, but to devise a method for thinking each moment in its relation to its Other. In this his philosophy reflected the emptiness that opened Japan to universal experience.[45]

Unfortunately, Nishida's conception of cultural self-affirmation seems to have gone well beyond the search for fruitful dialogue and embraced military struggle as a positive moment. In conclusion, I must discuss this disturbing aspect of his thought. This discussion is, however, limited by the confusion that surrounds Nishida's role in the War; he does not appear to have had any official or even semi-official post, and the texts from the period are so abstract they might be accommodated to rather different political positions. Hence the inconclusive controversy between those who hold Nishida, as a leading intellectual, in some measure responsible for Japanese imperialism, and those who see him as a moderate who dissociated himself from the worst ideological excesses of the time.[46] Nevertheless, I will argue that his late texts point at least to provisional conclusions, which I put forward below in the hope of provoking further research and discussion.

GREEKS OR JEWS?

Hegel argued that war is a means of spiritual self-affirmation for modern nations. Today this view has become shocking, but for several generations Hegel's doctrine merely articulated the common sense of nations in Europe and North America. Recall, for example, the vulgar Hegelianism of our own concept of "Manifest Destiny." In a later time, conservative Japanese philosophers defended war on just such Hegelian grounds without understanding that it was too late in the day to launch a colonial enterprise and carve out a sphere of influence of the old type.

It seems that Nishida shared this view. Several future national leaders (Konoe, Kido) attended his classes and in 1941 he was even invited to give a speech to the emperor.[47] It is not surprising, then, that he was consulted by the government. He opposed war with the U.S. and he emphasized the

---

[45] NKZ 14:407.

[46] Hiromatsu, *Theories on "Overcoming Modernity,"* 207–8; Pierre Lavelle, "The Political Thought of Nishida Kitarō," *Monumenta Nipponica* 49/2 (1994); Yusa Michiko, "Nishida and the Question of Nationalism," *Monumenta Nipponica* 46/2 (1991).

[47] "On the Philosophy of History" (NKZ 12:267–72). This was a great honor but not quite the union of philosopher and statesman a Straussian might imagine. Other prominent intellectuals were invited to address the emperor on what was essentially a ceremonial occasion.

importance of cosmopolitan cultural interaction to an unusual degree, but otherwise his occasional comments on world politics appear to follow the conventional opinion of the day.[48] Although he never explained how to achieve it, he supported Japanese hegemony in Asia and he was an enthusiastic advocate of the emperor system. Indeed, for Nishida the imperial house lay at the center of both the political and cultural systems. As such, he called it the "identity of contradictions," situating it mysteriously beyond the reach of his own concept of action as a system of reciprocities.[49] This would seem to absolutize the state as an expression of the emperor's will; only the sustained ambiguity of politics and culture in Nishida's thought distances it somewhat from the crude statist nationalism of the day by signifying that will as a place (*basho*) of nothingness without particular content.

The flavor of his position, and much of the reason for our difficulty in evaluating it today, is clear from the following thoroughly symptomatic passage from his speech to the emperor:

> Today, due to the extensive development of global transportation, the world has become one. Today's nationalism must be conceptualized from this standpoint. It is not a nationalism in which each nation turns in on itself, but rather in which each nation secures a position of its own within the world, that is to say, each nation must become globally aware. When diverse peoples enter into such a world-historical (世界史的) relation, there may be conflicts among them such as we see today, but this is only natural. The most world-historical nation must then serve as a center to stabilize this turbulent period. What do I mean by a nation having a global character? It means that this nation embraces holism yet at the same time does not deny the individual and, indeed, takes individual creation as its medium. Today we usually conceive of individualism and holism as opposed to one another, but by itself, individualism is outdated, and any holism which denies the individual is also a thing of the past.[50]

In the context of the ongoing War these remarks can, but need not necessarily, be read as a euphemistic defense of Japanese imperialism, yet at the same time Nishida also appears to contest totalitarianism in the name of the creativity of independent individuals and cultures.

On reading Nishida's war writings, the comparison with Heidegger immediately springs to mind. But this comparison is misleading. It is true

[48] See his "Principles for a New World Order," NKZ 12.

[49] NKZ 12:336. In Heideggerian terms, this is to ignore the ontological difference and to identify Being itself with a particular being. As we know, Heidegger himself was not above making a similar mistake.

[50] NKZ 12:270–1.

that, like Heidegger in his Nazi phase, Nishida could be heard repeating imperialist slogans. But unlike Heidegger, whose "private National Socialism" was expressed for a time in the official language of the Nazi state he represented as a government official, the private thinker Nishida always qualified offensive expressions of nationalism from his own culturalist standpoint. Here, for example, is a passage in which, without actually questioning the Imperial Way ideology that justified the Pacific War, Nishida attempted to reformulate it culturally.

> Japan's formative principle must become the formative principle of the world as well.... But it is most dangerous to subjectivize Japan. That merely militarizes the Imperial Way (皇道) and transforms it into imperialism (帝国主義化).... In contrast we must contribute to the world by discovering our own principle of self-formation in the depths of our historical development; that principle is the identity of contradictions. This is the authentic...Imperial Way. This is the true meaning of "All the world under one roof" (八紘一宇).[51]

There is an even deeper distinction to be made between Nishida and Heidegger in terms of their historical situation. Although Heidegger claimed to look toward the future, he was unable to give any positive content to his notion of a distinctively authentic modernity, and eventually he fell victim to the deluded hope that Germany could be the agent for his reactionary program of affirming man against technology and mass society. This was the basis of his Nazi adventure, to which he never counterposed another comprehensible, much less credible, alternative.[52] Heidegger's later thought of Being offers an oracular discourse that strives nobly to reenchant the world but it falls far short of a concrete alternative.[53]

By contrast, as a non-Westerner in a newly developed country Nishida seems to have experienced no particular anxiety about scientific-technical progress. He was untouched by the gloomy mood fostered by Weber, Jünger, and Spengler, and looked hopefully to the emergence of an alternative modernity defined in the rich terms of his own living Japanese culture.

[51] NKZ 12:341. Pierre Lavelle ("The Political Thought of Nishida Kitarō") dismisses this apparently anti-war statement and assimilates Nishida's views to the moderate ultranationalism of the Konoe faction on the grounds that anti-imperialist rhetoric was common even in the military at the time. I believe this goes too far toward disambiguating the ambiguities Nishida appears to have purposely introduced into his public statements.

[52] Herf, *Reactionary Modernism*, 109ff.

[53] Unbelievably, Heidegger's last interview expresses his conviction that "Only a God can save us" from modern technology. For a thorough study of Heidegger's views on technology, see Michael Zimmerman, *Heidegger's Confrontation with Modernity: Technology, Politics, Art* (Bloomington: Indiana University Press, 1990).

Accordingly, he had no need of a "politics of being" to break with a despised present.

It was this hopeful conception that became entangled with Japanese imperialism in his 1943 response to the War Cabinet's request for a paper on the New World Order. There Nishida can be found telling the old Hegelian story of national identity. According to this text, the Pacific War would lead to the appropriation of modernity by Eastern cultures that had so far participated in the modern world only as objects of Western conquest. The War was interpreted here as a kind of struggle for recognition out of which a new form of global community should emerge.

Nishida did not explain why Japan would have to mimic Western colonialism to achieve this laudable goal, and his understanding of events appears strangely anachronistic. He naively compared the War to the Greek struggle with Persia, as the military precondition of a triumphant cultural self-affirmation of world-historical significance: "Just as the victory of Greece in the Persian War long ago set European culture on a path it has followed up to this day, so too the contemporary East Asian war determines a path of development for the coming epoch of world history."[54] From that standpoint Japan's defeat would seem to represent the destruction of a cultural universe, indeed of the very possibility of cultural plurality in the modern world.

There is something of the Meiji man in this position. In the Meiji period Japanese militarism had a much clearer anti-imperialist content than later on. It is easy to sympathize with Nishida's enthusiasm for Japanese victories against the Russians in 1905, when Japan was still subject to national humiliation by the Western powers. It is not so easy to understand his apparent support for the War with China in the 1930s and 1940s, when Japan was a great power.

Perhaps Nishida's understated position reflected awareness of this difference. No doubt he hoped that emphasizing Japanese cultural rather than military leadership in Asia would contribute to an early end to the War. But he continued to think in terms of power blocs; his writings do not reflect until quite late a clear understanding that Japanese colonial policy was not simply a normal mode of participation in global politics, but the very death of his own cultural program.[55] In our time freedom, equality, and trade have cultural implications, not the military conquest of weaker neighbors.

---

[54] NKZ 12:429.

[55] Power-bloc thinking was not of course confined to Japan. As late as 1949, George Kennan could write that "realism will call upon us not to oppose the re-entry of Japanese influence and activity into Korea and Manchuria" to hold back Soviet expansion in Asia. Quoted in Bruce Cummings, "Japan's Position in the Postwar World System: Regionalism, the Korean War, and the Dawning 'Post-Postwar' Era" (1989 manuscript).

We can hardly miss this point today given the postwar experience of decolonization. Had Japan won the Pacific War, it would have founded an immense Asian empire at precisely the moment when Europe was giving up on colonialism. As honorary Europeans, the Japanese would have arrived too late at this banquet table to enjoy the fun. One imagines the consequences: Japan would have spent the next generation fighting guerilla wars all over Asia; fascism would have remained in power for another generation. Far from the conquest of Asia fulfilling Nishida's cultural program, it would have resulted in a terrible cultural catastrophe.

Toward the end of the War, Nishida seems to have understood his epoch better. He and his circle engaged in intense discussions of postwar policy in view of national-cultural survival. Several months before the surrender, he wrote a final essay entitled "The Logic of *Basho* and the Religious World-view," which hinted at a very different understanding of Japan's situation.

This extraordinary essay sharply distinguishes between the political and the religious dimension of human experience. The nation is an ethical-political unity in the Hegelian sense of *Sittlichkeit*, but as such it belongs to the "corrupt" world of everyday existence. Hence "the nation does not save our souls." Yet by the logic of the "identity of contradictions," immanence is transcendence and national life therefore also relates to the absolute:

> The reason that a nation is a nation lies...in its religious character as a self-expression of historical life. A true nation arises when a people harbors the world-principle within itself and forms itself historically and socially.[56]

The religious essence of nationality is both cultural and global and as such it contains the secret of international coexistence in the modern age.

These ideas represent a radical break with contemporary Japanese nationalism. Nishida's earlier political writings had followed conventional opinion in over-estimating the philosophical significance of the state, a natural enough tendency given the centrality of the state in reshaping Japan from the Meiji period on. However, this state nationalism had proven a false path, and Nishida's attempt to infuse it with his own culturalism was a disastrous failure, as he would no doubt have conceded had he survived the War.

As imminent defeat clarified the situation, Nishida innovated a new nationalist discourse based not on the state but on culture. That discourse was still continuous with the old state nationalism in many particulars, and, through the postwar influence of his followers, may have helped to provide the basis for the conservative reconstruction of Japan as an unarmed culture-nation. The important point is the shift to a principled affirmation of ethnic

[56] *Last Writings,* 122, 116.

identity, not of course on a primitive racialist basis but in terms of a global cultural mission that excluded militarism. This shift shows up in a change in historical metaphors for Japan's position in the world.

The implicit point of comparison was no longer the Greeks, but the ancient Jews. Their defeat and occupation by the Babylonians is recorded in the Bible, particularly in the prophetic book of Jeremiah. Nishida noted that, despite their conquest, the Jews maintained their "spiritual self-confidence" and transcended their merely ethnic limitations to create a world religion.[57] Just so, he argues, "the Japanese spirit participating in world history...can become the point of departure for a new global culture," but only if Japan overcomes its "insular" and "vainly self-confident" outlook.[58] Then Japan would no longer have to compete with the West by violence to make its cultural contribution, but could, like the Jews, learn to defend and spread its values from inside a system defined and dominated by the Other.

Nishida found in the Biblical texts a coded way of referring to the impending defeat he predicted more openly in his letters of the period. One easily understands the appeal of the prophecies in the midst of the bombing attacks of 1945: "For I have set my face against this city for evil, and not for good, saith the Lord: it shall be given into the hand of the king of Babylon, and he shall burn it with fire." Astonishingly, as MacArthur's ships approached, Nishida cited Jeremiah's warning that Nebuchadnezzar is also a servant of Yahweh.[59] Even the enemies of the chosen serve God's ends by chastening his people. In this bizarre passage Nishida seemed to anticipate a *meaningful* Occupation, which indeed it proved to be.

And none too soon! Japan's role in the modern world could not possibly conform to the old Hegelian model, but required a new one, the outlines of which were only barely visible in the months preceding the defeat. The Jewish example indicated a way out through cleanly separating cultural from politico-military self-affirmation. Nishida's surprising reference to the Jews suggests that he wanted Japan to accept its defeat and choose its fate. He seemed to promise that if it did so Japan would rise from the ashes as a great cultural force in the postwar world.

[57] *Last Writings*, 116. See also Nishida's letter to D. T. Suzuki of May 1945 (NKZ 19:426): "Lately, reading the history of the development of Jewish religion has made me think a lot. The Jews built the foundation for the direction of the development of their world religion in the Babylonian captivity. The true spirit of the people must be like this. The nation that combines self-confidence with militarism perishes when the military power perishes."

[58] *Last Writings*, 112.

[59] *Last Writings*, 116.

CONCLUSION

For Nishida the globalization of world culture challenged philosophy and science to recognize the contributions of non-Western peoples. He believed that Eastern culture could offer a new paradigm of historical understanding that would respond not only to the theoretical problems of the times, but also to the pressing need for a new mode of coexistence between nations and cultures. That paradigm was based on the notion of the identity of contradictions, global conflict grasped as a process of self- and world-formation. Japanese culture seemed to Nishida exemplary in this regard and capable of representing the new paradigm as a specific national instance, much as Europe represented the universal achievements of natural science to the world at large.

The contemporary relevance of these ideas is clear. The gradual decentering of the world system calls for renewed reflection on the equality of cultures. But it is not easy to reconcile that moral exigency with the powerful cognitive claims of the hegemonic science and technology. This is the dilemma Nishida faced. In responding to it, he showed that world culture is plural not simply in the variety of its dying traditions but in the very spirit of its distinctive modern experiments.

Nationalism as Dialectics

Ethnicity, Moralism, and the State in Early Twentieth-Century Japan

Kevin M. DOAK

NY DISCUSSION ON THE RELATIONSHIP of Zen Buddhism, the Kyoto school, and nationalism must immediately confront the problem that all three subjects involve their own peculiar host of internal contradictions and instabilities that potentially frustrate an understanding of each severally or collectively. The problem is only further complicated when one attempts to bring into the equation the ever-shifting sands of history. Yet, a historical analysis of the problem does have several advantages over philosophical or theological approaches. By framing the question at a particular time in a specific historical context, I hope to avoid the issue of whether or not Zen Buddhism and the ideas raised by the members of the Kyoto school were intrinsically nationalistic and would always be nationalistic. I also intend to show that nationalism as well cannot be simply essentialized, since the discourse on nationalism itself was also subject to historical changes. Consequently, the historical approach I have taken below is meant to reflect not merely personal interest, but my conviction that if discussions on Zen and the Kyoto school are to avoid simply repeating the beliefs of their advocates and actually attempt a critical reading of them, then a historical analysis of the social and political context in early twentieth-century Japan, particularly with regard to the development of nationalism, might be after all an advantageous place to begin.

Such a broader perspective might, I hope, contribute to an understanding of Zen and the Kyoto school in two particular ways. First, it might help avoid reading Zen merely as a transcendental entity not reducible to any particular historical or social context. Second, it might enrich our understanding of the relationship between religions and nationalisms in prewar Japan by uncovering the complex relationship that existed between Buddhism and nationalism. As I will argue, Buddhism was not merely the "victim" of a state-centered nationalism that privileged State Shinto and oppressed all other religions. The position of the emperor in religious ideology, the privileged position of State Shinto, and the "emperor-system" nature of the prewar Japanese state cannot be ignored. However, an overemphasis on these factors, coupled with too simplistic an understanding of the nature of nationalism in prewar Japan, have all too often led to the conclusion that Buddhism maintained an Asian, if not universal, value-structure in the face of state oppression. This was true, of course, in some cases. Yet, nationalist and religious sentiments were deeply rooted and often subtly intertwined to the degree that no religious group was totally immune from nationalist inclinations and no nationalist formulation could completely ignore the powerful appeals of Buddhism in all its sectarian forms. Liah Greenfeld has helped elucidate the complex relationship between nationalism and religion in general by questioning those narratives that see nationalism as a replacement of religion in industrialized and secularized societies. On the contrary, she points out that "nationalism emerged in a time of ardent religious sentiment, when questions of religious identity grew more, rather than less, acute, and faith became more significant.... It was able to develop and become established owing to the support of religion, and, if it later replaced it as the governing passion, in many cases it incorporated religion as part of the national consciousness."[1] How well Greenfeld's insight into the development of nationalism in Europe applies in the case of Japan rests, of course, on the argument I will develop below.

Consequently, in order to understand how Zen Buddhism came to represent itself as a Japanese, perhaps *the* Japanese, form of Buddhism, I will begin with the historical struggle over what constituted the Japanese nation. Discussions on nationalism in Japan have often proceeded under the assumption that the "nation" was a fairly obvious thing and that the relationship between "nation" and "nationalism" was also a relatively clear one. But, as an ideological project involved in creating identities, nationalism is best conceived not as a specific identity but as a field of political contestation. As Harry Harootunian has noted, "the production of ideology is inevitably rooted in the propensity of groups to make 'authoritative' claims to know and to fix the boundaries between real and unreal."[2] Nationalism was itself caught up in this contestation over which representation of Japan was "real" and most "authoritative" as it attempted to assert either what Japan was or who the Japanese people were. There were opposing groups with opposing representations of the nation in the 1930s. In order to reconceive the field of nationalism as contested terrain, one might begin with Abe Hirozumi's revision of

---

[1] Liah Greenfeld, "Transcending the Nation's Worth," *Daedalus* (1993): 49.

[2] Harry Harootunian, "Ideology as Conflict," in Tetsuo Najita and J. Victor Koschmann, eds., *Conflict in Modern Japanese History* (Princeton, N. J.: Princeton University Press, 1982), 26.

Maruyama Masao's chronology of fascism. Abe emphasizes the post-1935 period as the formative period of fascism, as he maintains that the years from 1935 to 1940 witnessed the suppression of popular movements that sought to reorganize the state from below. The subsequent success in promoting fascism "from above" by the so-called "reform bureaucrats" and elements in the army was premised, he writes, on the co-option of the energy of the populist movements.[3] My argument seeks to revise Abe's analysis slightly. Whereas Abe focuses on ideologues such as Kita Ikki who had in mind plans for reorganizing the "nation-state" (国家 *kokka*), I will suggest that a more radical, if less violent, challenge during these years came from other quarters. In particular, an alternative form of nationalism stemmed from those who drew on spiritual and cultural values to reinterpret the nation as fundamentally an ethnic-nation (民族 *minzoku*), rather than, and often in hostility to, the political structure of the nation-state.

The problem of nationalism and religion in prewar Japan, then, might best be seen in this light as representing the dialectical process, or perhaps better (to borrow a metaphor from Inoue Tetsujirō),[4] the specific collision between two distinct fields of identity formation: nationalism, as a contestation between alternate visions of the "nation" rooted either in the nation-state (国家) or in ethnic people (民族); and religion, as comprising symbolic and spiritual practices that were forced to constantly realign themselves in response to changes in the modern nation-state's view of what it considered native and foreign. The historical unfolding of the dynamic between these two highly charged fields should help resituate Zen Buddhism within a specific historical context. The trajectory of collision between religion and nationalism has had noticeable peaks and valleys, points at which the two converged and diverged, over the course of the last one hundred twenty years.

Two in particular stand out: the rehabilitation of "New Buddhism" during the 1890s, and the state's attempt to regain control over religion during the 1930s and 1940s. In either case, it should be clear that the ability of the Japanese state, with its ideological roots in the emperor and State Shinto, to co-opt Buddhism and the facility with which Zen (Ch'an!) Buddhism could project itself as the most Japanese of religious expressions should not strike us as especially strange or paradoxical for, as John Hall has pointed out, in

[3] 安部博純 Abe Hirozumi, 急進ファシズム運動論 [An explanation of the swift rise of fascism], in 体系, 日本現代史 [Contemporary Japanese history series], as cited by 由井正臣 Yui Masaomi, 赤沢史朗 Akazawa Shirō, and 北河賢三 Kitagawa Kenzō, 解説 [Commentary], in 資料日本現代史 [Sources in contemporary Japanese history] (Tokyo: Ōtsuki Shoten, 1981), 6:543–4.

[4] 井上哲次郎 Inoue Tetsujirō, 宗教と教育の衝突 [The collision of education and religion], cited in James Edward Ketelaar, *Of Heretics and Martyrs in Meiji Japan: Buddhism and Its Persecution* (Princeton, N. J.: Princeton University Press, 1990), 132.

the end "there is no firm sociological mooring to the nation, not in language, not in religion, and not in ethnicity."[5] Neither, one might add, was there any ontological prior condition limiting how Zen Buddhism could develop within its own historical context in twentieth-century Japan.

Let me emphasize the interactive character of nationalisms and religions with one final example before concluding this introduction. Sheldon Garon has indicated the limitations of the emperor-system approach to Japanese nationalism that

> invariably traces all suppression back to the pre-1945 Japanese state—a state which appears omnipotent and eager to unilaterally define what is orthodox. Historians of Europe and America have recently argued that such theories of "social control" neglect the input of societal forces. In Japan, as well, rival religious organizations and progressive intellectuals were often as likely as bureaucrats to call for the strict regulation of certain sects. I propose that we reexamine relations between the Japanese state and civil society in terms of a more interactive model.[6]

In the pages below, I will draw from Garon's insight that a more interactive model with more attention to the input of social forces is necessary, but my focus will be different. Whereas Garon's attempt is to show that elements within civil society negotiated with the state in a manner that ultimately led to a stronger state, I will argue that the powerful social control the state achieved by the 1940s was also the result of a dialectic relationship of contestation, co-option, and in some cases cooperation with, forces that were at times indifferent, if not hostile, to the state. The result of this dialectic between religion and nationalism was not only a transformation within religious theology but also a metamorphosis of the state.

THE DEVELOPMENT OF NATIONALISM IN MODERN JAPAN

Before proceeding to a discussion of the critical period of the 1930s and 1940s, I will offer a brief description of the historical character of nationalism in Japan during the period from the Meiji Restoration of 1868 until the end of the First World War in 1918. This is a necessary step in order to grasp both the historical difference between the discourses on nationalism in the Meiji and Shōwa years, as well as to come to terms with the shift in relationship between religion and nationalism in these two historical moments.

[5] John A. Hall, "Nationalisms: Classified and Explained," *Daedalus* (Summer 1993):4.

[6] Sheldon M. Garon, "State and Religion in Imperial Japan, 1912–1945," *Journal of Japanese Studies* (Summer 1986): 276.

Concomitant with victory over the loosely confederated *bakufu* (幕府) in 1868 was the necessity perceived by the imperial government to redefine a sense of national unity that would meet the requirements of a modernizing nation-state. The resultant struggle over how to define the nation, most noticeable in the violent rebellions of the 1870s and the constitutional debates of the 1880s, resulted in the triumph of the views of the moderniz-ers as they were encoded in the Meiji Constitution of 1889. The nationalism that followed, whether termed *kokkashugi* 国家主義, *kokuminshugi* 国民主義, *kokusuishugi* 国粋主義, or otherwise, was an attempt to incorporate the "peo-ple" (民) into the new modern nation-state (国家), to broaden traditional al-legiances beyond regional domains in order to focus on the new nation-state. This indoctrination of the values of the nation-state often involved, as Carol Gluck has shown, the active participation of many of "the people" them-selves.[7] Gluck's work has broadened our understanding of the source of nationalist ideology, but it has not challenged the general consensus behind Kenneth Pyle's conclusion that the essence of Meiji nationalism was "a process...by which large numbers of people of all social classes are psycho-logically integrated into active membership in and positive identification with the nation-state."[8] No clear distinction between a sense of nation rooted in the emerging nation-state and a sense of nation rooted in the people as an autonomous source of national identity, separate and distinct from the state, emerged at this time.

Just as Meiji nationalism represented the incorporation of the people into a new relationship with the modern nation-state, one finds a parallel devel-opment in the way Buddhism accommodated itself to the new Meiji nation-state. After the persecution of Buddhism (廃仏毀釈) in the 1860s and 1870s, large numbers of persons within organized Buddhism reorganized themselves as "New Buddhism" to incorporate many of the rational, modern demands of the Meiji state and its promotion of the values of "civilization and enlight-enment" (文明開化).[9] This reformation was so successful that when Shaku Sōen, a Rinzai Zen abbot, journeyed (first class) to the 1893 World's Parliament of Religion in Chicago, he delivered himself of opinions that were characterized by a social Darwinism and evolutionary thrust remarkably sim-

[7] Carol Gluck, *Japan's Modern Myths: Ideology in the Late Meiji Period* (Princeton, N. J.: Princeton University Press, 1985). This argument is the crux of Gluck's study and may be found throughout her book, but a summary of her contrast of the "officials" (官) and the "people" (民) may be found on pages 60–7.

[8] Kenneth B. Pyle, "Introduction: Some Recent Approaches to Japanese Nationalism," *Journal of Asian Studies* (November 1971): 516.

[9] See Martin Collcutt, "Buddhism: the Threat of Eradication," in Marius Jansen and Gilbert Rozman, eds. *Japan in Transition: From Tokugawa to Meiji* (Princeton, N.J.: Princeton University Press, 1986): 143–67. See also note 10 below.

ilar to the ideas of Katō Hiroyuki, one of the Meiji state's chief ideologues.[10] In retrospect, this may not seem so surprising given "institutional Buddhism's active support of involvement in the Sino-Japanese (1894–1895) and, to a lesser extent, the Russo-Japanese (1904–1905) wars,"[11] but the contrast between this Zen Buddhism and that later popularized by D. T. Suzuki is rather striking.

The late Meiji years have often been seen as a period of withdrawal by a successful "secular" state from religious affairs. For example, Sheldon Garon has pointed out that

> unlike the ambitious Ministry of Rites and Education (教部省) of the 1870s, the succeeding Bureau of Shrines and Temples (1877–1900) and Bureau of Religions (1900–1913) were simply low-ranking divisions within the Home Ministry.... Rather than harnessing the spiritual influence of the religions, the authorities preferred to socialize the people directly through agencies of the secular state.[12]

But on closer inspection, the distinction between sacred and secular with respect to the state and Buddhism in late Meiji may not be a fruitful one. A nation-state whose very legitimacy was secured in part by an ideology based on a sacred emperor could never completely distance itself from religious concerns.[13] And indeed, the reshuffling of bureaucratic agencies responsible for the oversight of religious activity was also a recognition of New Buddhism's incorporation of modern, nationalist values. These New Buddhists had already taken it upon themselves to write a history of their faith that would "accentuate the long and intimate relation between Buddhism and the Japanese national spirit."[14]

[10] Ketelaar, *Of Heretics and Martyrs*, 159–66. The comparison to Katō is mine. Ketelaar leaves it implicit, merely noting that, in describing the "progress of the universe," Shaku argued that "since the Karmic Law, like Darwin's own, is applicable to all beings, the moral life of human beings is thereby equally determined by a logical calculus of evolution driven forth by the actions of particular individuals" (165).

[11] Ketelaar, *Of Heretics and Martyrs*, 133.

[12] Garon, "State and Religion in Imperial Japan," 278.

[13] Bernard Silberman argues that the development of rational bureaucracy was designed precisely to provide an alternative to the emperor as the source of legitimacy of the new state. See his "The Bureaucratic State in Japan: The Problem of Authority and Legitimacy," in Najita and Koschmann, eds., *Conflict in Japan*, 226–57. But his brief discussion of the rise of the military during the critical 1936–1945 period remains more descriptive than analytical as it does not sufficiently explain why the military felt compelled to intervene in parliamentary politics or indeed why the framers of the Meiji state order allowed the military to remain outside of the checks in the constitutional order and in direct relationship to the emperor.

[14] Ketelaar, *Of Heretics and Martyrs*, 135.

What might have seemed like success to the architects of the Meiji state was merely a momentary stabilization in the ongoing contestation between spiritual and national values. While the state had succeeded in managing its own survival in the critical years of the late nineteenth century, it did so at great cost. By anchoring its concept of nation to the modern nation-state, centered in the new image of an active, European-style emperor, the state had also provided guidelines for Buddhism and other religions to reorganize themselves for their own survival as well. But the very survival of Buddhism preserved the potential for a challenge to the state's authority over knowledge. As Ketelaar has noted, "The failure to eradicate Buddhism guaranteed the failure of the state's attempt to establish a universally accepted doctrinal apparatus."[15] Just as the state had failed to monopolize religion, so too did it fail to monopolize conceptions of the nation. Many of the Meiji populist movements that Irokawa Daikichi has chronicled stemmed from a different political tradition that maintained that

> "the realm belongs to the realm" (天下は天下の天下なり) and not to the emperor alone. Imperial authority resided not in the emperor's personal possession but in his rule in accordance with the "kingly way" (王道), which implied the assent of the people.[16]

And, as Irokawa concludes, "the old question of whether the realm belonged to the ruler or to the people was not resolved by the early Meiji leaders."[17]

The unsolved riddle of Meiji—whether "Japan" referred to a timeless people or to the historical achievement of the Meiji nation-state—resurfaced with renewed vigor in the years following World War I. Throughout the Taishō period, an undercurrent of populism gained strength and broke free of manipulation by state nationalists, gradually overwhelming both the rejuvenated socialist movement and the limited liberalism embodied in the Taishō party system and franchise growth. It was linked to the popular rights movement by "a shared skepticism about bureaucratic government" and stressed "emotional" links between the people and the emperor, who was reconceived "as a popular and aesthetic institution."[18] Certainly, the social turmoil of the time concerned ministers of state. Tokonami Takejirō was perhaps the most perceptive of these state servants who quickly grasped the need for a new relationship with organized religion. In 1912, Vice-Minister for

[15] Ketelaar, *Of Heretics and Martyrs*, 131.

[16] Irokawa Daikichi, *The Culture of the Meiji Period,* trans. and ed. by Marius B. Jansen (Princeton, N. J.: Princeton University Press, 1985), 252.

[17] Irokawa, *The Culture of the Meiji Period*, 253.

[18] Tetsuo Najita, *Japan: The Intellectual Foundations of Modern Japanese Politics* (Chicago: The University of Chicago Press, 1974), 116–17.

Home Affairs Tokonami summoned representatives of Buddhism, Shinto, and even Christianity and promised to respect their religious authority in exchange for their cooperation in improving social conditions by enhancing public morality. The real utility of this new relationship between church and state became apparent when the rice riots of 1918 signalled that the mass movements and populist revolutions that had engulfed much of Europe in the wake of World War I might threaten the Japanese state as well. Tokonami acted quickly. In 1919 "Home Minister Tokonami occasionally consulted Buddhist representatives on how to ameliorate tensions between labor and capital...(and the chief of the Bureau of Religions) encouraged the spread of general religious instruction in an effort to roll back radical thought."[19] Buddhism, along with other major religions, was now offered a chance to work with the nation-state to defeat attempts to divide the Japanese people along class lines.

Not all religious groups received the invitation, and not all that did responded positively. The New Religions that found fertile ground among those most affected by industrialization were excluded as "pseudo-religions." Yet there is little indication that they were inclined to cooperate with the modern nation-state. Deguchi Onisaburō, the leader of Ōmotokyō, one of these new religions, liked to "enrage the public yet awe supporters by reviewing the sect's paramilitary organizations from atop a white horse—an act conventionally reserved for the emperor himself."[20] This act of political parody was a stunning revelation of the power of populist religions to prefigure in symbolic language a repossession of the emperor by the people. Nor did it go unnoticed by the authorities, who arrested three leaders of Ōmotokyō in 1921 and charged them with lèse-majesté.

That Ōmotokyō, like many other New Religions, had its origins in the Kyoto area could hardly have been merely accidental. Kyoto's significance as a central and sacred ground for resistance against Tokyo dates from before the restoration, and with the emperor relocated to the hub of politics, rationalism, and "civilization and enlightenment," Kyoto gradually became the focus of a host of practices that were often self-consciously cultural, non-rational, and nativist. Whereas Tokyo defined the very practice of modern politics in Japan, Kyoto became a powerful symbol of an enduring cultural tradition that, possessed of the potential to unite all Japanese, remained as alienated from that national unity as the emperor was from his ancient hometown.

Intellectuals in the Kansai area often appealed to the symbolic importance of Kyoto as a localized alterity in modern Japan that formed the basis of a "humanist" critique of the modern state. Yasuda Yojūrō, whose ethnic

---

[19] Garon, "State and Religion in Imperial Japan," 281.

[20] Garon, "State and Religion in Imperial Japan," 288.

KEVIN M. DOAK

nationalism I discuss below, best grasped the irony of Kyoto's tradition of resistance to Tokyo when he recalled that the influence he felt from Kyoto was the tradition of European continental philosophy, particularly the works of Husserl and Heidegger, that underlies what he called Kyoto University's "humanism." By "humanism," Yasuda did not mean humanism in a narrow sense, as he recognized that Kyoto University often pioneered the critique of humanism as well. Rather, he sought to identify an emphasis on cultural issues at that university which he contrasted with the emphasis on politics and elitism that allegedly characterized education at Tokyo Imperial University.[21] It is significant that he only uses the adjective *imperial* in connection with the university in Tokyo, as the word refers not to a traditional emperor but to the new, imperial state (大日本帝国) and, as I argue below, equates Japan's modern governmental structure with imperial states elsewhere, especially in the West. This "humanist" tradition of Kyoto University apparently included communism as well, as relations between Kyoto University and the Japanese state suffered when in 1928 the university was forced to dismiss Professor Kawakami Hajime because of his communist beliefs. Only five years later, when Education Minister Hatoyama Ichirō 鳩山一郎 demanded the dismissal of law professor Takigawa Yukitoki 滝川幸辰 for alleged communistic sympathies, he set off a bitter struggle between the bureaucratic state and the university that soon resulted in the collapse of Kyoto University's precarious sense of autonomy.

THE RISE OF AN ETHNIC NATIONALIST CRITIQUE
AND THE RESPONSE OF THE STATE

Isolating a critical ethnic nationalism in Japan during the 1930s is fraught with difficulty. While there is little doubt that ethnic nationalism was a vital part of the political discourse of that time, there is no agreement on the existence of a concept of the ethnic nation that was distinct from, and critical of, the state. Ishida Takeshi has provided perhaps the strongest argument against the existence of a critical ethnic nationalism through a comparison with Germany, noting that in Japan the conceptual distinction between ethnic nation (*minzoku*) and the nation-state (*kokka*) was not as clear as it was in Germany and that the shift in people's interests from class to ethnic nation in Japan was immediately connected to the strengthening of state nationalism.[22]

[21] 保田與重郎 Yasuda Yojūrō, 日本浪漫派の時代 [The age of the Japanese romantic school], in 保田與重郎全集 [Collected works of Yasuda Yojūrō], 36:16–17, 100–25.

[22] 石田 雄 Ishida Takeshi, 日本の政治と言葉—平和と国家 [Japanese politics and language: Peace and the nation] (Tokyo: Tokyo University Press, 1989), 2:208.

182

Ishida is correct in pointing to how a concept of ethnic nationalism was often used to critique Western liberalism and in noting the ultimate failure of this critique to prevent the state from co-opting it and utilizing the ethnic-nation to enhance its own position. But it is first necessary to recognize that there were influential voices, on the political left and right, who were aware of the "ethnic nation" as a concept distinct from, and critical of, the nation-state. Moreover, both political wings of the ethnic nationalist discourse shared an assessment that the modern Japanese nation-state was coterminous with modern, Western liberal values and both condemned that aspect of it.

One of the earliest and most influential sources of a critical theory of ethnic nationalism can be found in the journal *Under the Banner of the New Science*, which was founded by Miki Kiyoshi and Hani Gorō in late 1928 as an attempt to suggest a broader, more humanistic understanding of science than Newtonian paradigms of a universal natural science would permit. Miki and Hani had only returned from study in Heidelberg a few years earlier and introduced much of what they had learned in Germany in the pages of the journal. Miki in particular was influenced by the "absolute spiritual anxiety" (全く精神的不安) that he found in postwar Germany and responded with theoretical attempts to articulate a "specificity" or "particularity" that might resolve spiritual ideals with material reality.[23] But it was Nagashima Matao's "On the Ethnic Nation and Ethnic Nationalist Movements" published in the April 1929 issue of the journal that most concretely connected the theoretical discussion of "specificity" with the historical realities of ethnic nationalism. After introducing the theories of Rudolph Springer, Otto Bauer, and Joseph Stalin on the definition of an ethnic nation (*minzoku*), Nagashima concluded with Stalin's definition that "an ethnic nation is unified through the commonality of a traditional mentality that is revealed as a common language, territory, economic life and culture—a commonality that has a permanence historically constructed by humans."[24] By situating ethnic nations as historically contingent phenomena, Nagashima placed the problem of nationalism within the New Science group's focus on "specificity" as a critical force against the modern state.

But what makes this essay most significant is Nagashima's argument that the ethnic-nation and the nation-state are theoretically and historically distinct. Arguing that the relationship between the ethnic-nation and the nation-state is determined by history, he pointed out that in Europe, "the formation of ethnic-nations (*minzoku*) was simultaneously the formation of

[23] 渡辺一民 Watanabe Kazutami, 林達夫とその時代 [Hayashi Tatsuo and his times] (Tokyo: Iwanami Shoten, 1988), 1–16.

[24] 長島又男 Nagashima Matao, 民族並びに民族運動について [Race and racial movements], in 新興科学の旗のもとに [Under the banner of the new science] (April 1929): 28.

ethnic nation-states (*minzoku kokka*), as those ethnic nations were able to establish their own independent state .... But in Eastern Europe, the situation was different. In Eastern Europe, a single nation-state (*kokka*) was often formed over various ethnic-nations (*minzoku*)."[25] And in the countries of Asia, the situation was different again:

> The various ethnic nations (*minzoku*) of this region are totally dominated, i.e. oppressed, by Imperialism. Yet, the development of capitalism, and along with it the development of commerce and the means of transportation in these colonial countries, will give them an economic identity and drive them on to the formation of their own independent, ethnic nation-state (*minzoku kokka*). Nonetheless, they will at the same time encounter powerful opposition. That is, the oppression of the dominant ethnic nation (*minzoku*). This is how the struggle among ethnic nations, the ethnic nationalist movement, arises.[26]

Although Nagashima left it implicit, the message here was undoubtedly that Japan was a mixed-case: as a late developing nation, Japan did not belong in the category of the European ethnic nation-states. But given its own history of colonization of other Asian nations, particularly after the 1919 nationalist movements against Japanese colonization in Korea and China, Japan could no longer lay claim to simple victim's status as oppressed by foreign imperialists.

In the years following Nagashima's essay, and especially after the Japanese Imperial Army began mobilizing nationalist sentiment for their aggression in Manchuria, others began to appeal to ethnic nationalism in a more populist vein. In April 1934 Yanaihara Tadao published in *Chūōkōron*, one of the two most influential journals of the day, an essay on "Peace and the Ethnic Nation" that criticized the state by arguing that those who would use ethnic nationalism to promote the state's interests or to suppress individualism were guilty of "murdering" the ethnic nation.[27] A year later, Yokomitsu Riichi argued in his essay "A Theory of the Pure Novel" (published in *Kaizō*, the other leading journal of the 1930s) for a concept of the ethnic-nation as the matrix of Japanese artistic creation. Yet it bears repeating that this discovery of a native identity, a Japanese specificity, was only first made possible through a study of the West, in this case, the French author André Gide. Yokomitsu drew from Gide's analyses of self-consciousness and the desire to liberate the Ego to arrive at his own concept of a fourth gram-

[25] Nagashima, "Race and Racial Movements," 29.

[26] Nagashima, "Race and Racial Movements," 29–30.

[27] 矢内原忠雄 Yanaihara Tadao, 民族と平和 [Peace and the ethnic nation], cited in Ishida, *Japanese Politics and Language,* 2:68.

184

matical person, the "Self that views the Self" (自分を見る自分). By thus suggesting a consciousness of consciousness, an identity that contextualized identities, Yokomitsu sought to rehabilitate aesthetics by grounding literary production in a historical connectedness between authors and their readers. Invoking the need to develop a writing that conformed with Japan's specificity, Yokomitsu concluded that "the time has finally come to think about the ethnic nation (*minzoku*), which up until now has mostly been overlooked."[28]

In March 1935, just one month after Yokomitsu implored his fellow writers to reconsider the ethnic nation, Yasuda Yojūrō announced the formation of the Japan Romantic School. Yasuda and his fellow romantics turned to German romantics, especially Hölderlin, Novalis, and Friedrich Schlegel, as a means of "discovering" a traditional culture that would signify a Japanese identity free from the corrupting influences of modernity. Modernity for Yasuda could encompass both European culture and, as shown by his recognition of the necessity of mediating present and past through the German romantics, the reality of Japan's own modernity as represented by the post-Meiji nation-state. Although his romanticism was criticized for contributing to the rise of fascism in the late 1930s, Yasuda vehemently denied that he was a fascist, noting his innate distrust of the "bureaucratic temperament," and adding that "fascism is the annihilation of things through the power of the state."[29] Yet he recognized the dangers involved in recovering a critical ethnic nationalism since some would argue such attempts would only support the "preservation of the essence of the state" (国粋保存). As a rather feeble example of his own resistance to the mobilization of tradition for modern goals, Yasuda noted how he had written three letters to the newspapers expressing his indignation over a rumored abridged version of the Tale of Genji. "While the Japan Romantic School may be ineffective, it contests the basis of such rumors in the name of the Japanese ethnic-nation (*Nihon minzoku*) and commits itself to the defense of this culture." And this need to understand and defend Japan's cultural past was nothing less than a "moral obligation."[30]

Yasuda expanded his critique of the state's mobilization of culture in a 1939 essay that offered a teleology of the Meiji state, succinctly captured in the essay's title, "On the End of the Logic of Civilization and Enlightenment." Shrewdly grasping how the Japanese state continued to use cultural

[28] 横光利一 Yokomitsu Riichi, 純粋小説論 [The theory of the pure novel], 改造 [Reconstruction] (April 1935), reprinted in 平野 謙 Hirano Ken et al., eds., 現代日本文学論争史 [A history of literary debate in contemporary Japan], 3:76–9.

[29] Yasuda Yojūrō, 「日本的なもの」批評について [On things Japanese], 文学界 [Literary world] (April 1937): 83–4.

[30] Yasuda, "On Things Japanese," 91.

issues as ideology and equating its nationalism with yet another attempt to impress the West, Yasuda noted that it was not surprising that such an "objectivistically simplistic Japanization" would leave the impression of the corruption of "Japanism." But it was important, he concluded, to distinguish this "Japanization" from the true "Japan," which "from the beginning of time to the end of time, resides in the Japanese national soil and in the people; it flows in our veins. It knows neither corruption nor ruin."[31] Returning national identity back to the people themselves, he condemned those whose opportunism led them to join the nation-state's mobilization of Japanism, which he dated from September 1938 when

> the government completely transformed the literary and scholarly world by sending writers to accompany the army. At that point, literature as such completely disappeared.... Writers of major novels converted to government literature...by rewriting some shameless parts of their work to fit bureaucratically approved ethics—an ideology like the Greater Japan Youth Association. Thus began the corruption of Japanism.[32]

By the late 1930s, Yasuda had retreated from his earlier acceptance of the irony of representing tradition in a modern world and had begun to settle on the appeal of a natural "blood and soil" as a more authentic expression of the Japanese soul than such historical constructs as the modern nation-state.

It is at this juncture that the contribution of the Kyoto school of philosophers can best be assessed. In contrast to the Romantic School, the Kyoto school was less troubled by the ambiguities of nationalism and argued for a historical perspective that would reappropriate "moral energy" for the state.[33] By explicitly connecting "blood and soil" with the Japanese state, the Kyoto school played such a critical role in asserting a clear and unequivocal identification of nationalism with the nation-state that Najita and Harootunian have concluded that "no group helped defend the state more consistently and enthusiastically than did the philosophers of the Kyoto faction, and none came closer than they did to defining the philosophic contours of Japanese fascism."[34] While Nishitani and others described the state as the locus of absolute nothingness for the individual, Tanabe Hajime explicitly addressed

---

[31] Yasuda Yojūrō, 文明開化の論理の終焉について [The end of the logic of civilization and enlightenment], コギト [Cogito] (January 1939): 13–14.

[32] Yasuda, "The End of the Logic of Civilization," 19–20.

[33] See for example, Nishitani Keiji,「近代の超克」私論 [My own theory of "the overcoming of modernity"], in NKC, 33. See also the discussion by Nishitani, Suzuki Shigetaka, Kōyama Iwao, and Kōsaka Masaaki on the "ethicality of world historical ethnic nations" in CK, 127–30.

[34] Tetsuo Najita and H. D. Harootunian, "Japanese Revolt against the West: Political and Cultural Criticism in the Twentieth Century," in *The Cambridge History of Japan* (Cambridge: Cambridge University Press, 1988), 6:741.

the challenge of ethnic nationalism to the state. Investigating what he called the "logic of species," Tanabe attempted to restore the rational state above the emotionalism of the ethnic nation through a synthesis of the rational individual and the irrational claims of ethnicity:

> During the years 1934 to 1940 I pursued research into the dialectical logic of what I myself called the logic of species, and through this I tried to investigate logically the concrete structure of nation-state society (*kokka shakai*). My motivation was to treat, as a philosophical problem, the ethnic-nationalism (*minzokushugi*) that had arisen in those days. While criticizing the liberalist thinking that had dominated us for some time, I simultaneously negated the so-called totalitarianism that was based on a simple ethnic-nationalism. Through the mediation of a mutual negation of the former's individual as subject and the latter's fundamental concept of the ethnic-nation (*minzoku*), I tried to discover...a rational basis for the nation-state as the practical unity of the real and the ideal.[35]

For Tanabe, "species" carried with it a more rational, universal element that could more easily be absorbed into the modern political structure of the nation-state. It also served effectively to deflect attention from ethnicity as an alternative biological metaphor for group identity.

While Tanabe's writings provided support for state nationalism in philosophical discourse, the state itself did not remain inactive in the face of threats to its claimed monopoly on national identity. Two moments in the state's counterattack might be isolated: the first is the period from the outbreak of war with China in 1937 to the construction of the "New Order in East Asia" in November of 1938; the second begins with the declaration of a "Greater East Asian Co-Prosperity Sphere" in 1940 and reaches a peak in the years immediately following the broadening of the war with the United States and Great Britain. Throughout these seven years from 1937 to 1943, the state recognized the challenge posed by ethnic nationalism and attempted to neutralize it by absorbing much of the ethnic nationalist appeal. In the end, the result was the spectacle of a modern nation-state engaging in a moral critique of modernity itself—the very foundation of an earlier, Meiji, national pride.

On June 4 1937, less than four months after the House of Peers proposed to consolidate religious groups around State Shinto through the Bill on Religious Organizations, Prince Konoe Fumimaro formed a cabinet and took over the government. This selection of a member of the court nobility as head of government, only a month before the Marco Polo Bridge Incident brought open hostilities with China and renewed pressure for national solidarity, reaffirmed the indelible ties between the emperor and the modern

---

[35] Tanabe Hajime, "The Dialectical Method of the Logic of Species," THZ 7:253.

state. A few months later, the Konoe cabinet called for national unity and in December set up the National Spiritual Mobilization Central League as an auxiliary organ of the cabinet to mobilize popular sentiment behind the state.

During this period, from late 1937 to early 1938, the Greater Japanism Movement held a series of meetings in a central Tokyo hotel that brought together over fifty participants, including the former prime minister Hayashi Senjūrō (1876–1943), Hiranuma Kiichirō, Home Minister Suetsugu Nobumasa (1880–1944), and Justice Minister Shiono Suehiko (1880–1949). Yoshida Shigeru drafted a plan for the group[36] that, after describing an "unprecedented world historical crisis" of nation-state struggle for survival, offered the following assessment of ethnic nationalism:

> While England, America, and France are busy at work defending the status quo from their stronghold of liberalism, and the Soviet Union upholds communism in its plan to paint the world Red, Germany and Italy are trying to break the status quo from their own positions of ethnic-nationalism, and right next door China's dreams of knocking down Japan have finally led to the recent Incident.... If we are to break through this unprecedented crisis and realize our great mission as an ethnic-nation, we must first fundamentally dissolve all our rivalries and quickly put in place and express the true spirit of Greater Japan of "one ruler for the multitudes, the people's hearts beating as one" (一君万民億兆一心錠). That is, ...(rejecting selfish liberalism and the moral bankruptcy of communism) we must understand that the essence of what is required of us at this urgent hour is to permeate all aspects of the life of our nation (国家生活) with that pure Japanese spirit that emanates from the national polity (国家) and that fuses together all individuality.[37]

In this call to national unity, Yoshida and his group recognized a variety of different national styles in the world and, implicitly, a contestation within Japan over what constituted national unity. Yet, while reaffirming the unity of the Japanese nation around the nation-state through the core concept of the *kokutai* (国体), this manifesto did recognize, and legitimize, the appeal of ethnic nationalism so long as it was not used to divide the national polity.

The declaration on November 3 1938 of a "New Order in East Asia" marked a highly visible attempt by the state to co-opt ethnic nationalism in what Miwa Kimitada calls the first victory of "nativistic idealism" over "polit-

---

[36] Yet Yoshida could not have attended the meeting in person since he was still serving as Ambassador in London at the time.

[37] 吉田 茂 Yoshida Shigeru, 大日本運動趣意書 [A prospectus of the Great Japanism Movement], in *Sources in Contemporary Japanese History*, 6:27–8.

ical realism." Miwa illustrates the contrast through two members of the Diet: Saitō Takao, who, in his "anti-military" speech of February 1940, condemned the ideological attempts to mask military aggression in China through moralism; and Kimura Takeo, member of the House of Representatives Disciplinary Committee, whose "nativistic idealism" led him to censure Saitō and remove him from the Diet. Miwa notes that "believing in the idea of *minzoku kyōwa* (民族共和) or multinational cooperative harmony, Kimura had supported Konoe's New Order proclamation, and construed Saitō's criticism as a materialistically motivated argument for a crass power-political settlement."[38] Both Kimura and Saitō were nationalists, but of a different breed. The difference between these two nationalisms is illustrated in Saitō's view that wars are essentially fought for the profit of nation-states and their peoples. In contrast, Kimura maintained that "the notion that Japan should support its life at the cost of China...is absolutely incompatible with the moralistic national policy that reflects the founding spirit of Japan."[39] From 1938 to 1940, then, one can begin to discern a shift from the state's attempt to co-opt ethnic nationalism to the incorporation of elements of ethnic nationalism within the very centers of state power.

But even the "New Order in East Asia" may have been too Western to meet the changing needs of the state as it increasingly incorporated ethnic nationalism. Indeed, the very conception of the "New Order" may have been derived from a direct suggestion to Konoe by Edward M. House, a close advisor to Woodrow Wilson, that if Japan would not recognize the world order established by the Washington Conference, then Japan ought to propose a new order that would be acceptable to other nations.[40] The formation of the "Greater East Asia Co-Prosperity Sphere," a concept that grew out of the Shōwa Research Association and took shape between April and August of 1940, marked an even greater concession to the demands of ethnic nationalism. In 1938, when the New Order in East Asia was proclaimed, the nation-state still referred to itself as an "empire" (帝国), a word that, encoded in the Meiji Constitution itself, suggested continuity with the Meiji political construct as well as comparability with Western nation-states.[41] But by July 1940, the term "empire" was "promptly dropped in favor of the more particularistic term *kōkoku* (皇国, the Land of the Tennō) ...indicating a move away from

[38] Kimitada Miwa, "Japanese Policies and Concepts for a Regional Order in Asia, 1938–1940," in James W. White et al., eds., *The Ambivalence of Nationalism: Modern Japan between East and West* (Lanham, Md.: University Press of America, 1990), 145.

[39] Kimura Takeo, cited by Miwa, "Japanese Policies and Concepts for a Regional Order in Asia," 145.

[40] Miwa, "Japanese Policies," 145–6.

[41] Miwa, "Japanese Policies," 152–3.

internationalization as defined by the advanced Western nation-states." This change in terminology was historically significant. For although Japan had declared war against China, Russia, and Germany in the name of the *kōtei* 皇帝, a term for emperor that was also applied to all other emperors throughout the world, when Japan declared war on the United States and Great Britain on December 8 1941, it did so in the name of the *Tennō*, a term reserved exclusively for the Japanese divine ruler. Whether this change in terminology represented the completion of "the idealistic transformation on the governmental level" as Miwa Kimitada maintains,[42] it does suggest something of the difficult compromise that the nation state—which had, in spite of all the rhetoric, of course remained a political construct—had made with ethnic nationalism.

Even as it co-opted more and more aspects of the ethnic-nationalist critique, the nation-state did not lessen its surveillance and suppression of nationalist movements that threatened its own authority to define the national community. A report prepared in October 1942 by the Public Peace Section of the Police Security Bureau of the Home Ministry makes this clear. No longer willing to recognize ethnic nationalism as a distinct form, the report focused on what it called "the Nationalist (*kokkashugi*) Movement and its supervision." It opened with a historical analysis of the rise of nationalism in Japan, tracing the "irrationalities" and "contradiction" that resulted from

> the appearance of various movements with many different ideologies and beliefs that necessarily arose when, over the long course of the life of our nation-state (国家生活) social conditions progressed and developed to the point where we left nature and ancient traditions and tried to create something compatible with this new society.... Moreover, the effect of these movements has been to improve our social lifestyle and, in turn, to contribute to the development of the nation-state (国家). When, on the other hand, these movements and ideologies are designed to interfere with the social order and destroy the life of the nation-state, then...we must firmly suppress them.[43]

One finds here a clear expression of the nation-state perspective that upholds the state as a product of modernization and is, implicitly, a rejection of any appeal to an ethnic nation that might lay claim to a national identity that predates the Meiji Restoration or is rooted in a timeless, natural community. In addition, the report attempts to lay claim to nationalist movements by suggesting that they generally have had a beneficial influence on the nation-state.

[42] Miwa, "Japanese Policies," 153–4.

[43] *Sources in Contemporary Japanese History,* 6:185. Emphasis added.

Indeed, the report notes that when social criticism is offered by nationalist movements that are based on protecting the "glorious *kokutai*" or on "Imperial House-ism" (皇室中心主義) there is no need, "from a nation-state point of view" to oppress them. But constant vigilance was warranted since there were many nationalists

> especially since 1930 or 1931 [who]…hid behind the nice words of loyalty to the emperor and love of country [but whose] regular habit was to commit the so-called acts of "squeezing," such as fraud and intimidation, or who tried to settle things through violence.[44]

Under the heading, "a grasp of the conviction that terrorism is absolutely unacceptable," the report notes:

a. the temporary popularity of the slogan, "Let's not become the *Shinsengumi*[45] of the Shōwa era";
b. from ancient times, domestic squabbles have had no influence on the fortunes of ethnic nations (民族);
c. to allow domestic squabbles to engulf us at this point in time is, regardless of the reasons for them, to become fifth columnists for the enemy.[46]

Finally, the report recommends a tolerant attitude towards nationalist movements, recognizing that these "pure nationalist movements" do not need to be completely suppressed like the leftist movements. Rather, officials should bear in mind that the goal is "constantly to guide them in a proper way" so that certain elements within them do not adopt means that ignore the national polity or destroy the constitution.[47]

By the early 1940s the Japanese state had in place a classified project oriented towards control of ethnic nationalism through its various administrative agencies. Evidence of how the state attempted to supervise and influence the potentially dangerous concept of the ethnic-nation is provided by the eight-volume research report carried out by the Ministry of Health and Welfare and published between December 1942 and July 1943. The last six volumes carried the title *An Investigation of Global Policy with the Yamato*

---

[44] *Sources in Contemporary Japanese History,* 6:186.

[45] The Shinsengumi (新撰組, recently selected brigade) was a group of swordsmen and assassins hired by the bakufu during the turbulent 1860s to restore order to Kyoto by hunting down and killing those who supported the emperor and sought the downfall of the bakufu. Symbolically, they could serve as villains both for the Meiji state, whose leaders fought them, or for ethnic nationalists, who saw the modern Japanese nation–state as analogous to the *bakufu*.

[46] *Sources in Contemporary Japanese History,* 6:186.

[47] *Sources in Contemporary Japanese History,* 6:187.

Race [sic] *as Nucleus.* As John Dower notes, "the report was not a polemical work meant for public consumption, but rather a practical guide for policy makers and administrators. One hundred copies, classified secret, were circulated within the government."[48] The report adopted an apparently ambivalent attitude towards the "ethnic nation," or what Dower calls "race" (*minzoku*): suggesting in places the need to transcend racism and in others how "in the modern world...racism, nationalism, and capitalist expansion had become inextricably intertwined."[49] Moreover, as Dower admits, the authors of the project drew a sharp distinction (one that Dower does not recognize) between "race" (*jinshu*) and "the ethnic nation" (*minzoku*), between Rasse and Volk.[50] The distinction was an important one for a nation-state that was attempting to assert its distinctive place in a Co-Prosperity Sphere with other Asians. But the ambivalence centered on the relationship between the ethnic nation (*minzoku*) and the nation-state (*kokka*), and the impression that these two concepts of the nation were "inextricably intertwined" was one that the state actively encouraged.

TOWARDS SYNTHESIS: MORALISM IN THE SERVICE OF THE FAMILY STATE

The modern Japanese state had never fully abandoned its original concern with religious ideology. But, as I argued above, its preoccupation with a nationalism centered on the recent nation-state and its rehabilitation of religion, particularly Buddhism, along rationalist and universal lines towards the close of the nineteenth century had left in their wake a weakening of the state's preoccupation with spiritual forms of social critique. All this began to change in the years following World War I, when populism emerged as a powerful social critique and increasingly acquired new forms in ethnic nationalism and among the new religions. By the "cultural crisis" of the 1930s, it was becoming increasingly clear that the state could not simply direct these forces against communism, but needed to establish an entirely new relationship with them. What emerged was a peculiar process, actually quite reminiscent of the Meiji settlement, in which movements that the state attempted to control actually had a good deal of influence over the subsequent character of the nation-state itself. The result was a highly efficient, rational state, deeply engaged in an aggressive war against its Asian neighbors as well as Western

---

[48] John W. Dower, *War without Mercy: Race and Power in the Pacific War* (New York: Pantheon Books, 1986), 263.

[49] Dower, *War without Mercy*, 264–6.

[50] Dower, *War without Mercy*, 267–8.

powers, that increasingly intoned moralistic and traditional sentiments while denouncing modernity *tout court.*

Almost simultaneous with the state's absorption of "nativistic idealism" in the declaration of a "New Order in East Asia," it "asserted a monopoly over the definitions of orthodoxy and the social order.... Speaking before a Diet committee on February 8, 1939, Prime Minister Hiranuma Kiichirō codified the new definition of orthodoxy: 'Let me emphasize that all religions must be one with the ideal of our national polity; they cannot be at odds with the spirit of our Imperial Way.'"[51]

To that end, the Peace Preservation Law was revised in 1941 "with the specific purpose of rooting out those religions, mainly Shinto, which previously could not be convicted of aiming to 'overthrow the national polity.' Under the revised law, officials could and did destroy such groups for propagating beliefs that simple 'denied' (i.e., varied from) the national polity."[52] Not only did the state recognize the possibility of threats to its concept of the national community from within even "nationalist" religious groups, but it also put into place heavy sanctions for those who would use religious practice to mask anti-state rhetoric.

Alongside suppression of "unorthodox" religious beliefs, the state also sought to direct, if not incorporate, the force of moral critique. The 1942 symposium on "overcoming modernity," sponsored by the "Council on Intellectual Cooperation (知的協力会議), is a good example of the state's attempt to provide "proper guidance" to moral and nationalist critiques. Indeed, the very purpose of the symposium was, arguably, to co-opt much of the force of these ethnic nationalist critiques within the state structure by appealing to a morality that united all Japanese against a materialism and amoralism that purportedly stemmed from foreign culture. No one expressed the bond between moralism and the state better than Nishitani Keiji, who explained the role of the moral state in the paper he prepared for the symposium:

> Why does the nation-state (*kokka*) demand a professional service from the people (*kokumin*) that extinguishes their private sense of self? *It is, quite simply, because of the need to strengthen, as much as possible, its internal unity as a nation-state.* And this unity is necessary for the nation-state

[51] Garon, "State and Religion in Imperial Japan," 300–1. Internal quotes are attributed to 渡辺 治 Watanabe Osamu, ファシズム期の宗教統制—治安維持法の宗教団体へ法発動をめぐって [The control of religion in an age of fascism: Legal activities of the security laws against religion], in ファシズム期の国家と社会—戦時日本の法体制 [Nation and society in an age of fascism: The legal system in wartime Japan], ed. by the Tokyo University Institute for Social Sciences (Tokyo: Tokyo University Press, 1979), 160.

[52] Garon, "State and Religion in Imperial Japan," 301.

193

to concentrate its total power as an individual totality and to act with a high level of energy. Moreover, the concentration of that total power is fundamentally impossible without a profound ethicality that would lead each and every Japanese to extinguish their private selves and be reduced, as a totality, to the nation-state.[53]

Nishitani's valorization of the state as a totality seems to contradict Tanabe's belief that totalitarianism stemmed from a "simple ethnic-nationalism." But in fact both agreed that ethnic nationalism needed to be replaced by a new, enhanced foundation for the nation-state as the only unity of the real and the ideal.

While Nishitani's emphasis on the "ethicality" of the state was the most explicit expression of the attempt to wed moralism and the modern state, others at the symposium responded with equal vigor to the perception that modernity meant a loss of religiosity. Kamei Katsuichirō focused on "spirit" (精神) to represent the modern Japanese in a way that skillfully avoided the question of whether they were an "ethnic nation" or members of a "nation-state": in the end, he concluded, they were merely "Japanese who have lost sight of their gods (*kami*)."[54] His fellow romantic, Hayashi Fusao, refined this "spirit" to "a heart that seeks purity" and he found it ultimately in a "heart that serves the Tennō" (勤皇の心), for after all "the denial of the gods (*kami*) is...the denial of the divine country Japan (神国日本)."[55] And even the Catholic theologian Yoshimitsu Yoshihiko was able to agree that the first order of business for Japanese in 1942 was "a repentance of the soul."[56] While there were profound differences among these men as to whether modernity was foreign or Japanese, the symposium on overcoming modernity did succeed in providing a new moral mission to the wartime state and thereby distract some attention from the contradictions that rested at the heart of its aggression in Asia.

The state's renewed concern with Buddhism can best be understood in the context of this attempt to incorporate moralism and idealism and not simply as a battle between State Shintoism and its religious rivals. That struggle was solved in the aftermath of the Buddhist persecutions of the late nineteenth century and the construction of rehabilitated New Buddhism. But just as ethnic nationalism had a stronger grip than state nationalism on the hearts

[53] Nishitani Keiji, "An Essay on Overcoming Modernity," KC, 27. Emphasis added.

[54] Remarks attributed to Kamei in KC, 200.

[55] Remarks attributed to Hayashi in KC, 106–10.

[56] 吉満義彦 Yoshimitsu Yoshihiko, 近代超克の神学的根拠—如何にして近代人は神を見出すか [Theological grounds for the overcoming of modernity: How can people today see God?], in KC, 79–80.

of many Japanese, Buddhism remained the most vital religious force for the majority of Japanese. When, in September 1942, Kaburagi Kihei revived the heterodox theory, expounded earlier by Ogasawara Jimon in 1934, that the Buddha was merely a manifestation of the Japanese native gods (神本仏迹), his sense of timing could not have been better. Kaburagi's attempt to redefine Buddhism for the wartime state held particular significance, as it came in the midst of Shimonaka Yasaburō's campaign to have all "war heroes" buried in Shinto rites. Both the struggle over burials and Kaburagi's theological debates suggested the tremendous power Buddhism retained over the Japanese people even during the heyday of State Shinto ideology. Yet, following so closely after the symposium on overcoming modernity, this theological debate helped situate Buddhism in the early 1940s within the Japanese state-directed "pan-Asianism" by restoring Japanese essence, represented by the priority placed on native *kami,* at the core of a religious tradition that otherwise might have absorbed Japan into an Asian whole.

With Kaburagi's heterodox theories in the background, one can gain a sense of the historical context of D. T. Suzuki's conversion of Zen Buddhism into the best expression of Japanese religious sensibilities. Although Suzuki belonged to a generation that was deeply influenced by the universal New Buddhism of the Meiji period, his interest in Zen as a particularistic, Japanese form of Buddhism shares in the realignment of religion that took place after the mid-1930s, when cultural and ethnic nationalism were widely discussed. Certainly, by 1942 his views converged with Kaburagi's theories when, in *Oriental "Oneness"* (東洋的 "一"), he expressed reservations concerning some forms of nationalism, while at the same time he "endorse(d) Japan's attempt to take the lead in restoring the consciousness of oneness among the peoples of Asia."[57] Here again is a manifestation of Japan as "the leading ethnic nation" (指導民族) a concept promoted by the wartime state as a means of, among other things, regaining control over the inherent polysemy of national identity by restoring the appearance of an inextricable connection between ethnic nation and the state—a solution that was expressed in the concept of the nation as a "family-state" (家族国家). The "family-state" restored the emperor to his rightful place as nominal and patriarchic head of the modern state, thus absorbing the "natural" community of the ethnic nation while dissolving it into the stronger, and more "natural," unit of the family. Thus, Suzuki's promotion of the paradoxical kōan may be seen as a response to the earlier, more rational, forms of New Buddhism and grew out of a society and a time replete with other, more historical, paradoxes—a moral state at war, a Japan in Asia but not of Asia, and the artificial nation-state appealing to the natural bonds of the family, while debating which rites

---

[57] Dower, *War without Mercy,* 227.

KEVIN M. DOAK

should be used to bury the remains of so many family members consumed in its wars.

To recapitulate, it was not that a clear distinction between the state and ethnic-nation was lacking in prewar Japan, but that the state quickly became aware of the threat posed by ethnic nationalism and intervened by creating ambiguity over the two terms at a critical, historical moment. Ethnic nationalism had tremendous appeal through its promise to raise the level of dignity of all Japanese, both in the aftermath of class-based theories such as the proletarian movement and especially in contrast to the privileged status of those most closely associated with the state—the bureaucrats themselves. It hoped to transcend the distinction between bureaucrat and subject by envisioning an organic moral community outside of the state structure. In the end, the state structure and its bureaucrats were skillful enough to co-opt much of this appeal through their own claims to native ethics and morality that redirected nationalism for state goals. In the process, however, the very nature of the modern Japanese state was changed, and changed in ways that some pragmatic politicians resisted. But co-option was not subjugation, and the dialectic between ethnic nationalism and state nationalism, and its intersection by Buddhist faith, has continued on into the postwar period, providing contemporary reminders of the spiritual depth of nationalist sentiment and the political passion of religious conviction.

196

The Symposium on "Overcoming Modernity"

MINAMOTO Ryōen

I N JULY 1942 A GROUP of Japanese intellectuals was brought together by the
magazine *Literary World* (文学界) in symposium to discuss modern Western civilization and its reception in modern Japan. The papers and discussions, subsequently published under the title *Overcoming Modernity*, present
an interesting portrait of thought during wartime Japan and the position of
the Kyoto school. In this essay I propose to introduce the main thrust of those
discussions, focusing in particular on the contribution of Nishitani Keiji.

THE CONTEXT OF THE SYMPOSIUM

Ever since Takeuchi Yoshimi's critical 1959 essay on the symposium,[1] the
"overcoming modernity" debate has been linked to the well-known
Chūōkōron discussions on "The World-Historical Standpoint and Japan,"[2]
but as a later revival of interest in the symposium has shown, the papers and
discussions deserve attention on their own merits.

Takeuchi has forced intellectual historians to have a second look at the
symposium, which had previously been dismissed as "infamous" and not
worthy of serious discussion. As to why he did this, Matsumoto Ken'ichi
speculates that the incentive was his belief "that the postwar intellectual
atmosphere, in which the question of overcoming modernity was being
ignored or blithely identified as 'wartime fascist ideology,' could lead to a
weakening of democracy in the postwar period."

I am not in a position to second-guess Takeuchi's psychological motives,
but I agree with Matsumoto that the historical importance of his work rests
on "its distinction between the symposium, the ideas, and those who exploited

---

[1] 竹内 好 Takeuchi Yoshimi, 近代化と伝統 [Modernization and tradition] appeared in volume
7 of 近代日本思想史講座 [Lectures on the history of modern thought in Japan] (Tokyo: Chikuma
Shobō, 1959).

[2] See the discussion by Horio Tsutomu in this volume, pages 289–315.

the ideas."[3] Takeuchi made it possible, for the first time, to treat the issues objectively by removing the bias of "wartime propaganda" that had previously surrounded the term *overcoming modernity*, whose very mention created such a surplus of animus (or in some cases, nostalgia) that serious discussion was impossible. As the years went by, however, and the symbolic meaning of the phrase faded, Takeuchi's work was also largely forgotten and eventually displaced by the ebb and flow of opinion about modernity—a new enthusiasm for the modern age, followed by a turn to postmodernism, followed by a drift towards reaffirming prewar thinking.

As mentioned, Takeuchi's approach was to link the debate on "overcoming modernity" with the *Chūōkōron* discussions of the Kyoto-school thinkers on Japan's place in world history. The philosopher Hiromatsu Wataru also took an interest in the debate, shifting the focus of the critique away from Japanese Romanticism and on to the Kyoto school. His interest was not simply to resurrect the wartime debates but also to sift the wheat from the chaff to see what might be of use to us in our own times.[4] Hiromatsu's work was followed by Karatani Kōjin's extensive work.[5] More recently, Ōhashi Ryōsuke, a young heir to the Kyoto school tradition, has tackled the topic of "overcoming modernism" from a different perspective. To begin with, he rejects Hiromatsu's Marxist critique of the Kyoto school as "lacking serious research in the historical and social foundations of the thought of the modern period, getting completely wrapped up in abstract sermons purporting to give a philosophical grasp of what it is that is supposed to be overcome.[6] Ōhashi argues that an examination of the contributions of the Kyoto school philosophers prior to the war brings out an important insight with which I find myself in agreement:

[3] See 松本健一 Matsumoto Ken'ichi's concluding "Commentary" to Takeuchi Yoshimi, 近代の超克 [Overcoming modernity] (Tokyo: Chikuma Sōsho 285, 1983), 271, 280.

[4] See his 「近代の超克」論—昭和思想史への一視角 [Theories on "overcoming modernity": One perspective on the intellectual history of the Shōwa period] (Tokyo: Kōdansha, 1980).

[5] 柄谷行人 Karatani Kōjin, 「戦前」の思想 ["Prewar" thoughts] (Tokyo: Shunjūsha, 1994). After completing the present essay, I read Karatani's and found myself in agreement on two points. First, the fascination with Yasuda Yojūrō's Romanticism is a result of its posture of disinterestedness. And second, the *Literary World* circle did their best to warn against political statements, which even today is clear in reading the "Overcoming Modernity" symposium and which was made possible by the magazine's "standpoint of literary liberalism." This second point is particularly significant. I believe this is the first time for a critic to separate the symposium from the *Chūōkōron* discussions and treat it on its own merits. It is this very position that I have argued for here. However, I have my doubts about Karatani's view that at the time of the symposium (July of 1942) the members of the *Literary World* circle had predicted Japan's defeat in the war.

[6] Hiromatsu, *Theories on "Overcoming Modernity,"* 246.

That Europe is only one, relative world, neither the only world nor the center of the world. Quite the contrary, no matter how much the non-European worlds modernize or are influenced by Europe, there remain cultures and traditions that do not ultimately derive from Europe.[7]

The Organization

The idea for a symposium on "Overcoming Modernity" was conceived by Kawakami Tetsutarō, Kobayashi Hideo, and Kamei Katsuichirō, all members of the circle that formed around the magazine *Literary World*. Kawakami took care of the organizational details and chaired the sessions, while Kamei delivered a paper. All three of them, along with Nakamura Mitsuo, Miyoshi Tatsuji, and Hayashi Fusao, took part in the discussions, which were held in Tokyo in July 1942. The papers were printed in the September and October issues of the magazine. The entire collection, including a paper by Nakamura and an edited transcript of the discussions, was published in July of the following year by Sōgensha of Tokyo.

Unlike the *Chūōkōron* debates, which dealt more with the philosophy of history, the "Overcoming Modernity" symposium dealt with the nature of civilizations. Of the thirteen participants, only two were members of the Kyoto school, whereas all the participants in the *Chūōkōron* debates belonged to the Kyoto school. The two in question, Nishitani Keiji and Suzuki Shigetaka, were also part of the *Chūōkōron* discussions. Shimomura Toratarō, though not a member of the Kyoto school strictly speaking, moved in academic circles that had ties to it. In addition to the six members of *Literary World*, other participants included Moroi Saburō, a music theorist and composer, Kikuchi Masashi, an atomic physicist, Yoshimitsu Yoshihiko, a Catholic theologian, and Tsumura Hideo, a movie critic. The criterion for selection of the group is not clear, but the invitations seem to have been extended to specialists who were also in some sense cultural critics.

Kawakami Tetsutarō explains that the symposium was modeled on a number of similar conferences sponsored in Europe by the League of Nations Committee for Intellectual Cooperation. During the mid-1930s the atmosphere of free thought began to erode as the Japanese military (led by the Army) and its sympathizers started advocating the empty slogan "the promotion of the Japanese spirit." The symposium was conceived and its topic chosen, therefore, at a time when the cultural spheres of Europe and Japan

---

[7] 大橋良介 Ōhashi Ryōsuke, 近代の超克—京都学派 [Overcoming modernity and the Kyoto school], in his 日本的なもの、ヨーロッパ的なもの [Things Japanese, things European] (Tokyo: Shinchōsha, 1992), 156.

were growing increasingly isolated and estranged from one another, in the hopes that it might provide a beacon for the intellectual community.[8]

This does not mean that Kawakami and others of the *Literary World* circle had come to any conclusions about the modern age or how to "overcome" its problems. Moreover, the variety of opinion among the participants was too diverse to speak of any consistent pattern of thought emerging from the papers and discussions. I recall reading a criticism of the symposium as "a giant free-for-all," but matters are not so simple. There is no question that it represented a common wish by all concerned to reflect on Japan's situation during a time of anxiety over the acceleration of the war effort and a time of momentous cultural change when the norms of civilization itself had come up for question, and to consider how best to set the compass for the voyage ahead. In a sense, the symposium may be characterized as a premature challenge to the questions that have yet to be answered today, fifty years after the end of the war.

Basically, the participants were middle-of-the-roaders, including Kamei Katsuichirō and Hayashi Fusao, who had converted from communism. Hayashi Fusao was the most nationalistic of the group and sympathetic to the rightist cause, though he was not himself a member of any rightist organization.

Right-Wing Japan, Left-Wing Japan

Historically, the right represents a resistance against the policies of rapid modernization and Westernization taken by the Meiji government. Hiraoka Kōtarō, Tōyama Mitsuru, and others formed the Gen'yōsha (玄洋社, Dark Ocean Society) in 1881 to express their protest. In 1901 a splinter group broke away under the leadership of Uchida Ryōhei to set up the Kokuryūkai (黒龍会, Black Dragon Society). Subtle differences aside, these groups aimed at being non-governmental "patriots," and held to nationalism, the centrality of the imperial family, and the construction of a Greater Asian sphere.

The success of the Russian Revolution and the subsequent rise of the socialist movement within Japan, the revelation of the social contradictions that accompanied the rapid growth of capitalism in the country, the social unrest that followed on the economic recession after the First World War, the intensification of the anti-Japanese movement in China, the penetration of individualism in Japan—each such new development made the young generation sympathetic to a rightist movement more and more dissatisfied with the inability of the old right to do anything, and led them to think that there was no way out except through "restructuring the nation." The right-wing movements of Japan were faced with a new situation.

---

[8] See 河上徹太郎 Kawakami Tetsutarō, "Closing Words," KC, 167.

200

Their response included such things as a turn to the divinization of the emperor and an absolutization of his present authority, an amalgamation of nationalism and sociality, an acceptance of German *Geopolitik*, and an alignment with the military, particularly the Army, as a strategy to realize the ideals they held so fervently. They also enlisted lower-ranking officers to carry out what needed to be done, were not adverse to assassination for practical ends, and supported the proponents of "agriculture-first" as a check against capitalism. Those they faulted most for the state of the country were the elder statesmen that surrounded the emperor, liberalist politicians, financial cartels, military cliques, liberals, the individualistic intelligentsia, and the advocates of socialism and communism.

In order to bring down these elements in society, the rightists believed that it was necessary to rely on Japan's traditional religion and philosophy. Some turned to the Japanese classics and to Shinto and Confucian ideas in the Hirata school, the Kimon school, and the later Mito school as the best way to crystallize a politico-religious nationalism. Representative leaders of this direction at the time include Hiraizumi Kiyoshi, professor of national history at the Tokyo Imperial University, and Imaizumi Teisuke, president of the Nihon Kōsei Gakkai (日本皇政学会). On the other hand, rightists attracted to Buddhism, like Kita Ikki, Inoue Nisshō, and Ishihara Kanji, turned to Nichiren for support, in particular to the interpretations propounded by the line of Tanaka Chigaku.[9]

Those interested in management theory turned to the late Edo thinker Satō Nobuhiro's theory of continental management as a precedent. Meantime, a legal foundation for absolutizing the emperor was provided by Uesugi Shinkichi's *Theory of the Divine Right of the Emperor* (天皇神権論). On this basis certain rightists succeeded in having Minobe Tatsukichi (1873-1948)—whose *Imperial Organ Theory* was the dominant interpretation of the constitution during the late Taishō and early Shōwa periods—removed from his teaching post in 1935. Another object of the attacks of the nationalistic right were the studies in ancient history of Tsuda Sōkichi (1873-1961), which undermined their thinking by liberating the *Kojiki* and the *Nihonshoki* from hitherto dogmatic interpretations. As was the case with Minobe, his works were banned and he was forced to retire from teaching in 1940. We should not forget that Watsuji Tetsurō was among those to defend Tsuda's scholarship during the court trial that resulted.

A third example of academic conscience and scholarly excellence persecuted at the time was Kawai Eijirō (1881–1944), one of the few historians of

[9] I would note, however, that since the celebrated writer and devout Buddhist Miyazawa Kenji became a disciple of Tanaka Chigaku and remained a follower of Nichiren, one must not simply identify Tanaka Chigaku nationalism with Nichirenism.

Western social thought. Besides being conversant in English utilitarian theory and the idealistic ethics of T. H. Green, he had an interest in the thought of the Fabian Society and liberalism, taking as his own position a kind of Fabian socialism from which he courageously attacked Japan's militarism as "fascist." As a result, he was attacked from the right by the nationalists and militarists and from the left by Marxist economists, and in 1939 was forced to resign from his post. When a court found him guilty, the publication of his books was banned.

The demagoguery for the right was provided by Minoda Muneki (1894-1946), who relied on the support of the *Genri Nipponsha* (原理日本社, Japan Principle Society) founded in 1925. His way of arguing and style of criticism were so eccentric as to earn him the name "Minoda the Crazy" (a pun on the reading of his personal name 胸喜 and the word 狂気), but he was hated and feared. Having studied under Uesugi Shinkichi and the poet Mitsui Kōshi, president of a group known as *Sumeramikuni* (Land of the Emperor), he presided over the magazine *Genri Nippon* and in its pages developed the case against Marxism and democracy. During the Taishō period he dug his claws into the "Taishō democracy" of Yoshino Sakuzō, and in the Shōwa period he railed against democratic trends in the universities, including the theories of Takikawa Yukitoki of Kyoto University and Minobe Tatsukichi. He instigated the so-called "Takikawa Incident" and "Imperial Organ Theory Incident" and sent shock waves throughout the "academic freedom" that the Shōwa academic leaders had worked to build up. One after the other, Suehiro Izutarō, Kawai Eijirō, Nishida Kitarō, Tanabe Hajime, Kuwaki Gen'yoku, Hasegawa Nyozekan, Sugimori Kōjirō, and others like them fell prey to his wiles.[10]

During my high-school years, a friend passed on to me a copy of something Minoda had written called *The Restoration of Scholarship* (学術維新). I had a look at it, but did not find much in it in the way of criticism or see anything particularly scholarly in its content. In fact I remember putting it down in disgust because I couldn't make heads or tails of it. Once I was in university I had completely forgotten about it, but on 30 January 1946, after Japan had been defeated in the war, my eyes fell on a short piece in my home town Kumamoto newspaper, reporting that Minoda had committed suicide. I was surprised that it was someone so close to home, but somehow it did not strike me as unexpected, almost as if it had happened to someone unknown, from a distant country. Perhaps it was because at the time I did not have a

---

[10] The entry on Minobe in the 国史大辞典 [Cyclopedia of national history] (Tokyo: Yoshikawa Kōbunkan, 1992) relies heavily on the essay of 大島康正 Ōshima Yasumasa, 大東亜戦争と京都学派—知識人の政治参加について [The Greater East Asia War and the Kyoto school: The political participation of the intellectuals], 中央公論 80 (August, 1965). This essay is an extremely valuable resource on the activities of the Kyoto school during the war, written by someone on the inside.

very good idea of the role these people had played in Shōwa history. I never did pick up that book again, but I wonder what impression I would have if it were to fall into my hands a second time.

Saitō Tadashi, Saitō Shō, Toyokawa Noboru, Satō Tsūji, and other right-wing nationalist philosophers who advocated a "philosophy of the imperial way" criticized the Kyoto school's view of history for its lack of historical will, for not having sacrificed itself to the historical process, for being content to do an analysis from the sidelines, and for being a speculative philosophy that runs the danger of classifying the Empire as a particular historical archetype.[11]

Strictly speaking, the left referred to the Marxists and anarchists. De facto many of those who joined social movements were communists and anarchists, but since Communism had become illegal and anarchism was being actively repressed, not many would have used these labels for themselves in the years around 1935. The spread of Marxism among the intelligentsia was considerable. In the generation just above mine, hardly anybody seems to have escaped baptism in the waters of Marxist thinking, whether or not they eventually agreed with it. The influence was especially strong in the fields of economics and economic history, but there was an immense intellectual assault on ideas of history in the name of a broad-ranging materialistic view of history, and on the philosophical front those who had grown comfortable in the world of idealism were shaken to the roots.

Tosaka Jun, one of Nishida's brilliant disciples, became a communist. Miki Kiyoshi, though not going that far, raised the banner of a "new science" to which young people sympathetic to Marxism rallied. This was the backdrop against which Nishida penned his poem:

> It is because of Marx
> that sleep comes hard to me.[12]

The influence of Marxism did not stop at moral questions but also touched on the problem of how to understand present-day Japan. The book *Lectures on Japanese Capitalism* (日本資本主義講座) published by Iwanami was so influential that people were divided into the camps of "lecturists" and "laborists" depending on where they stood on modern Japanese society. Marxism clearly had an important part to play in the tumultuous debate that resulted.

---

[11] This group seems to have had ties to the army. The entry also relies on Ōshima's essay (see note 10). In any case, I report all of this second-hand, since, although I recall browsing the bookshelves during the war and reading the names of their books on the spines, I never actually read them.

[12] See NK, 30.

By the mid-1930s, the impact of the Marxists had diminished, but given the many contradictions and irrational elements that persisted in Japanese society, along with the prolonged war with China that seemed to have the country trapped in a swamp and the harassment by the Higher Special Police, large numbers of liberal intellectuals, though not strictly leftists themselves, continued in their sympathy for the Marxist program. Nor should it be forgotten that one of the hallmarks of the left and its sympathizers was its opposition to the nationalist system of the Meiji constitution, dubbed "the emperor system."

When trying to place the Kyoto school, it is important to note that among those who rushed to the left and those who stayed behind there was no break in relations (as witnessed in the friendly ties that Nishitani and Tosaka maintained, despite their differences),[13] and they remain united in their stance against the common enemy: the narrow-minded nationalists. Where relationships between the Kyoto school and the left are concerned, we must not forget that the opposition was based on differences in worldview that grew out of the common base of an open-mindedness to the world.

The Middle-of-the-Roaders

If we may lump together the remainder of Japan's intelligentsia who did not belong to the right or the left as we have defined them, those close to the right would be the Japanese romanticists like Yasuda Yojūrō. They considered all of modern Japan after the Meiji Enlightenment to be a "decline" and made a strong appeal for a radical return to an aesthetic Japan. Many literary movements were drawn to them, including a number of my close friends who were intoxicated by Yasuda's *A Coronation Poet* and *The Bridge of Japan*. Because of their "aesthetic nationalism," the Japanese Romantics, unlike the

---

[13] See Nishitani's "Remembrances of Tosaka Jun," NKC 21:129–33. At the conclusion of this piece, Nishitani comments:

The last time I met him was just before he was put into prison. He was in Kyoto for something to do with the translation of a Catholic dictionary, and stopped by the house. At the time I, too, was considered one of the members of the "Kyoto school." It was after I had also been attacked by rightists from behind the shield of the army. Even then, journalists of the very magazines that were attacking me would come and invite me to take part in discussions they were sponsoring. Their meanness was transparent and we refused to go along with them, but somehow they had gotten under my skin and I even thought about going with them on my own and speaking my mind. When I told him this, he stopped me in my tracks, telling me to give up such nonsense and have nothing to do with that pack of mad dogs. He also said he thought the war would be over soon. Shortly thereafter a postcard came from Tokyo. They had finally put him in prison, it said, but he would soon be out and we would meet again. I understood him to mean that he would be released once the war was over. But when the war did end, he did not get out after all. I often wonder if his spirit is looking down on us today and what it is thinking.

right wing, are not associated with any political movement. Their position was narrow and biased, but it remained a literary, artistic movement rooted in a romantic longing for "things noble and passionate."

If we consider Japanese Romanticism to represent the form that Japanese nationalism took in the world of aesthetics, then the people associated with the *Literary World* were even more diverse and are therefore hard to categorize. The basic difference comes to this: the Romantics were narrow but threw themselves intuitively and precipitously into the world of traditional beauty, whereas the latter were trained in the study of Western literature and therefore were better grounded intellectually and critically. Rather than work for breadth they exerted themselves more in discovering the core of their own literary studies.

Within the *Literary World* circle, the closest to the Romantic movement was probably Kobayashi Hideo. He was the one most deeply preoccupied with the difficult task of maintaining identity as a Japanese while studying Western thought and literature. In his youth he was enchanted with Rimbaud, captivated by Bergson, fascinated by Dostoevsky's power as a writer, and was quite content to give his life over to these pursuits. Then his interests took a turn back to the world of the Japanese classics, and in his late years he found himself most at home in the world of Motoori Norinaga. He stressed that the way to discover the classics of Japan is to press ahead diligently in the study of Western literature. In this he differed from Yasuda's fleet-footed leap directly into the world of Japan. Be that as it may, the point distinguishes those in the *Literary World* circle in general from the Romantics.

In terms of the social dimension, the most important relationship to postwar Japan was is seen in the "Group of 27" that gathered around Kiyozawa Kiyoshi and was set up by Ashida Hitoshi, Ishibashi Tanzan, and the then president of the Chūōkōron publishing house, Shimanaka Yūsaku. According to Ōshima Yasumasa, they were resigned to the fact that Anglo-American liberalism would finally emerge victorious and for that reason did not collaborate in the war effort.[14]

In the religious world we may mention the group of non-Christian liberals at the former First Higher School, including Takeyama Michio, Ichihara Toyota, and their president and backer Abe Yoshishige. During the war they were engaged only in translation and expressed no opinions of their own. As for Christian liberals, we may mention Nanbara Shigeru, who published an indirect attack against the Japanese state during the war,[15] Yanaihara Tadao, and Mitani Takamasa.

---

[14] It is not clear to me just why this "Group of 27" merits the extensive treatment it has been given, but I imagine it has something to do with the impressive list of members that made it up.

[15] See below, pages 257–9.

The most pointed relationship to the times is to be seen in Kawai Eijirō, whom we referred to earlier, and his sympathizers. An anti-Marxist but not a rightist, Kawai was receptive to the ideas of John Stuart Mill and turned to Thomas Green for his self-reliant ethical standpoint. He had a profound knowledge of English thought, but grew dissatisfied with capitalistic liberalism and opted for social democracy. He was a spirited man and criticized head-on the policies of the army on the Chinese mainland. Caught between the attacks of the army and the right-wing forces on the one hand, and the Marxist economists who disagreed with him on the other, he was driven out of the university. He died without seeing the end of the war. One may perhaps associate him with the liberal left. In any case, his books were a voice of conscience for many students at the time.

In this same left-of-center position were liberalists like Ōtsuka Hisao, a Christian and a follower of Max Weber who did not lose his sympathies for the Marxists. Non-Christian liberals included the likes of Maruyama Masao, a devotee of English nominalism and follower of Hobbes who sought a direction for Japan in the line from Ogyū Sorai to Fukuzawa Yukichi. Knowledgeable about Marxism as well, he produced a standard work called *A History of Japanese Political Thought*. Also standing left of center were a large number of Marxist sympathizers and fellow travelers whom we may call "hidden Communists." Without them the intellectual history of the postwar period would not make sense.

The participants in the "Overcoming Modernity" symposium, as I mentioned earlier, all belong to this middle-of-the-road faction. One of them, Kamei Katsuichirō, was associated with Japanese Romanticism and was a core element in the *Literary World* circle. As noted earlier, two others belonged to the Kyoto school (Nishitani Keiji and Suzuki Shigetaka), and one had scholarly ties to it (Shimomura Toratarō). The others had no such affiliation.

One has to suppose that the members of the *Literary World* circle chose partners whom they considered congenial to their own ideas.[16] I further surmise that they would have had to fulfill the following general requirements: an understanding of Western civilization and recognition of its significance, a sense of the problematic areas in modern Western civilization or of the problems Japan faced in accepting Western modernity, an appreciation of the *raison d'être* and value of the traditional civilization of the East in contrast to that of the West—in a word, people with a feel for looking critically at civilization.

In terms of social composition, as far as we have seen the participants were restricted to persons within the sphere of Japan's intellectual world.

---

[16] I base this suspicion on remarks made during the discussion by Kawakami to Kikuchi (KC, 204–6).

Their common concern was modern Western civilization and its acceptance on the one hand, and the possibilities for Japanese and Eastern traditions on the other. At least in this symposium, the question of the Greater East Asian War was not central for them. In the case of the Kyoto school representatives, Nishitani and Suzuki, it is clear that the question of the East Asian Coprosperity Sphere was also a serious concern, but this does not show in their comments and discussion here. No doubt the outbreak of war was an important psychological factor in the background, but in the pages that follow I shall restrict remarks on the war to what was actually said in the papers and discussion.

"MODERNITY" AND ITS "OVERCOMING"

We must begin with some account of how the participants understood the term *modernity* and then whether or not they thought it was something to be *overcome*. The underlying assumption throughout was that modernity was a European phenomenon and that modernity in Japan was the influence of Western European civilization.

We may classify the participants' understanding of modernity and its overcoming into several types. The physicist Kikuchi Masashi's view that "there is neither modernity nor antiquity in science," while a not uncommon view, was not shared by the others at the symposium, who were convinced that modern Europe was an age with a meaning all its own. Yoshimitsu Yoshihiko, a Catholic theologian from Sophia University, was clearest in this regard, rejecting the modern West and calling for a return to medieval Catholicism. Despite the strong impact of the Catholic theologian Jacques Maritain and of Nicolai Berdyaev with his "New Middle Ages," the predominant influence on Yoshimitsu was the French poet and philosopher Charles Péguy. In his late twenties Yoshimitsu became disenchanted with Western modernity when he saw the atheism to which it finally led. To avoid this, he threw himself back to the Middle Ages and argued for the need to restore the unity of culture and religion, of knowledge and spirituality, that he found there. In Yoshimitsu's view, the spirit of Western modernity does not represent a "rejection" of the medieval spirit but a "schizophrenic result" of the breakdown of the medieval world. Given this opposition, a return to the Middle Ages was a matter of course.[17]

Since none of the other participants shared Yoshimitsu's Catholic faith, it is not surprising that their attitudes to modernity differ from his. The group was by and large split between those who argued that modernity is some-

[17] KC, 9.

207

thing to be overcome and others who argued for a recognition of its value. A few others did not mention the modernity of the West at all but spoke of the need to overcome modernity in Japan.

Modernity and Music

For me, the most interesting position among those who argued for going beyond Western modernity was that of the musician Moroi Saburō. "For some time now," he explained, "I have been concerned with the problem of how to overthrow modern music and rescue music from the art of sensory stimulation and restore it to an art of the spirit. To this day that concern has not changed in the least."[18] Living in the present as we do, Moroi noted, we are caught up in modern music. Granted we are born into it, we have still to decide whether to follow it unconditionally or to resist and bring into question its essence.

Moroi opted for the latter course. One reason was his sense that modern composers did better work in their youth than when they were more advanced in age, so that their musical compositions did not mature as they themselves matured in life. Modern music for him is guilty of a fundamental error, namely the idea that music is the art of the pleasure of sensory stimulation. This brought him to think of returning to music as an art of the spirit.

In the history of music, the term *modern* refers to the early decades of the twentieth century. Specifically, it is said to refer to what are called impressionism, expressionism, and primitivism. By noting transformations in the idea of music, Moroi argued persuasively that the beginnings of modern music lie rather in romanticism. He saw signs of hope in the neoclassical trend that appeared after the First World War. If "analysis" is the basic principle at work in the music of romanticism and modernity, its form of musical expression is "harmonic." In contrast, neoclassical music begins by retrieving the monistic quality and continuity of sound, and stresses the formal element of unity in music (not in the concrete sense but in the sense of the principles of form). He sees the neoclassical movement as still incomplete, but acknowledges that it is a step towards defeating modernity in European music.

Even with my little knowledge of music, I find it easy to understand what he is trying to say. As a Japanese, he finds something unsatisfying about Western music, and he attributes this to a different "feel" for music. Western music is rooted in the feeling of the "song," while the music of the East is rooted in "narration." In his own composition, Moroi said, he tries to be narrative.[19] Besides a knowledge of the essence of Western music—he refused to reject it outright—such composition requires familiarity with the ongoing spirit of

[18] KC, 38.
[19] KC, 213.

Japanese music and the elemental spirit of the Japanese people that gave it birth. It is not merely a matter of modernizing *gagaku* (雅楽, court music) or rewriting the music of traditional *naniwabushi* (浪花節, narrative ballads) for Western instruments. It means the attempt to express one's grasp of the elemental spirit of the Japanese people through Western composition and instruments. For Moroi, only such creativity can "overcome modernity" in music.

I do not know what Japanese musicians today think about Moroi's views. But I was most impressed to see someone trying to do in the world of music what Nishida was attempting in the world of philosophy. I find it a serious effort by a Japanese to come to terms with Western culture. Of course, one way to comprehend the West is to become completely Westernized, as Mori Arimasa and others like him did, but I am more persuaded by Moroi's approach. I find it surprising that readers of the symposium did not make more of it. Perhaps the ideological lens through which they were filtering its contents was too thick for its subtleties.

Suzuki on Modernity

The "Memorandum on 'Overcoming Modernity'" that Suzuki Shigetaka delivered to open the symposium was, at his own request, withdrawn prior to the publication of the proceedings. It was not to resurface in published form until 1980.[20] As it stands, the program that Suzuki laid out seems to be highly valuable, but he apparently felt that it did not fit in with the general direction of the symposium. Since my focus is on the published proceedings, I refer to his piece only briefly.

As a historian, Suzuki understood overcoming modernity as the rejection of "historicism" and the idea of "development." This is easy to argue philosophically, he notes, but quite another thing to demonstrate with the tools of historical research and description. Suzuki speaks from practical experience when he insists on the difficulty of such an undertaking. I had frequent occasion to hear him speak when he was alive, and I am sure that this was a lifelong concern of his.

Suzuki's "Memorandum" notes the need to clarify just what it is that is supposed to be overcome: "Is it the nineteenth century or is it the Renaissance?" One cannot help feeling here the influence of Christopher Dawson, who traced the mistakes of modernity to the Renaissance. Indeed, in the course of an exchange with Yoshimitsu, Suzuki remarks:

> The Renaissance was basically something born out of the Middle Ages in the sense that it was to reverse what the medievals had done. And here

[20] Hiromatsu restored the short text of the "Memorandum" in his *Theories on "Overcoming Modernity,"* 18–19, 22–3.

we come to a basic question. Apart from the fact of whether the beginnings of modernity can be traced *objectively* to the Middle Ages, I think there is something to the view that *subjectively* speaking, the modern individual began from the rejection of the Middle Ages. This is the contradiction of the modern age. Do we not need to overcome this contradiction? If there is something wrong with the spirit that rejected the Middle Ages, perhaps reflection on what we owe to the Middle Ages...is one way to overcome modernity.[21]

On the one hand, we have Suzuki's idea of associating modernity with the Middle Ages by way of the Renaissance. On the other, we have the views of Hans Freyer, Emile Durkheim, and others who locate the actual birth of modernity in the eighteenth century with the introduction of the idea of "scholarly methodology" by which scholarship ceased to be simply truth and came to be seen as a definition of the character of society and civilization.[22] For the historian, Suzuki's position on overcoming modernity raises the important question of whether modernity should be understood as the outgrowth of the Renaissance or as an eighteenth-century phenomenon. But the participants did not take up this question and attempt to answer it. Nor have any of the later commentators on the symposium.

The movie critic, Tsumura Hideo, argued that even if parts of modernity were worth taking up, "Americanism" was not. This seems to have been the general view among the general population at the time, though there was a considerable gap between the general population who enjoyed watching American movies and the intellectuals who were uninterested in American culture. Suzuki's response to this broadside, pointing out the importance of the Puritan element in America, showed a grasp of American culture rather advanced for his day. I will return to his remarks in the conclusion to this essay.

Shimomura and the Problem of Science

In contrast to those who saw modernity as something to be overcome, Shimomura Toratarō represents the opposite side who argued for the positive elements in modernity. The question of overcoming modernity in Europe arises from the idea that modern culture had fallen externally into mechanized civilization in which people are enslaved to machinery. But Shimomura

---

[21] KC, 186.

[22] For a long time, I could not understand how Suzuki, a specialist in Western medieval history, could publish *The Industrial Revolution* (産業革命), an impressive volume of reflections on science, technology, and civilization from the modern age to the present. In reexamining the symposium for this essay, I finally see the reason. I discovered that even after the war he continued thinking about the problem of "overcoming modernity."

notes that there were more slaves prior to the invention of the machine, and suggests that the enslavement of people to machinery is a result of the institutional structure—and hence ultimately the human spirit—that uses the machines. In one sense the building of machinery signifies a victory of the spirit. If there is a problem, he concludes, it lies in the imbalance between the physical sciences and the mental sciences.[23]

This leads him into a discussion of "nature" and "spirit." If the essence of nature lies in necessity, the essence of spirit lies in freedom. The superiority of spirit to nature is self-evident to the spirit. The problem is freedom. The wisdom of the ancient sages sought freedom in disciplining the spirit to obey nature (subjective freedom). Modern philosophy came up with the idea of "objective idealism," whose transformation into an "idealism of objective freedom" represents the real culmination of the self-awareness of the modern spirit that shaped modern philosophy. For Shimomura, the experimental method of modern science is a method for disclosing what does not exist naturally, or is not present in nature. The knowledge it aims at is not the intuition of essential forms but the development of nature's potential. Modern machines are the product of this method. This is not simply the application or use of nature but the restructuring or making over of nature. What results from this modern process of creation is not a simple subjective independence from nature, but a truly *objective* independence. Here, for the first time the objective idealism was given a basis for becoming concrete reality.[24]

Concerning the question of "body and soul," Shimomura notes that in antiquity the soul was considered a spirit in contrast to the body, whereas in the modern age that body no longer exists:

> Today the body is an organism whose organs are provided by machines. The tragedy of the modern age is that the old soul can no longer keep up with this "new body." A new metaphysics is needed for this new body-mind. The body today is at once gigantic and delicate. It can no longer be measured on the yardstick of ancient psychology with its talk of inner awareness and personal disciplines. It requires a political, social, even a national measure. Or perhaps better, a new theology.[25]

It is not easy to know what Shimomura had in mind with this "new body." Was it the structured body of society? Or perhaps an organization with a certain goal? In any case, prior to mechanized civilization, methods used for improving the "soul" like introspection, persuasion, asceticism, and

---

[23] Shimomura uses his own English terms to distinguish what today are known as the "natural" and "human" sciences.

[24] KC, 114–15.

[25] KC, 116.

discipline are no longer effective. Shimomura argues that finding a way to overcome modernity entails an awareness of the notion of spirit and the conceptualization of a new "theory of spiritual cultivation" in line with contemporary structures and contemporary insights. This includes the idea of overcoming modernity in a modern body and in a form that pushes ahead along the lines in which modernity has developed. He notes here that, by and large, the knowledge of the Japanese intellectual is "literary," not "scientific," or what he calls "vegetable sentiment."

The problem Shimomura set before the symposium was extremely important, but perhaps because the other participants in the symposium were not well versed in science, it did not get very far in the discussion. The medievalist Yoshimitsu argued that the fusion of science and the spirit of antiquity would bring about a unity of the natural sciences and natural philosophy and a harmony of science and Christian doctrine, even to the point of proving the existence of God. Shimomura countered that the differences between ancient science, which was based on geometry, and modern science, which is based on mathematics and physics, yield a different idea of proof. The methods of modern science came about through a union of causal necessity and the experimental method. As a branch of study modern science is fundamentally "positivistic" in nature, unlike the nature of learning in antiquity, which consisted in "ratiocination." From the standpoint of science, he argued convincingly, a return to the Middle Ages is difficult.

Shimomura's ideas of a "new body" and a "machine-creating spirit" for a mechanized civilization are extremely important and bear comparing with Norbert Wiener's "cybernetics," which were only published later. Nevertheless, Kawakami Tetsutarō booted aside Shimomura's ideas of a "new body" and a "machine-creating spirit" for a mechanized civilization: "Mechanical civilization cannot be an object to be overcome. It is not among the things the spirit overcomes. The spirit is not interested in machines." Kobayashi agreed.[26] Shimomura's ideas of the "modern body" as an organic extension of the machine and the need for a new soul to accommodate it, were not pursued in the discussions.

JAPANESE MODERNITY

Four papers in the symposium took up the question of Japan's relationship to modernity. Two of the presenters, Kamei and Hayashi, were "converts" from Communism and spoke in personal terms from their own experience. "The war we are engaged in at this moment," remarked Kamei in his short essay,

---

[26] KC, 261.

"is aimed outwardly at the destruction of the British and American forces. But internally it is a kind of basic therapy aimed at curing the psychological malaise...brought about by modern culture." His argument heats up, however, when he comes to a second problem. In his own words:

> In the name of a "battle of ideas," two clichés, a hero known as "the Japanese spirit" and a villain known as "foreign ideas," are pitted against one another.... The villain falls and the hero is showered with applause. This is the puppet-show fantasy that is being drummed into the psychology of ordinary people,....a feeble spirit captivated by a display of bravery.[27]

Admitting the importance of the classics, Kamei nevertheless objects to interpreting their contents and the sayings of the sages by means of the ruling slogans and catch-phrases. "The greatest enemy of the classics," he claims, "is a spirit that feeds on quick compliance and short memory." From the day that Japan took in the last stages of Western culture known as "modernity," the spirit of this civilization has violated the Japanese spirit in its innermost recesses, its enchantment far surpassing the hostile ideas said to come from England and America.

Kamei's critique focuses on three points: *the crisis of words* (specialized or technical vocabulary taken out of context and turned into "labels" to think with), *the deterioration of sensitivity* (outspokenness and the loss of respect for silence), and *the impact of speed on the spirit* (the desire to get things finished as quickly and efficiently as possible, which accompanies progress in mechanization). In a section entitled "The Illusion of Victory," Kamei notes:

> In the background of the present war, another war is going on. We see it in the pressure of a civilization moving relentlessly ahead with an apparently natural force of persuasion, in our trust in the machine and all the maladies and debilities of the spirit this brings in its wake, in the self-destructive behavior of people who have lost all sense of moderation. It is not sure whether we will perish in this fight or be saved, but at least as we count our victories in the war we can see, let us not deceive ourselves into thinking that this deeper war, hidden to the eyes, is a mere fantasy.[28]

There is much merit in what Kamei has to say as a criticism against the deterioration of the spirit that had surfaced under the sham excuse of "war time." Indeed, it reminds me in some ways of what Karl Jaspers had to say in *Man in the Modern Age*. But at this point his argument takes a turn to the abstract:

[27] TC, 5.
[28] TC, 6.

The illusion of "peace" that victors often carry around with them glosses over this abyssal war....Behind the mask of "peace" the poison of civilization spreads. More frightening than war is peace....The present disturbances are a war in the name of that abyssal war. In those battlefields the rise or fall of the Japanese people will depend on the clarity of their insight to drive away all delusions and on the irradicable fearlessness of their belief. Rather a war of kings than the peace of slaves![29]

It is as if Kamei had somehow confused actual warfare—in which people slaughter each other—with the demanding struggle of each of us with ourselves in the spiritual and intellectual realm.[30]

Hayashi's presentation on "The Heart of Loyalty to the Emperor" is totally different from the others and left me with the sense that it did not belong there. Still, it does represent one strain of thought among the Japanese intelligentsia of the day.[31] Hayashi begins by observing that loyalty to the emperor is distinct from mere patriotism and from allegiance to a landlord or shōgun. It is also not to be confused with Chinese or Western ideas of loyalty.[32] Rather:

Kneeling before the Gods and the emperor, I call to mind my sinfulness and something blossoms in my breast, my bowels, my limbs, and my senses one and all—this is the heart of loyalty to the emperor.... And only this heart can make a true patriot with true love of country.[33]

In the discussion, the question of Japan's spiritual condition from the Russo-Japanese War to the time of the Second World War was not taken up. Instead attention was turned to the "civilization and enlightenment" of the Meiji era. According to Hayashi, the Meiji Enlightenment was a utilitarian culture strong enough to defeat all its critics—among them Uchimura Kanzō, Okakura Tenshin, Saigō Takamori, and Nogi Maresuke—and to make victors ever after of all those who championed its cause.

---

[29] TC, 17.

[30] In saying this, I am left with the doubt that there might be something more behind his rhetorical flourishes than I was able to see.

[31] Asano Akira 浅野 晃 is like Hayashi in this regard. He is also a convert and another of the Japanese romanticists. In his interesting personal account, Hayashi, who was born in a small town in Kyūshū the year before the Russo-Japanese War, recalls how he passed his childhood indifferent to the Gods and the emperor, later argued against the national polity, and finally became a left-wing *littérateur*.

[32] The English word *Royality* is printed in the text, apparently a spelling mistake for *Royalty*, which is in turn a spelling mistake for *Loyalty*. The "new edition" preserves the mistake intact, though it does correct another on page 88.

[33] KC, 109–10.

There is something to what he says, but neither he nor any of the participants make any mention of Fukuzawa Yukichi's *Outlines of Civilization*, which spoke out against the Meiji enlightenment during its height, criticizing its shallowness even as it stressed the need for positive efforts to learn from Western civilization.

Hayashi's distorted knowledge of modern Japanese history shows up also in his reply to a question of Nishitani Keiji's concerning the role that Western individualism played in eliminating the feudal class system in the early Meiji period. For Hayashi, Western individualism played no role whatsoever. The fall of the feudal system was entirely the result of the Meiji Restoration and the restoration of the ancient emperor system.[34] Here, and indeed throughout the symposium, the question of individualism, liberalism, capitalism, socialism, and other fundamental questions facing modern Japan were by and large passed over. The study of social thought may have been late in arriving to Japan because of its negative association with the emperor system, but the disciples of Kawai Eijirō and young Japanese modernists like Maruyama Masao show that this was not entirely the case. In any case, it would seem that the staff of *Literary World* did not think of including such people and their ideas in the discussion of "overcoming modernity."

As the exchange between Nishitani and Kobayashi Hideo to be taken up later will show, not all the debate was so lacking in content. The paper by Nakamura Mitsuo also merits mention in this regard.

Nakamura specialized in French literature at university, but as his postwar *History of Meiji Literature* attests, along with his interest in literary criticism, he brought a broad perspective to carefully documented studies on modern Japanese literature and the history of the modern spirit that lay behind it. He was dissatisfied with the flow of the discussion, and seems to have maintained silence from beginning to end. Afterwards he submitted an essay, whose main points we may summarize here.

Nakamura begins with a discussion of the difference in attitudes towards modernity between Europe and Japan. In Europe, he finds both "a healthy despair and a healthy self-confidence, rooted in the things of life," that results from having lived through the modern age. In Japan, however,

> modern culture is no more than a superficial import. To speak of overcoming modernity forgetting this unique character of our country's "modernity"…is nothing more than toying around with abstractions.[35]

[34] KC, 243.
[35] KC, 52.

The speed with which the Japanese lifestyle changed after the Meiji period can only be called "miraculous," but on the other hand:

> Who knows what sacrifices this miracle cost? How much confusion of spirit has this abrupt change of lifestyle brought us, forced upon us as something we "needed"! How badly have the heartless demands of the times twisted the spirits of those who had no choice but to accommodate themselves to it! Surely this is the most serious question our country's modernity puts to us.[36]

Regarding the relationship between the West and modern Japan, Nakamura observes that many in Japan mistakenly suppose "modernity" to be synonymous with Western Europe, confusing the West with the modern West. This leads him to ask why Japan continues the insanity of pursuing what is "new" in ignorance of Europe's past, and how such a serious distortion of perspective could have arisen in Japan's commonsense view of Europe. For Nakamura, the answer begins with a careful consideration of how Western civilization was imported to Japan during the Meiji period.

Nakamura points out that in the years immediately after the reopening of Japan to contact with the outside world, in order to guarantee its survival as a nation against pressures from the West, it felt the urgent need for military and economic parity. This could only be achieved by importing a scientific, that is to say Western, civilization.

A scientific civilization based on "utility" does not constitute a foundation for true science and technology. What was forced on the Japanese of the Meiji era was a ready-made knowledge and technology, the antithesis of true scientific endeavor. Meiji "scholars" were no more than hasty importers of new and ready-to-wear knowledge from the West. They lacked the capacity to think for themselves. This kind of "reckless and lax mind set,"[37] out for the maximum results with the least amount of effort, spread like an irresistible fashion among the Japanese academic community. Even in this time of war, Nakamura complained, the simple "rush" to adapt to the superficial moods of the times has not let up, and the ranks of those who have lost the habit of thinking on their own is on the increase. Noting that numbers of such spiritually handicapped are also notable among those calling for a resurrection of the classics or preaching tradition and history, he finds it hard to imagine how the serious business of a country's cultural self-awareness can be carried out as such a casual pursuit (a point made also in the essay of Kamei referred to earlier and in Miyoshi Tatsuji's contribution, "A Brief Account").

[36] KC, 155.
[37] KC, 160.

Nakamura's conclusion regarding the "overcoming of modernity" is this:

> If this is the harsh reality of the "modernity" as we live it, the first concrete step to overcoming it seems to lie in the clear consciousness that the enemy with whom we must do battle is the spiritual crisis within us and among us.[38]

Nakamura's argument follows the same line as the ideas Natsume Sōseki developed in his lecture "The Blossoming of Contemporary Japan" (現代日本の開花) and in his novels. Having spent the years of my youth during the war frustrated by the endless stream of short-circuited ideas that filled the newspapers and books, I feel a sense of relief at knowing that there were "normal minds" like this around.

I do not know how Nakamura Mitsuo understood Japanese or Eastern tradition. He was probably an advocate of the West. There were others of his contemporaries, like the specialist in ancient Greek philosophy, Tanaka Michitarō, who pursued this standpoint more radically in his own field. Such persons took a step back from their times and were able to look at things with a calmer and clearer eye. As much as I appreciate this, I still have my doubts about the absoluteness of Western civilization and wonder what it is that Japan and the East have to contribute to the culture of all humanity.

The keynote of the thinkers of the Kyoto school, as persons educated in the traditions of Japan and the East despite all they have learned from the West, has been the attempt to bring the possibilities latent in traditional culture into encounter with Western culture. With this in mind, we may look more closely at the contribution of Nishitani Keiji to the symposium.

NISHITANI ON OVERCOMING MODERNITY

Nishitani's brief but well-structured contribution to the symposium, "My Idea of the Overcoming of Modernity," suggests that Japan's adoption of European culture is characterized by the importation of disparate elements with little or no connection to each other. This contrasts with the introduction of Chinese culture in ancient times, which was done more organically. Part of the blame lies with Japan's picking and choosing things from the West with no concern for relationships among them, but a more fundamental reason lies in the fact that Western culture itself had lost its sense of cultural connectedness.

According to Nishitani, Europe's modern age was a time that saw the crumbling of the foundations that had once made possible a unified view of

[38] KC, 164.

the world. Specifically, he singled out three streams of thought in modern Western Europe: the Reformation, the Renaissance, and the rise of the natural sciences. It is a mistake to see these as merely three tributaries flowing from a single intellectual mainstream. They are in essence independent of each other and radically at odds with one another because each holds within itself a completely different view of the world.

Nishitani argues for the need to lay new foundations if we are to face the basic questions of today and forge a new worldview. He poses the problem in terms of religion:

> What kind of religiosity will it take to give culture, history, ethics and so forth, all of which entail a complete affirmation of the human, the freedom to pursue their own standpoint, while at the same time insuring equal freedom of activity for the sciences, whose standpoint is one of indifference to the human, and then to unify the two standpoints?[39]

The answer, for him, lies in "the construction of an ethics based on religion." This standpoint of religiosity, which can be discovered only by "probing into our own subjectivity," he calls "the standpoint of subjective nothingness."[40]

Subjective nothingness, Nishitani explained, is not some *thing* that can be grasped objectively. It can only be grasped in an act of free spontaneity as a reality belonging to the interiority of the self. It entails a denial of the conscious self, a "no-self" or "no mind" that extinguishes the petty ego. In a word, it is the True Self. Having said that, Nishitani hastens to add that awareness of this True Self is *inseparable* from the body, the natural world, the mind, and the world of culture. The point is rather that this self-awareness does not come about as the work of conscious mental activity but as the work of the subject *qua* nothingness. As a result,

> the absolute negation of all things, including culture and science, is converted directly into an absolute affirmation. The subject that creates culture or engages in science had not yet reached self-awareness at the standpoint of subjective nothingness. This standpoint, from its position of transcendence, can become immanent in the subject that creates culture or engages in science as a true subjectivity.[41]

This is Nishitani's proposal for the unification of science, culture, and religion.

What is more, Nishitani proposes this standpoint of subjective nothingness as something distinctive to Eastern religiosity, which he sees as the only

[39] KC, 23.
[40] KC, 24.
[41] KC, 25.

form of religion able to resolve the difficult relationship that science and culture have come to in the religiosity of the modern West. He believes further that this global religiosity of subjective nothingness can be developed into an ethic for the people. The standpoint of subjective nothingness makes it possible to integrate the skills refined in various occupations (technology in the broad sense of the term) and the selfless devotion to one's occupation (popular ethics), and in so doing to raise the level of "moral energy" among the people at large. The context leaves no doubt that it is the Japanese people he has in mind:

> Even in the East itself, there is no country other than Japan where Eastern religiosity has been so closely bound to national ethics as to become the cornerstone of the nation and tap its primal energies.[42]

He singles out as the most immediate problems facing Japan at present "the establishment of a new world order" and "construction of Greater East Asia." Regarding the former, he insists that the new order be a just one, and regarding the latter, that activity in Asia must in no way be taken to mean the acquiring of colonial territories.

For Nishitani, establishment of a new *and just* world order is not only an inevitable development in world history, it is also the "destiny" of Japan. "Our country is the only strong non-European country, and therefore we are pressed to challenge Anglo-Saxon domination in Asia."[43] That Japan succeeded in escaping Anglo-Saxon rule he attributes to its strong unity as a nation and the moral energy that results therefrom.

The term *moralische Energie*, taken over from the German historian Leopold von Ranke, was a byword in the social thought of the Kyoto school, but Nishitani's use of the term was somewhat different in that he expanded it to cover not only the ethics of the people or the nation but also a "world ethic." If it is only a Japanese ethic,

> it has no connection to the ethics of the world, and in certain circumstances can be linked to injustices like making other peoples and nations objects of colonization. It can be put at the service of the personal grudges of a nation, as it were. In our country today the moral energy that is the driving force of national ethics must at the same time directly energize a world ethic.[44]

We must not forget that in speaking of the actual problems that arose once the war was underway, Nishitani's aim was a world ethic that went

[42] KC, 29.
[43] KC, 32.
[44] KC, 33.

beyond the national level and he warned against colonization. This sets him apart from collaborators who fanned enthusiasm for the war among the people.

He expounded a "correlation between nation and world" and argued that the nation must get beyond a standpoint centered on itself alone and direct itself to the establishment of international relations that open up into a "horizon of the communality of nations" based on the nonduality of self and others (自他不二) and benefiting oneself in benefiting others (自利利他). He concludes that the actual task of overcoming the spirit of modernity consists in securing an ethic of moral energy, based on a religion of subjective nothingness and infusing the individual, the nation, and the world.

Among the responses, the Catholic theologian Yoshimitsu Yoshihiko, not surprisingly, criticized the first part of Nishitani's paper. But there was almost no reaction concerning the second half. One surmises that the participants and the sponsors from *Literary World* deliberately wanted to avoid touching on the question of the war. There was, however, a lively exchange on a number of other questions between Nishitani and Kobayashi, to which we shall next turn our attention.

TWO VIEWS OF HISTORY

It was Kobayashi Hideo who raised the question that started him and Nishitani off on their immensely interesting exchange. It struck him, he said, that the history of Japanese literature after the Meiji period is a history of the misunderstanding of Western literature, and that when solid research into the real history of modern thought and literature in the West had finally caught on, the country was visited by a time of political crisis insisting on the discovery of some kind or other of "Japanese principle." The discussions on "overcoming modernity," he went on, grew out of this impasse.

Kobayashi himself settled on a thoroughgoing study of Dostoevsky as the most problematic giant of modern Western literature. His concern was not to find a Japanese Dostoevsky but to make every effort to get back to the original, and as a result he discovered that Dostoevsky was not a representative of modern Russian society or Russia in the nineteenth century, but rather a writer who fought with his times and won.

From there Kobayashi came to see the way in which positivistic, scientific literary criticism falls into the trap of reflecting the conventions of a given society or age, and at the same time to recognize how all first-rate thinkers seek a meaning in life by trying to overcome the age in which they live. This brought him to challenge the ruling theories of history. In opposition to "theories of historical change" Kobayashi emphasized "theories of what does not change in history." He located the weakness of moderns in their captivation by the dynamic side of historical forces and their forgetfulness of the static side:

> Literature and the arts always take the form of harmony or order—not the form of the transformation of power but the equalizing of power. Is not the harmony and order achieved by those writers who, permanently at odds with their age, strike a balance between opposite forces a great blessing? In this sense one can speak of certain artists conquering their age. Masterpieces do not kowtow to their age but neither do they flee it. Theirs is a kind of state of static tension."[45]

From there he draws an analogy between the Japanese classics and the great writers from East and West that have come down to us through the ages. If, he suggests, "it is a serious mistake to see history as ever changing or progressing," then those figures that have passed through a history of the same people struggling with the same things are "eternal." He suggests that the history of Japan and Japanese classics be reconsidered in the same way.

While acknowledging the point, Kawakami Tetsutarō questioned whether this should be called something like "universal anthropology" rather than "history." Kobayashi preferred to consider it a form of "aesthetics," when Nishitani turned the question back again to history. This is the point at which their exchange begins.

For Nishitani history contains both change and something unchangeable, and the question is whether these two aspects are separated or permanently bound to one another. If bound, then even what the world of literature considers "eternal" is really a product of history. In the case of great authors whose works live beyond their own age, they transcend history from *within* history and this roots them still more deeply in history. He suggest that it is better to speak of this as "the more fundamentally historical" than as an "anthropology."

Kobayashi retorted that he found this a "modern dialectic of history" which falls under what he had called "theories of historical change." There is a "form" in history that cuts off interpretation—be it causal or dialectical—and this form manifests history. For example, when the form of the Kamakura age is visible, the Kamakura age can be understood. This is different from current historicism. For Kobayashi it confirmed him in the awe-inspiring greatness of Plato's theory of Ideas.

Nishitani took issue with this idea of seeing the eternal in a particular historical form, drawing attention to the human spirit that created this so-called eternal form or aspect. Form and aspect are things from the past, things made, and the human effort and spirit that went into them is something we must also possess. We find ourselves face to face with that spirit of old when we have to pull ourselves beyond our own times. This is not a matter of form or aspect but of something that must be appropriated. It is a question of seeking in the past what does not lie in the relics of the past, of seeing the spirit of former times as spirit.

Along with *constant* eternal forms and aspects, the *inconstant* spirit is also at work in history. It comes down to us and we must make it our own. In this sense the inconstant spirit must be at work in its very inconstancy. It may be all right for historians to contemplate the eternal form in what lies before them, but this is not enough for those concerned with philosophy and religion. They must break their own trail, tripping on the present as they go. This is why the inconstant things continually throw themselves up at us from the midst of what is constant. If one removes oneself from the midst of history, the idea of history is no longer possible. The changeable and unchangeable are woven warp and woof together. This was Nishitani's reply.

To compare these two views of history, Kobayashi is looking at the "form" of history as a *spectator* (as his own express affinities for Plato's theory of Idea and Forms makes patent), feeling that history has been understood when its form has become visible; Nishitani takes more the standpoint of a *player* concerned with taking hold of history, and thus takes more seriously the "mind" of the player. This confrontation is one between form and mind on the one hand and "artistic creation" and "religious praxis" on the other—or perhaps we might say, between Plato and Zen.

Nishitani's point was not lost on Kobayashi, but his perspectives were too different for the discussion to go anywhere and he therefore changed directions, taking up the question of "creativity." From the standpoint that what's past is past, and that Plato would have come up with something different had he been born today just as we have no choice but to make something new, he began, it is hard to know what is being created in all of this. Does not the standpoint of creativity eliminate the need for novelty? The achievements of the ancients stand. The problem is that today we lack the humility to realize that we cannot surpass them, having forgotten that the only reason we are able to create something different is that the resources at our disposal are different.

The mere fact of having been born today is a ridiculous reason to feel superior. We flatter ourselves to think that there is something that only we can do because we live when we do. The distinctive mark of the work of powerful artists is precisely that they lack that self-infatuation. In this way Kobayashi argued for a standpoint where the classical element in the classics comes to light.

Kobayashi makes a strong case for the "classicism" of his literary position. It is the same standpoint preserved intact today in the world of Noh drama,[46] but this is rarely to be seen in the world of literature or art in general during the modern period, where creativity is seen in terms of "individuality" and "freedom." Since Kobayashi's position is far removed from modernity in this sense, his "return to tradition" is actually an "overcoming of modernity" and not a simple traditionalism. This helps explain the appeal of his position for many who were loyal to his vision, though he was never without his critics.

Nishitani did not, of course, belong to the camp of scientism and positivism that Kobayashi was criticizing, but he did once again voice objections, which started the two off on a new debate focused on their respective ideas of literature, philosophy, and the arts.

Nishitani began from his own experience, noting that everyone begins philosophy with an immersion in the classics. Predisposed to the greatness of thinkers like Plato and Kant, one studies their works with the aim of feeling something of their spirit. At the same time, as soon as one stops to reflect on oneself, it is clear that there are things that Plato and Kant cannot satisfy. And from there the feeling arises that only by leaving the trail that others have made can one resolve one's own questions. As one trips and stumbles out on one's own, one discovers the footprints of Plato.

This does not mean that one has wild ambitions of achieving something that ancients were not able to achieve. If someone is caught entirely in Plato's web, such ambitions would even be out of place. Indeed, it would be satisfaction enough if one were able to walk in all honesty the way of great thinkers of old. But there is something in the essence of philosophy that precludes this, even forbids it. In the case of artistic appreciation and religious belief, things may be different, Nishitani notes, but when it is a question of truly stepping into the footsteps of the ancients, there is no other way than to walk one's own path.

Without wishing to ignore the standpoint of philosophy, Kobayashi shifted the discussion to aesthetics, beauty, and expression. He made clear his allegiance to Bergson, in whose position on aesthetics he found none of the equivocal use of language one finds, for example, in Hegel's talk of the

---

[46] 喜多六平太 Kita Rokuheita, the fourteenth successor in the Kita line of Noh, performed for the first time in the temple of Dōjō-ji on 3 March 1892. Some forty years later, on 28 April 1935 he performed for the last time. On that occasion he was sorely tempted to change the form he had used up until then, but when he paused to think what it would mean to destroy the ritual form of his lineage, he danced his last as he had always danced, without the slightest change. See 六平太芸談 [Artistic discussions with Rokuheita] (Tokyo: Shunjūsha, 1942), 219–20. This example shows up the conspicuous respect for form in Noh, which may be due to its relatively early perfection as an art form and its achievement of a world of classical art. See my 型 [Form] (Tokyo: Sōbunsha, 1989), 245–7.

"concrete universal." Captivated by Bergson's view that "if one were able to remove all the inevitable obstacles imposed by life in society and immerse oneself in the true shape of reality, one would grasp beauty," Kobayashi claimed that "this is the way to forge a metaphysics directly—beginning with an analysis of pure perception, aware that the historical and social persona is a mere mask."[47]

Once this problem of "expression" had been introduced, he launched a severe question at Nishitani, the scholar of French letters irritating the sore spot of Japanese philosophy:

> For example, your paper and that of Yoshimitsu are most difficult to understand. To put it in the extreme, they have none of the sensuality of the Japanese language. We have the sense that philosophers really care very little for the fact that fate has given them a native language to write in. However conscientious and logical one's expression, it seems to me that beyond merely using the traditional Japanese language, the style should possess the flavor that only a Japanese can give it. This is something that those of us in literature are always conscious of in our work.... But on this point the philosophers are extremely nonchalant. I do not see any way for reviving the philosophy in Japan as truly Japanese philosophy if this problem is not surmounted. What do you think about this?[48]

The question is not new to those who have struggled with translation and the incorporation of new scholarly disciplines from Western civilization, but in the case of Japan's acceptance of philosophy, it has not been taken as seriously. Nishitani acknowledged the complaint and admitted that he felt it himself:

> For those engaged in philosophy...it is extraordinarily difficult to step into a current flowing from the West and express ourselves with only our given Japanese language. One must not force things on the language, but at the same time one must be able to make oneself understood, and this means trying to express ourselves naturally in Japanese by forging a new language. Really, there is no time to bother writing in a way that the general Japanese readers can easily understand. To be frank, we feel as if we are writing for Western intellectuals, but at the same time we want to take our thought further than Westerners have been able to go. More important than worrying about whether we are making ourselves understood is breaking through the deadlocks that people over there have

---

[47] KC, 230.
[48] KC, 248.

landed themselves in. For the present, I do not see any other way to forge ahead.[49]

It is not that Nishitani was generally misunderstood or that his philosophy took shape only through contact with German philosophy. His graduation thesis was on "Schelling's Absolute Idealism and Bergson's Pure Duration," and when the publishing house of Kōbundō put out the *Anthology of Western Philosophy* he was so fond of Bergson and held him in such high esteem that he personally prepared the section on Bergson. In 1980, when he was already well up in years, he wrote a lucid and clear précis of Bergson's major works for Shunjūsha's *Bibliographical Resumes of Great Philosophers*. The readers of Nishitani's essays can hardly fail to notice the rich artistic sensibility and uncommonly strong intuitive insight running through them. On this score he has much in common with Kobayashi.

Be that as it may, the style of his early essays is dense and difficult. I do not think the analogy of French aesthetics and German philosophy is fair for contrasting Nishitani with Kobayashi. There is a real delicacy in Nishitani's speculations and sensitivities. He took them too seriously to entrust them to a fixed vocabulary or style of argument. This is why his expression was so dense and why he was never a systematizer. Nevertheless, there is no denying the fact that in the years after the war his style gradually lost its dense quality. As the years went he matured and in his own way paid more attention to questions of style. Fine nuances of expression had a strong impact on his style. In my view, Kobayashi's criticism took their toll on Nishitani.

To return to their discussion, the topic turned next to artistic discipline and the theories of Zeami, and from there broadened out into a variety of artistic theories. Kobayashi's view of the classics as "form" brought him to the mimetic theory of Noh drama as developed through Zeami's *Transmission of the Flower-Acting Style* and *Flower Mirror* with its stress on learning by imitating. In response to a question of Suzuki Shigetaka, he admitted that he agreed with the view of the German historian, Eduard Winkelmann, that "creation is imitation."[50]

It was not easy for Nishitani to enter into this discussion. The basis of philosophy is thought rooted in inner need, and this does not lend itself to a viewpoint based on "form." But even in philosophy, the study of figures one holds in esteem is taken seriously at the introductory stages. Here Nishitani alludes to the stages of artistic discipline proposed by the Edo-period Omote Senke tea master Kawakami Fuhaku: keeping, breaking, and leaving (守, 破, 離). On this scheme, Nishitani's study of the forerunners of Western philoso-

[49] KC, 249.
[50] KC, 232.

phy and his own teachers Nishida Kitarō and Tanabe Hajime was the stage of *keeping* the form. But even as he was under the influence of such great figures, he had to pass through a ten-year "period of stringent groping"[51] in response to his own interior needs. This was his period of *breaking* the form. His writings on Nietzsche's *Zarathustra* and on Meister Eckhart were a voyage of self-discovery, bringing him to the stage of *leaving* the form. He had already passed through these three stages at the time of preparing his paper for the symposium. His standpoint of "subjective nothingness" may be called his attempt to "overcome modernity." But this was not a final resting place for Nishitani, as his later writings attest. Again and again he broke through the forms he made for himself in a continual cycle of breaking-and-leaving, until at last he came to a fourth stage, his *great departure*: the world of "emptiness."

In comparing Nishitani and Kobayashi, we see how these two figures of the Shōwa intellectual history, each faithful to the demands of his own interiority, experimented with bringing a "religious praxis" (修行, 修道) formed in the intellectual history of Japan into contact with the civilization of Western Europe. On the one side we have Kobayashi, brushing aside the idea that the overcoming of modernity meant only the overcoming of Western modernity, that there was no Japanese modernity to overcome in Japan, and anchoring himself instead in a return to the classics and the affective world of Motoori Norinaga. On the other stands Nishitani, whose concerns revolved about the problem of nihilism inherited from the modern West, and who tried to overcome the modernity of the West by way of modern Japan from the perspective of "absolute nothingness" that Nishida Kitarō had opened up. In these two completely different ideas of transcending the times, we have two models of overcoming modernity.

CONCLUSION

The discussions on "Overcoming Modernity" have rightly been criticized as disjointed and inconclusive, but this does not mean that they amount to no more than idle talk. In a variety of ways the participants were able to express themselves frankly on modern Europe, without which the existence of modern Japan would have been impossible, and their own relationship to Europe and the West.

No doubt there were major issues that were not touched, but still the discussions were far more fascinating than the usual sort of simplistic debate

---

[51] Nishitani refers to this in a foreword to his 1940 book 根源的主体性の哲学 [A philosophy of elemental subjectivity], NKC 1:3.

going on in wartime Japan and in many respects they were an outstanding contribution to the statement of the issues. Given the fact that the discussions were held by specialists from different fields, one misses the excitement of in-depth treatment, but at the same time questions were raised that even postwar Japan has not been able to resolve. If there were some way to go back in time, it would surely be worth our while to gather the participants together for another round.

The views of Shimomura Toratarō and Nakamura Mitsuo concerning positive evaluation of the modern West and its culture are first-rate and hold up well today against the test of time. Moreover, the papers and comments concerning "culture and creativity"—the contributions of Moroi Saburō, Nishitani Keiji, and Kobayashi Hideo in particular—on the whole have lost none of their appeal and continue to pose challenging and as yet unanswered questions. There is still much in them that merits reviving today.

Not a few commentators have expressed regrets that Shimomura's questions regarding scientific-technological culture in the modern and contemporary world were not adequately pursued. This may be the biggest failure of the discussions. This, and the related problem of "science and religion" touch on the foundations of contemporary civilization, and one wishes that Shimomura and Nishitani had had a chance to lock horns on this question the way Kobayashi and Nishitani did.

The presentation of Kamei Katsuichirō, though infamous for its concluding remarks, ranks with Nakamura's as a splendid critique of the intellectual conditions in wartime Japan, as does Miyoshi Tatsuji's critique of the timeserving opportunism of Japan's classical scholars. Not even their support of the war effort should be allowed to eclipse their contributions.

A concluding word is in order about the place of the Kyoto school in these discussions. In the case of Suzuki Shigetaka, the paper he delivered at the symposium and subsequently withdrew from publication shows his skills as a historian. All but a few of the participants lacked the capacity to take it up and develop it further in discussion. Although Suzuki fielded the questions of the others well, his special quality does not shine through in these discussions the way it did in the *Chūōkōron* discussions on "The World-Historical Standpoint and Japan."

That having been said, Suzuki's remarks on America stand out from what the others had to say, as evidenced in the following passage:

> In present-day Japan, most people are used to thinking in terms of a simple confrontation between the world of the colored races and the world of the white race. But America is not an extension of Europe. It is giving shape to a unique world all its own, which means that the white world is becoming two....This seems to me a world-historical problem of

immense proportions. In traditional, European-centered Western culture, America seemed no more than a colony at the edge of the world. But when we look at things from the context of *world* history, it takes on a new meaning.[52]

Suzuki further chided European and Japanese intellectuals for taking the idea of "Americanism" lightly. He stressed the need not to forget the two faces of "Americanism": on the one hand, the flow of capital, mass production, and movies that have had such an important influence on Japan; and on the other, the "puritan spirit" that rejects modernism and introduces prohibition.

Suzuki, though a specialist in Western medieval studies who had never been to the United States himself, has a knack for getting at the heart of things. For example, taking off from Tsumura Hideo's view that both American democracy and its material, mechanized civilization are "egalitarian movements," Suzuki adds that the distinctive thing about America is not its ideal of equality, but the high level to which it has been able to raise the standard of equality.[53] From our present-day vantage point of developments in research during and after the war and of a greater knowledge of America in general, Suzuki's views of America are hardly adequate, but as someone who tried to free world history from its Europe-centeredness and see it as *world* history, his perspective was a relative rarity in his own day. Of course Japan had top scholars of America at the time (Takagi Yashaku, for example), but the general view of America among the intelligentsia was shallow and their insight feeble. Suzuki's knowledge may not have been rich, but his instincts were solid.

As for Nishitani, it is worth noting that among the participants who recognized the importance of "tradition," he was the only one who considered Japanese culture not only as something Japanese but also as containing elements from the East. No doubt the practice of Zen helped to broaden his horizon. In matters touching on the West, Nishitani was well versed not only in the modern West but also in Greek and medieval thinkers, and it was from this global perspective (though at the time he had not yet broadened it far enough to include America) that he took up the question of the self. On this point, Nishitani inherited from the Kyoto school, beginning with Nishida, the problem of transforming the essence of Eastern thought through the encounter with European ideas into something accessible to all of humanity. Of all the symposium participants, Nishitani stands out as the one who spoke most confidently and forcefully of the value of "tradition."

[52] KC, 257.
[53] KC, 260.

There is no denying the fact that Nishitani was a nationalist and that he supported the war. Still, we cannot leave the fact that he was a universalist out of the picture. As I mentioned earlier, at the same time as he made a case for a "national ethics" in his presentation to the symposium, Nishitani recognized the pitfall of a national egoism and argued also for a "world ethic." When he alludes to a spontaneous harmony (冥合) between Mahāyāna Buddhism and the Shinto idea of the "clear, bright heart" (清明心), it is not the exclusivist State Shinto centered on Hirata Shinto he refers to, but rather the medieval Ise Shinto of Kitabatake Chikafusa, which stressed a purity of "heart" that included Confucian and Buddhist teaching, and was held to be innate to ancient Shinto. Nishitani emphasizes the universal and global character latent in popular Shinto and insists on the need to "awaken to the global aspect that the Way of the Gods has possessed from the beginning."[54] The mere fact that he refers to Shinto hardly makes him a nationalist.

The major difficulty with Nishitani's ideas in the discussion lie in the range of efficacy he assigned to the idea of "subjective nothingness." I have no quarrel with the idea as a philosophy of individual human existence; indeed, I find it admirable. The problem is whether it can be extended to all aspects of human and societal existence. However one brings the marvelous intellectual and religious traditions formed in the East and the West into relation, is this not something to be carried out in the forum of humanity? Is not our task to cooperate intellectually on a scale that includes all humanity?

[TRANSLATED BY JAMES W. HEISIG]

---

[54] KC, 31–2.

PART FOUR

Questioning the Kyoto School

Kyoto Philosophy—Intrinsically Nationalistic?

Jan VAN BRAGT

STROKE FELLS KIYOHARA TANAKA, 87
EX-LEFTIST, RIGHTIST LEADER DIES.

Tanaka...joined the JCP in 1927 while a student in the aesthetics department of the Imperial University of Tokyo. In July 1930, he was arrested for leading the armed May Day struggle. While in jail, his mother, after voicing an apology to the Emperor and society over her son's activities, committed hara-kiri. Having learned of her suicide, Tanaka renounced communism while still behind bars. In 1941, he was released through an amnesty. He then went through spiritual training at a Zen temple and acquired what he termed the concepts of "becoming one with the emperor" and "absolute nothingness without left, right, or center." (*Japan Times*, December 12, 1993)

A S ONE OF THOSE WHO has a certain stake in the fortunes of the Kyoto school, I am not unaware of the accusations raised against its philosophers of complicity in Japan's nationalism and its military adventures during the first half of the Shōwa period.[1] The difficulty is knowing just how to deal with such claims. On the one hand, academic honesty seems to require that those of us who have been in some measure instrumental in

---

[1] It may be significant that the problem of the nationalism of the Kyoto school has been taken up not only in America, which until now has shown by far the strongest interest in Kyoto philosophy, but even in the French-speaking, Spanish-speaking, and German-speaking worlds. In French, there are Nishida Kitarō, *La culture japonaise en question* (日本文化の問題), translated and introduced by Pierre Lavelle (Cergy: Publications orientalistes de France, 1991); Bernard Stevens, "Sur la spécificité philosophique du Japon," *Revue philosophique de Louvain* 91 (1993): 275–95; and Bernard Stevens, "En guise d'introduction: une présentation de l'Ecole de Kyôto," *Etudes Phénoménologiques* 9 (1993): 7–62. In Spanish we have Agustín Jacinto Z., "La derecha en la escuela de Kioto," *Avances de Investigación* 1/4 (Colegio de Michoacán, 1992): 1–110. And in German, I know of one strong criticism: Ruth Kambartel, "Religion als Hilfsmittel für die Rechtfertigung einer totalitären Staatsideologie in Nishitani Keijis *Sekaikan to kokkakan*," *Japanstudien* 1 (1989): 71–88.

JAN VAN BRAGT

introducing their thought to a wider audience outside Japan should face the question squarely. On the other hand, the long years of personal involvement seem to compromise our judgment from the start. I confess that rarely, if ever, have I undertaken a scholarly task that has cost me as much soul-searching as this one has. I beg the reader to indulge my personal comments as I find my way into the principal subject matter of this essay.

THE SCOPE OF THE QUESTION

In my study of the Kyoto school I have tended to pass over the political dimension as "just one of those things" that one is vaguely aware of but that somehow distracts from the main point—in my case, the encounter of Buddhism and Christianity. Did the current brouhaha awaken me to a culpable blindness, like someone shaken by the feminist movement into realizing longstanding habits of male chauvinism? Have I been wrong all along not to recognize the connections between the "nationalistic stance" of the Kyoto philosophers and their religious thought?

The Broader Context

Only after I had been invited to write on these questions did it dawn on me how important the question is, first because nationalism in general is a crucial issue for humanity as a whole, and secondly because the "nationalism" of the Kyoto philosophers is not simply a question about the past but equally a question about the present. Recent world events—mainly in Eastern Europe and Russia, but also in Sri Lanka and elsewhere—have once more illustrated the explosive force and disastrous effects of nationalism, which Marx seemed to have considered a thing of the past. These events appear to reconfirm Arnold Toynbee's thesis that nationalism, seen as a kind of "collective egoism," constitutes the greatest danger for humankind. "The sin of pride becomes mortally dangerous," he writes, "when it is translated from the singular into the plural, from egoism into what, to coin a word, one might call '*nosism*'."[2] Toynbee goes on to argue that curbing that collective egoism is the principal common task of all religions. If we agree with his diagnosis, and also with Nishitani Keiji's conviction that only religion can "provide the force to eradicate the deepest roots of the 'ego',"[3] the question then becomes: Is religion after all capable of doing the job on the collective level? Even with

[2] Arnold Toynbee, *Christianity among the Religions of the World* (New York: Scribner's Sons, 1957), 97.
[3] Nishitani Keiji, 世界観と国家観 [View of the world, view of the nation], NKC 4:201.

234

the aid of the supposedly cool and rational thinking of philosophy, is religion any match for the social passions of an age?

History seems to tell us that religion has indeed enabled certain rare individuals in time of national crisis to distance themselves from collective, tribal egoisms. But seldom, if ever, has it been able to prevent the social passions of a people from flaring up into open warfare. On the contrary, it has more often provided the rallying cry—*Gott mit uns*. As Toynbee has it, "we are always relapsing from the worship of God into the worship of our tribe or of ourselves."[4] On the whole it is only after the battles had been fought and passions had cooled that religion was able to begin exercising its powers of reconciliation. It is good to keep this in mind when asking whether and to what degree the Kyoto philosophers kept their distance from the nationalism of the Shōwa period of crisis as a result of their philosophy (and religion), and what their teachings might possibly have done to stem the tide of Japanese nationalism.[5]

The question also came to seem important to me because its scope extends beyond a mere "judgment" about the attitude of a group of wartime philosophers who have since died and should perhaps be allowed to rest in peace. The accusation raised against the Kyoto philosophers is not that they were the original instigators of a Japanese nationalism whose practical adventures brought untold suffering to other countries in Asia and was ultimately catastrophic for Japan itself. To the best of my knowledge, the point of the criticism is rather that their philosophy did not keep them from being swept up into the prevailing whirlwind of nationalism, that it did not enable them to "keep their heads" when people all about them were losing theirs but rather turned them into accomplices insofar as they provided rationalizations for that nationalism. It seems to me that the more basic problem is this larger Japanese nationalism,[6] rather than any particular philosophical statement of it, and this at once lifts the critique of the Kyoto school out of the past and

---

[4] A. Toynbee, *Christianity among the Religions*, 94.

[5] Writing about the life and character of Pope John Paul II, Peter Hebblethwaite has the following to say: "During World War I, his father heard propaganda lectures from Max Scheler, the phenomenologist. Scheler claimed the Central Powers were defending Christian civilization against the godless French, the autocratic Russians and the mercantile Protestant English." See "Pope Soldiers on…," *National Catholic Reporter* 30/1 (22 October 1993): 10.

[6] The importance of the understanding of such a background has been emphasized also in connection with Heidegger's Nazism. "What needs to be better comprehended is German intellectuals' disenchantment [in the early nineteenth century] with Enlightenment principles.... I think that only by appreciating the lure of anti-Enlightenment thinking...can we begin to make sense of Heidegger's conviction that Nazism had an 'inner truth and greatness' that could inspire and transform all Germans." Alan Paskov, "Heidegger and Nazism," *Philosophy East and West* 41 (1991): 526.

into present history. Time and again one sees signs that the people of Japan, or at the least its leaders, have not fundamentally broken with nationalism or repudiated its past effects. One need only think of the massive conspiracy of silence in school textbooks and elsewhere that enshrouds the foul deeds of the war, or of the vehement reactions provoked from influential figures when a mayor or prime minister dares to speak explicitly of Japan's guilt. "The Japanese people consider it a virtue to forget the past, but this becomes a wrong when it serves the evasion of responsibility."[7]

Ienaga Saburō, who has been waging a solitary war against this state of affairs for more than thirty years, stands as an important witness in this regard. Speaking in a recent interview of how the truth was kept from the people of Japan during the war, he observed:

> Many things have now been disclosed to the people. The new democracy under a Japanese constitution...played a large role in improving the consciousness of the Japanese people. At bottom, however, continuity with the prewar era has been strong. There has been no true overturning of the roots of the thinking process that existed before the war. A large number of people still believe that the war was for the sake of the nation, or that Japan was driven into a corner and had no other choice. I don't know whether they really believe this consciously, but they still believe in a "Japanese-style spirit," as in prewar days.[8]

In this connection, something that Robert Bellah wrote nearly thirty years ago may still be worth pondering:

> The humane and gracious figure of Watsuji Tetsurō would not be problematic for modern Japan were it not for the fact that partly behind the cloak of just such thinking as his, a profoundly pathological social movement brought Japan near to total disaster. The ideology of that movement [in its explicit version] ....was so deeply repudiated in the post-war period that it can probably never reappear. But it is of the essence of Japanese particularism that it exists as a tacit assumption more than as an explicit ideology.[9]

If this more general Japanese nationalistic or particularistic trend is indeed the basic problem, then the question of the nationalism of the Kyoto school must always be located in this broader context. In other words, the

---

[7] Inukai Masakazu, in *Informatio Catholica* 70 (1989): 3.

[8] Ienaga Saburō, "Teaching War," in H. T. Cook and T. F. Cook, *Japan at War: An Oral History* (New York: The New Press, 1993), 444.

[9] Robert Bellah, "Japan's Cultural Identity: Some Reflections on the Work of Watsuji Tetsuro," *Journal of Asian Studies* 24 (1965): 593–4.

question may be rephrased to read: *To what extent did Japanese nationalism penetrate the philosophy of the Kyoto school?*

A Renewal of Reflection

In this way I came to see the need for a renewed reflection on "Japanese nationalism." Are the Japanese people particularly nationalistic, and if so, in what sense? Directed in part by the conclusions of Robert Bellah, whom I have just cited, I arrived at a number of tentative conclusions which I shall try to lay out as succinctly as I can.

I believe that nationalist feelings are especially strong in Japan, but I at once wish to qualify what I understand by the term *nationalism*. In its strictest sense, as the word itself suggests, the term refers to a certain relationship to or a disposition towards a "nation-state" whose sovereignty rests in the people who make it up. In that sense, one can only speak properly of Japanese nationalism after the Meiji Restoration, and perhaps then only with reservations. In any case, what I mean by nationalism is something more basic—perhaps I should say more primitive—that is not bound to the structure of the state as such but can be traced much farther back in Japan's history. We might call this a "particularism" or a concentration on what Tanabe meant by 種 or "species," which entails a corresponding belittling of both the individual and the universal or transcendent. It is a question of the preponderance of the social nexus over the individuals and over the transcendent of which Nakamura Hajime speaks. One sees here the two elements of which Bellah speaks: "Correlative with the sense of uniqueness is a strong feeling of identification which Japanese people feel with their culture."[10] Under *culture* I mean to include also race (血縁, ancestors) and soil (氏, 神国), which then, in historical perspective, allows us to speak of a prevalence of the Shinto ethos (which, as a "tribal religion," is particularist) over the Buddhist ethos (which, as a "historical religion," is supposed to be centered on a transcendent universal and on the individual). I would then add, as a final qualification, that this Japanese particularism is strongly pervaded by a remarkably flexible notion of the family that was able to radiate from the center of the "Imperial Family." Thus Bellah concludes: "If there was any structural reference at all [in Japanese particularism] it was not to the nation but rather...to the imperial dynasty."[11]

The next question is unavoidable: why should the Japanese people be more nationalistic than most other peoples? Although it is hard to find a really satisfactory explanation, it is not an entirely unintelligible phenomenon. As

[10] R. Bellah, "Japan's Cultural Identity," 573.

[11] R. Bellah, "Japan's Cultural Identity," 574.

for why it should be so difficult to explain, this is at least in part due to the mystery of how, despite the successful implantation and centuries-long presence of a historical religion, Shinto and its ethos as a tribal religion should have survived for so many centuries. In looking for factors that help us to understand, one thinks first of the term *shimaguni* (島国, island country), which Japanese even today point to as a distinguishing trait. But more cogent than geographical circumstance are the historical conditions that come into play. Affirmations of the particularity (or superiority) of the group to which one belongs are, after all, a way of satisfying the psychological need for self-respect and defending one's identity against what are perceived as outside threats. Throughout its history Japan seems to have felt the menace of outside forces overshadowing it or threatening to absorb it. The greatest and most enduring intimidation lay of course in China, to which Japan owes most of the elements of its culture. In order to strengthen its self-identity and reaffirm its *yamato-damashi* (大和魂), Japan needed a number of long periods of seclusion during which it closed its doors to Chinese influence.

The introduction of Buddhism into the picture further compounds the mystery. Although received by Japan as part of the Chinese cultural package, Buddhism never lost the vestiges of its birth in India. In the Buddhist scheme of things, Japan is a latecomer, a small backwater off the mainstream of religious history. Judging from Japanese literature, especially its Buddhist literature, this consciousness must have been very strong among the ancient Japanese. Indeed, the survival of Shinto may have something to do with a rebellion against this self-image.

When we come to modern times, especially since the end of feudalism in Japan, Western culture with its technical and military superiority replaces China as the force that keeps Japan in a position of inferiority and makes its identity problematic. Forces that had once stood in opposition join together to form a bulwark against the new threat. Things Chinese and things Japanese come to be seen together as Eastern culture; Buddhism and Shinto form the common, native religious front against Christianity, the religion of the West. Meantime, the need for a particularly *Japanese* identity within this larger Eastern identity remains as strong as ever. In the early years of the Shōwa period, this two-sided problem of Japanese identity reached a high pitch. As Bellah writes, "The Pacific War posed for Japan the profoundest problems of its cultural identity—the relation of Eastern to Western culture and the relation of the Japanese past to the modern era."[12]

All of this, I repeat, is not meant to "explain" Japan's nationalism. But I find it relevant that each of these ingredients resurfaces in the official nationalistic rhetoric of the war as well as in the writings of the Kyoto school.

[12] R. Bellah, "Japan's Cultural Identity," 579.

238

Nowhere is this as blatant as in the so-called *nihonjinron* (日本人論) literature. I cannot go as far as Robert Sharf when he writes that "Suzuki, like Nishida, placed his reading of Buddhist history in the interests of the most specious forms of *nihonjinron*."[13] But at the same time, there is no denying the fact that the same preoccupation with Japan's identity and unicity, albeit on a higher level of sophistication, pervades the writings of the Kyoto school, especially in the critical years of the war.

To try to understand nationalism is not, of course, to approve of it. In healthy doses it may merit the more acceptable labels of "patriotism" or "love of country," but an overdose quickly breaks out in the "group egoism" of which Toynbee spoke. On the one hand, a rational, objective view of the outside world is made impossible; on the other, individual citizens within the country are made subservient to a greater, national totality.

Assumptions

For my part, I have no wish either to play the devil's advocate or to lend my voice to a simple *apologia pro schola kyotoense*. On this latter point, I begin by conceding at least the following two points.

First, the Kyoto philosophers did not, during the period in question, keep a philosophical composure but were swept up in the general nationalistic tide, even to the point of making some rather irrational declarations that they would not have made in calmer circumstances. One thinks particularly, though not only, of the famous *Chūōkōron* discussion. On this point, I find a defense of the Kyoto philosophers in question, like the one offered by Hanazawa Hidefumi (in the course of an otherwise most instructive essay), not only unconvincing but counterproductive. I cannot agree with Hanazawa in dismissing out of hand Ienaga Saburō's impression of these conversations as no more than "the tall talk of drunkards."[14] Here we see a group of intellectuals stumbling about in a kind of euphoric daze, groggy with the excitement of a war and its coming adventures. In their paean for the war effort, no mention is ever made of the immense suffering it is inflicting. No doubt, however faint, is raised concerning the rightness of its cause or the certain victory that awaits Japan. No one bothers to question the right of one people to judge itself superior and destined to dominate the East Asian sphere. What kind of a detour must conscience make to go along with Nishitani's plea to make other Eastern high-quality peoples into "half-Japanese,"[15] or the musings by the participants about the destiny of the Korean people, capped off by

[13] Robert Sharf, "The Zen of Japanese Nationalism," *History of Religions* 53 (1993): 24–5.

[14] 花澤秀文 Hanazawa Hidefumi, 高山岩男の思想と行動の研究 [A study of the thought and activities of Kōyama Iwao], 岡山県立邑久高等学校研究紀要 13 (1987): 12.

[15] CK, 262–3.

Kōsaka's declaration that "by becoming Japanese in a broad sense, the true historicity of the Koreans will come to life"?[16] Had they bothered soberly to consult their own philosophies, surely these men would have spoken differently. To be sure, their high erudition is everywhere in evidence; and to be fair, many of the points they make are well taken and, in hindsight, even look at times prophetic. I refer, for instance, to Nishitani's wish that "all-out war" be seen as transcending wartime and peacetime: "Seen as the energy to fight, military strength transcends the traditional, narrow understanding of 'fighting' and continues into the so-called 'postwar' period."[17] Given the current world situation, it is hard to deny that, after all, the fighting spirit of the Japanese in the postwar period did in a sense make them the "real winners of the war."

A comment of Himi Kiyoshi seems to suggest, however, that the *Chūōkōron* discussions are not the only case in point. Noting that one might have expected the "rationalist" Tanabe to see through the official emperor ideology, Himi notes:

> In fact, Tanabe did not remain free from the spell of the dominating ideology of modern Japan…. Thus, because of subjective limitations, he sacrificed his rationalist thought to the affirmation and praise of the Japanese state.[18]

A second point I wish to concede from the start is that the attitude and writings of the Kyoto philosophers during the critical period were on the whole supportive of national policies in general and of the war effort in particular. It is true that they distanced themselves from certain of the excesses of the totalitarian nationalism and warned of the dangers, thus incurring the wrath of extremist factions (especially among the ground forces). In contrast to the irrationalistic tenor that pervaded the official ideology, they advocated clear reasoning; in opposition to an exclusive focus on the Japanese state, they insisted on the need for individual creativity and a global, world-historical outlook; against the absoluteness of state Shinto, they upheld the importance of the Buddhist contribution. Moreover, it seems that some of the Kyoto philosophers collaborated with political forces aimed at moderating some of the excesses of the war policy. Still, one must say that by and large their ideas and pronouncements were sufficiently in line with the national polity to have wrought a reassuring effect on intellectuals too sophisticated to swallow the

[16] CK, 339.

[17] CK, 291.

[18] 氷見 潔 Himi Kiyoshi, 田辺哲学研究 [A study of Tanabe's philosophy] (Tokyo: Hokuju, 1980), 126.

raw form in which the war ideology was being rationed out, and to have offered students an honorable cause for which to die fighting.

In making these concessions I do not, however, mean to offer them as evidence on which to assess the personal integrity of the Kyoto philosophers or from which to apportion guilt. I find myself unable to detect in them any sign of clear duplicity—speaking directly against their better judgment—or opportunism or cowardice. Subjectively, we can say no more than that they served their country in the state it was in, as loyal subjects (and for those at imperial universities, as employees).

In this respect, their attitude after the end of the war is telling. Nishida did not himself outlive the war, of course. Those who did, such as Nishitani and Kōyama, never made a public apology for their wartime activities. Indeed, Kōyama insisted that what he did during the war, and especially his collaboration with the navy, was done "on the basis of deep reflection and resolve, and my evident duty as an intellectual employed by a state university."[19] Once the war was over, Tanabe began to talk openly and at length of the need for metanoia, and in that sense seemed to have acknowledged guilt both personal and collective. I say "seemed to," because in all honesty I cannot pin down for myself just what those ideas meant in the concrete. Was his metanoetics basically anything more than an expression of the shock brought about by direct encounter with the fallibility and gullibility of human reason? I have a difficult time reading much more into even his clearest admission of "guilt":

> All my teachings on this matter [the state and its relationship to religion] have failed to be really concrete, and it cannot be denied that, because of their abstractness, they have given rise to the trend of the absoluteness of the state .... I cannot gainsay that they contained the possibility of being used as a rationale for a particular state [policy].[20]

As for Watsuji, Bellah argues that he may not have made any clear apology but that his views on Japanese history certainly underwent a great change.[21] Nishitani, on the other hand, is something of an enigma. Are we to conclude from his silence that Nishitani never retracted his wartime ideas? Or perhaps that he simply left behind the "extravagancies" of his youth as a matter of course, but, rather than publicly alter his basic ideas about the state, preferred to avoid the question and devote himself more exclusively to meta-

---

[19] As quoted in Hanazawa Hidefumi, "Kōyama Iwao," 1.

[20] 種の論理の弁証法 [The dialectics of the logic of species], THZ 7:336–7.

[21] R. Bellah, "Japan's Cultural Identity," 589–90.

physics and religion, at least after 1952? If so, James Heisig's remark may be to the point:

> The irony is that, in a sense, the failure of Japan's nationalistic aims was a victory for the true aims of the Kyoto philosophers, calling them less to a laundering of their image than to a return to their fundamental inspirations.[22]

To sum up, then, I am suggesting that the judgment that is ours to make is not on the Kyoto philosophers as persons—whether they were nationalists or not—but only on the relationship of their philosophy to nationalism. This brings me to the principal query of this essay: Is Kyoto philosophy as such instrinsically nationalistic?

IS KYOTO PHILOSOPHY INTRINSICALLY NATIONALISTIC?

On the basis of my preliminary remarks, I would like now to draw the question closer to home. It is not merely a question of the nationalism that may or may not be present in the Kyoto philosophers, but also of what remains of it in our own attempts to work with the legacy of their ideas. In this sense, the nature of the investigation shifts from witch hunt to exorcism, from autopsy to disinfection.

Harking back to the first lessons I learned in philosophy, that half the answer lies in understanding the question, I would like to try to tease out various possible meanings to the statement, "Kyoto philosophy is nationalistic" and only then try to refine an answer.

I suggest we begin by eliminating a reading of the phrase as an instance of a general rule that *all* philosophy (and for that matter, all religion) is in part ideological and therefore bears within it covert agenda and hidden loyalties to nation, sect, class, gender, and so forth. Surely this kind of blanket condemnation is unsuitable as a working norm.

---

[22] James Heisig, "The Religious Philosophy of the Kyoto School," RPTH, 15. In several essays written between 1946 and 1952 Nishitani expressed views on political questions, on the war, and on the "narrow nationalism" at work in it. In these essays he generally takes an objective point of view, without the slightest reference to the role he himself may have played in the course of events. To the best of my knowledge, there are only two exceptions to this. In a private memorandum originally composed around 1946 but published for the first time in 1987 as an afterword to the reissue of *View of the World, View of the Nation* (1941) as volume 4 of his *Collected Writings*, Nishitani defends the soundness of his intentions. And in direct response to an attack by Ichikawa Hakugen aimed mainly at Nishitani's pronouncements in the *Chūōkōron* discussions, he defines the nature of his "collaboration in the war" and defends it as right. See 自衛についての再論 [Another argument on self-defense], 中央公論 (1 May 1952): 21–32. After that, again as far as I have been able to determine, there is only silence.

In the first place, then, we have the strongest, most direct reading of the statement: that nationalism is *the* fundamental inspiration of a particular thought system. In other words, abstracting from its nationalism, there is no system left. I have never read Hitler's *Mein Kampf* myself, but I imagine that it would qualify for just such a judgment.

Secondly, the phrase may be taken to mean that nationalism, while not the *fundamental* inspiration of the thought system, is one of its main determinants. In this case, the nationalistic element must be taken fully into consideration by anyone who wants to understand the system as such. It may be possible to pry the nationalistic elements loose from the philosophy as a whole without serious loss of content and meaning, but even so the possibility of a subtler, undetected taint can never be discounted.

A third reading of the statement is that nationalistic elements are to be found in at least *some* of the texts in question, but are judged out of line with the thought as a whole, a mere accretion at the periphery or a temporary deviation from its principal aims. There are two possibilities here. On the one hand, nationalistic accretions could be considered a pure and simple betrayal of everything the philosopher's thought stands for, products of a temporary myopia or stress.[23] While absolving the philosophical system of all blame, this reading tends to cast a dark shadow on the personal integrity of the philosopher in question. On the other hand, nationalistic accretions could be judged secondary, adventitious elements that might have been prompted by unusual historical circumstances but that nevertheless are linked organically to the philosophical system. In this case one looks to the deeper layers of the thought either for a positive propensity to nationalism or for the absence of sufficient defense against the onslaught of nationalistic ideas.

As soon as one tries to lay this schema on the history of the Kyoto school, the luxury of logical distinctions soon becomes an inconvenience. For one thing, not all the philosophers associated with the school can be placed in the same slot. For another, not all these thinkers maintained a consistent position during the period in question. In view of the diverse ways in which each of them developed, in greater or lesser proximity to Nishida, the origi-

---

[23] Since the disclosure of Heidegger's rather close and long-standing links with Nazism appears to lie at the bottom of the accusations against the Kyoto school in the West, the following observations may be especially relevant here: "When I was a young graduate student in the '60s..., I was told that Heidegger's involvement with the Nazis was an unfortunate, short-lived dalliance. It was to be understood as the outcome of political naiveté, a momentary lapse not to be held against this great thinker." And: "Farias' book [*Heidegger and Nazism*, 1989] raises a single overwhelming question—one that cries out for an answer: Is there anything in Heidegger's philosophy that would have made his involvement with the Nazis impossible? The answer, tragically, is no...." Joseph Grange, "Heidegger as Nazi—A Postmodern Scandal," *Philosophy East and West* 41 (1991): 515–16.

nal inspiration of what we are calling "Kyoto philosophy," we have no choice but to take each case individually or at least divide them into groups, in order to shade their several assocations with "nationalism." Clearly this is a task too large for a single essay—and in any case, too demanding for my own resources. I will therefore limit my remarks to the trunk-line thinkers of the Kyoto school, who also happen to be best known outside of Japan: Nishida Kitarō, Tanabe Hajime, and Nishitani Keiji. I shall furthermore begin with the presupposition that some meaning of the term *nationalistic* can be applied to these scholars, and shall assume—until evidence to the contrary persuades me otherwise—that each shared the same kind of nationalism.

The first question is whether the thinking of Nishida, Tanabe, and Nishitani can be called nationalistic in the first and strongest sense. I submit that it cannot, since the central preoccupations of these thinkers, the fundamental inspiration of their philosophy, do not belong to the social, political, or even ethical realms but rather to the "transcendent," metaphysical, religious, and in some sense therefore to the aesthetic realm. Theirs is not a philosophy of "objective spirit" but of "Absoluter Geist."

This is clear enough for Nishida himself, who came to questions of the state only late in his career. The same holds true for Nishitani, though I qualify this by noting that in the critical period of Japan's military adventures, much of his thinking turned around history and the state. I do not agree with R. Kambartel, who sees in Nishitani's 1941 book *View of the World, View of the Nation* a pure ideology of the state:

> ...In the end, what is developed in this book is not philosophy of religion but ideology of the state: Nishitani here uses his philosophy of religion ....for the promotion and justification of a totalitarian usurpation of the individual by the state, of a total sacrifice of the individual to the state.[24]

Moreover, I believe we can say of Tanabe as well that, notwithstanding his valiant efforts to bring his thinking down to earth by shifting the focus to "species" or "objective spirit," his primary concerns were far from sociopolitical. At the same time, given the importance of the state this implied, Tanabe may have been more vulnerable to nationalistic temptations than Nishida and Nishitani were. In a different context, Nishitani substantially makes the same point:

> Indeed it is my impression that a close examination of the points of Nishida's philosophy that Tanabe criticized reveals that Nishida's views

[24] Ruth Kambartel, "Religion als Hilfsmittel," 72.

often are surprisingly similar to Tanabe's own. In particular their philosophies share a distinctive and common basis that sets them apart from traditional Western philosophy: absolute nothingness.[25]

Having made this claim of Nishida, Tanabe, and Nishitani, however, I do not assume that this is true across the spectrum of Kyoto-school philosophers. For example, despite his frequent use of Nishida's basic terms, Watsuji's thinking focused directly on the ethical realm and the social nexus in a way that is absent in Nishida. Or again, Kōyama, Kōsaka, and Suzuki Shigetaka, whose prime interest seems to have been the philosophy of history, belong to a different branch.

The second step in our inquiry is rather more delicate. If the three trunk-line thinkers of the Kyoto school are not nationalistic ideologues in the strong sense of the term, how shall we classify the nationalistic elements they contain? The further I have delved into this question, the clearer it has become to me that the nationalistic-sounding pronouncements[26] of Nishida, Tanabe, and Nishitani are not simply turns of phrase or idle thoughts without any organic link to the body of their philosophical thinking. I therefore answer the title question of this essay in the affirmative. *Kyoto philosophy is intrinsically nationalistic.* The problem for me is rather with the nature of the intrinsicality. Was it strong enough to be one of the major inspirations or determining elements in Kyoto philosophy, or was it merely an adventitious and secondary element in it?

The question does not limit itself to whether or not certain declarations by the Kyoto philosophers made during a time of high crisis must be called nationalist or not, but rather extends into a question about the nature of the Kyoto philosophy *per se* as a historical endeavor. I realize that I am not qualified on my own to answer the question, and that even to try would take me well afield of the material I have gathered for the present essay. I content myself therefore with a summary presentation of why academic honesty compels me to find Kyoto philosophy "intrinsically nationalistic."

Engaged Philosophizing

In my view, it was one of the principal virtues of Kyoto philosophy that made it most vulnerable to nationalism. In other words, the very point that makes this philosophy most interesting and worth studying for the Western scholar

---

[25] NK, 161.

[26] It seems that it is the nationalist talks and writings of the Kyoto philosophers, and almost never their activities, that are brought into question. This contrasts with the case of Heidegger, in whose writings it is hard to discover pronouncements that come near to Nazi tenets, but whose Nazi activities seem by now well documented.

is the point of its strongest affinity to the nationalistic agenda. That is, the Kyoto-school thinkers, as distinct from the purely historical approach pursued at most Japanese faculties of (Western) philosophy, aimed at an "authentic" or "existential" philosophizing. Theirs was a philosophy born of reflection on human existence in the concrete, which included both the general and particular historical, religious, and cultural background as well as individual experience and circumstances.

I mentioned earlier that the fundamental inspiration of the central Kyoto philosophers was metaphysical and religious. I would add that therefore—especially from their Buddhist perspective—their central concern was not with the state but with the individual and its authentic existence, with what they call the "true self." Like most Japanese scholarship since the Meiji Restoration, the Kyoto philosophers cultivated a voracious appetite for Western materials. But as philosophers of a country that had become *the* crossroads of Eastern and Western cultures, and was consequently threatened with a loss of identity in the face of the imposing Western presence, their very openness to Western ideas required the counterbalance of their own heritage. By engaging in philosophy from the standpoint of a particular Eastern tradition, they were able to see Western ideas and systems with new eyes, to detect many shortcomings that had escaped the Western keepers of the philosophical tradition. What is clear to us today is that this new eye was not entirely innocent, but in part—perhaps inevitably—predisposed to defend the identity and glories of Eastern culture, especially in its Japanese forms.

In this connection, I have often been struck (and have said this on a number of occasions) by a certain strain of ambiguity in the writings of Nishitani Keiji, the Kyoto philosopher with whom I am most familiar. In general, his formulations seem to go like this: both Eastern and Western cultures, nothingness and being, Buddhism and Christianity, have their strengths and weaknesses; both are part of our present problems and neither suffices by itself to lead us into the future; therefore, a higher synthesis of the two is needed. At the same time, Nishitani often intimates that this higher synthesis is, in fact, already present, whether only in principle or already in embryo, in Eastern culture. At times he suggests that while Japan is part of the problem, it already has a solution at hand in its own tradition.

This tendency is not restricted to Nishitani alone. In Nishida's lecture to the Emperor of 23 January 1941, he argued that the nation-state that present-day history requires must be a synthesis that takes up into itself totalism (全体主義) and individualism. He then goes on to say:

> In the history of our country, the whole does not stand in opposition to the individuals, nor the individuals to the whole, but the whole and the

individuals have known a lively development while mutually negating one another with the imperial family as their center.[27]

Tanabe's "logic of species," as Himi Kiyoshi points out, contains a comparable ambiguity. Although ostensibly writing a general philosophy of the state, Tanabe had only the current Japanese state in mind. In this way he conflated the ideal state and the actual state of Japan. His reference to the ideal state as an "avatar-existence of the Absolute" or an "absolute relative" in fact glorified the warring Japanese state of his own day.[28]

As for Nishitani, long ago and in a context completely unrelated to questions of nationalism, I wrote the following:

> It is Nishitani's conviction that Japanese traditional culture, and especially its Mahāyāna Buddhist component, carries the necessary elements for a solution of the modern problems not only of Japanese society, but also of Western culture.[29]

A few examples may help to illustrate the point. In taking up the problem of religion and science, Nishitani argues that traditional religions have yet to tackle this problem seriously. "I am convinced," he adds, "that the basis for overcoming this difficulty has long since been laid in Buddhism."[30] In *Religion and Nothingness*, one finds a similar line of argument. After a rather sweeping statement to the effect that "up until now, religions have...put the emphasis exclusively on the aspect of life," he at once discloses the missing aspect of death in Buddhism.[31] Or again, in more direct relation to Japanese culture as such, we find remarks like the following:

> There is no turning back to the way things were. What is past is dead and gone, only to be repudiated or subjected to radical criticism. The tradition must be rediscovered from the ultimate point where it is grasped as containing in advance "the end" or *eschaton* of our westernization and of Western civilization itself.[32]

---

[27] NKZ 12:271–2.

[28] Himi Kiyoshi, *A Study of Tanabe's Philosophy*, 121–4.

[29] J. Van Bragt, "Nishitani on Japanese Religiosity," in J. Spae, *Japanese Religiosity* (Tokyo: Oriens Institute, 1971), 274.

[30] Nishitani Keiji, "Die religiöse Existenz im Buddhismus," *Proceedings of the IXth International Conference for the History of Religions* (Tokyo: Maruzen, 1960), 577.

[31] RN, 50. I have omitted the words "tended to," because, while making the English more elegant, they are not present in the original.

[32] Nishitani Keiji, *The Self-Overcoming of Nihilism*, transl. by G. Parkes and S. Aihara (Albany: The State University of New York Press, 1990), 179. Translation slightly altered.

The clearest example, and one that applies to all three philosophers with only minor differences of emphasis, is the notion of absolute nothingness. The idea is fraught with ambiguity from the start. On the one hand, it is presented as transcending (Western) being and (Eastern) nothingness. On the other, it is located in the Eastern tradition, most clearly in the form of Buddhist emptiness, which sometimes merits it the name of "Oriental nothingness" (東洋的無). It is on this point that David Dilworth has accused Nishida of "regionalism" in his reasoning, of "an ambiguous mixture of metaphysical pronouncements and cultural-regional underpinning," and "an appeal to a privileged and unique experience, based on a special historical and geographical standpoint."

> Such a mixture is present in the term "Oriental Nothingness," which we encounter frequently in the works of Nishida and his disciples. This concept becomes the basis for an apologetic and exclusivist attitude—an attitude which may be interesting in its own context, but is misplaced on the level of philosophical discourse.[33]

A variation of the same tendency appears in the presentation of Japanese Buddhism, especially the "New Buddhism" of the Kamakura Era, as the zenith of perfection of Mahāyāna Buddhism, and, at the same time, in the identification of Mahāyāna Buddhism (especially Zen) with the "true spirit" of Japan and its religiosity or "spirituality." The suspicion that this is merely a covert way of elevating Japanese particularity to a higher, more universal status is irrepressible. Examples of this kind of statement are legion, but I limit myself to a few:

> Present-day Buddhists have forgotten such a true meaning of the Mahāyāna (Great Vehicle). Eastern culture must arise again from such a standpoint. It must contribute a new light to world culture. As the self-determination of the absolute present, the national polity (*kokutai*) of Japan is a norm of historical action in such a perspective. The abovementioned true spirit of the Mahāyāna is in the East preserved today only in Japan.[34]

> I think that Japanese Buddhism, Japanized as it is by Japanese polity (*kokutai*) thought, contains in itself the spirit needed to carry on the creation of a new age.... In this sense the principle for the building of the

[33] David Dilworth, 西田の思想における地域的存在主義 [Regionalism in the thought of Nishida], 理想 536 (January 1978), 97–8.

[34] Nishida Kitarō, "Towards a Philosophy of Religion with the Concept of Pre-established Harmony as Guide," *The Eastern Buddhist* 3/1 (1970): 36. Nishida wrote this text in 1944, about a year before his death.

new age shows up within the spirit of Japanized Mahāyāna Buddhism. In this way we recognize the great significance for world history of the building up of East Asia under Japanese leadership.[35]

As for Nishitani, a clear and elaborate example can be found in the fourth chapter of his *View of the World, View of the Nation*. There, he distinguishes Eastern intellect from its Western counterpart, and finds the difference to lie in the absence of any separation in the East between worldview and (religious) practice. Nishitani sees this Eastern intellect as having reached its culmination in Japan, which naturally leads to a simplification that permits it to pervade the daily life of the people as an ethos. This ethos is visible in Shinto's "way of the Gods" (随神の道), but even more so in Kamakura Buddhism.[36]

Among the philosophers of the Kyoto school, I have the impression that this line of reasoning is strongest in D. T. Suzuki, though Watsuji may also join him here:

> In *Ethics as the Science of Man* (1931) and the first volume of *Ethics* (1937), Watsuji developed in detail the dialectical negation of individual and group in the absolute whole, which is then related to an essentially Buddhist metaphysical underpinning on the one hand, and the specifically Japanese *gemeinschaft* community and its emperor on the other.[37]

In view of their existential style of Kyoto-school philosophizing, it is not surprising to find more and more attention being given to the "philosophical position" of the state as Japan found itself in a deepening period of crisis and as ultranationalism grew stronger. I have already noted what I consider the influence of the general mood of the time on their philosophical thinking. For the sake of balance, I would only repeat that they never mustered their writings to the bugle of the ultranationalists or kowtowed to the concrete political agenda of the official party line.

In this context, it is worth noting that where the idea of the state was concerned, the Kyoto philosophers did not draw on the philosophers of the phenomenological school, whose influence in other respects was considerable. Klaus Held attributes this to the fact that "in Husserl's and Heidegger's analysis of the human being's openness to the world, a particularly significant kind of world was not recognized *as* world: the political dimension."[38] In other words, since the leading phenomenologists saw "public life" as just

[35] THZ 8:166–7.

[36] Nishitani, *View of the World, View of the Nation*, NKZ 4:167–71.

[37] R. Bellah, "Japan's Cultural Identity," 584.

[38] Klaus Held, "Eigenlijke existentie en politieke wereld," *Tijdschrift voor Filosofie* 55 (1993): 634.

another instance of the inauthentic existence of *das Man,* the Kyoto philosophers turned to other sources of a more nationalistic stamp: traditional Japanese ideas, some twentieth-century theoreticians of the state (mainly German), and Hegel (who, after all, was thought to have absolutized the Prussian state). While this argues against any direct link between Heidegger and the Kyoto philosophers on the idea of the state, it only highlights the irony of the fact that both sides, each in its own way, betrayed the centrality of the authentic individual in a state-centered totalitarianism. Again, Held:

> Surely it must serve as food for thought that it was precisely Heidegger, the phenomenologist of authenticity, who could come to think that the movement led by Hitler would end up as the awakening of an entire people to the epochal authenticity of political life.[39]

One can hardly resist the thought that the two philosophical systems shared a common weakness.

Immanent Transcendence

> "For Japan, however, the state is not simply objective spirit, but is objective spirit as the expression of the Absolute Spirit."[40]

I am persuaded that a calm reading of the texts of the principal Kyoto philosophers at the height of the critical years of the war will show them to have been utterly sincere in departing from the official nationalist ideology to stress the importance of the individual as a creative agent, to urge an international, world-historical outlook, and to relativize the position of state Shinto. The question is whether this sincerity was solidly anchored in their basic philosophical ideas or not. Here again, I begin with my own conclusion.

It seems to me that Kyoto philosophy did not in fact contain a sufficiently critical stance against nationalist tendencies to be able to take a stance in time of crisis. In saying so, I mean to stress again that establishing links with nationalism was not a necessary consequence of the ideas of the Kyoto philosophers, and yet that the bonds that did eventually form are not as surprising, unnatural, or illogical as they perhaps should have been.[41] I begin with two texts that reflect the same conclusion:

> We cannot shut our eyes to the fact that in essence Nishida's philosophy is intrinsically such that it could not work effectively to restrain the pre-

[39] Klaus Held, "Eigenlijke existentie en politieke wereld," 636.

[40] Nishitani Keiji, CK, 395.

[41] Might we not say that it is easier to find a basis for the charge of nationalism, even if only in negative form, in the Kyoto philosophers than it is in Heidegger's writings?

war course that led to a militarization of the country, and that eventually it would end up affirming and sanctioning the existing situation.[42]

Yet Watsuji, as he himself was later fully aware, made no effective resistance to the tendencies leading Japan to disaster. Indeed, the position which he had worked out did not give any basis for individual or social resistance.[43]

In digging around for the roots of this lack of power to resist, I find myself coming back again and again to what I can only call the "Mahāyāna character" of Kyoto philosophy. I base this judgment on the idea that the rise of historical religions with a clear concept of transcendence made possible for the first time the de-absolutization of the tribe and the emergence of the individual; and that, while original Buddhism posited a clear transcendence in its idea of nirvana, that clarity was weakened in Mahāyāna by a stress on nirvana-*sive*-samsara. No doubt the shift made possible great gains for Buddhism, but I also feel that something momentous was lost or at least endangered—namely, the refusal to identify the Absolute with anything this-worldly and with it the "absolute" grounding of the individual. Reference could be made here to the historical fact that "it was the idea right from the beginning of its transmission to Japan, that Buddhism is the Dharma for the protection of the state,"[44] and the relative ease with which Buddha Law and King's Law were joined together and even identified in the Buddhism of Japan.

Two points are worth recalling here. First, Kyoto philosophy is root and branch a religious philosophy, which means that it also views the state rather directly from the standpoint of religion. In this sense it always stands perilously close to sacralizing the state. Second, as a philosophical tradition it clearly situates itself within the ambit of Far Eastern Mahāyāna with its "immanent" (and one must add, often ambivalent) transcendence. Taken together, these two elements account for the tendency, visible in the relevant works of the Kyoto philosophers, to nudge the state in the direction of the Absolute—whether as a mediating force or as a concrete embodiment—or conversely to see the Absolute as immanent in the state. In Tanabe's later writings we find an explicit recognition of this:

[Before my metanoia], Nothingness [in my thinking] lacked transcendence. This unavoidably brought about the following consequences: on

---

[42] 山本誠作 Yamamoto Seisaku, 無とプロセス [Nothingness and process] (Kyoto: Kōrosha, 1987), 118.

[43] Robert Bellah, "Japan's Cultural Identity," 589.

[44] 金子大栄著作集 [Selected writings of Kaneko Daiei] (Tokyo: Shunjūsha, 1985) 5:200.

the one hand, it usurped the character of the individual as subject, and for that very reason made its transcendence immanent in and one with the individual as subject; on the other hand, nothingness became identified with the species-like substratum, and in so doing absolutized the state.[45]

Examples of this conflation of the Absolute and the state wherein the self-negation demanded by (religious) nothingness is conveniently aligned to the self-negation that the totalitarian state demands of its citizens, are not hard to find. The statement from Nishitani with which I opened this section is typical. To prepare the way for my next and final point, however, I prefer to draw attention to the danger to which the idea of absolute nothingness or emptiness (including its most current interpretations) all too easily exposes the individual subject. When emptiness is seen onesidedly as *nondual* (不二) instead of *not-one not-two* (不一不二), and when it is interpreted as an "absolute totality" instead of as an infinite horizon, its absolute negation can never return to an affirmation of the individual. This kind of interpretation is especially clear in Watsuji. For example:

> ....*established betweenness* is, in its extreme, an absolute totality in which self and other are not-two. It is the authentic face one had before one's parents were born. In other words, when all is said and done this is the authenticity out of which we emerge. Moreover, *potential betweenness* is ultimately that same absolute totality of the nonduality of self and other.... And the more close-knit a society is, the stronger does it [authentic absolute totality] become.[46]

In such a view, emptiness or absolute nothingness condemns all multiplicity and otherness as inauthentic and finally disposable. What we end up with is an ontological monism or totalism, which in turn readily leaves itself open to the support of state absolutism.

Absolute Nothingness and Human Rights

This brings us to one final defining mark of Kyoto philosophy that might also be construed as facilitating nationalism, or at least as eroding the status of the individual within the state. The point is put succinctly by Kitamori Kazō: "Absolute Nothingness makes it impossible in the end to consider the 'contradictions' of this world as tragic contradictions; it slants one in the direction of esthetic contemplation."[47] In other words, the sweeping, all-encompassing

[45] THZ 7:367.
[46] Watsuji Tetsurō, 倫理学 [Ethics] (Tokyo: Iwanami Shoten, 1937), 316.
[47] 北森嘉蔵, as quoted in Yamamoto Seisaku, *Nothingness and Process,* 118.

negation of absolute nothingness seems to take away all opposition, all tension and evil. It seems to wipe away every imperfection of actual human life by proclaiming a higher standpoint from which all such things are seen to be non-existent or illusory. I do not wish to challenge the value, the incalculable value, of such a standpoint for religion—*provided that* it opens a path back to a heightened awareness of the actual contradictions, beautiful or tragic as they may be, *provided that* it elaborate this path in sufficient detail to constitute a norm for our imperfect attempts at being fully human.

In this regard, one thinks at once of the contradictions between I and Thou, between individual and state, between good and evil. Did Kyoto philosophy, for example, live up to this ideal in countenancing the contradiction between the individual and the state? Did they take seriously the centuries-long history of the struggle for the rights of individuals within the state? Did they even consider such a struggle as truly real and authentic? The evidence suggests that, at least where Japan was concerned, they were rather inclined to think of a direct harmony (*wa,* 和) between individual and state, and to gloss over its tragic elements; and as a result, to look down on imported ideas of equality, individual freedom, and democracy, and the actual struggles of real good against real evil of which these ideas speak.[48]

In a short reflection on ethics in Nishitani's *Religion and Nothingness*," David Little has looked at the ongoing international battle on behalf of human rights and asks where one can find a solid basis for that struggle in Nishitani's thinking.[49] From his own experience in the United Nations, he points out that historically this struggle has been waged on the basis of a rather commonsense, Kantian ethic that presupposes "other selves whose autonomy and integrity ought to be respected and promoted in harmony and mutuality." Thus, when he sees Nishitani trying to "radicalize" this Kantian ethic from the standpoint of emptiness with its negation of the otherness of the I and Thou,[50] he cannot help fearing that the imperfect, but somehow functioning, normative base has been taken away with nothing to replace it. Particularly problematic for him is the following passage from Nishitani:

> We have to kill the self absolutely…, breaking through the field where self and other are discriminated from one another and made relative to one another. The self itself returns to its own home-ground by killing every "other," and, consequently, killing itself.[51]

[48] This tendency appears in its strongest form in the *Chūōkōron* discussions. See, for example, CK, 349–57.

[49] "The Problem of Ethics in Nishitani's *Religion and Nothingness*, RPNK, 185.

[50] RN, 272ff.

[51] RN, 263.

I have to agree with Little when he suggests that Nishitani does not step down far enough from the lofty heights of emptiness to reach the human condition in its concrete actuality. "While I understand what Nishitani is saying (the formulations are intelligible in one sense), I do not understand what they mean for action, and especially for the web of dutiful relations."[52] Nishitani's texts indeed give the impression—something which, I might add, he would have fiercely denied—that he does not particularly care about imperfect principles and norms being abolished because ideally they well up spontaneously from that deepest, pure core where the self is one with emptiness.

I also share Little's discomfort with the sweeping and symmetrical negation of I and Thou in the quoted passage. "Dutiful relations" are not, after all, focused on the rights of the I (they rather limit them) but on the "absolute" rights of the Thou, the Other in its irreducible individuality. Elsewhere Nishitani vents his negative feelings toward all the talk about "human rights" much more explicitly, stating that they seem to him only to underline the will and power of the I.[53] But why cannot human rights be seen, as I believe indeed they are seen, as first of all stressing the rights of the Other?

The symmetrical negation of I and Thou leaves the individual with no ground to stand on, neither towards other individuals nor vis-à-vis the state. I further resist the attempt to equate the I-Thou relationship—as Buddhist theory and Kyoto philosophy both constantly do—with the subject-object relationship. True individuality can be sustained only in a context where "otherness" is final and not reducible to any totality, be it history, absolute nothingness, or (a pantheistic) God. I conclude with two brief citations from Emmanuel Lévinas, whose writings have reconfirmed me in my convictions:

> If it [history] claims to integrate myself and the other within an impersonal spirit, this alleged integration is cruelty and injustice, that is, ignores the Other.
>
> ...the relation with the Other does not have the same status as the relations given to objectifying thought, where the distinction of terms also reflects their union. The relation between me and the Other does not have the structure formal logic finds in all relations. The terms remain absolute despite the relation in which they find themselves.[54]

[52] Little, "The Problem of Ethics," RPNK, 185.

[53] NKC 17:22–6.

[54] Emmanuel Lévinas, *Totality and Infinity: An Essay on Exteriority*, trans. by A. Lingis (Pittsburgh: Duquesne University Press, 1969), 52, 180.

Tanabe's Logic of the Specific and the Spirit of Nationalism

James W. HEISIG

IN SEPTEMBER OF 1931 JAPAN'S colonial army in Southern Manchuria, impatient with the indecision of their government back home, unilaterally attacked the Chinese garrison in Mukden. Within fifteen months they had assumed control of Manchuria. The aggression not only widened the rift between Japan and China, it also prompted the Russians to a military buildup in Siberia and brought the Japanese government general censure from the nations of the world. This in turn further hardened the extremist elements within Japan in their resolve for military hegemony in Eastern Asia. Step by step they began to tighten their grip on the country's resources, material as well as intellectual.

At the time that Japan's army was launching the first stages of its fifteen-year campaign in Asia, Tanabe Hajime, full professor in the Department of Philosophy at Japan's prestigious Kyoto Imperial University and designated successor to Nishida Kitarō, laid the groundwork of his "logic of the specific" in a series of lectures devoted to social philosophy. By 1934 Tanabe had published his first draft of the idea; and by April of 1937, just three months before the incident at Marco Polo Bridge that triggered all-out war between China and Japan, he had published his theory of the racially-unified society as a specific substratum that mediates the relationship between particular individuals and the universal ideals of the human community. Two years later, in 1939, when Japan's writers and intellectuals were still reeling from the loss of freedom of expression, Tanabe applied his new logic to argue that the Japanese nation, with the emperor at its head, has the status of a divine, salvific presence in the world.

A small resistance of thinkers, Marxist as well as Christians, were quick to identify this new "logic" as cut from the same cloth as the rhetoric of the ultra-nationalist government. Once the war was lost and the government disgraced, the ranks of the critics swelled liberally, and the same ideological fever that had sent the country blindly to the battlefields was turned mercilessly against the errant intellectuals who had supposedly given substance to many of the slogans of mass deception. Leading scholars of the Kyoto school were relieved of their posts as part of a wider purge. Tanabe, who had already retired five months before the end of the war in 1945, was labeled a "racist," a "Nazi," and a "fascist."

In a public act of repentance issued during the final stages of the Pacific War, Tanabe acknowledged his lack of strength to speak out against what he knew in his heart was wrong. He called for a complete overhaul of the notion of philosophy, which had betrayed itself in opting for expedience over truth. Months later he made an attempt to resurrect his logic of the specific, insisting that he had designed the idea for the exact opposite purpose his critics supposed—namely, to hold back the dark tide of nationalism and put the idea of the nation in a larger context of moral responsibility.

Today, half a century later, Japan's intellectual historians have yet to administer justice on the contradiction between Tanabe and his accusers. As with the rest of the Kyoto-school philosophers, the image of his philosophical contribution remains a chiaroscuro of fact and fiction, and may well fade away into the shadows altogether before the century that saw it come to life has had a chance to test its genius properly. Meantime, the introduction of the ideas of Kyoto philosophers to the West, for all the promise it holds out to the next generation of philosophers, has already begun to echo doubts of its own. The bearers of the tradition in Japan and their disciples watch bewildered as the moral agenda of the Western intellectual grows to a measure of confidence that is no longer as intimidated by claims about the "uniqueness" of Eastern culture and wisdom as it might have been a decade or more ago.

Against this backdrop, the present essay aims only to bring the contradiction between Tanabe and his accusers into sharper relief by chiseling deep into the main outlines of the logic of the specific and the main complaints raised against it. I make no apology for the nuance of detail that is lost in the effort. The text is no more than the hasty record of an early explorer, jotted down in the hope of aiding the more serious work that remains to be done. And, as those who are already familiar with the material will realize at once, the footnotes demonstrate far less than the dignity of their form might suggest, and are hardly suitable justification for the modest batch of intuitions I shall offer by way of conclusion.

FIVE CRITICS

I would begin by singling out five critics who seem to me to represent the main lines of criticism leveled against the logic of the specific. Only the first of them published their remarks during the war. Their arguments are of varying quality and insight, but I will let them stand by and large without comment.

Nanbara Shigeru

In a 1942 book entitled *State and Religion*, Nanbara Shigeru linked Tanabe's logic of the specific with the racism of the Nazis. Speaking with a courage that led Ienaga Saburō to speak of him as "our pride for having protected the smoldering wick of conscience in the Japanese academic world,"[1] Nanbara ended his book with a direct attack on Tanabe, whom he singles out by name for having put Japanese philosophy at the service of the quest for the "uniqueness" of the Japanese spirit. Though Nanbara's is not an especially sophisticated argument, it is a good indication of how those opposed to the wartime aggressions read the writings of the Kyoto philosophers.

In particular, Nanbara sees Tanabe's ideas of Absolute Nothingness and absolute dialectic as "marked by the attempt to revitalize the historical content of Eastern culture on the basis of racial self-awareness." In his engagement of the support of Buddhism, in particular Zen, "religion, philosophy, and the state are united in a way different from the West." For Nanbara, Tanabe's notion of the "absolute society," which distills species and individual, through a process of mutual negation, into a nation that makes concrete the generic universal, amounts to a simple "faith in the nation" based on a "belief in dialectics":

> "Absolute nothingness" is elevated to the status of a supreme faith, the source into which all things flow back through the self-negation of the individual.[2]

The chief stumbling block for Nanbara, as a Christian, lay in the fact that Tanabe tried to explain the nation as the incarnation of the absolute in time, in effect conceding it the role that Hegel had given to Christ. Not only does this eliminate the *ought* from history (which Nanbara, like others of Tanabe's critics, attributed to his Hegelian leanings[3]), but it also does away with the

---

[1] 家永三郎 Ienaga Saburō, 田辺元の思想史的研究—戦争と哲学者 [Studies in the history of Tanabe Hajime's thought: War and the philosopher] (Tokyo: Hōsei University Press, 1988), 143.

[2] 南原 繁, Nanbara Shigeru, 国家と宗教 [State and religion] in 南原繁著作集 [Collected writings of Nanbara Shigeru] (Tokyo: Iwanami, 1972), 1:264–5. Nanbara was drawn to Christianity, in particular the No-Church movement of Uchimura Kanzō, who was still more outspoken during the war years. After the war, Nanbara served a term as president of Tokyo University. An appendix was added to the book for its inclusion in Nanbara's collected works and an apparently expurgated phrase restored. See Ienaga, *Studies*, 142–3.

[3] On this point, Furuta has leveled a general accusation against the thinkers of the Kyoto school. See 古田 光 Furuta Hikaru, 十五年戦争下の思想と哲学 [Thought and philosophy during

critical distance between reality and our perceptions of it. For Nanbara, Kantian dualism was preferable in that it maintained the transcendence of the divine order over the human. His sensitivities are further offended by Tanabe's attempt to twist the dialectic of the Christian myth of incarnation to the point that the Japanese nation would be a mediator of salvation in the world order, thus reducing the idea of God to a logical negation:

> In such an Eastern pantheism, the race is elevated even higher than it is in Nazism, and the rationalizations for the spirituality of "race" and "nation" are dragged still further down. Given the way the idea of the racial state is thriving today and the religious foundations have weakened, what a broad and profound foundation such an idea offers compared with the Nazi ideal of the totalitarian state![4]

The fact that Nanbara's attack was not limited to Tanabe's logic of the specific was not lost on the Kyoto-school philosophers. In reviewing the book some months after it came out, Nishitani Keiji recognized it as one of the most important religious works of the year, but criticized it for "leaving one feeling alienated from historical realities." The problem for Nishitani lay not in the distance that Nanbara had set up between the religiously ideal and the politically actual, but in what he saw as its "general failure to take into account the subjective element," in its failure to point to just who—or what—is supposed to bear the burden of history. Clearly this was not a task for "humanity" as such. Nanbara's critique of Tanabe is passed over without comment.[5]

As for Tanabe himself, he seems to have been deeply touched by the explicit attack. In a later essay on the logic of the specific, he alludes to the critique and thanks its author, without alluding to the contents or to Nanbara's closing plea for saving the true universality of Christianity so that it can help Japan find its place in the world.[6] Yamamoto Seisaku suggests that in fact the critique spurred Tanabe on to develop his idea of "metanoetics" and to reconsider the possibility that latent authoritarianism in the nation

---

the fifteen-year war] in vol. 4 of 近代日本社会思想史 [The history of social thought in modern Japan], ed. by Furuta Hikaru et al. (Tokyo: Chikuma Shobō, 1959), 278.

[4] *State and Religion*, 268–9, 274. At the time the original was published, Japan had already signed a treaty with the Nazis. As Ienaga Saburō points out, a close reading shows that Nanbara in fact judiciously avoided an explicit attack on the Nazis (*Studies*, 143). I use the word *race* rather than *ethnic nation* or some such variant to translate the Japanese 民族, reckoning that it better glosses over many of the distinctions we are driven to by our modern sensibilities, which, for all their importance, are after all by and large anachronistic.

[5] 西谷啓治 Nishitani Keiji, 哲学年鑑 [Philosophical yearbook] 2 (1943): 93–4.

[6] 田辺元全集, THZ 7:366–7. The essay was composed during the war but only published in 1946.

needs to be submitted to a higher, divine judgment of history.[7] Yamamoto fails to mention, however, that after the war Nanbara sent Tanabe a collection of his own poems lamenting the war. This, together with Tanabe's response praising Nanbara for his efforts on behalf of freedom of thought, indicates that there was no lasting ill will between them over the public criticism.[8]

Nanbara's complaint that Tanabe's logic had slackened the tension between the ideal and the real was hardly original. In the same year that his book appeared, Akizawa Shūji raised similar doubts about the implicit "totalitarianism" of Tanabe's dialectical method.[9] Takizawa Katsumi would later see this as an abiding flaw in Tanabe's philosophy, one that weakened the idea of death-in-resurrection that was central to his metanoetics. Writing in 1972, Takizawa went so far as to intimate that this was why Tanabe's dialectic and logic of the specific had been completely forgotten within ten years after his death.[10]

Umehara Takeshi

This brings us to a second line of criticism, which focuses on a certain abstractness and distance from the real world in Tanabe's thinking that not only made his ideas easy prey for political ideologues but also clouded Tanabe's own perception of the events going on around him. Umehara Takeshi offers himself as a representative of those who felt themselves cheated by the philosophers at Kyoto—first herded off to war and then brought back to the pure heights of speculation as if nothing had happened.

Umehara recalls in retrospect that the Kyoto philosophers filled a need for many of the young students of his generation.[11] After the Manchurian Incident, it was only a matter of time before the whole country would be at war. All the efforts made at sitting in Zen meditation and studying existential philosophy were supposed to help them find a standpoint beyond life and death, but none of this was any match for the raw anxiety of young students

[7] 山本誠作 Yamamoto Seisaku, 無とプロセス—西田思想の展開をめぐって [Nothingness and process: The development of Nishida's thought] (Kyoto: Kōrosha, 1987), 122.

[8] Cited in Ienaga, *Studies*, 196, note 13.

[9] 秋沢修二 Akizawa Shūji, 田辺哲学と全体主義 [Tanabe's thought and totalitarianism]. The article appeared in a special issue of 科学ペン [Science magazine] devoted to Tanabe's philosophy.

[10] 滝沢克巳全集 [Collected works of Takizawa Katsumi] (Kyoto: Hōzōkan, 1972), 1:456–7, 460, 472. Takizawa's several essays on Tanabe deserve a closer reading than I have been able to give them.

[11] 梅原 猛 Umehara Takeshi, 京都学派との交渉私史—天ぷらと哲学 [A personal history of dealings with the Kyoto school: Tempura and philosophy], 思想の科学 [The science of thought] 8 (1959): 31–8. The essay centers on remarks supporting the war made by the four principals of the *Chūōkōron* discussions: Kōyama Iwao, Kōsaka Masaaki, Suzuki Shigetaka, and Nishitani Keiji.

facing the prospect of being sent to war. Only a philosophy that could prepare them to die for a cause would do, and eventually this was what their
teachers gave them.[12]

Umehara places himself among the philosophy students of the time who
knew too much of modern thought to be taken in by the official imperialist
philosophy[13] and for whom the idea of the emperor as a living absolute divinity beyond criticism was the "supreme insult" to their intelligence. At the
same time, Nishida and Tanabe were a "godlike presence" that lent credibility to what their principle disciples were saying in class. For example, the
recondite and mystical philosophy of Nishitani, as difficult as it was to understand, at least succeeded in communicating that the moral thing to do was to
sacrifice the self to the fascist state.[14]

Not without a certain animus of regret, Umehara admits that the Kyoto
philosophy of a "world-historical standpoint" offered an answer to the question that he and others like him had at the time. Indeed, after the war he
returned to study under the very people who had forged that philosophy—
until an edict from the American Occupation that had them purged—and
who continued to advance its truth in spite of the circumstances of Japan's
defeat at the hands of the West. At the time, Tanabe and Nishida remained
the chief gods in the Kyoto pantheon, and every attempt to correct or
advance their philosophy was based on the assumption of continuity with
their absolute dialectic. Umehara, on whom much of Tanabe's subtlety was
admittedly lost, describes the ruling position as a barren middle ground
between existentialism and Marxism that forfeits the very elements it is trying
to relate dialectically:

> Existential philosophy is the standpoint of the individual. But the indi-
> vidual that is not mediated by the specific—that is, by society—is abstract
> and without concrete actuality. Thus existential philosophy must be
> mediated negatively by society. At the same time, Marxism is a stand-
> point centered on society and fails adequately to generate the individual.
> But a society that does not create free individuals is an evil universal, and
> therefore socialism must be mediated negatively by the individual.

[12] 高山岩男 Kōyama Iwao recalls the weakness philosophy teachers like himself felt in trying to
face their students in class after the attack on Manchuria. See the preface to his 世界史の哲学
[Philosophy of world history] (Tokyo: Iwanami, 1942).

[13] This 皇道哲学 is associated with figures like 紀平正美 Kihira Tadayoshi and 鹿子木員信
Kanokogi Kazunobu.

[14] Umehara's conclusion that "Nishitani was a believer in the myth of the emperor's divinity"
(34) squares clumsily with the claim that Umehara himself was taken in by the ideology and yet
was too sophisticated to swallow the idea of the emperor's centrality.

Aside from the fact that Umehara is content to wrap Nishida's logic of absolute self-identity in the same bundle, this is not an inaccurate picture of Tanabe's position as far as it goes. In any case, the abstractness of it all was too much for Umehara, who found himself longing for something closer to his own lingering preoccupation with the problem of death that he carried back with him from the war. The appearance of Tanabe's *Philosophy as Metanoetics*, not to mention the apparent idol-worship that surrounded its somber call for religious conversion, was not in the end metanoia enough to persuade Umehara otherwise.

Yamada Munemutsu

A third line of criticism, and the most severe, comes from the Marxist quarter, where the clash of ideologies is at its rudest and most inflexible. If the dialectic of absolute mediation gradually became a kind of tacit assumption for Tanabe, the socialist idea of critique of the state-individual relationship through an analysis of class struggle and control of the means of production was equally so for Japan's Marxists. But there is more at work here than a simple disagreement over principles. Tanabe had attempted a rather feeble critique of socialist philosophy which failed to convince the Marxists but which had some influence in the prestigious circles of philosophy and may have contributed to the persecution of philosophers sympathetic to Marxist thought during the war. The counterattack that Yamada Munemutsu represents needs to be read, at least in part, as retaliation for those events.

While the war was still in progress, Yamada Munemutsu, then a student in Kyoto's Department of Philosophy, was given special permission from the munitions factory where he had been mobilized to work, enabling him to attend Tanabe's "Metanoetics" lectures. Looking back over his notes at the time, he finds that he was not convinced by Tanabe's assertion that his only failure was a failure of strength. Yamada felt there were problems in the philosophy itself that kept its epistemology from facing social realities head on.[15] In his book-length critique, however, Yamada does not take his own point seriously—or even mention the notes he took at the time. All nuance is eclipsed by his conviction that Tanabe was not just philosophically incomplete but politically fascist.

Yamada basically accepts the idea of a shift from the liberalism and individualism—or "culturism"—of the Taishō era to the social awareness and politicization of the Shōwa period. He finds taints of Nishida's culturism in Miki's humanism and humanistics, in Kōyama's study of cultural patterns, in Kimura's expressionism, in Tanigawa Tetsuzō's cultural theory, and the like.

---

[15] Cited in Ienaga, *Studies*, 185.

JAMES W. HEISIG

In contrast, the core of Tanabe's critique of Nishida lay in his rejection of this culturism.[16]

Basically, Yamada's starting point is this: The racism of Tanabe's logic of the specific was a natural result of his having been "born and baptized" in bourgeois society. Instead of establishing a link between the universal and the particular as Nishida had done, Tanabe's stress on the nation as the "specificity" through which transformation takes place in the historical process actually provoked a conflict between the two thinkers. This conflict in turn added fuel to the rise of the militaristic ideology that lay behind the Manchurian Incident of 1931, the military coup of 1936, the Sino-Japanese war of 1937, and eventually the Pacific War that began with the attack on Pearl Harbor.

Yamada does not provide very much detail as to just how these connections are made, but assures us that Tanabe's logic was more appealing than Nishida's idea of the "self-definition of history," which kept the reality of history from being identified with any particular nation. On the positive side, Tanabe's position cut closer to the bone and mobilized the Kyoto school as a whole to come to terms with what was going on. Unfortunately, they accepted the standpoint of Japanism and a nationalism based on the emperor system as a platform from which to resist militarism to the right and Marxism to the left. In Yamada's view, within this commonly accepted nationalism,

> Tanabe stood at the right, seeking a more classical interpretation of the state, while Miki and Nishida himself stood at the left, aiming at limiting the nation. At the initial stage, the centrist faction was made up of Mutai, Kōsaka, and Shimomura, followed by Yanagida later and perhaps Kimura. Still later, Kōsaka, Nishitani, and Kōyama shifted over to the right to advance a philosophy of all-out war, while Shimomura preserved rationalism in the "overcoming Modernity" discussions, and after the war Mutai and Yanagida gradually stepped over into socialism.[17]

As Yamada sees it, Miki tried to limit nationalism through a kind of globalism, and Nishida, agreeing with him but more in direct response to Tanabe, worked on a logic of the historical process in conjunction with the centrists Mutai, Shimomura, and Kimura. As Konoe Fumimaro, who presided over Japan's transformation into a "national defense state," steered the ship of state closer and closer to the Pacific War, the relations among the three factions changed shape:

---

[16] 山田宗睦 Yamada Munemutsu, 昭和の精神史—京都学派の哲学 [Intellectual history of the Shōwa period: The philosophy of the Kyoto school] (Kyoto: Jinbun Shoin, 1975), 46. Tanabe's critique of culturism surfaces immediately again after the war. See PM, lxi.

[17] Yamada, *Intellectual History of the Shōwa Period*, 61.

262

Aggravations between Nishida and Miki brought about a change in the Kyoto school as a whole, with the centrists shifting to the right. Miki's comments on current events dried up while those in the center who had turned right—Kōsaka, Nishitani, and Kōyama—spoke out on current events. Nishida, as if one possessed, argued various particular points from the fundamental standpoint of the self and came out with one philosophical collection after the other. Miki sunk into a logic concerned with the power of ideas.[18]

Determined to keep Tanabe at the opposite extreme from Nishida, Yamada does his best to shift the blame for the fate of Nishida's theory of "moral energy" to disciples who had misunderstood their teacher's aim of limiting the state. No such slack is given for Tanabe, who is made to stand alone at the far right.

There is far too much to sort out here without a careful look at the writings and records of the time, but Yamada gradually leaves his sources as he tries to draw the bigger picture. He returns to the texts with Tanabe's *Metanoetics*, which he sets aside summarily as a "super-metaphysics" fabricated by someone caught in a pinch between his ideal of the nation and the stubborn realities of nationalism at work. For Yamada, it seems to have been no more than the final, parting gesture of the right wing of the Kyoto school as it strides off haughtily into complete philosophical irrelevance.[19]

Katō Shūichi

Contrasting sharply with Yamada's reproach of Tanabe as an inveterate rightist, the Tokyo philosopher Katō Shūichi accuses him of a simple naiveté. He summarily lumps the rationalist Kyoto philosophers together with the irrational "romanticists" of the age as offering support from opposite quarters for the Japanese invasion of China and the Pacific War.

For Katō, Tanabe was at home discoursing on the pure abstractions of logic, but "when he spoke of the meaning of Japan in world history, it was pure nonsense."[20] Thus, when Tanabe applied his logic of the specific to the actual political situation and referred to the emperor as Japan's symbolic way of transcending totalitarianism; or again, when he credited service to the emperor with breaking Japan out of the closed, tribal society and into the

---

[18] Yamada, *Intellectual History of the Shōwa Period*, 87–8.

[19] Yamada, *Intellectual History of the Shōwa Period*, 99.

[20] 加藤周一 Katō Shūichi, 戦争と知識人 [War and the intellectuals], in 近代日本思想史講座 [Lectures in modern Japanese thought], vol. 4, 古田光·作田啓一·生松敬三編 Furuta Hikaru et al., eds., 知識人の生成と役割 [The emergence and role of the intellectual] (Tokyo: Chikuma Shobō, 1959), 346.

wider human community,[21] Katō sees him rather out of touch with the events that were transpiring around him. Even after the war, in a short 1946 book that appeared just two months after *Metanoetics*, Tanabe clung to the monarchical model as the guarantee of democracy:

> The emperor is the embodiment of the ideal of the unity of the people as a whole. Only nothingness is able to unify things that stand in opposition; simple being cannot do it. The absolute inviolability of the emperor is a function of transcendent nothingness. Thus understood, the symbolic presence of the emperor should be seen as the principle that unifies through absolute negation both democracy and the opposition that it contains.[22]

Tanabe did realize, of course, that support for this application of the logic of the specific could not come from within the logic itself but must rest on objective fact. Tanabe's version of what constitutes such evidence, Katō concludes, amounts to this: "The majority of the people today are of one mind about retaining national polity through continuing the emperor system." For Katō, not only was the idea of retaining the unity of the state through its identification with the emperor "pure fantasy," but Tanabe should have seen that the "majority" of which he spoke was no less a fantasy, planted in the minds of people by a half century of education since the Meiji period. He concludes that both during the war and after, Tanabe was out of touch with the real world. His words cut with a bitter air of sarcasm:

> Tanabe's logic is a technique for justifying the ideas of the "majority of the people" in a given age. With no other interpretation of reality than "the majority of the people," the experience of reality is no more than so much barbershop banter. It begins with a Sanba-like experience of "the world of the baths," followed by dialectics, and then by the unity of opposites in nothingness. Tanabe's philosophy, in a word, is a philosophy of dialectical bath-talk. With a dialectics from the West and the baths from the Edo period, it united East and West in nothingness. On one hand, it appeals only to the head; on the other it appeals to earthy, vital sentiments. The result is a unity of body and spirit in the self-unity of absolute contradictories.[23]

---

[21] 歴史的現実 [Historical reality], THZ 8:166.

[22] 政治哲学の急務 [The urgent task of political philosophy], THZ 8:370. Tanabe turns around the demand of the West that the emperor accept responsibility for the war to show how this implies the very thing he is arguing (370–1).

[23] Katō, *War and the Intellectuals*, 347. The literary reference is to 式亭三馬 Shikitei Sanba, an early nineteenth-century satirist who wrote of conversations in the public baths.

While this does not qualify as imperialism of the usual political sort —nor does Katō claim that it does—neither does it qualify as the sort of reasoning that political philosophy expects. The simple fact for Katō is that Tanabe remained aloof from the facts, seeing them from the distant mists of the philosopher's podium, where, the implication is, the simple facts of life could not oblige him to review his assumptions.

Ienaga Saburō

Perhaps the most sympathetic of the critics is Ienaga Saburō, whose thoroughgoing study argues that Tanabe's relationship with nationalism alternated between resistance and cooperation, until in the end the pattern was broken in a final act of repentance. Ienaga's mustering of the facts on the one hand, and his decision to suspend judgment on the accuracy of Tanabe's various philosophical critiques on the other,[24] lead him to reject a simple conclusion. This alone sets him apart from most of Tanabe's other critics.

In 1922 Tanabe published an essay on "The Notion of Culture." In it he accepted socialism's critique of bourgeois culturism and its idea of democracy, but at the same time rejected what he saw as its wholesale dismissal of the philosophic enterprise.[25] The fact that so voracious a reader as he never bothered to base his views on a serious study of Marxist-Leninist thought, and that he seems to have maintained to the end his initial suspicions that its economic theory and data were simply a "secondary means" to enhance the philosophical ideas, makes it clear that socialist thought never worked more than a marginal stimulus on his own thinking.

Tanabe's first direct confrontation with the fascism of the Shōwa period came in 1933 when the government intervened to call for the dismissal of a professor of law, Takikawa Yukitoki, for supposedly dangerous remarks against the state. Tanabe led a small contingency in the Faculty of Letters to oppose the interference as being against academic freedom. The *Chūōkōron* brought the details to the public eye, and by October Iwanami Shigeo had

[24] See Ienaga, *Studies*, 32.

[25] Tanabe had trouble with drawing a straight line from Taishō democracy to Taishō philosophy, which for him was a humanism and a cultivationism and did not represent a true basis for the ideals of Taishō democracy. The political Taishō democracy and cultural Taishō humanism and cultivationism ran parallel but rarely communicated with each other. Apart from a slight overlap in the "concept of culture," the waves of Taishō democracy hardly reached Tanabe at all. Ienaga argues that he accepted the term *culturism* only in the sense of a metaphysical culturism that broke through the crude antipolitical and antisocial culturism he saw as distinctive of Taishō thinkers. See *Studies*, 5–6, which draws on the analysis of 船山信一 Funayama Shin'ichi, 大正哲学史研究 [Studies in the history of Taishō philosophy] and compares it with Tanabe's essay on "The Concept of Culture" (THZ 1:423–47).

published the account in book form.[26] Despite the widespread attention the incident attracted, Tanabe did not force his own views to any extreme extent.[27] Still, his position seems to have aroused the displeasure of Nishida, who also turned down Iwanami's offer for support, fearing to endanger the university as a whole for just this one case.[28] More importantly, it led him to seek a philosophical explanation for what takes place when the state exercises its will against the individual.

Two years later, in 1935, Tanabe voiced public opposition against the Ministry of Education's drive to isolate Japanese culture from the West, and the following year argued his case in print in the context of a more pointed assault on the emerging militaristic ideology and a defense of the need for Western science.[29] Tanabe is reported to have said that he felt his life was on the line for his remarks.[30] Though this may have overstated the facts, his comments did elicit sharp, ad hominem, and immediate accusations of infamy from Minoda Muneki in the pages of *The Japan Principle*, an ultra-rightist magazine founded to defend the emperor system against the inroads of Marxism and Western democracy. Among other things, Tanabe was suspected of providing support to the Marxist revolution. The following month, the magazine printed a similar attack by Matsuda Fukumatsu.[31] Nishida

[26] The book 先輩の見た京大事件 [The Kyoto affair as seen by senior colleagues] appeared in July of 1933, just three months after the affair broke out.

[27] Just how important Tanabe's role was is difficult to say. His name is not mentioned in the account of Takikawa and those immediately involved, which was published in October as 京大事件 [The Kyoto incident] under the editorship of 滝川幸辰 Takikawa Yukitoki and six others involved in the events (Tokyo: Iwanami, 1933). One has only to glance through the account of the events to realize how ridiculously complicated the Ministry of Education made things, and to understand perhaps something of how ideologies flame passions on the slimmest of pretexts. The only intellectual content has to do with the supposed danger of Takikawa's views that crimes against society do not emerge merely from some evil in the individual but can also be the result of society itself. Particularly interesting is how the government substituted the term *nation* for *society* in representing Takikawa's views (101); and also how the counterargument that runs through the book, once all the political maneuvering is set aside, is that the reason for making criticisms against the state was really to strengthen the sense of the "people's" identity (16). This seems to have been the mood of the time: a choice between ultranationalism and nationalism.

[28] Ienaga quotes from the diary of 岩波茂雄伝 Iwanami Shigeo here (*Studies*, 50).

[29] The account appears in the postwar reflections of 中島健蔵 Nakajima Kenzō. See Ienaga, *Studies*, 51, notes 5 and 6; 53.

[30] The comment is reported by 上田泰治 Ueda Yasuharu in an explanatory afterword to THZ 5:110. In *Metanoetics* Tanabe makes a similar remark about being ready to die (189), which Ienaga surmises refers to this essay. Concerning the exaggerated fear of dying for his views, see the comments cited in Ienaga, 65, n.15.

[31] 蓑田胸喜 Minoda Muneki, 田辺元氏の科学政策論の学術的誤謬を分析す [An analysis of the academic fallacy in Tanabe Hajime's theory of scientific planning] 原理日本 [The Japan Principle], November 1933; 松田福松 Matsuda Fukumatsu, 科学的精神と新スコラスティク打破—

encouraged him not to reply, but once again Tanabe refused the advice and sent his reply to the magazine, where it was printed in May of the following year. In it he stressed the peril of Japan's isolating its intellectual culture from the scientific progress of the rest of the world.[32]

Within two years Tanabe's philosophical reflections had turned seriously to the question of the state. He was still convinced that a simple stress on subjectivity would not do to assure individual freedom. Something had to be done to locate the reality of the state in the rational scheme of things. He offered such a scheme in a series of essays over the next few years that outlined his new logic of the specific. Ienaga's conclusions, when pieced together, show a studied ambivalence:

> Acknowledging the rationality of the state, Tanabe did not oppose the current state head-on. He did not step forward and fight to stop its policies. For this reason, he does not deserve to be included in the small number of those who, from a variety of intellectual persuasions, risked the little they had in wartime and continued to resist. But at least in the early stages of the fifteen years of war and within the sacred precincts, Tanabe did show courage to the point of publicly issuing a severe criticism, limited though it was, against the state authority run wild.
>
> ....
>
> Tanabe's philosophy in 1935, seen as the wartime thought of an intellectual, shines out proudly, as rightly it should, but there is another side to the picture that cannot be forgotten. Subjectively sincere though he was, there is an objective tragedy to Tanabe that cannot escape severe criticism....
>
> ....
>
> Beginning with a resistance that tried to correct from within a military policy that was heading blindly down the path to extreme irrationalism and inhumanity, by and large his efforts did not prevent him from cooperating in such a way as to justify philosophically the very things he was set against.[33]

In the end, the ambivalence of Ienaga's verdict seems to rest on two factors. On the one hand, at the time the logic of the specific was being formed, the political drive to reinforce national unity was already a fact to be reckoned with. No simple cause-and-effect relationship can be drawn from one to

---

田辺博士の所論に因みて [The spirit of science and the overthrow of neo-scholasticism in connection with the theory of Dr. Tanabe].

[32] 蓑田氏及び松田氏の批判に答う [In reply to the criticisms of Minoda and Matsuda], in THZ 8:11–31.

[33] Ienaga, *Studies*, 50, 64–5, 178.

the other. On the other, the strongest opponents to Japan's military adventures looked at weaker, compromising opponents, and of course as *ex post facto* critics, as collaborators. Given the courage it took the former to speak out, one hesitates to dismiss their judgment too quickly.[34]

TANABE'S RESPONSE

Tanabe did not take well to the criticisms that reached him during the war. Accusations of totalitarianism understandably hurt him, as it did others in the Kyoto school.[35] In his first defense of the logic of the specific, composed in 1937, he wrote:

> My view, which at first glance appears to be no more than an extreme nationalism, is in no way simply and directly an irrational totalitarianism or racialism. Rather, it is like a "self-sacrifice"-in-"self-realization" or a unity-in-freedom whose aim is to build up the nation in the form of a subjective realization of the whole through the spontaneous cooperation of each member.[36]

In later years he was to repeat the claim that he had been misunderstood. In reply to his critics, Tanabe published more on the logic of the specific in a book published in 1947, the year after the publication of *Philosophy as Metanoetics*. Its opening essay, which originally appeared only four months after *Metanoetics*, speaks of the period just before the virtual five-year silence[37] he maintained at the end of the war:

---

[34] One thinks here particularly of Tosaka Jun, who referred to the Kyoto philosophers as a "high-level phenomenology" that amounts to "the most courageous bourgeois speculative philosophy in our country or in the world for that matter," and singled out Tanabe as a "fascist" even before Tanabe had made his political views clear. See the two sections on the Kyoto school and Tanabe's philosophy in his 1934 book *Talks on Contemporary Philosophy*, in 戸坂潤全集 *Collected Works of Tosaka Jun* (Tokyo: Keisei Shobō, 1970), 3:170–84. See also the short piece 思い出の一端 [Fragments of a memory] by 相原信作 Aihara Shinsaku in the leaflet appended to volume 12 of Tanabe's *Collected Works*.

[35] Ienaga, *Studies*, 71.

[36] 種の論理の意味を明にする [Clarifying the meaning of the logic of the specific], THZ 6:452. This foreword should be compared with the afterword Nishitani appended in 1946 to his 1941 book 世界観と国家観 [View of the world, view of the nation], the structure of whose apology follows much the same pattern as Tanabe's. See NKC 4:381–4. For his part, Ienaga was not impressed by Nishitani's efforts to distinguish what he believed from what he was accused of believing, and finds his lack of self-criticism puts a "large gap" between him and Tanabe. See *Studies*, 146–7, note 9. I am not so persuaded.

During the years 1934 and 1940 I pursued a study of a dialectic logic that I called the "logic of the specific" and by means of which I tried to explain logically the concrete structure of the society of the nation. My motive was to take up the philosophical question of racialism that was emerging at the time. Together with a critique of the liberalism that had come to dominate us at the time, I rejected a so-called totalitarianism based on a simple racialism. Mediating by mutual negation the race that formed the substrate of the latter and the individual that was the subject of the former, I took a standpoint of absolute mediation as substrate-in-subject, subject-in-substrate and thought to discover a rational foundation for the nation as a practical unity of the reality and the ideal.[38]

Leaving aside the technicalities for later, the passage makes it clear that Tanabe wants to present himself as an enemy of nationalism or racialism from the start, and that for reasons grounded in his logic of the specific. What he fails to mention is that his "logic" had undergone a rather important shift as a result of the war experience. Where before he had characterized the state in Buddhist terms as an "absolute incarnation," he now refers to it as an "expedient means" for a higher end.[39] Tanabe was never very forward about transformations in his thought, with an almost pontifical habit of insisting on consistency when it is clear there was none. The dramatic conversion he announces in *Metanoetics* did not change this. Tanabe's self-criticisms, then, were not so much theoretical as they were pedagogical, religious, and practical. We may consider an example of each.

Farewell to Cadets

In a piece published in the *Kyoto University Newspaper* under the title "Farewell Words to Students on the Way to War: Realize the True Meaning of Conscription!" Tanabe told his listeners that they all knew the day that was upon them would come, and that "this late hour is not the time to waver over the problem of life and death." He pauses for a moment to consider the wider significance of the government's unprecedented enlistment of hundreds of thousands of students, insisting that refinement of thought and cultivation of the arts are also "indispensable elements in all-out war." Bowing to necessity, he sets the question aside and instead encourages the young recruits to enter the army as representatives of Japan's intelligentsia. I quote

[37] THZ 7.382.

[38] THZ 7:253.

[39] The point is noted by 大島康正 Ōshima Yasumasa in his explanatory afterword to THZ 7:384.

JAMES W. HEISIG

from the core of the piece because it contrasts so sharply with the style
Tanabe is better known for:

> War today, as all-out war, is not exhausted in mere fighting in the narrow
> sense of the term. It is hard to expect final victory without engaging
> intelligence and technology through and through. Moreover, in order
> to demonstrate positively the results of the fighting, there is a need to
> back up with deep thinking and high insight the making of culture for
> races in the lands and the moralization of the everyday life of people con-
> nected with the war effort. This has become for us common sense....
>
> But to ward off misunderstanding, I ask you to pay particular atten-
> tion to this: I am not saying you should enlist in the army with the aim of
> intellectualizing the army. I am only encouraging your self-awareness by
> speaking of the natural and inevitable results....
>
> First you are to learn the spirit of the imperial army, ...which is none
> other than the quintessential flowering of the spirit of the nation. To take
> up the spirit of Japan as a member of the armed forces is the gateway by
> which a Japanese becomes a Japanese.... Aware of your heavy responsi-
> bility as military cadets, take the lead in breaking through the brink of life
> and death. Actualize the spirit of the imperial army, which sees that living
> or dying is only for the sake of the Sovereign.... In this way, by serving
> the honorable calling of the Sovereign as the one whose person brings
> together country and God, you will share in the creation of the eternal
> life of the state. Is this not truly the highest glory?[40]

At the time, 1943, the question was rhetorical for Tanabe. Thirteen years
later the bottom had dropped out of its self-evidence. In a 1956 essay titled
"Memories of Kyoto," Tanabe takes the same phrase that he used to close his
remarks to the students off to war, "highest glory,"[41] and uses it to describe
the teacher who is able to embrace in the classroom a great number of students "burning with the love of truth." The connection between the two,
which rather leaps out at one today, was probably lost on most of his readers
at the time. The content of the article leaves little doubt that it was more than
coincidence.

Tanabe admits that the glory has not been without hardships. The peren-
nial task of philosophy does not consist in transmitting accumulated knowledge but in reassuring the love of truth. This demands a special relationship
of mutual criticism between teacher and student for which reason and not
rank provides the basis. He thinks back to the waves of socialist thought that

[40] 征く学生におくる贐の言葉—入隊の真義を自覚せよ [Farewell words to students on the way to
war: Realize the true meaning of conscription!] THZ 14:415–6. As far as I have been able to
ascertain, the piece was not delivered orally.

[41] 無上なる光栄.

270

had washed across the campuses and fired the imagination of Japan's young intellectuals, admitting that for him personally it had been a test of his commitment to philosophy.

Tanabe admits that he was not without sympathy for the theoretical consistency of socialist thought and its demand for social justice, and even that to some extent it answered the demand for a philosophy of social justice. What he resisted was the introduction of politics into the philosophy classroom, not to mention that "reactionary thinking" and irrationalism that were used against those like himself who resisted reducing everything to class struggle. With the Manchurian Incident in 1931, things grew still more complicated. On the one hand, the intellectual confrontation with socialist thinking grew more intense; on the other, the government began to step up its monitoring of teaching at public universities. Together, these two forces threatened the existence of the rational forum that philosophy depends on. In these circumstances, Tanabe says that he opted to focus on classical German philosophical texts and not to take up the vital political issues of the day, in order the better to face the basic existential questions of philosophy. Looking back at this decision he writes:

> In the face of the gradually worsening pressures of the Second World War, and the ever increasing strict control of thought, I was too faint-hearted to resist positively, and more or less had no choice but to be swept up in the tide of the times. On this point I cannot reproach myself deeply enough.

The thought of the students rushing to the battlefields, some of them to die there under the banner of a "blind militarism," leaves him, he says, with "a strong sense of regret for my own responsibility. I can only hang my head low and confess my sin."[42]

The conclusion one would expect Tanabe to draw, that he was wrong about keeping politics out of the classroom, or at least naive to think that it was possible, is not drawn. I have yet to find a passage in his works where it is. His call for a metanoesis in philosophy does not challenge this fundamental point, but rather shifts the accent to religious consciousness. The oversight is telling.

The Metanoetics

Philosophy as Metanoetics is not Tanabe's lament for what he *did* do but only for what he did *not*. Rather than a recanting of particular ideas, it calls for a general reform of the philosophical enterprise itself.

---

[42] 京大の憶出 [Memories of Kyoto], THZ 14:439.

After the surrender of 1945, many of Japan's writers broke their pens in shame. Others reupholstered their memory to find a consistency in their ideas that never was there. Some even doctored their collected works to hide the stains.[43] In such a mood, the idea that the Kyoto philosophers had made the best of an oppressive situation, that against impossible odds they had tried to encourage more moderate elements, could hardly get a fair hearing. To some extent, the *Metanoetics* did. Granted it did little to answer the direct criticisms against Tanabe himself or the other Kyoto philosophers, it does seem to have attracted considerable sympathy in both philosophical and religious circles. Tanabe's distance from Nishida throughout the fifteen years of war, though in no way related to their respective views on the war or Japanese nationalism, prevented his ideas from being cited to back up any political position of Nishida or his closest disciples. There is, for instance, not even a hint of his logic of the specific in the *Chūōkōron* discussions. No doubt this fact, too, though entirely circumstantial, had a role to play in the enthusiastic reception of the *Metanoetics.*

This may not have been entirely to Tanabe's advantage. Takeuchi Yoshinori laments the extent to which the circumstances of the book's origins "overshadowed its true origins and caused it to be absorbed into the general atmosphere of mass appeals for national repentance being generated by opportunistic politicians."[44] For, all things considered, the *Metanoetics* is a supremely nonpolitical book. Even when it tilts towards the concrete in "despising the shamelessness of the leaders primarily responsible for the defeat who are now urging the entire nation to repentance" and expressing a belief in "the collective responsibility of the nation,"[45] its call is for a religious change of heart, not for a reform of social institutions.

For the logic of the specific, this meant "a new and deeper basis," not a radical restructuring.[46] Even his crowning idea of the ideal of an "existential community" through collective repentance does not depart from his original idea of the nation.[47]

[43] Akashi Yōji has gathered together an expressive essay on the subject, "The Greater East Asian War and *Bunkajin*, 1941–1945," *War and Society* 11/1 (1993): 129–77.

[44] "Translator's Introduction" to *Metanoetics*, xxxvi.

[45] *Metanoetics*, lx, lviii.

[46] *Metanoetics*, lviii.

[47] See Yamamoto, *Nothingness and Process*, 123. 辻村公一 Tsujimura Kōichi notes that what happens in *Metanoetics* is not that the logic of the specific disappears but that it is given different expression. "The three elements of absolute dialectic—individual, species, genus—each show up in a new form in the ideas of 'death-resurrection,' 'nothingness-in-love,' and the 'fellowship of mutual forgiveness'." 田辺哲学について [Tanabe's philosophy], in 田辺元 [Tanabe Hajime] (Tokyo: Chikuma Shobō, 1965), 47.

A Proposal to the Emperor

Finally, Tanabe's self-criticism took the form of practical action, where his refusal to part with former ideas takes a curious turn. In 1945 Tanabe, already retired to Karuizawa, wrote what was to be his last letter to Nishida. In it he laid bare his genuine concern for the future of Japan and the emperor system. Given his idea of the emperor as a symbol of Absolute Nothingness on the one hand and the difficult conditions that had fallen on the population at large on the other, Tanabe proposed that initiatives be taken before the arrival of the occupying forces to ward off the impending deposition. Concretely, he suggested that the emperor publicly renounce all possessions associated with his position and return them, in the form of a salvific offering, to the Japanese people. In so doing the emperor would embody the Buddhist principle of nothingness—"without a single thing"[48]— and perhaps prevail on the West to leave the emperor system intact.

In highly formal prose, Tanabe asked Nishida for permission to communicate his plan to the emperor as representing Nishida's own views. His letter reads in part:

> The danger our nation finds itself in today is unlike anything in the past, and like you I am most anxious about it. There is no need repeating that without clear thinking nothing can save us. I am an old and powerless man in a weak frame, and as always full of my own opinions. But I cannot repress the hope that perhaps there is something in those opinions that might help to save the country. As often as I have expressed them to you and heard your criticisms, if there be something of truth to be had in my plan, I would like to ask your power to help see it realized....
>
> With your kind leave, I would like whatever you find useful to be presented to Prime Minister Konoe, and from there have it brought to Takamatsu no Miya [the emperor's younger brother] for handing over to the emperor. Under normal circumstances, such a request would be unreasonable, but the anxieties of the moment make time of the essence. I am convinced that whatever may come of it all, there is something here of service to the emperor and the nation, and that steps should be taken to pursue its realization. I know this is asking a great deal, but I would be grateful if you would give this matter your serious consideration.[49]

[48] 無一物. Tanabe uses the same phrase later to refer to Japan's starting over with democracy after the war (8:319–21). In this context he refers to the Japanese people and the imperial household as forming "a single body above and below" (322).

[49] NKZ 19:3–4. I have simplified Tanabe's rather stilted prose.

Kōyama Iwao, who in the main agreed with Tanabe's idea, went to Tokyo in June of 1945 to start the process.[50] He first consulted with Yabe Teiji, whose diary mentions the visit by Kōyama:

> Argued strongly that the only road to promote all-out war in the true sense of the term was through some positive steps from the imperial household. Asked my opinion.
>
> ....
>
> Agreed to discuss the matter that night with a young paymaster lieutenant and others in the offices of the research division.

Apparently there was a consensus, as later entries in the diary speak of the need for "extreme steps for the very foundations of a genuine national community," the "fatal error of separation of the imperial household from the people in order to save the future of Japan's group unity," and "the unthinkability of omitting the confidence in the nation's internal system and the moral strength of the Japanese race."[51]

In the end, there was no time to put the plan into action and it came to naught, although Tanabe's views on the emperor system were eventually communicated directly to the emperor by the minister of education.

Actually, the idea of having Nishida collaborate in his plan was doomed from the start, as there was talk among certain military officials of having both him and Konoe arrested. In his reply to Tanabe of 20 May Nishida wrote (in friendlier prose) his agreement that "there is no other way than for the imperial household to get out of the situation," indicating at the same time that he was aware of the danger to his own person. As for Konoe, he remarked that he considered him a man of "sufficient insight" but lacking the clout to do anything in the present circumstances. The rest of the politicians he dismissed as "awfully weak."[52] A month later Nishida died.

THE LOGIC OF THE SPECIFIC

The space of a short essay dims from the start any hope of distilling into a few short paragraphs an idea that matured during the years when Tanabe was at

---

[50] 花澤秀文 Hanazawa Hidefumi, 高山岩男の思想と行動の研究——知識人の立場と太平洋戦争の時代 [A study of the thought and activities of Kōyama Iwao: The standpoint of the intellectual and the age of the Pacific war], 岡山県立邑久高等学校記要 8 (1976): 27. For additional information, see also Ōshima Yasumasa's remarks in the explanatory afterword to volume 8 of Tanabe's *Collected Works*, 482.

[51] The passages from the diary of 矢部貞治 Yabe Teiji are reproduced from Hanazawa, "Thought and Deeds of Kōyama Iwao," 27–8.

[52] NKZ 19:669.

the peak of his powers, and whose elaborations take up the better part of two large volumes in Tanabe's *Collected Works*. Relying in part on studies that have already been made of the idea,[53] I will try only to sharpen the general *form* of the idea as best I understand it.

The logic of the specific was no mere speculative flight, but neither did it flow from Tanabe's pen in response to Japan's militaristic expansion. Already in 1922, years before Japan's military buildup and at the height of Taishō liberalism, Tanabe had published an essay on "The Notion of Culture." In it he stressed the development of a "racial state" as Japan's "duty" to the international community of nations. He expressed there his disappointment with Taishō culturism for rushing from its stress on the individual to humanity as a whole but "ignoring respect for the race and forgetting the important significance of the nation."[54] The further step to a new logic cannot be attributed to any one single factor. In 1926 Tanabe began to show clear signs of a shift away from the critical philosophy of Kant and towards the Hegelian dialectic of the *Phenomenology*. The shift was accelerated by Nishida's announcement of his "logic of locus" in the same year, and culminated in Tanabe's first systematic and open critique of Nishida in 1930 and his own alternative: the dialectic of absolute mediation.[55]

The Dialectic of Absolute Mediation

For Tanabe, the dialectic of absolute mediation was the keystone to the metaphysic of Absolute Nothingness that arched over his mature work. In essence, it accepted Hegel's idea that the particular beings that make up the real world are granted their individuality not by virtue of some mysterious essence or thing-in-itselfness that is permanently obscured from view by biases built into

---

[53] The two most reliable accounts I know of in recent years were prepared by Himi Kiyoshi 氷見 潔 in his book 田辺哲学研究—宗教哲学の観点から [Studies in the philosophy of Tanabe Hajime: A view from the philosophy of religion] (Tokyo: Hokuju, 1990), 94–127; and 大橋良介 Ōhashi Ryōsuke, 「種の論理」再考 [Rethinking the logic of the specific] in 武内義範, 武藤一雄, 辻村公一編 Takeuchi Yoshinori, Mutō Kazuo, and Tsujimura Kōichi, eds., 田辺元—思想と回想 [Tanabe Hajime: Thoughts and reflections] (Tokyo: Chikuma Shobō, 1991), 104–30. Very little of Tanabe's writings on the subject are available in Western languages. An uneven English translation of the first chapter of 弁証法としての種の論理 (THZ 7:257–69) was published under the title "The Logic of the Species as Dialectics" by David Dilworth in *Monumenta Nipponica* 24/3 (1969): 273–88. An annotated German translation of 種の論理の意味を明にする (THZ 6:447–521) was prepared by Johannes Laube under the title "Versuch, die Bedeutung der Logik der Spezies zu klären" and printed in R. Ōhashi, *Die Philosophie der Kyōto-Schule: Texte und Einführung* (Freiburg: Karl Alber, 1990), 145–95.

[54] THZ 1:444.

[55] See the remarks in the leaflet appended to vol. 11 of Tanabe's *Collected Works* by Kitamori Kazō 北森嘉蔵.

the structure of mind itself, but rather by virtue of relationship with other individuals. In this self-other relationship, a self affirms its own individuality by negating its identity with an other, and in the process thereby affirms the individuality of the other as something that in its turn negates the first self as its own other. Thus the individual is radically relative and, depending on which standpoint it is viewed from, functions as both self and other, as both identical with itself and not-identical with the other. This "affirmation-in-negation" or "self-in-other," whose model is the relationship between conscious human beings, is applied backwards to all objects in the material world and forwards to the customs, institutions, and social structures that govern relationships among human beings.

The next step is to see this mutual determination of correlatives—things, persons, institutions—as belonging in turn to a grander, universal scheme of things working its way out in time. History takes on the character of a kind of super-self whose identity does not consist in the negation of some super-other (which would land us in an infinite regress of histories), but rather in the single story of selfs and others coming into being and passing away in relationship with one another. History defines itself as a dialectic, that is to say as process of entities giving-and-taking their identities through conflict, resolution, and new conflict. Or put the other way around, as individuals—again, we include social structures here—live and die through time, it is not only particular relationships that are changing shape from one moment to the next or one age to the next, but history that is defining its identity. Science has provided us today with metaphors of history that make it possible for us to look at a scientist viewing an atom under a microscope and see an atom having evolved to the point that it can look at itself. In much the same way, the Hegelian dialectic provided the metaphors for seeing present historical events as an unfolding of the past that is somehow lifted up out of a *time* writ small and into a *Time* writ large.

The question, of course, is whether history was running around in a treadmill of endlessly repeating cycles or was actually going somewhere in the process. Laying his scheme over the facts of recorded history and the events of the present, Hegel was convinced that there was a self-unfolding going on, and that the vocation of human consciousness was to participate in it. The final destiny of consciousness was neither simply to be washed along by the unfreedom of its massive tides nor simply to direct it along the arbitrary currents of free will, but rather to become one with history, to be the concrete subjectivity of an objective universal. It was here that Hegel melded the symbols of Christian theology to the self-unfolding of history, thus transforming the mere "cunning of history" into a "divine providence."

To all the critical questions and creative thinking such a scheme inspired in the philosophical world after Hegel, Tanabe added his own: the dialectics

276

of absolute mediation.[56] To begin with, Tanabe was wary of falling into any form of historical necessity that would submerge the individual in the whole. This is how he explains his rejection of both Hegel's conceptualism and Marxist dialectical materialism (a position towards which his sympathies had not yet completely soured) as too one-sided. The conscious subject was not to be harnessed to the will of overriding social institutions, but neither were those social institutions ever to be granted the privileged status of absolute will over history. This same view shows up in a scattering of comments on the state that appear in these early years before the actual introduction of the notion of the logic of the specific.[57] Even though he was to be accused of identifying the providential advance of history with the Japanese nation, as late as 1936 even so astute a critic as Takahashi Satomi could criticize him for slipping a Kantian subjectivism back into the picture.[58] In any case, from the very start his use of the dialectic was headed in a direction quite different from that of either the Hegelian or the Marxist recipes.

At the same time as he resisted the diminution of the subject in history, Tanabe was not prepared to give subjective consciousness (or its pure form of "immediate experience" in which the subject-object dichotomy falls away) the inflated role in history that he thought Nishida had done. What then is left to account for the unfolding of history? What is it that is working itself out in time through the interplay of the concrete subject and the social order? Is history's "dialectic" an ultimately meaningless hydraulics of energy flowing back and forth between self and other to give each its identity by negating the other, or is there some reality to which the myth of a divine providence making its will concrete in history corresponds? The fact that the question itself may have been wrong, or at least misguided in the sense that its answer could never be given us to know, never seems to have occurred to Tanabe any more than it did to Nishida. At the same time, it was not as if Kant had never existed or as if Hegel had satisfactorily discharged Kant's critique. For Tanabe the only answer capable of satisfying all the critical demands lay in the

---

[56] It should not be forgotten that from early on Nishida was also swept up in the imaginative power of the Hegelian idea and its aftermath. His own response focused mainly on the relationship between transformation of consciousness and the self-transformation of the world. The similarities with Tanabe's response are far more striking than the differences, though the particular circumstances in which their two philosophical systems took shape tended to obscure the fact during the years of Tanabe's mature work. On this point, see Nishitani's important essay, "The Philosophies of Nishida and Tanabe" in NK, 210–1.

[57] Ienaga has brought many of these together nicely in his *Studies in the History of Tanabe's Thought*, 35–46.

[58] See note 80.

Buddhist notion of nothingness, which Nishida elevated to the status of an Absolute Nothingness.[59]

As Tanabe understood it, Absolute Nothingness functioned somewhat like a mirror image of the Judeo-Christian God of Being, and yet was something more than that. As *nothingness*, it was not merely a shorthand for an apophasia or aphasia towards an ultimate reality. It was also a rejection of the concept of being as a suitable ground for correlatives to stand in order to identify and determine each other. As *absolute*, it meant that there is nothing that is not mediated. Therefore, if absolute mediation is merely the form of a more fundamental dynamic process of coming into being and passing away, then neither can there be any unchanging Entity or unchanging substrate of Being giving ultimate content to that form. Hence, only an absolute (that is, a non-mediated) nothingness (that is, a non-being-ness) can qualify as ultimate.

Now if all things exist in relation to other things, and if there is a common, absolute ground that mediates the existence of all things but is not itself mediated, then we are logically obliged to conclude that ultimately everything is related to everything else. The Buddhist concept of ultimate reality as a perfection achieved by seeing through the absolute relativity of a world of becoming, a world in which all things arise co-dependently, was thus well suited to fill the gap left vacant by the Supreme Being that exercized its will over the course of history.

For Tanabe, then, history was the story of beings mediating each other enveloped in a process of growth into Absolute Nothingness, and in that story human consciousness enjoyed the privileged capacity to realize what was going on. But that realization, fueled by innate impatience with the frustration of personal desires in the larger order of things, made no sense without the capacity to distinguish between what *is* going and *should be* going on. Human consciousness may be the concrete subject of universal historical process whose ground has shifted from Absolute Being to Absolute Nothingness, but the ethical questions remained as before. Within the world of absolute mediation, what does it mean to have free will and to exercise it in order to direct the course of history? Against what more concrete, visible background does it make sense to talk of what free will can do and what it cannot? For Tanabe, the answer to this question lay in logic, which was the critical link between the ideal and the actual.[60]

---

[59] As Nishida's questions were framed somewhat differently from Tanabe's, the connotations of Absolute Nothingness were correspondingly different. For economy of argument, we may leave this aside here.

[60] I find the attention given to this relationship one of the most interesting aspects of Ōhashi's essay, "Rethinking the Logic of the Specific."

The "Logic" of the Specific

Tanabe's search for a novel logic was not only a function of the questions that his dialectic of absolute mediation left open. Even less was it merely a matter of establishing a position to vie with Nishida's. Cross-grained though his critical spirit may have been at times, the fact that Tanabe kept an eye on philosophical questions in the West also provided him with a different perspective on Japan's current preoccupation with self-identity in the order of history. Tanabe left us no diaries or clear account of the evolution of his thought, but it is possible to telescope his writings in the early 1930s into a reasonable argument for why the new logic became necessary and why it went astray as it did.

While the absolute dialectic and its grounding in Absolute Nothingness may have been a direct result of his reading of Hegel and his reaction to Nishida's logic of place, the catalyst to the introduction of the "logic of the specific" seems to have come from outside, namely from Bergson's idea of an "open society." It was an idea whose persuasive power for Tanabe was enhanced by Japan's current condition.

In *Two Sources of Morality and Religion,* which came out a mere two years before Tanabe introduced his logic of the specific, Bergson draws on Durkheim's sociology to distinguish between "open" and "closed" societies. Tanabe immediately recognized that Japan's engagements in Asia were grounded on the ideology of a racially based, totemically sealed clan mentality of the closed society; and that it would never be able to join the great open societies of the world without first recognizing that fact.

The obvious, and simplest, solution would have been to follow Bergson and encourage an openness to the whole human community not bound by the constraints of one's particular tribal unit. But for Tanabe it was more important first to make the irrationality of tribal bias as transparent as possible if it was ever to be replaced by the rationality of the open society. He hit on the idea of identifying the logic that the closed society used to think its thoughts. This he called the "logic of the specific."

When Tanabe introduced the notion of the idea in a lengthy 1934 essay called "The Logic of Social Existence,"[61] it was clear that the subject was much too large to be confined to a single essay. The overt purpose was, as he said, to get a philosophical hold on the primordial fact that humans organize themselves into societies. At the same time, his choice of the name set important parameters that may not have been clear to all his readers, but should be borne in mind as we watch where he took the idea, or at least where it looked

---

[61] 社会存在の論理—哲学的社会学試論 [The logic of social existence: In search of a philosophical sociology], THZ 6:61–167.

to some as if he had taken it. In particular, the logic of the specific had two functions, a negative and a positive one. Tanabe did not make any such distinction, but drawing it seems to clear up some confusion.

In its negative function, the logic of the specific was less like the dialectic of absolute mediation than a "logic" in the classical sense of the term. That is, it was an attempt to describe the circumstances under which inferences were drawn and which determined what constituted evidence and self-evidence and what did not. In this way, Tanabe felt it would be possible to determine what it was that a society—the "specific"—did to close itself and keep itself closed. The racial society could then be seen to function as a sort of unconscious fiction that stood between the concrete, living individual and the universal, ideal human community. Not unlike Kant's categories, the closed society filtered the way reason processed the interplay between the actual and the ideal in such a way as to protect its closure from the compelling reasons for opening up. He saw examples of this in the Nazi ideology of *Blut und Boden*[62] and in Heidegger's search for German uniqueness, both of which he criticized.[63] In the sense of its negative or critical function, it may have been better to speak of it as the "illogic of the specific."

In practice, Tanabe's use of this function remained purely formal. Little effort was ever made to refer the critique to the problem that prompted the idea in the first place, namely the the irrational habits of thought that made Japan a closed society. It was the mere *possibility* of the existence of such an irrational logic that seems to have satisfied his interests. Still, at the theoretical level, the texts leave little doubt that Tanabe was very much aware of the limits on how the "specific" society thought. Indeed, it was for him the bedrock on which many of the irrationalities that infect thinking at the highest levels rest. It is also clear that he in no sense meant to absolve Japan from the criticisms. On the contrary, the closed mentality of contemporary Japan that showed up in its culturism (and to a limited extent, also in its militarism) constituted his clearest concrete example.

The Logic of the "Specific"

The second, positive function of the logic was to enable a move from a critique of the closed society to modes of thought constructive of an open one.

---

[62] Himi is right that a careful reading shows that Tanabe used the phrase as an example of a closed totemic society; I do not find reference to the term, however, in the 1934 essay Himi is citing (*Studies in the Philosophy of Tanabe*, 97–8), but only in a later essay dating from 1940 (THZ 8:146). After the war, when it was clear where Tanabe's new logic had eventually led him, the phrase *Blut und Boden* was cited as proof of his rightist tendencies, without regard for its original context. Thus, Yamada, *Intellectual History of the Shōwa Period*, 47.

[63] THZ 8:8.

The term *specific* is intended to guide the logic out of its confinement in the irrational by locating it in a broader frame of reference.

Tanabe felt that the method of classification traditional to philosophy had tended to focus attention on individuals and universals (or genera) to the neglect of the intervening sub-classes (or species).[64] While such classification may aid in locating the one in the many, it tends to engender expectation of theories that see the many as somehow derivative of or emanating from the one,[65] or that see the interplay of concrete reality and abstract ideals as descriptive of the real world. For Tanabe, the logic that guides and misguides common sense is incomplete without taking into account the culturally specific foundation and considering how it can be overcome. In a word, it is the specificity of culture that alienates one culture from another, from the universal ideal, and from respect for its individual members.

Not only was the logic of the specific not directed critically against the vital irrationalities of his time; it was applied positively to support what turned out to be the most fatal of those irrationalities—the idea of the Japanese nation united under the emperor. To see the "reason" behind its argument, laying aside all political agenda, we need to begin with a formal problem left over from the dialectic of absolute mediation.

If Absolute Nothingness is not bound by the world of becoming and yet is "at work" in some sense wider than as a rational cement to hold beings together in mutual mediation, that is to say if in any sense it is engaged in the

---

[64] Takeuchi Yoshinori explains clearly how Tanabe relates the logic of classes and the logic of the syllogism, something that is not always clear in the original essays (for instance, 6:485). The "species" accounts for the middle term of the classic syllogism—Humans die. *Socrates is human.* Therefore Socrates will die.—and thus mediates the connection between the "universal" possibility and the "individual" reality. "Recollections of Professor Tanabe," in RPTH, 8–10. It is interesting to compare Bertrand Russell's criticisms of Aristotlean logic in his *History of Western Philosophy* (New York: Simon and Schuster, 1945), 197:

> Metaphysical errors arose through supposing that "all men" is the subject of "all men are mortal" in the same sense as that in which "Socrates" is the subject of "Socrates is mortal." It made it possible to hold that, in some sense, "all men" denotes an entity of the same sort as that denoted by "Socrates." This led Aristotle to say that in a sense a species is a substance.

Although strictly speaking what Russell calls *species* (namely, "all men") corresponds to what Tanabe calls *genus*. In classifying the cultural society as species, Tanabe intended to make it the kind of actual substrate that "human race" could never be, thus adding an important qualification to Russell's criticism.

[65] This is not unrelated to his criticism of Nishida's logic of locus as a kind of mystical neo-Platonism (see *Philosophy as Metanoetics*, 45, 80) that neglected the role of negative mediation. As is well known, Nishida never challenged Tanabe on this directly in print, but 小坂国継 Kosaka Kunitsugi has recently argued that the idea of "inverse correlation" (逆対応) was Nishida's attempt to answer Tanabe's criticism. See his 西田哲学と宗教 [Religion and the philosophy of Nishida] (Tokyo: Daitō Shuppansha, 1994), 281.

unfolding of history, then there must be some way to speak of it as incarnat-ing itself in time. Obviously this incarnation cannot lie in mere individual subjectivity, since this would elevate consciousness beyond the law of absolute mediation. But neither can the Absolute embody itself in the collec-tive memory and modes of thought of a specific race or culture, since this would do away with the very thing whose transformation makes up the advance of history. Nor again is the universal human race a suitable locus for the Absolute to direct history from, since it is no more than an abstract ideal. The one remaining reality that qualified as a blend of the real and the ideal made concrete in time and history was—the Nation.

His position is already clear from the essay in which he first introduced the logic of the specific:

> In the sense in which the nation achieves unified form as an absolutely mediated unity of the specific and the individual in religion, the nation is the only absolute thing on earth.[66]

In line with the shift from the Judaeo-Christian myth to the Buddhist one, Tanabe was thus able to speak of the nation of Japan as moving beyond the Judaeo-Christian idea of ethics incarnated in Jesus to an Eastern ethic that sees the nation as the embodiment or *nirmāṇakāya* of the Buddha. In the process, we see him leap to a startling conclusion in an uncharacteristic breach of logic:

> My philosophy of the state may be said to possess a structure that radi-calizes the dialectical truth of Christianity by liberating it, as it were, from the confines of myth and by putting the nation in the place of Christ.... Such a comparison, I think, helps better explain what I mean by asserting that our nation is the supreme archetype of existence and that, as a union of objective spirit and absolute spirit, it manifests the absolute as a Buddha-embodiment.[67]

From the very first, Tanabe stood in line with the political ideology of the day, or at least without any intention to counter it. In a sense, it is not surprising to find him end up identifying the corporate unity of the emperor and the Japanese people as the "salvific will" that will transform the individ-ual "will to authority" into a true moral will, and culture's "will to life," which expresses itself in the irrational drive for conformity, into a true will to unity.

[66] THZ 6:145.

[67] THZ 7:30–2. I find it important that he avoided mentioning the *corpus mysticum* theolo-gy of State Shinto that saw the emperor as the 現人神 *arahitogami* or God-appearing-in-human-form, who was the living soul of the Japanese nation.

At the same time, there are no formal, rational grounds in Tanabe's thought to warrant the conclusion that the Japanese nation so viewed deserved a place of honor as a "supreme archetype" in the larger scheme of things. The community of the human race is made up of a community of nations that have found a way to transcend their specificity. And this is something that definitely does *not* transcend time and culture. Each nation may come about as *an* instance of the generic universal,[68] but nothing in the logic of the specific allows any one instance to lord it over the others. It is as if Tanabe were quoting himself out of context.

In any case, it is not a position he develops further or allows to interfere with his general orientation to a community of nations united in equality. Thus, in an essay on "The Morality of the Nation," published in *Chūōkōron* for 1941, the same year that saw the first of the famous discussions on *The World-Historical Standpoint and Japan*, Tanabe wrote:

> In order for the state to make itself concrete through the mediation of individuals, it gives rise to the autonomy of the individual and at the same time unifies that autonomy to itself.... Only in a self-conscious autonomy of coexistence in a universal order with other nations, can the nation express its absoluteness.[69]

Tanabe himself says that it was his dissatisfaction with Nishida's intuition of a basic unity between the contradictories of individual and human race that drove him back to the realities of history, to see the calling of the nation as

> *without*, consisting in mutual cooperation and mutual respect among the various countries united at the level of genus; *within*, fulfilling the desires of each individual; and *within and without*, mediating fulfillment and cooperation and love in the individual.[70]

To base a nation only on racial or cultural specificity, he says, is to risk leading it into communism or totemism. Only in the intercommunion of specific states can the human community truly become a concrete reality. In other words, the logic of the species as such did not see the national polity of Japan either as an alternative to the human community or as occupying a central role in that community. At the same time, neither did he himself draw that conclusion in so many words.

Tanabe's idea of opening the closed society, therefore, was to see it as one nation among many in the human community. The concrete execution

[68] THZ 7:362, 79.

[69] THZ 8:207–8.

[70] THZ 6:232–3. The passage is an attempt by Tanabe to locate himself in counterposition to the "humanitarianism" of Kōyama Iwao and the "individualism" of Nishida.

283

of this idea requires individual will grounded in something larger than itself: "Through service to the nation and submission to the orders of the nation, moral autonomy does not disappear but is rather made possible."[71] Conversely, should a society turn in on itself in totalitarianism and oppression, morality requires that the individual resist it and lead it back to its true destiny in the society of universal humanity.

In arriving at these conclusions, sound though they be in their fullest context, Tanabe let loose a brood of ideas that seemed to flock right into the nests of the ultranationalists in a way that Nishida's thought never explicitly did. This seems to have confused Tanabe himself. At the time that Tanabe was framing the core essays of his logic of the specific, Nishida was arguing that the mutual determination of the individual and the world was manifest biologically in a specific race and that this in turn, through the contractual relationship among individuals and between the individual and the race, forms the *Gesellschaft* into a civil society.[72] Moreover, Nishida had stated clearly that "we become concrete personalities through the state," and further hints that each species is a kind of world, and that there are also conditions appearing where species and species cross swords with each other."[73] He even described the state as the concrete form of the ethical substance in which each individual can fulfill himself. Nothing Tanabe could say criticizing Nishida's goal of the harmonious fusion of the many in the one for having effectively eliminated the basis for resistance against the state seemed to matter to those in Nishida's circle. Considering how Tanabe had dragged the concept of Absolute Nothingness into the profane space of national polity, the indifference is not without reason.

From the hindsight of the historian, the logic of the specific may be said to have opened a new stage in Tanabe's thought, bridging his early interest in the dialectic and his later turn to religion. But to Tanabe himself, it was anything but a bridge. It was a groping in the dark for an answer to the spirit of the age, an answer that could not rest on the consolation that it was leading him just where he wanted to go. In the end, it did not. His response was the metanoetics.

Tanabe's postwar writings on the logic of the species did not correct its fundamental problems as a logic. They did, however, reorient the manifestation of Absolute Nothingness away from the nation and closer to a nonpolitical, Buddhist-Christian "compassion-in-love." At no time did he repudiate the logical status he had given the nation as a universal relative to other uni-

[71] THZ 7:41.
[72] NKZ 8:288–9, 451.
[73] NKZ 9:146, 144; 9:113.

versals, but neither did he explicitly look to it any longer as a concrete realization of the ethical substance of history. Because he did not address this question directly in his self-criticism, the reorientation meant less of an advance for the logic of the species itself than a retreat back into a safer level of abstraction, leaving him free to concentrate on more personal, existential questions. That religion occupied his principal attentions in his declining years and that he withdrew into virtual isolation to do his writing is hardly to be wondered at.[74]

HINTS OF AN APPRAISAL

Wherever Tanabe's idealistic sights may have been focused, it seems clear that he did trip badly over the nationalistic rock at his feet; and that he did so not in the pure innocence of philosophical absent-mindedness, but at least partially as a result of the path he himself chose to walk. A conscientious appraisal of Tanabe, his critics, and the intellectual atmosphere in which each of them worked requires fuller detail on nearly every point. Further, such an appraisal must at least aim for the same critical self-awareness that it is predisposed to accuse Tanabe and others of the Kyoto school for having failed to achieve.

The question of whether to agree with the emperor system and the war, and what relation to see between country, emperor, Japan on the one hand and the free self on the other was, as Furuta Hikaru notes, a kind of *fumie* for many of Japan's leading intellectuals at the time.[75] Like the choice given to the seventeenth-century Nagasaki Christians of trampling on the images of their faith or being condemned as enemies of the ruling powers, the challenge of Japan's fifteen-year war to the country's intellectuals produced both its martyrs of conscience as well as its apostates. At the distance of 350 years from the early Edo period, the modern mind feels secure enough to applaud a certain freedom in those who outwardly trampled on the images but inwardly clung to their faith, as if possessed of a wisdom beyond the constraints of absolute principles that have shaped the Western idea of conscience. But when it comes to the context of a real war whose scars are with us still, the conscience is wont to stiffen again, to narrow its aim, and to draw more quickly on the trigger.

---

[74]Immediately after the war, he did write a number of essays on the political situation at the time. These are gathered together in volume 8 of his *Collected Works*.

[75] "Thought and Philosophy during the Fifteen-Year War," 259. His own conclusion is that the "tragedy" of the Kyoto philosophers was that, in effect, they contributed to the "internal embellishment" of the slogans that carried to the people the very thing those philosophers themselves were opposed to: namely imperialism, racialism, and a holy war.

JAMES W. HEISIG

Still, it is not Western moralism but the Kyoto philosophers themselves who decided that the proper place for Japan's traditional values and modes of thought was within the horizon of transcendent principles. At least in their case, a hasty retreat to Eastern uniqueness seems to deride their original motivations.[76] The question of their complicity in the war may not be their own question, but it is very much at their own request that we frame it as a question about *human* strength and weakness, about *rational* insight and oversight, not as a cultural confrontation between East and West.

Tanabe's own philosophical project, and the critical rigor with which he pursued it, argue against looking to a mere failure of will for an answer. We have to look at the ideas themselves and to read between the lines of his writings if we are to understand what it was that allowed the logic of the specific to be pried loose from the momentous challenge that faced it. It is not simply a matter of how a formal logic was applied to a concrete situation, but also of how it bounced back from the application to reorient itself. Tanabe's metanoetics did not answer the question of the relationship between the logic of the specific and the spirit of nationalism because it did not ask it. Granted, much of our moral understanding of war and peace today took shape only after the events in question. But Tanabe's turn away from the critique of social existence to work at the limits where reason breaks down and religious consciousness comes to birth inverts the very goal that he had set for the logic of the specific. There is no doubt the metanoia was radical. The problem is that he also saw it as a redemption of his ideas from the fate that had befallen them.

As many of his critics, and not a few of his disciples, have pointed out, even at his most concrete Tanabe was still too abstract. The language in which the logic of the specific was proposed made it benignly ineffective, thus also making it all the more susceptible to spreading the disease it had been concocted to diagnose. This is not to say that he did not realize what was going on and what was at stake in taking a position.[77] What it does say is that to brush him aside as a right-wing fascist or Nazi or ultranationalist is simply an abuse of the wealth of facts and ideas we have to work with.

Paradoxically, Tanabe's fondness for abstract expression and his aversion to social analysis seem to have escorted him uncritically into what Whitehead

[76] For a good example of this in Tanabe, see the opening two sections of his 1939 essay on "The Logic of National Existence," THZ 7:27–53. See also 8:173.

[77] As Yamamoto Seisaku points out, "In the context of the second world war, the nation that oppressed fundamental human rights at home and displayed a demonically authoritarian form of racial exclusivism abroad, looked to each individual for support; the confrontation between species and species, species and individual, individual and individual had already become too serious for Tanabe's philosophy to gloss over." *Nothingness and Process*, 112.

has called the "fallacy of misplaced concreteness." Whitehead's paradigm of fallacy is Plato's tendency to see the Ideas as concrete and immediate realities.[78] In Tanabe's case, the more he brought the abstract, timeless attributes and relationships of the dialectic of absolute mediation to bear on the reality of national consciousness, the more concrete that ideal became, until finally the critical difference between what *is* and what *ought to be* faded from view. The concrete nationalism of his day in effect *became* an ideal internationalism.[79] The only conclusion we are left with is that Tanabe did not apply the negative, critical function of his own logic of the specific to a critique of the irrational specificity of his own idea of Japan as a religious manifestation of the Buddha ideal.[80]

As we have seen, the logic of the specific grew up in answer to a particular intellectual environment, and carried its birthmarks with it to the end. For it to be reborn, an account must be given of its nationalistic blemishes. And these blemishes must be shown not to be symptomatic of a structural affliction. My own feeling is that, freed of the distractions of personal disputes within the Kyoto school, the idea of an irrational, epoch-specific substratum to thought will survive critical demonstration of where it took a

---

[78] Whitehead also saw the fallacy at work in Aristotle's doctrine of a static, primary substance, which led to a confusion between the bare individual with the actual concrete (or con-crescent) individuals that make up the world. Tanabe seems less guilty on this count. I would note that Tanabe was familiar with *Science and the Modern World*, the book in which Whitehead introduced the idea of the "fallacy of misplaced concreteness" (see THZ 8:29). It is also worth noting that Tanabe himself explicitly refers to Plato's Ideas as "immediately" corresponding to the realm of the specific (6:102).

[79] "The nationalists of our country need to give profound thought to the fact that nationalism is at the same time internationalism." Cited from an undated letter to 原田熊雄 Harada Kumao cited in Yamada, *Intellectual History of the Shōwa Period*, 50.

[80] In this connection, I would like to draw attention to the far-sighted critique that Takahashi Satomi made in 1935 of the logic of the specific. For Takahashi, Tanabe was too quick to claim historicity for his notion of the racially specific society, and thus wavered between reforming it in the direction of universal ideals at one moment and confusing it with existing realities at other moments. 高橋里見全集 [Collected works of Takahashi Satomi] 4:221–67. The fabric of Takahashi's argument is too delicate to reproduce here, but his main point is that Tanabe's "specific" sometimes served to provide the immediacy that Nishida had given to the individual, and sometimes worked to reduce the individual to the self-determination of the universal. The essay is carefully constructed, and I am disappointed that neither Himi nor Ōhashi (see note 53 above) takes its criticisms into account.

Takahashi's wider critique of the Hegelian currents in Japan at the time is based on his own view that it is time and not the dialectic that is the final basis of history. This he finds lacking first in Nishida and then throughout the Kyoto school. His corrective takes the form of counterbalancing Absolute Nothingness with absolute love, a position that prefigures Tanabe's own turn in later thought. His own views are neatly summarized in the article in volume 3 of his *Collected Works*, 138–50.

wrong turn in the practice. At the same time, the lingering intrigue of its Buddhist flavor and its distinctive perspective on Christianity, not to mention the growing suspicion that the idea of the nation, after a lifetime of barely more than 200 years, is drawing to a close, all suggest that the possibilities of the logic of the specific have yet to be spent. The only conclusion on which this suspicion rests can be stated forthright: *Tanabe's political conclusions are in no sense a natural outflowing of the logic of the specific; they are a refusal by its author to take the idea as seriously as it deserved.*

Tanabe's logic of the specific was an experiment in self-criticism that, for a number of reasons, failed in its own lifetime. There is of course no way to inoculate oneself against the criticisms of the age. And even if there were, the very thought of trimming one's thinking to such a measure offends the very spirit of philosophical inquiry and forecloses the possibility of ideas coming to birth posthumously. To allow our judgment of his ideas to be dominated by the fate they met in postwar Japan is no less an error than to uproot them from their native soil altogether. In the end, the story of Tanabe's logic of the specific is also a story about what our age expects of its thinkers. If any part of it is allowed to perish under the weight of historical research or moral righteousness, it can only mean that those expectations have not been understood. No doubt, the words and ideas and moral aims of each age work a certain enchantment on the minds of those who are born into it. Time pulls hard against our noblest attempts to find a place and time beyond our own to see clearly and to decide what is morally acceptable and what is not. The story of what happened to Tanabe's logic of the specific is no less susceptible to that enchantment than his idea itself. But perhaps, like the magical lance of Achilles, those very words and ideas have the power to heal the wounds they invariably inflict. At least it seems to me that this is the hope on which philosophy rests.

The *Chūōkōron* Discussions, Their Background and Meaning

HORIO Tsutomu

ROM NOVEMBER 1941 TO November 1942 the journal *Chūōkōron* (中央公論) published the transcripts of a series of three round-table discussions held with four young scholars from Kyoto Imperial University: Nishitani Keiji, Kōsaka Masaaki, Suzuki Shigetaka, and Kōyama Iwao.[1] After the war an aura of infamy came to surround the so-called *Chūōkōron* discussions, which were denounced as symbols of the intelligentsia's cooperation in the Japanese war effort. The critics—primarily Marxists, other leftist thinkers, and progressive intellectuals first awakened to humanistic and democratic thought during the political liberalization that followed Japan's surrender—saw the central theme of the discussions, "Japan and the Standpoint of World History," as a thinly disguised glorification of war, and accused the participants of having provided the philosophical underpinnings for Japanese fascism. These criticisms were fueled in part by the resentment of thinkers who, as young people during the war, had been strongly influenced by the contents of the discussions, but who in the postwar period had come to feel that they had been betrayed.

THE POLITICAL BACKGROUND

At the time of their original publication the discussions, though criticized by certain ultranationalist elements, were enormously popular with young intellectuals facing military service. When the transcripts of all three discussions were compiled into a single volume and published in 1943 under the title *The World-Historical Standpoint and Japan* (世界史的立場と日本), the book's

---

[1] 高坂正顕 Kōsaka Masaaki was Professor and Director of the Institute for the Humanities; 高山岩男 Kōyama Iwao was an Assistant Professor, lecturing on the history of philosophy in the Department of Philosophy; 鈴木成高 Suzuki Shigetaka was a Lecturer and taught Western history; 西谷啓治 Nishitani Keiji was Assistant Professor in the Department of Philosophy and lectured in the field of religion.

first run of 15,000 copies sold out almost immediately, as did a second imprint of 1,000 copies.[2]

The influence these discussions had is reflected in the fact that intellectuals of the time assigned an almost symbolic significance to certain of the discussions' key terms, such as "the world-historical standpoint" and "the philosophy of world history." The idea of "overcoming modernity," the theme of another round-table discussion held at about the same time, enjoyed a comparable popularity.[3]

One of the reasons for the impact of these discussions was that they conveyed a certain sense of intellectual and spiritual liberation to thinkers already weary of Japan's endless military involvements. The country had been at war since the Manchurian Incident in 1931, and the constant tension of maintaining a state of martial readiness had lent a sense of oppression to the national mood. The wide-ranging debate of the three-part round-table discussion let some fresh air into this stifling intellectual atmosphere and awakened hopes that there might be a way to give some meaningful direction to the state of the nation. Given the climate of the times, such hopes were far from unreasonable. The spirit of objectivity in which the four participants discussed the problem of world history during the first session was seen as an expression of free thought. Indeed, *The World-Historical Standpoint and Japan* was hailed in the national press (the Mainichi and Asahi newspapers) for its free-thinking outlook.[4]

In a sense, this show of freedom was only skin-deep. To be sure, not a few of the opinions voiced by the participants during the actual discussions were bold enough, given the tightening of government control over intellectual activity at the time. But what was actually published in the pages of the *Chūōkōron* were not full or accurate transcripts. Political conditions at the time left the publishers with the choice of either "veiling statements in two or three layers of cloth"[5] or facing suppression by the authorities (in particular, elements associated with the Army).

[2] 花澤秀文 Hanazawa Hidefumi, 高山岩男の思想と行動の研究―知識人の立場と太平洋戦争の時代 [A study of the thought and activities of Kōyama Iwao: The standpoint of the intellectual and the age of the Pacific war], 岡山県立邑久高等学校記要 8 (1976): 15.

[3] KC, 276. For further information on this subject, see Minamoto Ryōen's essay above, pages 197–229.

[4] See 粕谷一希 Kasuya Kazuki, 京都学派と世界史の哲学 [The Kyoto school and the philosophy of world history], in 戦後思想―知識人達の肖像 [Postwar thinking: A profile of the intelligentsia] (Tokyo: Nihon Keizan Shinbun, 1981), 15. I am also drawing here on personal discussions held with Nishitani Keiji.

[5] 大島康正 Ōshima Yasumasa, 大東亜戦争と京都学派―知識人の政治参加について [The Greater East Asia War and the Kyoto school: The political participation of the intellectuals], 中央公論 80 (August, 1965).

Even despite these precautions, however, what was published in the *Chūōkōron* was attacked by nationalist "Imperial Way" philosophers as "from start to finish the analysis of disinterested bystanders, ivory-tower speculations that risked reducing the Empire to simply one more category of world history." The ideas expressed were seen as seditious and as anti-war.[6] Following the publication of the book, the Army put pressure on the government and in June 1943 the activities of the "Kyoto school" were stopped and subsequent printings of the book were outlawed.[7]

Indicative of the military government's attitude toward the Kyoto school is an incident that took place in 1945 and was reported in the newspapers. A certain Army officer named Kimura commented during a speech that in preparation for the coming invasion of Japan by America, all American and British prisoners of war, all Koreans, and all Kyoto school philosophers should be put to the spear.

Years later Nishitani Keiji remarked, "During the war we were struck on the cheek from the right; after the war we were struck on the cheek from the left." His comment summarizes the historical shifts in the position of his attackers. It also points to a certain tendency common to all criticisms of the *Chūōkōron* discussions, namely to regard the content of the discussions as pure ideology, and to evaluate it solely on those grounds. Only in very few cases has the "philosophy of world history" developed by the four young thinkers been seriously analyzed for its value as *thought*.

This imbalance in the critiques is all the more marked when one examines the other wartime writings of the four participants, to which virtually none of the critics have devoted any serious attention. The fact that the participants nevertheless kept silence in the face of postwar criticisms may reflect a reaction against the unrepentant bias and partiality of their attackers. As Nishitani seems to have been conscious of in his remark about the shift in the attack from right to left, the very world-historical standpoint advanced in the discussion may be said to be "seated in silent judgment" on critics before and after the war. I will return to this question later in my essay.

PROBLEMATICS

The principal concepts and themes of the *Chūōkōron* discussions make sense only in light of the domestic and international situation that Japan found itself in following the 1868 Meiji Restoration. There are three principal rea-

---

[6] Ōshima, "The Greater East Asia War and the Kyoto School," 131.

[7] Hanazawa, "The thought and activities of Kōyama Iwao," 15. I rely also on a personal communication from Nishitani.

sons for this. First, the intent of the discussion was, to some extent, to express the position and mission of modern Japan within the context of world history; this was, to say the least, a critical topic at the time the discussions were held. Second, the participants themselves clearly defined their standpoint as world-historical. Third, the criticisms directed at the participants were, as mentioned above, largely reflections of Japan's historical circumstances at the time the criticisms were made. A complete historical analysis is beyond the scope of this paper. I shall accordingly limit myself to those developments most directly related to the discussions, and on that basis analyze the significance of the "world-historical standpoint."

The first systematic intellectual analysis of the round-table discussions appeared in a 1959 essay by Takeuchi Yoshimi. More recently Oketani Hideaki has examined the discussions from the perspective of intellectual history. Both scholars avoid the ideological approach so common in other studies—be it that of the wartime "opportunists" or the postwar "victims"—and investigate the discussions for what Takeuchi calls their "de facto thought." As a body of ideas, the discussions belong very much to the attempt of Japan to come to terms with its own modern history and all its contradictions, a history that was severed or redirected by its defeat in World War II.

Underlying the approach of Takeuchi and Oketani is the belief that the Tokyo War Crimes Tribunal failed to clarify the true significance of the Greater East Asia War, and that this crucial episode in Japan's history has been shunted to one side without adequate attention. The basic judgment of the Tokyo Trials was that the war in Asia was a barbaric challenge by a militarist Japan against the forces of world civilization as represented by Great Britain and the United States. Such a simplistic understanding of history hardly does justice to the real reasons for which the war was fought. Admittedly, in some sense it was a "challenge to the forces of world civilization," but not *only* in the sense taken by the trial judges. There is another meaning to the war, one that entails the combination of at least two elements.

Internationally, the Greater East Asia War represented an attempt by the nations of Asia to create a new, pluralistic world order in which the hegemony of modern Western culture and its values would be overthrown, and in which the influence of capitalism and imperialism—the concrete expressions of Western civilization in Asia—would be replaced by a national commitment to self-determination and a renewed respect for traditional values. This aspect of the war was touched on in the Imperial Declaration of War when it stated that the conflict was being waged for the purposes of self-defense, self-preservation, and the establishment of eternal peace in Asia.

Domestically, the policy of modernization that Japan had pursued since the time of the Meiji Restoration under such slogans as "Civilization and

Enlightenment" and "Enrich the Country, Strengthen the Military," had succeeded in raising Japan to the level of most industrialized Western nations, but it had also left in its wake problems like the weakening of traditional culture and ethos and a widening gap between rich and poor, not to mention all the cultural and psychological turmoil that inevitably accompanies sweeping social change.

In this sense the challenge against the forces of world civilization was actually a challenge against the value system of *modern* civilization as such. This was seen, in part, as an attempt to create a new value system, one in which people could find new purpose and a new sense of spiritual integration, and in which society could discover a new basis for stable development. This aspect of the conflict, referred to as the "domestic war of ideas," was of course just as subject to abuse as the military aspect. In particular, the creation of an orthodox "empire-centered" view of history, based on State Shinto, as a counterfoil to the historical view of the modern West, provided an ideological foundation for much of the militarist government's repression of the Japanese people.

Japan's conflict in Asia was thus being fought on two fronts: an "internal war" directed against many of the cultural innovations brought into Japan during the "Civilization and Enlightenment" of the Meiji era, and an "external war" against the imperialism of the modern West. Together these two challenges lent symbolic weight to the expression "the overcoming of modernity" in wartime Japan.

The obvious contradictions that this entailed go all the way back to Japan's emergence as a modern state. The military strength that allowed Japan to declare its autonomy and proclaim a distinctly Japanese set of values was actually an outgrowth of the nation's drive for modernization. What is more, in its attempt to overthrow Western imperialism, Japan opted for an imperialist system of its own based on the historical centrality of the emperor. Takeuchi takes these questions up in his discussion of the "twofold structure" of the Greater East Asia War. He distinguishes between Japan's war with China and Asian nations, which he sees as an imperialistic invasion, and Japan's war with the nations of the West, which he sees as basically an act of self-defense.

Be that as it may, what is clear is that the war being waged in Asia entailed a self-contradictory solution to a historical situation that was itself self-contradictory. The question before us here is how the participants in the *Chūōkōron* discussions responded to this conflict and how they interpreted it in the broader context of world history. Takeuchi locates the significance of the discussions this way:

The Kyoto school thinkers were the ones who did the most to put logical order into the three pillars [of wartime thought]: "all-out war," "eternal war," and the "founding ideals of the nation." Of all the efforts of the Kyoto school thinkers, the three-part round-table discussions held by Nishitani, Kōsaka, Suzuki, and Kōyama and subsequently published as *The World-Historical Standpoint and Japan*, stand out in particular.... Never during the entire period of the war was a more impeccable explanation given for the Imperial Declaration of War.... Even the Imperial Way philosophers, who denounced their "philosophy of world history" and would have ordered the entire Kyoto school rounded up had the Navy not protected them, were unable to come up with so complete an explanation.

While "admiring" the "structure" of their philosophical position, Takeuchi assesses the role it played as thought:

They did not produce an ideology for fascism and the war. All they did was *formulate* public ideas, or perhaps we should say *interpret* them. The ideological function that this played was due to other causes. Their ideas did not affect the actual situation.

Takeuchi is thus of the opinion that the round-table discussions—and the Kyoto school itself—was incapable of developing a system of thought that might influence the course of events, but merely formulated a logical framework for the Imperial Declaration of War. He concludes:

The Kyoto school was able, on paper, to come up with an explanation for "eternal war," but it was incapable of really responding to the issues.... Perhaps it is possible to transcend the "low-level confrontation between war and peace" through a philosophy of Absolute Nothingness, at least as long as one stays on the conceptual plane, but that was not the issue. The real question was: What kind of logic would it take for a system of thought to act effectively on reality? No one was able to discover such a logic during the war, and no one has been able to discover one since.[8]

Oketani views the significance of the discussions from a slightly different perspective:

The round-table discussion was perhaps the first successful attempt to situate the Greater East Asia War in the developmental context of modern world history. If this dialectic of historical philosophy had limited itself to the necessary system of world history, it would have amounted to

[8] KC, 316–21.

little more than a kind of relativistic historicism. But these proponents of the world-historical standpoint, clearly intending to supersede the logic of historicism, proposed a metaphysic of *moralische Energie* as historical self-formation linked to the "eternal now" or to Nishida's philosophy of Absolute Nothingness. This system of thought, in which world history and nation, nation and individual were linked by intimation to something eternal, caused a stir among many Japanese.[9]

Oketani's conclusion is that the discussions were an example of "ideas overcome by events, prophecies stumbling into endorsement." This latter expression alludes to the fact that the first session of the discussions, which took place a mere thirteen days before the outbreak of hostilities between Japan and the United States on 8 December 1941, contained utterances that were later seen to be prophetic of the upcoming conflict.

Takeuchi and Oketani may be correct in characterizing the discussions as mere "explanation" and their intellectual effect as one of simple "intimation." But we have to wonder why it was, at a time when every Japanese intellectual must have been aware of the historical crisis of the nation, that only the Kyoto school thinkers were able to formulate a rational framework for what was going on. What does this say about Japan's other intellectuals? The fact that they were unable to come up with a logical elucidation of what was, after all, their own existential plight raises questions about their position as members of Japan's intelligentsia. The fact that the discussions were able to come up with a systematic explanation of what was the reality of the times is, in a certain sense, one of its most essential characteristics, a characteristic that by itself sets it apart from the activities of the rest of Japan's intelligentsia. Faced with a situation in which the destiny of their nation hung in the balance, yet unable to come up with a reasoned response, some intellectuals joined the ranks of the ultranationalists with their sentimental appeals to the *kami* and the "Japanese spirit." Others simply refused to get involved and retreated to the sidelines. Still others wandered about in the intellectual wastelands between the two positions. The contrast with the standpoint represented by the *Chūōkōron* discussions is telling.

Neither Takeuchi nor Oketani gets to this point in their analysis of the discussions. Their interests are limited to the factual content of the talks and the influence it had on the society at large. But it seems to me that without some understanding of the "world-historical standpoint" that the four participants were trying to describe, the true intent of their discussions is bound to be no more than a "paper explanation" or a vague "intimation."

---

[9] 桶谷秀昭 Oketani Hideaki, 昭和精神史 [An intellectual history of the Shōwa period] (Tokyo: Bungei Shunjūsha, 1992), 429.

PHILOSOPHY AT A WORLD-HISTORICAL STANDPOINT

The symposium described its standpoint as "world-historical." The idea of "world" the participants had in mind was an objective, universal horizon that transcends the standpoint of particular nations. This horizon brings about a scholarship or culture based on humanity and a history that is truly history. To the extent that a people or nation sees itself in some sense as the center of the world and the world as a mere periphery (typically this appears as a sense of ethnic particularity rooted in the myth of a chosen race), that people has not arrived at a true awareness of itself as subject. For such a people or nation the "world" is no more than a conceptual abstraction. There is no true *Thou* for the *I*, and hence no understanding of self through other. Where this is the case, action is not subjective action performed vis-à-vis other subjects, and there is no possibility of activity responding realistically to objective conditions in the world. The awakening to the subjectivity of the *I* that can only come about through a *Thou* is bound up with an awakening to the "globality" of the world (i.e., its character as a world). Self-consciousness of the globality of the world is an awakening to a horizon wide enough to transcend the *I* and the *Thou* and yet embrace it (in other words, a world that subsists objectively in itself). But at the same time it is the self-awareness of the historical world insofar as it awakens to a true inter-subjective I-Thou relationship in the context of a plurality of peoples and nations. The globality of the world is the locus at which peoples and nations are able to awaken to themselves objectively, and in their activities to awaken to true reality and historicity. This is also the locus at which the possibility of scholarship and culture based on humanity opens up, a possibility that is realized only insofar as scholarship and culture appropriate that openness into their very essence.

In conducting the symposium from a "world-historical standpoint," the idea of the participants was, in their own unmistakable terms, that "we needed to position ourselves on a standpoint of a high-level, world-historical reality that would hold for times of war and times of peace." From the very first they positioned themselves against the ever more forceful national educational policy of instruction in the idea of Japan as a "land of the Gods" based on the myth of the "founding of the nation."[10] Their comments make it clear that they were questioning "an educational policy that developed only the muscles of Japanese history," stressing themselves "the need to rewrite the history of Japan more in terms of world history and political history" and

---

[10] Nishitani commented as follows in the course of a conversation: "About that time I gave a talk at the high school in Matsumoto where Mutō Kazuo was teaching. I was suprised at how far to the right the students had moved, with their talk of Japan as 'the country of the *kami*.' And not only the students—the teachers, too, found it odd to think of Japan from the standpoint of the world."

to "get a better grasp of the history of Japan by approaching it through historicism."[11] This helps clarify the sense of statements like the following made in the symposium:

> To assume the simple, narrow perspective of national history [a view of history based exclusively on a Japanese interpretation of the history of Japan] is to allow unscholarly tendencies to enter in. The standpoint of world history gives scholarly attention to such things.[12]

The symposium tries to locate the problem of the Japanese nation in a context where the nation could be seen as a truly subjective nation, and to think about history from a position in which history could be seen as history in the true sense. This was what it meant by its "world-historical standpoint."

At this point another difficulty arises. Insofar as the world-historical standpoint stops at an objective, universal view of the world's "globality," it fails to provide a standpoint from which to relate, in truly subjective manner, to the individual history and conditions of the participants' own particular country, Japan. Here the general question of culture and nation comes into the picture, engaging the intelligentsia in a fundamental and existential way as citizens of a particular country. The criticisms leveled against the symposium that it was the "speculative philosophy" of "standers-by" cut to the bone of the world-historical standpoint.

In connection with the problem of "philosophy's leadership in the present," the symposium argued that the creation of a "new image of the world" in line with the world-historical situation of the present moment was possible for a philosophy "pushed into being by historicism," namely "a philosophy of world history mediated by the study of world history."[13] In other words, the kind of philosophical leadership that was needed, they insisted, was not a "metaphysics of world history" that treated history from the start as an ideal to be treated at an idealistic level, but a philosophical ideal shaped by a spirit of learning that throws itself without reserve into the inner recesses of historical reality, and out of those inner recesses of the dynamics of history comes to a self-awareness coincident at all points with the historical manifestations of history.[14] The idea of being "pushed by historicism" obviously means more than being caught in superficial descriptions of historical "facts," but also more than the further step of viewing history in terms of an inner "meaning" of the facts that gives provisional unity to the wealth of data. It means push-

[11] CK, 73–4.

[12] CK, 82.

[13] CK, 94–9.

[14] "Philosophy must be mediated through historical reality." CK, 94.

ing ahead to a historical "ideal" that penetrates beneath the realm of the factual to the ground of historical facts, where it effects a greater unity and hence provides leadership. Such an ideal cannot be grasped through a mere objective knowledge of the facts. It is, rather, an ideal that comes to birth in the self-awareness of the subject from the inner recesses of its own activity as it tries, from within the historical world, to create a new history by breaking through the relationships among historical facts. In this sense philosophy, under the pressure of history, pursues a consciousness of history all the way to the creation of a historical ideal. A "world-historical philosophy" would then consist in the historical praxis of bringing a world-historical ideal of the world to the clarity of self-awareness. Only when the world-historical *standpoint* at which nation is perceived truly as nation and history as history begins to function as a world-historical *philosophy* in the retrieval of the dynamic of world history from its own inner recesses to the light of self-awareness, can we speak of a standpoint that has grasped the life of the globality of the world as it is, at its most elemental and most truly real.[15]

What does it mean to speak of *universality* in the academic discipline of such a world-historical philosophy? Simply put, it is not an abstract, conceptual universality but a concrete (actual) and practical (subjective) one. Scholarship and culture, as we said, are rooted in a "world" that surpasses and yet embraces the *I* and the *Thou*. They become concrete in each individual person living in the world cultivating herself or himself *from within*. In this sense scholarship and culture are truest to themselves when they are through and through historical, which means fully specific (in the ethnic sense) and objective, and at the same time fully subjective. The true essence of scholarship and culture requires breaking through a mere abstract universality that transcends individuals, races, and nations to an actual self-embodying cultivation of the inner dynamic that permeates individual, race, and nation. Any scholarship and culture that does no more than make direct ties between individuals and the world, reducing ethnic groups and nations to a level where intellectual activity is satisfied with merely "standing by," only betrays its own abstractness and lack of thoroughness, sinking in effect to the level of the lowest common denominator.

In a preface added when the discussions were published as a book, the participants reply to the complaint that the discussions had "lacked Japanese subjectivity" by making it clear that they "were trying to expose, in logical fashion, the self-righteous and dogmatic quality that do not belong in the subjectivity of Japan":

[15] "The philosophy of world history is the unfolding of the very ideal of the world, a clarification of its genealogy." CK, 178–9.

At bottom, the reference we make to world-historical necessity is not merely a matter of natural inevitability, but of a subjective necessity that is unfolded through the self-awareness and praxis of Japanese subjectivity, and at the same time carries the added significance of a world-historical *ought*.

In the preface, they also reply to the criticism that the symposium had "glamorized the reality of Japan" by taking the same standpoint of historical subjectivity:

We ourselves believe that the truth of Japan is gradually unfolding through the Greater East Asia War. We are, moreover, convinced that through the praxis of that truth, distortions of reality are being corrected.

At first glance, the remainder of their response to criticisms might be seen as a statement in support of the war. But as before, their references to the "truth of Japan" relate to the moral obligations of Japan that coincide with the *ought* of world history. At present that moral obligation lay in overcoming modern Western civilization (the capitalism and imperialism based on a scientific-mechanistic culture), which the realities of world history were showing to have been a dead-end, and in its place creating a new, true culture. As a country that digested modern civilization while managing to hold on to a traditional culture of its own, quite different from that of the West, Japan was charged with the "world-historical task" of using modernity to overcome modernity. Fully conscious of this task, Japan had therefore to muster its *moralische Energie* in the service of correcting its own imperialistic tendencies and breaking the unilateral world dominion of the imperialism of Europe and America. It had to exert itself in the construction of a new "pluralistic world order" that would "have a place for each and every people." The "truth of Japan" lay precisely in the fulfillment of that task.

The details of this idea I will leave for later. For the moment, it is enough to be clear about the fact that as far as the radical engagement of scholarship was concerned, the members of the symposium understood the duty of the intellectual to consist in correcting distortions of reality brought about by the implementation of the truth of Japan. This need for a deeper involvement of scholarship in history is present in the call among the participants, each from his own standpoint, for "more philosophy to be done" in the particular sciences. Only the radical engagement of a world-historical standpoint functioning clearly as a world-historical philosophy can generate an "explanation" of what is morally acceptable in a time of historical crisis such as Japan was facing. If this be no more than a "paper solution," at least it should suggest a radical intellectual standpoint cut to the measure of a "world-historical philosophy."

BACKGROUND TO THE DISCUSSIONS

Before presenting a synopsis of the actual contents of the "philosophy of world history," a brief review of the historical circumstances surrounding the round-table discussion seems in order. The first real attempt to clarify the background of the discussion was made by Ōshima Yasumasa of Tsukuba University thirty years ago. A disciple of the Kyoto philosopher Tanabe Hajime, Ōshima was in charge of clerical affairs for a "secret organization" formed, at the request of the Japanese Navy, within the Department of Philosophy of the Kyoto Imperial University. It was members from this group that took part in the *Chūōkōron* discussions.

Ōshima's article appeared only two decades after the war. Why did none of the four actual participants, all of whom were still alive at the time, ever attempt to answer the attacks against them? In spite of the fact that after the war newly formed left-wing groups publicly censured them as war criminals, and that all of them were banned from public employment by the Occupation authorities, none of them "attempted to offer excuses for his actions; they all accepted dismissal without comment or complaint."

In the climate of postwar Japan any attempt of theirs to explain the simplest facts about the discussions would probably have been taken as hypocritical posturing. To some extent this climate is still with us today. The four therefore kept silence, entrusting to history the final judgment for what they had said and done. Perhaps, too, their silence represented a desire to share somehow in the fate met by those of their students who had been driven to the battlefields to die.

This question was touched on in one of the short memorial pieces written on the occasion of Nishitani's death in 1990. The author, Doi Michiko, was a long-time student of Nishitani and aware of the various political intrigues that had led to his being purged from Kyoto University after the war. When she pressed him to set the record straight and explain the facts of his wartime activities, he responded sharply: "What are you talking about? So many of my friends and students died. Do you really think I could do that?"[16] Like the others, he put his hand over his mouth and left the interpretation of the discussions to the intellectual current of the day. As it turns out, this was something they had all anticipated.

According to Ōshima, the "secret organization" referred to was formed in response to a request by the Japanese Navy six months before the attack on Pearl Harbor. The Navy's aim was to restrain the Army from its reckless escalation of the war and to avoid conflict between Japan and America. "At the

---

[16] 土井道子 Doi Michiko, 黄葉誰がために飛ぶ [For whom the autumn leaves fly], プティスト 38 (1991): 10.

time," writes Ōshima, "the civilian authorities no longer had the power to control the Army. The Navy was the only hope." But the Navy lacked the Army's political clout, and there were a number of officers among its ranks sympathetic to the position of the Army. Unable to present a unified front, the Navy moderates decided to utilize public opinion as a potential ally.

Why did they turn to the Kyoto Imperial University Department of Philosophy ? One reason was the wide influence of the Kyoto school, whose chief representatives, Nishida Kitarō and Tanabe Hajime, were held in high regard not only in the Japanese intellectual world but among the general public as well. Furthermore, both Nishida and Tanabe had voiced serious apprehensions about Japan's sudden turn toward militarism. Nishida was in retirement in Kamakura, absorbed in his studies and writing, but was still considered by the majority of Japanese to be the thinker best qualified to formulate a response to the historical impasse Japan had come to. This very esteem for Nishida had already led to an attempt to co-opt his ideas as a way to tighten intellectual control on the people at large. Meantime, other more radically nationalistic elements perceived his influence as a threat, and launched an all-out attack against his views on Japanese tradition, culture, and nationhood.

Another reason for the Navy's selection of the Kyoto philosophers, Ōshima suggests, has to do with the former prime minister Konoe Fumimaro (1891-1945), who by virtue of noble birth had always been at the center of political power and who, as a philosophically minded student at Kyoto Imperial University, had known Nishida personally. It was thus hoped, even in some quarters of the Kyoto school, that Nishida might somehow persuade Konoe, and through him the very centers of Japanese power, to turn the country in the direction of peace:

> Many in the Kyoto Department of Philosophy, particularly Tanabe, felt that Nishida could help convince Konoe to put a stop to the excesses of the Army. Tanabe even wrote a letter to Konoe, which he hoped to have Nishida transmit to him. Nishida, however, had little hope for Konoe. "Konoe is a court noble," he said at the time. "Court nobles are by nature indecisive and one can't rely on them." Quite as Nishida had foreseen, Konoe ended up being pushed around by the Army.[17]

In any event, the "secret organization" held quiet meetings once or twice a month. Among the meetings were those later published as the *Chūōkōron* round-table discussions. According to Ōshima, the main theme of the first session, which took place on 26 November 1941, was "How to

---

[17] Ōshima, "The Greater East Asia War and the Kyoto School," 129.

avoid war (with the United States)."[18] By the time the discussion had found its way into print, however, the fighting had already broken out, and the participants' words were seen by most readers as having been a forewarning of the upcoming conflict. Ōshima notes that the change in circumstances meant shifting the theme of the secret meetings to "How to bring the war to a favorable end as soon as possible, in a way rationally acceptable to the Army."[19] Obviously the participants selected their themes on the basis of the historical trends of the time, hoping somehow through their discussions to nudge those trends in a certain direction. With those historical transitions behind us now and only the words on paper before us, it is not hard to see how Oketani can see in them "ideas overcome by events, prophecies stumbling into endorsement."

As noted earlier, those of the secret discussions that were printed in the *Chūōkōron* needed to be veiled in two or three layers of cloth in order to disguise their true intent from the Army. "All of the rather extensive criticism of Tōjō Hideki was expurgated," writes Ōshima, "as was all censure of the Army." The impression this expurgation leaves, he concludes, was one of total support for the war effort among the Kyoto school thinkers.[20]

Even so, these precautions were to little avail. The Army had no use for the Kyoto school to begin with, and as the war drew closer to an end it began to exert pressure in various ways on the the school's thinkers. Even Nishida, on Tōjō's orders, was investigated by the military police.[21] Ōshima suggests two main reasons for the Army's antipathy:

1. The Kyoto school emphasized the standpoint of the philosophy of history, and attempted to steer the war in that direction.
2. The Kyoto school thinkers were unlike certain other intellectuals who, while ridiculing the government in private, wrote clever praise for public consumption. Such behavior rubbed the Kyoto thinkers the wrong way. In both the good sense and the bad, there was something quixotic about these Kyoto thinkers.[22]

The Kyoto school thinkers, intending to reform the system through a new idea of history, conducted their analyses of the government and the war from within the system. They remained committed to this position throughout the

---

[18] Ōshima, "The Greater East Asia War and the Kyoto School," 130.

[19] Ōshima, "The Greater East Asia War and the Kyoto School," 130.

[20] Ōshima, "The Greater East Asia War and the Kyoto School," 131.

[21] Nishitani commented as follows in the course of a conversation: "At that time a member of the Special Higher Police Force who lived nearby stopped by at my house and, underlining the term *self-negation* in red, grilled me on what it meant."

[22] Ōshima, "The Greater East Asia War and the Kyoto School," 131.

war, both as citizens of Japan and as scholars determined to establish a genuinely meaningful academic response to the country's situation. Ōshima notes that they kept a serious eye even on the ideas of the far right, refusing to the very end to yield to cynicism about the nation or people of Japan. This was that "something quixotic" that proved to be their undoing.

As already mentioned in passing, the political pressure by the Army and right wing continued after the publication of *The World-Historical Standpoint and Japan* in March 1943, resulting in an all but total muzzling of the press from June of that year with regard to the ideas of the Kyoto-school thinkers. Ōshima says that the secret meetings continued, with the discussions from the end of 1944 until just before the surrender in 1945 focusing on how to handle the postwar situation. The fate of the emperor system was of particular concern. Tanabe's view that "the Emperor should be regarded as a symbol of Absolute Nothingness" was met with "general approval" by the participants.[23]

A SYNOPSIS OF THE DISCUSSIONS

To complement the foregoing remarks centered on the philosophical consequences of the world-historical standpoint of the *Chūōkōron* discussions, I would like to offer a simplified outline of the main questions taken up in each of the three discussions. It is worth noting at the outset that in addition to the deliberate camouflaging of certain ideas referred to earlier, each of the discussions had its own hidden agenda not always visible to the reader. As far as possible, I shall present my summary in the actual vocabulary of the participants.

First Session, 26 November 1941

The first session, which was held shortly before Japan initiated armed hostilities with America, had as its hidden agenda the avoidance of just such an occurrence. In fact, there is no mention of the expansion of the war effort in the printed text. One only finds oblique statements such as the following:

> The Pacific problem is a central issue for world government today. The reason it is so important is not simply because of the pressure of time but also because of its historical nature.[24]

These are the only sort of comments made. Despite this "skirting" of the war question, the claim is made that if the Pacific problem and the new global

---

[23] Ōshima, "The Greater East Asia War and the Kyoto School," 130.

[24] CK, 9.

situation are to be understood, it can only be in a world-historical perspective that takes into account their profound cultural consequences. In this sense the title of the opening session, "The World-Historical Standpoint and Japan," may be read as its hidden agenda.

To begin with, the current world situation is introduced with an allusion to the German historian Erich Brandenburg (1868–1946), who remarks in his *Europe and the World* that in the true sense of the word the twentieth century marks the beginning of history. This is seen in the emergence of the League of Nations and the formation of nations outside of Europe but with the same rights, the outcome of which is that Europe is now only one particular region or cultural sphere and that a true world history is in the making. The present age, bearing within itself this heightened "significance of the world," begins as an age of analysis, of "self-criticism and self-examination."

This "world situation" is tied to the "crisis consciousness" of Europe brought about by the fact of having to "step outside of its accustomed position of viewing the world from the standpoint of Europe." In contrast, Japan's "consciousness of world history" is characterized by a "will to renewal."

The grounds for such differences of world-historical consciousness are to be seen in world history itself. Previously Europe had taken a "unilateral standpoint" and looked on Asia as merely a resource for its own activities. For Japan as an Asian country, however, Europe's activities stimulated its own activity. From the start its attitude was that of an "I-Thou relationship." Present differences between Japan and Europe in world-historical consciousness thus stem from their different ways of experiencing the same world and world history. The origin of the difference—in other words, the source of the strength that lay behind Europe's posture of superiority towards Asia—can be traced to Europe's actual role of leadership in world history, where we are able to discover something in European culture that gave it universal applicability, namely the foundation of a culture on the spirit of scientific positivism. This superiority took over the regional cultural sphere of Europe.

But the worldwide spread of this modern scientific (mechanistic) civilization and its new methods of production and capital-generation gave rise to two far-reaching consequences. First, it increased the dependency of Europe on its Asian colonial holdings; second, it put in the hands of those countries that took in the new civilization and means of production the same kinds of power. Meanwhile, within Europe the development of a mechanized civilization on the one hand and the human spirit on the other gave rise to a fundamental split that tore the culture down the middle, a split that we see crystallized in the "problem of science and religion."

This is the origin of the world situation today, which has broken free of the Eurocentric perspective and sees the world as a world. This cannot be understood merely as a crisis or a question of self-defense; it has rather to be seen as "renewal of the world." For such a renewal to be completed, "the will to mere subjective renewal" is not enough. What is called for is not a perspective that seeks to explain history in terms of a transhistorical principle like, for example, God. Its footings must be objective enough to keep the facts of world history ever-present before us. In order for it to become a "perspective of renewal," it must cultivate a keen insight into historical realities and enter deeply into European historicism and pursue that historicism radically until it uncovers at the ground of history itself the absolute fountainhead from which to animate and direct history. This is the kind of standpoint, "surpassing historicism by way of historicism" on the way to a "new historicism," that is needed.

Viewed in this light, the East Asian view of history and the world operates on different principles, and within East Asia there is a different "historical consciousness" in China from that found in Japan. One does not in general see in European views what one sees in Asia, beginning with China, namely a "consciousness of the world that includes a multitude of nations and peoples" and a view of history as "working through the interrelation of a plurality of centers." We see this, for instance, in the Chinese idea that "the nation *is* the world" (天下国家). Here "heaven" or "the will of heaven" functions as a transcendent metaphysical principle, such that even though the actual dynasty may change, a universal, unchanging, transcending principle lives on. In East Asia, therefore, one does not in general find the fall into relativism or skepticism that has become the crisis of historicism, or even an idea of "development" in which principles themselves unfold and advance historically. Instead we see, as in the case of China, a sense of history as fixed.

Already from ancient times Japan, which has lived historically through ties to China and Korea, had "a view of history unlike that of the Japanese of today, one which opened up from national [Japan-centered] history to include at the same time world history." Given this background, the historical consciousness of the Japanese does not land itself in the crisis of historicism "but may be thought to function developmentally, through renewal." This approach seems suited to think through the idea of a world "with a plurality of centers." A principle is being called for that can preserve the unity of a "world" while allowing for this pluralism, that can see history as truly history with its "continuity in discontinuity and discontinuity in continuity," a principle different from that of Europe, one that "makes possible a new historicism." Such a principle requires "an absolute nothingness."[25] Such a principle would provide the "historical potential" for advancing towards a renewal of history that would mediate a union of many centers.

[25] CK, 94.

As for just what this potential might consist in, the concept of *moralische Energie* was advanced. The idea came from Leopold von Ranke (1795–1886), who used it to explain what it was that France lacked, causing it to be defeated. "History is moved not only by the forces of economics and learning. There is a more subjective, more concrete life-energy in a people," and this is what is called *moralische Energie*.[26] This is not the same as what the French thinker Joseph Arthur Gobineau (1816–1882) referred to as "purity of blood." "*Moralische Energie* does not refer to an individual or personal morality, nor is it a matter of a purity of blood." It is a power "concentrated in the 'people of a country' culturally and politically," in a people subjectively self-determined.[27] Manifestations of this power include war, which may be called "the counterattack of a healthy life."

> As soon as one mentions the word *war* it is immediately thought to entail something immoral, as if war and ethics were eternally disconnected from one another. This is an entirely formalistic idea of ethics. But that only shows how far real moral energy has already dried up. As Ranke and others have said, moral energy is present in the midst of war.[28]

The new world history in the making needs to be fixed to this kind of *moralische Energie*. "Japan is being called on by the world to discover such a principle....This is the historical necessity that has been set on its shoulders."[29] Here and now that means that Japan needs to clarify the moral meaning of the war being waged against Manchuria and China. "This does not mean asking whether that significance was present from the start or not. It is rather a question of the new creation and endowment of our activities *from now on*." This self-conscious activity of ours is "the creation of a world in the eternal now."[30]

Such were the main points covered during the first session of the discussions. It concluded with a brief discussion on America.[31] "Europeans are in the habit of carrying around a heady notion of America as shallow. This has no doubt influenced us as well." The "heretofore lack of attention by Japanese historians to America" is "fundamentally due to the traditional influence of European historical studies." Today, however, there is a great interest in America from the viewpoint of the study of world history and there is a need to "rethink somewhat our one-sided judgment of its shallowness."

[26] CK, 101–2.
[27] CK, 107.
[28] CK, 102.
[29] CK, 126.
[30] CK, 124–8.
[31] CK, 119–24.

The discussion about America belongs clearly to the hidden agenda of this first meeting. Ōshima writes in this regard:

> In the opening discussion, the awareness that by some stroke of fate war had so far been averted was in the corner of everyone's mind.
>
> At the time the feeling was that if it came to war, the Americans, lacking the *yamato-damashii* (大和魂) of the Japanese, would fear for their lives and quickly surrender. America was perceived as a country where the women were proud, and where, if *they* were against the war, the country would be defeated. This was the unrealistic idea that the numbskulled soldiers in the Army carried around with them. Part of the aim of the discussion was to warn that they should know their enemy well before going to war.[32]

Second Session, 4 March 1942

The basic difference between the first discussion and the last two was the fact that the first had been held before the war with America, and the others after. The hidden agenda of these later discussions, as indicated earlier, was "how to bring the war to a favorable end as soon as possible, in a way rationally acceptable to the Army." This is clear in the title of the second discussion, "The Moral and Historical Nature of the Greater East Asia Co-Prosperity Sphere."

In the light of the "history-making power" of *moralische Energie*, the participants tried to shift the nature of the war from something aggressive to a defense of the *Lebensraum* and the actualization of a "world-historical ideal." The whole attempt was surely no more than tilting at windmills. Ōshima recounts an episode of interest here. A Tokyo intellectual asked him confidentially at the time, "But are they really serious? Don't they see how their actions are jeopardizing their futures? Wouldn't it be better for them just to keep silent?" Ōshima took the question was an admonition spoken in good faith, but reflects, "They were really serious and struggling to put the war on a moral track."[33]

The question of morality is present from the very opening comment of the second discussion:

> There is a sense in which the China Incident was a moral struggle. In particular, when we come to the present Greater East Asia War, this struggle broadens out into a struggle between the morality of the East

---

[32] Ōshima, "The Greater East Asia War and the Kyoto School," 132.
[33] Ōshima, "The Greater East Asia War and the Kyoto School," 137.

and the morality of the West.... The question is which morality carries greater weight for the future in world history.

Just what is this new morality of the East? "The concrete shape will emerge from a world-historical standpoint," unlike previous moral philosophy, including Kant's, which had consisted in a transcendental ethic detached from history. The problem is that "A nation cannot take shape in isolation from ethics." In the new stage of world history where peoples and nations will be the central issue, "history and ethics will be inextricably bound to-gether."[34] This "bond" is rooted in the world-historical turning point of today. It is a response to the "cry from within history," to the "world-historical *ought*," that echoes up from the depths of historical reality. "It is a morality driven out into the open by historical necessity," and in that sense it must be mediated by a relationship between a positivistic, world-historical standpoint and a philosophy of world history concerned with the ideal. At the same time, "an ethic cannot be an ethic unless it mediates between both poles."[35]

The question that world history raises for us today is the problem of plu-ralism or the construction of a "pluralistic world order." The *ought* that emerges from the reality of world history is "finding a place for all countries." "The basis of Japan's leadership in East Asia lies in its consciousness of this world-historical vocation." This "self-awareness" of Japan is one with the "vitality" of moral energy. Through it the Japanese can become a "world-historical people of the present." Unlike the old ideal of "simply expanding oneself through the whole wide world," the vocation entrusted to a world-historical people is "to renew the order of the world while recognizing the subjectivity of the other."[36]

In actuality, this self-conscious activity of the Japanese cannot avoid clashing with traditional Chinese thought. There is an "East Asian tragedy" in the fact that Japan and China were not really able to work together. In Japan's actions, "a problem remains that cannot be resolved simply by yield-ing the point about an imperialistic invasion." And that problem is, "Why [did Japan] protect China from being partitioned?" In this regard a kind of "unclarity" remains on the Japanese side as well, "something stemming from the limitation of Japan's world-historical position." There is no denying the "backwardness of Japan's economy and its dependency on Europe and America." At the same time, "the sad fact remains that had it not pursued this course, Japan would have lacked the necessary strength as a nation actually to prevent the partitioning of China." At the same time, "in the world-historical

[34] CK, 136-8.
[35] CK, 145–9.
[36] CK, 157–9.

position that it occupied at the time, Japan did not have a clear enough understanding of itself to stand up in the very midst of the world, as a world-historical people, and set about creating a new world." As a result, there is no point to glossing over the past or dragging it down in the dirt. What Japan had to do is "acknowledge it for what it was." Only then can the Japanese people themselves, "in clear awareness [of their historical vocation], come to terms with the *unclarity* in their consciousness of the past." The possibility must be considered, therefore, that "in order for Japan to proceed with the construction of a Greater East Asia order, what is true must rise to the surface straight out of the roots."[37]

How can the moral obligation of "finding a place for all countries" come about? This entails both "the profound problem of mediation among peoples" as well as that of the "wider sphere" of life activity. This latter problem is also a matter of historical necessity. In the aftermath of the worldwide recession (1929–1931) brought about by the essential dead-end of liberal economics, England began an economics of preferential blocs through the Ottawa Agreement of 1932, and Japan tried to follow suit. The problem was that this entailed "a certain excessive inattention to ethnic and moral ideals." In this context, "the Greater East Asia Co-Prosperity Sphere cannot be thought of merely in terms of resources." The need to "find a place for all countries" also comes into the picture.[38] The standpoint of Japan, in which world-historical consciousness was primary, not only differed from the standpoint of Nazism and fascism, both of which were fundamentally lacking such a perspective,[39] it also differed from the spirit of the Treaty of Versailles, which championed the ideal of atom-like ethnic states in which each people was free to determine itself.

But how was such a collaborative, mutual co-prosperity among autonomous and independent peoples and nations to be achieved? This is where "Japan's special vocation" comes in. With the exception of Japan, the peoples of Greater East Asia did not measure up to the high-level culture of the peoples and nations that formed Europe but were "by and large low-level peoples." Japan, on the basis of the position entrusted to it by history, carried the responsibility of "awakening each people to its ethnic self-awareness and converting each one into an autonomous active force."[40]

The root of the morality of the Greater East Asia Co-Prosperity Sphere lies in passing on to each people the *moralische Energie* of Japan, raising

[37] CK, 169–74.
[38] CK, 180–3.
[39] CK, 193–7.
[40] CK, 203–10.

their spiritual level to a height where they can cooperate with Japan, and in this way setting up a moral relationship among different ethnic peoples that can support the Greater East Asia Co-Prosperity Sphere.[41]

This kind of concrete inter-ethnic ethics is recognizable in the "household (家) spirit" that has been cultivated in Japan. The parent-child relationship in the household can apply to the relationships among peoples that the present stage of history requires. We have to think of the same kind of education that is given to children to raise them into independent persons. At the same time, the basis of this must be an "existential relationship" that transcends the ties between parent and child—a relationship resembling that between a married couple. The new meaning being given to the phrase "All the world under one roof" (八紘一宇) can only be based on such a spirit. "Is not what is needed today a relationship of educational guidance between parent and child that rests on the cornerstone of an inviolable, existential bond?"[42]

If the world is searching for such a new order, this means that the order of nation-society of Japan itself must take on a newer and more suitable form as well. In other words, the Japanese themselves need to cast aside their old structures and take on new ones. "The present war has this moral character," and therefore "we must always bear in mind that if that moral dimension is absent, the danger is that the war will sink to the level of a mere war over resources or a war of colonial competition."[43]

Commenting on this second discussion, summarized in the foregoing, Ōshima writes:

> In the end, sensing the moral responsibility that lay with the Army, their aim was to call back the voice of reason from within themselves and with that open the way to a speedy conclusion.[44]

Third Session, 24 November 1942

The hidden agenda of the third session was the same as that of the second. But the historical situation in the background, namely the war, was undergoing great changes. At the time of the previous discussion, the sphere of influence of the Japanese military was still on the increase. But in June 1942, six months before the third session, the Japanese Navy had suffered a major defeat at the hands of America at Midway. With that defeat, Japan's military expansion came to a halt and the road to defeat lay ahead.

[41] CK, 240.

[42] CK, 225–42.

[43] CK, 249–51.

[44] Ōshima, "The Greater East Asia War and the Kyoto School," 136.

Given this backdrop, the theme of the third of the *Chūōkōron* discussions, "The Philosophy of All-Out War," must have been a particularly burning issue for the participants. But the choice of the topic was not made with an eye to providing a new philosophical basis for an idea of "all-out war" presented to suit the pressing force of circumstances. Rather, they intended to draw a clear contrast between the idea of "total war" (*totale Krieg*) centered on military might alone on the one hand, and the war going on in Europe and the Pacific, which was rather an "all-out" war (*Generalmobilisierungskrieg*) that entailed a state ideology as well as a view of the world. Their aim was to clarify the world-historical nature and content of the Greater East Asia War. Once again, we let the participants express themselves in their own words.

"In most cases, there is a deep inner relationship between war and the structure of history in each age," but the war being waged at present cannot be treated in terms of the history of war and strategy up to now. Its essential new character cannot be grasped with past models. For what is going on in the war today is "a change in worldview being mediated by war." It is not only a "philosophical war" but one that has a world-historical character: "Nations structured on the bourgeois, capitalistic order are collapsing. The worldview of modernity is being destroyed." "Does this not call for a unique mode of war hitherto unseen, an all-out war in which the structure of society changes, the structure of the nation changes, and the very way the world is viewed changes?" In this sense, "it is an all-out war waged at the point that modernity has come to a dead-end; it is a war to overcome modernity." This is why a "national defense state" is also called for.[45]

In the sense that the current war represents a transition from the worldview of modernity to that of the present day, it may be called a "conflict between one order and another." If it is an all-out war that signifies a complete revolution of all systems of order in the world, it is a grave mistake to think of it as "a phenomenon of temporary adjustments." Rather, it must be thought of as "a war that has welled up from the deepest recesses of history, superseding the distinction between peacetime and wartime." Accordingly, there is no question of returning to peace as before once the hostilities have ended. Everything is in transition to a new and different order. In this sense, "the constructive core of the war as such makes it impossible to distinguish between a phase of war and a phase of construction." This "construction in the midst of struggle, struggle in the midst of construction" is the new mode of all-out war. It is therefore "necessary to built up a war system from a basis that runs along beneath wartime and peacetime.[46]

[45] CK, 267–75.
[46] CK, 284–8.

As a war that is essentially a war of ideas, the outcome of the present war will be decided "when the enemy concedes to our idea of a new order." But,

> in order to conduct an all-out war, it is not just a matter of persuading the enemy to accept the new order. The ideas, economics, government, and education within the country also need to be elevated above the standpoint of the old order of thought to that new order. Only then does the unlimited advantage of all-out war appear.[47]

Such "persuasion" is not won from a position of vengeance against the invasion, expropriation, and tyranny wrought on Asia by Europe and America. Such an attitude is out of character with the great ideal of an "imperial war." Rather, what is necessary is "the construction of an idea that will persuade the whole world, including the enemy: a manifestation of true moral purpose." It means stepping beyond the standpoint of good and evil that seeks the "salvation of the sins and failings of the other" to a "standpoint under the guidance of Mahāyāna [Buddhism]," and in this way coming to "the Japanese character and Japanese spirit that the present war of ideas is supposed to have."[48] Domestically, meantime, what must be built up is a "high-level integration" of the three dimensions of "economics, government, and ethics and thought"—government guiding economics, morals and thought guiding government—in order to rehabilitate the fragmented and scattered standpoint of modernity so that "each part can have its place and be given full play." In short, "the chief burden of leadership is to direct others to an all-out, creative spring to action, in other words to an *élan*."[49]

True all-out war is not the "all-out war of the nation" that the government talks about. It must be an "all-out war of the Co-Prosperity Sphere." In other words, "The all-out war that Japan is running must be an all-out war run by the Co-Prosperity Sphere. Only then will the all-out war reach its turning point." This means that "the self-awareness and confirmation of its own subjectivity is all-important for the Co-Prosperity Sphere." For a race or nation to think of itself as something fixed is nonhistorical. They are "always and everywhere fundamentally mediated" in the sense of being "shaped as a Co-Prosperity Sphere."

"Just as the Korean people at present have entered into Japan in a completely subjective fashion," so, too, "it is necessary to have a broader understanding of what it means to be a people (民族)." This kind of "Co-Prosperity Sphere" thinking is latent in the East from ancient times, as for instance in the case of Chin, which was a country without fixed borders. In contrast, the

[47] CK, 300–1.
[48] CK, 301–7.
[49] CK, 330–1.

312

"Atlantic Charter" that Roosevelt and Churchill have proclaimed is no more than an affirmation of an old order that opens the door to the self-determinism of peoples and free trade. "The self-determinism of peoples and imperialism are at bottom two sides of the same shield." If this is freedom, it is a freedom that implies free competition and nonintervention. It becomes no more than an open melee for the "survival of the fittest," which will end in an inequality of rights. "The very same principle of liberalism gives rise, on the one hand, to a self-determinism of peoples and a colonial imperialism that contradict one another; and on the other, to an abstract morality and rule by the powers-that-be." In this way, "even as the nations of Europe and America preach freedom, equality, and brotherhood and seek a way for the self-determinism of peoples, in the end these things only continue to feed their own imperialism and interventionism." This "ethical dividedness" is the "greatest malady of modern Europe." This is the basic contradiction in the standpoint of modern democracy, with its affirmation of the arbitrary freedom of the individual as central. The only order one can conceive in these terms is one that protects freedoms by the mutual limitation of freedoms. But from the viewpoint of "humanity" and "peoples," this kind of freedom is merely abstract and formal, with the result that the stronger continue to prey on the weaker in ever more underhanded ways.[50]

The English term "co-prosperity" does not carry the sense of what Japan means by the Co-Prosperity Sphere. It means "sharing moral honor in common." In order to respond in moral fashion to the world-historical *ought* of "finding a place for all countries," we might take up the suggestion of the Dutch cultural historian Johan Huizinga (1872–1945). In order to save Europe from its critical dilapidation, he argues for a "new ascesis," which, unlike the old world-negating asceticism, is oriented to overcoming the self, to a "purifying of the spirit." Such an ascesis—a higher consciousness gained by denying mere utility and hedonism—must spread to the people at large. "A culture purified through people that have undergone their own internal purification," born of a standpoint "that transcends wartime and peacetime," is the only way to a new spirit capable of fundamentally overcoming "the ideas of Anglo-Saxon democracy and a view of life as mere *prospering*."[51] Working from such a spirit, it is possible to build a true "national-defense state" able to withstand today's war of ideas.

The moral activity that flows from such a purified spirit "is of course something done by the individual, but it is not only something done but something that *must* be done because it is right." It culminates in "non-ego, no-self." This kind of "subjectivity of non-ego" extends beyond the self-

[50] CK, 348–57.
[51] CK, 358–62.

awareness of the individual to set up a truly effective structure in the common workplace of "acting that diminishes ego." In other words, it is important that this self-awareness of the individual be "objectified in an institution that fits it to a T." In particular, this objective is clearest when persons in positions of leadership exercise their responsibilities in a "subjectivity of non-ego." "It is mere insolence for the nation and its people not to aim for this higher standpoint, but only to think of the grandeur of that affair [the aims and motives for the war]."[52]

> The term *world-historical* should be taken less as an emotive phrase than as a reflective one. In this sense, we must give this term a fuller meaning and intellectual depth. This is the duty of the academic.[53]

BY WAY OF CONCLUSION

These discussions by four young scholars of Kyoto Imperial University expressed their idea of a "philosophy of world history" from a "world-historical standpoint." This represented not only a challenge to face squarely and to uproot the contradictions in the history of the modern Japanese nation, but also a challenge aimed at clarifying and resolving, in world-historical terms, the radical contradictions of the modern world that history has brought to light. This explains their decision to entitle the first session, and also the final volume, *The World-Historical Standpoint and Japan*. If there is one idea that captures the thoughts and claims made in the discussions, it is the idea of fulfilling the historical vocation of building a new and plural world order by raising consciousness of *moralische Energie*.

For those so intoxicated with the emotionalism of the "land of the Gods" that they had lost their perspective on where world history is going and what Japan's place in history is, this talk of a world-historical standpoint must have been like a bucket of cold water on their heads. For those who barely managed to maintain their sense of self-dignity and preserve their pride as intellectuals, the ringing out of a philosophy of world history must have reverberated with an irritating echo in their ears.

Were the participants "nationalistic" for having preached "Japan as the point at which a new world has come to consciousness," and "glamorized" the actions of Japan? If the term *nationalist* is used for persons who, out of love for their country, take the fate of their country on their own shoulders, exert themselves to the limit in order that the actions of their country and its life and death might be decided morally, then nationalists they were. To be

---

[52] CK, 414–24.
[53] CK, 425.

sure, they asserted that "there is a moral energy within war" and that "war is the most vital force in history." But does casting aside all sense of moral pride and thinking only of one's own tranquility really provide a stable *raison d'être* for the individual, let alone for an entire people or nation?

Are they nationalists because they claimed that Japan is the leading country in East Asia, and that "through its positive participation in the modern world Japan took over the truth of modernity and was able to see through its mistakes," thus putting them in a position of leadership to rank the various peoples of East Asia according to their respective degree of modernization and to "Japanize certain of the peoples within the Greater East Asia Co-Prosperity Sphere"? There is no question that they spoke of "Japanizing the Koreans" and said nothing of "Koreanizing the Japanese." Even if we grant that this shows an excess in the aim of realizing a "co-prosperous" autonomy and independence for the peoples of East Asia through a show of strength against the imperialist countries of the West, at the same time, it has to be read as a claim for the need to defeat "the existing Western way of viewing world history in terms of stages of development." It is an uncompromising assertion of the construction of a new, pluralistic world order, the formation of a Co-Prosperity Sphere in which peoples and nations exist in fundamental and mutual mediation in every respect. On this point, there is something incomplete about their overcoming of the modern West's view of world history. One cannot but feel here the "nationalism" of Japanese self-esteem.

For all its incompleteness, the standpoint and statements of the *Chūōkōron* discussions remain from start to finish an appeal to the reasonableness of a people issued from a position of reason. The fact that these discussions have been buried in the background of history not through rational criticism but by critics who gave themselves over to emotional protest and violence does not mean that they were a failure. Indeed, the construction of a new, pluralistic world order based on moral energy became a world-historical task in the postwar period of the "cold war." And with the fall of the Berlin Wall it remains a basic task for us today. The truth in the "world-historical *ought*" of which these discussions spoke is, I believe, something that world history itself is showing us.

[TRANSLATED BY THOMAS KIRCHNER]

Nishitani Keiji and the
Question of Nationalism

MORI Tetsurō

T HE TERM *NATIONALISM* IS anything but univocal, and depending upon which meaning we give it the "question of nationalism" in the thought of Nishitani Keiji changes rather dramatically. Rather than import a definition from the present arsenal of sociopolitical thought, I will restrict myself in this essay to the way Nishitani himself uses the term in various of his writings during the 1940s, in particular *View of the World, View of the Nation* (世界観と国家観, 1941) and *The Overcoming of Modernity* 近代の 超克, 1942).

In the years immediately following the war, Nishitani wrote a number of important essays on topics related to the question of nationalism. They include titles such as "Self-Awakening and Historical Consciousness in Ethnic Groups," "National Culture and Humanism," and "The Foundation of the Modern Spirit" (1946), and "The Duty to Criticize and the Problem of Fascism" (1949). But it is his earlier *View of the World, View of the Nation* that continues to provide the clearest, most consistent picture of his basic standpoint.[1] *The Overcoming of Modernity*, a transcript of round-table discussions held in 1943 and later published as a separate volume, gives us a good supplementary overview of Nishitani's thinking at the time.

In closing his afterword to the 1946 reprint of *View of the World, View of the Nation*, Nishitani lays out his fundamental motive for writing the book:

> In *View of the World, View of the Nation* I tried to explain the position of the nation in the world for the intellectual standers-by, and at the same time to open up a path in thought that might overcome from within the ideas of ultranationalism that were taking control at the time.[2]

---

[1] The book contains five essays, opening with the title essay and followed by "The Present as a Turning-Point for the World," "East Asia and World History," "The Worldview of the New Japan," and "Religion and the Nation." It was reissued in 1946 with a new afterword in which Nishitani presents a resume of its contents, and in 1987 as volume 4 of his *Collected Writings*.

[2] NKC 4:384.

316

Later in this essay I will take up the arguments aimed directly at the ultra-nationalists, but I think it better to begin with what Nishitani has to say about the "intellectual standers-by."

The term is as transparent to us today as to Nishitani's readers in 1946, for the simple reason that the existential and intellectual posture is still very much a problem today. In the case of Japan, the failure of the intelligentsia to participate in society and develop a sense of history has continued throughout the years after the Second World War. Indeed, the fact that it is not even an issue for most of the academic world shows how serious a problem it really is. As Nishitani remarked, "The history of Japan was cut off at the end of the war," but when one looks around at the "progressive," "critical" thinkers of present-day Japan, it is as if they carry on completely oblivious of the wound. For them history has begun all over again after the amputation. The "critics who have not suffered," are *Kritiker ohne Not*. They no longer know what it is to write out of a sense of historical necessity.[3]

For those of us born after the war, it is extremely difficult to understand the severance from history of which Nishitani speaks. Following Kierkegaard's suggestion that in each generation the history of sin begins all over again, perhaps we may look to religious ideas of sin and karma for help. In any case, we have at least to realize that if criticism of the war is to be genuine, it cannot entail a distancing of oneself from the events in question—perhaps with a latent sense of pride that, after all, these are deeds that *other* people committed—or a hunt for scapegoats on which to paste labels like "nationalism" and "the Kyoto school" and then to exile them from our midst. We cannot afford to be "standers-by" in dealing with the problem of nationalism today or pretend that it is something from a bygone era. Nationalism is, after all, *our* problem; or in Nishitani's phrase, we must "confront the past and make it our own past."[4] In writing about Japan's role in world culture and history, I am reminded also of Schelling's words: "Those who have not overcome themselves have no past."[5]

The central concept around which *View of the World, View of the Nation* revolves is *the world*. The term appears in the title of no less than four of its five essays. Its meaning cannot be understood without consideration of the related idea of *globality*, whose layers of meaning we will take up later. One cannot ask about the meaning of nationalism in Nishitani's thought if the question is framed merely, or even primarily, in the form of whether or not Nishitani himself was a nationalist. We need a broader perspective that allows

[3] NKC 4:461, 455.

[4] NKC 4:461.

[5] F. W. J. Von Schelling, *Die Weltalter: Fragmente,* edited by Manfred Schröter (München: Beck, 1979), 11, 199, 222.

us to see the connections between his "view of the world" and his "view of the nation," and one that also leaves room for the standpoint of religion.

THE PROBLEM OF MODERNITY

I begin with a review of Nishitani's ideas on modernity as presented in the opening lecture of *The Overcoming of Modernity*, since they provide a fuller context for the views worked out in *View of the World, View of the Nation*. In his lecture, Nishitani points out that the modern European culture which Japan began importing after the Meiji Restoration in 1868 itself lacked over-all integration. From there he turns to the wider historical perspective:

> Modernity is the age in which the foundations for an integrated world-view have broken down.... Modernity is, culturally speaking, the age in which the Reformation, the Renaissance, and the development of the natural sciences led to a definitive parting with the Middle Ages.... Moreover, if we consider a people's worldview to be its understanding of itself *in* the world and *with* the world, then we can say that modern humanity, stranded by the disintegration of the three movements that create worldview, is now faced with the fundamental problem of how to conceive of itself.[6]

During the Middle Ages a harmonious interrelation between the three fundamental concepts of God, the world, and the soul provided an unshakeable spiritual base. In the modern period the organic interrelation among the three is gone and the three pillars of human existence—religion, science, and culture—have fallen into a state of constant conflict with one another.

Nishitani sees this disintegration of the foundations of the human spirit reflected in the political sphere, where the relationship between the individual, the nation, and the world have deteriorated or broken down altogether. Insofar as we may view liberalism, the predominant political trend in western Europe, as grounded in "the assertion of the individual's right to independent existence within the world, then it may be said to represent a unification of individualism and globalism," but when the individual and the world face off against each other as polar opposites, the result is socialism, communism, or, in reaction against these latter, extreme forms of nationalism.[7]

For Nishitani, this style of modernity, with its twofold disintegration, came to dominate Japan as well in the years after the Meiji Restoration. Here he seems to share the verdict of Shimomura Toratarō expressed later in the

---

[6] KC, 19.
[7] KC, 21.

same volume: "Modernity is us, and the overcoming of modernity is the overcoming of ourselves. It is easy only if we imagine it as a kind of commentary about other people."[8] Near the end of his talk, Nishitani draws a conclusion important to our concern here:

> If we identify the basic problems of the contemporary age as rebuilding the foundations on which to create a new worldview and as the formation of a new, self-awakened human person, then surely these are problems we share with all of humanity.[9]

Nishitani was not interested in stopgap measures or in cobbling an arbitrary worldview that would safeguard the "special circumstances" of Japan at the time. The problem he had in mind was far more basic and creative. It had to do with locating the "place" (場所) at which the foundations could be laid for a new worldview and a new human being. In other words, he was seeking a "horizon of globality" to embrace the entire world. This is not to deny that his primary concern was with Japan, only that it was not restricted to Japan alone. The overcoming of *modernity* must not be equated merely with the overcoming of the *West*. It also entailed the overcoming of Japan and of the world. This was the sense of Nishitani's call for a transformation of *the world*.

Finally, the importance of the religious dimension in Nishitani's conclusions needs to be mentioned. Framed in religious language, the core question for overcoming modernity comes to this: How can religiosity—the inner urge to transcend our humanness by negating it in the name of what is Absolute—provide a common, unifying forum for culture, history, and ethics (which seek to affirm our humanness in as full and positive a manner as possible) on the one hand, and science (which is neutral towards humanness), so that each standpoint can express itself freely and interact with the others? What kind of religiosity is required of us to bring this about? And how do we reconstruct an ethics on the basis of such a religiosity so that our moral sense embraces the world, the nation, and the individual alike?[10]

THE OUTLINES OF THE GLOBAL HORIZON

Against this backdrop, we may turn now to the main arguments of the title article in *View of the World, View of the Nation*. Nishitani begins by pointing out the limitations and one-dimensionality of the idea of nation in traditional liberalism, according to which the state is seen as a "legal subject." From

[8] KC, 113.

[9] KC, 22.

[10] KC, 22.

there he examines a number of approaches, gradually building up a concrete understanding of the state as a living entity that rises and falls in the ebb and flow of history, a reality that exerts itself politically in the context of the power relationships that prevail at a given time among nations. Among the interpretations Nishitani reviews are Rudolf Kjéllen's *Staten som lifsform*,[11] which complements the usual emphasis on economics, society, government, and law with the "natural dimensions" of land and people as the basis of national existence; Friedrich Meinecke's *Die Idee der Staatsräson in der neuern Geschichte*,[12] which discusses the relationship between power and morality; and the work of Otto Koellreuter, which proposes the idea of a "community of destiny."[13]

I leave to others more knowledgeable than I the question of how accurate Nishitani's presentations are. What I find important is his discernment of a general historical pattern that "the nations of the modern world, no longer able to survive in liberalism, are being driven toward an authoritarian system with tendencies toward totalitarianism." He sees this pattern even in democratic nations like the United Kingdom where, like Christopher Dawson, he detects "a tendency toward a kind of democratic totalitarianism."[14]

But he does not stop at pointing to this trend toward increased politicization and control in modern nation-states. He argues that it is a matter of historical necessity. To elucidate the hidden contradictions at work here, Nishitani digresses into a brief history of the origins and developments of the idea of the modern nation-state:

> Absolutism fosters a free citizenry and a free citizenry in turn fosters community among the nation's people. One sees here a development first from authority to freedom and then from freedom back to authority. In the course of this historical process, rigid systems of class and other such extraneous elements pass away and in their place "the people" are brought into direct contact with "the nation." In this way we see a movement in the direction of a "nation of the people," at the center of which rests the immediate and mutual encounter of two contradictory principles: freedom and authority.[15]

[11] *Der Staat als Lebensform* (Leipzig: Hirzel, 1917).

[12] *Machiavellianism: The Doctrine of Raison d'état and its Place in Modern History*, trans. by D. Scott (New Haven: Yale University Press, 1957).

[13] See *Das politische Gesicht Japans* (Berlin: Heymann, 1940).

[14] NKC 4:381, 277.

[15] NKC 4:271.

This transition of history toward increased politicization and state activism required tight national controls not only over the economy and social order, but also over other dimensions of life, such as thought and religion, that have to do with the Weltanschauung of the individual and that had formerly been left to private discretion. At the same time, this dynamic worked a positive, unifying effect on people:

> Having arrived at a unified consciousness as a community, they sought to harmonize the nation so that it might faithfully express this unified communal consciousness. It was, in other words, a movement to make the nation into a single organism.[16]

Here we see what is for Nishitani the central paradox: the source of the very movement to curb freedom carries within itself the seeds of a new freedom. Given the convergence of the whole complex of relationships between the individual and the nation, the nation and the world, and the individual and the world in this contradictory connection between freedom and authority, the traditional approach of liberalism, seeking harmony by way of compromise, will no longer do. Rather, "if this contradiction is to be overcome, it will require a synthesis of thoroughgoing control by the nation and thoroughgoing freedom."[17]

Nishitani argues that a synthesis able to transcend this fundamental contradiction between control and freedom lies in "the dynamic relationship between the two approaches of subjectivizing the substrate (基体の主体化) and substrating the subject (主体の基体化)."[18] On the one hand, there is *control*: "the self-formation of the community of citizens," "the national will to incorporate the individual into the communal unity." Control represents the essence of the nation in the sense of "substrating" or grounding individuals in their relationship to the nation. On the other hand, there is *freedom*: the voluntary consent to such control as an expression of "each individual's desire not simply to sink into the natural substrate of the nation but to stand in a position of individual subjectivity." Freedom, in other words, represents the essence of the individual in the sense of "subjectivizing" the nation. Such freedom, Nishitani notes, "differs fundamentally from both absolutism (a pure substrate in which the people possess no subjectivity) and liberalism (a pure subjectivity in which the substrate is not present)."[19]

[16] NKC 4:271.
[17] NKC 4:381, 276.
[18] NKC 4:278.
[19] NKC 4:278–9.

The rotation between the substrative subject and the subjective substrate interacting at both "the outermost surface and the innermost depths" of the nation's existence gives rise to two elements not present in the historical models of Hegel or Ranke. The first is the increased politicization, referred to above, which takes place at the level of superficial controls. The other is "a globality immanent in the very existence of the state" and directing the state to the "abyss of free subjectivity" in its innermost depths. "This abyss is the ground of free subjectivity, and that very subjectivity in turn represents the horizon of a globality opening up within the substrate of a citizenry."[20]

Clearly Nishitani's idea of "globality" has a key role to play in this interplay and mutual transformation of the individual subject and the collective substrate. The term does not admit of a simple definition, but I believe we may single out three distinguishing elements:[21]

1. *Universal humanness.* Globality is the horizon within which people understand themselves as beings immediately in the world (*in-der-Welt-Sein*). It is against this horizon that "the perfect freedom and opening up of a worldview" takes place. "The spontaneous formation of a view of the world requires a horizon that stretches beyond the nation and beyond that world itself."

2. *World-historical world.* Globality is a conception of history in which the present age is seen as a turning point, or new epoch, in world history (a view that I will discuss in the next section).

3. *Transcendent openness.* Globality is the essence of spirituality, and in that sense perhaps we may even call it the standpoint of Zen or the "place of absolute nothingness."

The true nature of globality crystallizes only in the complex of relationships between and among each of these elements in which none is given privileged status over the others. To make this clearer, we may cite from the afterword:

Finally I reached the standpoint of national non-ego, or a horizon of globality, that becomes immanent in the nation through a self-negation of the nation's self-centeredness. The basic point at which my thought broke with nationalism is that it regarded the global nature of the nation as a subjectivity of non-ego brought about through self-negation, and that this standpoint must somehow open up not only within Japan but within all nations.... I spoke of this self-negation, which is necessary if the nation is to make the transition from modernity to a new mode of being, as a leap from the subjectivity of national "ego" to the subjectivity

[20] NKC 4:279, 281–2.
[21] See NKC 4:282–4.

of national "non-ego." I would like to stress that this is my fundamental standpoint.[22]

It is a mistake to read these words as merely an attempt by Nishitani to rationalize earlier views in the hindsight of the postwar period. Throughout the original work his standpoint is unequivocally clear and his philosophical argument astonishingly consistent. Most of the misunderstandings and simplistic critiques of Nishitani's work may be attributed, in my view, to the violent changes pressed on both the right and the left as a result of Japan's defeat in the war and its "severance" from history. In other words, it is in Nishitani's critics that one finds a deliberately ideological agenda, not in Nishitani himself.[23]

One can only imagine how brazen and challenging Nishitani's talk of a "global horizon immanent in the nation" must have echoed in the ears of the ultranationalists of the day. If nationalism feeds itself on the expectation of attack from without, it chokes on threats from within. The intellectual integrity required to risk exposing thoughts critical of ultranationalistic doctrine in a time of rising totalitarianism is not inconsiderable. Those of us who have never been faced with such a choice have constantly to wonder what we might do in similar circumstances.

In all probability Nishitani, who had fairly immersed himself in studies of the "dark nature" of Schelling and the nihilism of Nietzsche, had a good insight into the psychology of what was going on all about him, in particular the disenchantment with pure reason among anti-rationalistic movements and what he called their "hunger for the mythological."[24] In modern, secularized society there was no higher authority left to stand, as religion had once been able to do, against the dark side of the state and to denounce the perils of unbridled civil authority. The reason of liberalism had also fallen into disrepute and was unable to exert any influence. Living within a state that had regressed to its "natural, authoritarian roots," Nishitani's primary concern was how to get beyond the unreason of "intense naturalism" and promote in its place the ideal of reasoned "moralization." His idea of a "global horizon immanent in the nation" was an attempt to overcome this intense naturalism by putting it at the service of something higher. To do so the *humanness* of globality had somehow to be inspired to make the leap to a *transcendent openness.*

[22] NKC 4:382.

[23] A typical case is Ruth Kambartel, "Religion als Hilfsmittel für die Rechtfertigung einer totalitären Staatsideologie in Nishitani Keijis *Sekaikan to kokkakan,*" *Japanstudien* 1 (1989): 71–88.

[24] NKC 4:373.

In a 1946 essay on "Popular Culture and Humanism," Nishitani reworked his idea of substrate and subject. He states there that the global horizon the nation carries within itself points to something that it cannot quite completely encompass. He attributes this to the fact that the nation is by nature something universal manifested in limited form, and like all universals, that "something" resists and negates its specific determinations. At the same time, by taking on these limitations, the universal opens itself to the possibility of endless new specific forms. All things that live and grow can only do so through negation of their "self." To remain fixed within a given set of limits is to die. In this sense, infinite negation is the central principle of life.

Accordingly, the life of the nation, viewed in terms of its logical form

> always consists in a renewal of the self brought about by the breaking down of what has become fixed and the resulting transcendence of the self.... If one considers the *subject* as that which continually limits itself, and if one regards the *substrate of the self* as the *negation that is contained in this self-limitation as the principle of life* (because of its infinite potentiality), then the establishment of the self through a series of self-negations represents the continual return of the subject to its own substrate and at the same time a resubjectification of the substrate. The dynamic unity (or the unifying dynamism) of life comes about in this *cyclical movement of the substrating of the subject and the subjectifying of the substrate. The ego returns to its source in the substrating of the subject, and in so doing re-emerges in a freedom that embodies infinite possibility.* In the subjectification of the substrate, the ego acts autonomously to impose new limits on itself within the context of everyday life and in so doing limits the world around it as well.[25]

The nation's horizon of globality is visible in its "self-negation or self-transcendence." This is what he means by the "nation-transcending globality immanent in the nation," a phrase that he repeats from his earlier treatment.[26] This negation-and-transcendence is thus a "substrative" overcoming, a "transcendence of the self to itself, a return to the freedom of a new self-limitation." Nishitani insists that it is impossible for a nation to grow and develop without the freedom of willpower to negate itself. That freedom consists not only in radically affirming itself (the subjective dimension) but also in radically negating itself (the substrative dimension). It represents at once "a profound movement of nature at the spiritual core of the subject" and "a life force that wells up from the profoundest depths of our interiority."[27] Here is the point

---

[25] 国民文化とヒューマニズム, NKC 4:406–24. Citation on 409, emphasis added.

[26] See NKC 4:286, 409.

[27] NKC 4:410.

of contact with the "intense naturalness" and the possibility of giving it life as the substrate of the subject. Nishitani proposes this self-negation as "a third and new dimension of the nation distinct from naturalness and reason" and with it a "new "concept of the nation":

> Just as the individual ego manifests itself in its true form at the point of self-negation or no-self (that is, at the point of transcending the ordinary natural-rational mode of existence), so, too, the nation attains its true form only when it has transcended its ordinary mode of being and has discovered a new mode of being centered on self-negation.[28]

This idea of a "national no-self" is basic to Nishitani's thought, and his "horizon of globality" is simply a reformulation of it, particularly in terms of the leap from universal humanness to transcendent openness mentioned above. Grounded in this same analysis of no-self, Nishitani describes the "national polity" of Japan as "the principle that makes it possible to unite the highest degree of politicization as a nation with an openness that embraces the world." And again, on this same basis he refers apparently to the imperial family (without ever mentioning it or the emperor explicitly) as "the kind of transcendent center that expresses both globality and religious essence," as "an unmovable center that runs through the history of the country."[29]

The complexity of the language in which Nishitani couched his idea of "a return to the transcendent center" makes the idea rather forbidding and, not surprisingly, susceptible to misinterpretation. His use of the word *center* in this connection is perhaps easier to grasp if viewed in the context of a culture whose natural tendency is not towards centralized authority but rather towards an emptying of the center.[30] As for the relationship between globality and religious essence that this center is said to express, we shall return to this in the concluding section of this paper.

THREE IDEAS OF "THE WORLD"

Nishitani's concept of globality in the second sense—globality as world-historicity—is the central concern of the second and third chapters of *View of the World, View of the Nation*. There he argues that the times we live in represent "the age of global historical self-awakening." The idea recalls Nishida's reading of history:

[28] NKC 4:286.

[29] NKC 4:291, 294.

[30] This is a point that Karel van Wolferen has made in *The Enigma of Japanese Power* (London: Macmillan, 1989).

The eighteenth century was the age of individualism, the age of the self-awakening of the individual. The nineteenth century was the age of nationalism (or imperialism), in which the nation came to a self-awakening. But now we have entered *the age of global historical self-awakening, in which the world as such has become self-aware.* Our task is to find a way to build a *new world.*[31]

Nishitani took over this idea of the "self-awakening of the world," but his focus shifted away from Nishida's idea of the progression from individual to nation to world and towards what he saw as a global shift in the very *idea* of the world that has come down to us from ancient times through the modern period and into the present. If history may be divided into the Age of the Mediterranean, the Age of the Atlantic, and the Age of the Pacific, then the age that is coming to birth at present is the last of these. Ours is an age of a new globality in which the waters of the three great seas are flowing politically into each other. This new globality implies not only the awakening of "the politics of the Pacific" but also Japan's appearance on the stage of world history:

> The present age is one in which all the great seas of the world have become one, in which the body of the world has, as it were, awakened to itself as a single corpus, in which the world is gradually awakening to its own spiritual totality.[32]

The unity we find in the empires of the ancient world was a unity imposed through conquest. The prevailing idea of the world allowed for no autonomy within subjugated nations. The world was conceived of in terms of "a single universality that did not permit a plurality of individuals." The ancient world was "a world that was one with a particular nation," as we see in Rome's imposition of its own particularity on the conquered lands of its empire.

In contrast, the idea of the world we find in the modern age was that of "a plurality of individuals that did not permit any one universality." It implies a multitude of autonomous national monads, disparate and in conflict with each other. Since such a world was not able to achieve unity under any one particularity, its unity came to consist in "an abstract universality divorced from the plurality of individuals." In fact, however, strictly speaking it was no

[31] NKZ 10:336ff. Emphasis added. In this same passage, Nishida argues against the extreme ethnic-nationalists that "it is not that blood is noble, but that blood is the bearer of culture."

[32] NKC 4:298–9. I am reminded here of the remark of W. I. Thompson to the effect that the present is also effecting a shift towards a global cultural ecology that puts the Pacific Ocean where the Mediterranean used to be. See his *Pacific Shift* (San Francisco: Sierra Club Books, 1986).

more than a greatly expanded version of the European world, a "universality integrated under the specificity of Europe." It was, as Nishitani says, "a world assimilated into a specific sphere of unity enveloping the struggles of a multitude of individual nations for independence."[33]

The contemporary age has left the idea of European centrality. Today's world is bound by no one periphery. It is a "completely open world" that can no longer be identified with any particularity or specificity, and that has arrived at the "concrete universality" of self-identification. Nonetheless, even though the idea of the world may have broken free of its former model of Europe-centered assimilation, it "has still to reemerge as something that includes a number of distinct unified spheres by recovering some continuity in its discontinuity with the historical past." The self-identity of the contemporary world can only be achieved as "a community of individual nations made up of a plurality of self-sufficient and distinct spheres striving for unity."[34]

Nishitani analyzes these three distinct ideas of the world and draws attention to some of the fundamental problems they incorporate. In this context, for example, he compares the Stoic concept of nature in ancient times with the abstractness of nature in the modern age. Similarly, he contrasts the spirit of the ancient and modern age—their sense or consciousness of the world—in the former's notion of *pneuma* and the latter's *pneuma*-free rationality. Turning to the "open" character of the modern world, he speaks of "naked" *in-der-Welt-Sein*, of the sharp correlation between the self-limitation of the world and the self-limitation of the individual, the interrelation of global politics and the concentration of spheres of unity, and the face-off between nations and individuals. As a way to overcoming these problems, he proposes a standpoint of "a universality of nothingness" that he describes as "a spirit of no-self permeating the individual, the nation, and the world."[35]

For Nishitani, one of the factors that helped transform the modern concept of the world into the contemporary one was Japan's sudden rise to power. This is the main topic of his third chapter on "East Asia and World History." Besides looking at Japan's appearance on the stage of world history, he also takes up the resulting trend towards a "new East Asian order," which he sees as part of the general global trend toward multiple spheres of unity. He sees this idea of a new order emerging in East Asia not as an ideological strategy but as a dynamic "grounded in the reality of the world." As a historian he tries to provide a factual basis for his conclusion, and as a philosopher

---

[33] NKC 4:301–5.

[34] NKC 4:304–5.

[35] NKC 4:319, 382.

he tries to define the form and spirit it should assume. Although he was not without misgivings about the baldly aggressive policies of the government at the time, he nevertheless believed that the concept of the new East Asian order possessed an "ethical dimension of a global scale":

> It constitutes a rejection of the colonization of East Asia; as an expression of the will toward communal independence based on the commonality of our historical culture, it signifies a demand for justice directed at the world.[36]

In Nishitani's view, a new East Asian order represented not only a strategy for self-defense, but an expression of Japan's responsibility towards the destiny of East Asia. But more important than these political concerns was its significance as a "purely cultural or spiritual movement." Of all the nations of Asia at the time, only Japan had successfully modernized and achieved equality with the powers of the West. One of the reasons for its emergence into world history, Nishitani argued, was its possession of a living East Asian cultural tradition that had kept both "the breadth of its spiritual horizon and the depth of its history." "Only in Japan," he claimed, "does East Asian culture and spirituality animate everyday life and provide the source of the ethos and spiritual nurture of the people."[37] This living tradition enabled the leaders of the Meiji Restoration to

> make contact with Western culture from a broad spiritual horizon and existential depth. It also enabled them to draw living strength from the culture of the West.... In this way one large segment of humanity was able to comprehend another.[38]

Nishitani saw Japan as the locus of this great encounter between the cultures of East and West. Even if the two worlds within Japan were still in a state of chaos, this very chaos was "a mark of superiority." At a time when Western culture had spread throughout the world, Nishitani foresaw a corresponding spread of Eastern culture to the West. In these circumstances, Japan could not afford to risk falling apart because of its internal cultural chaos. A certain order had to be imposed to protect it from disintegration. At the same time, for Japan to draw strength from its own historical tradition, like any nation it had first to awaken to a sense of the uniqueness of its culture. This rooting in culture and history was necessary, he saw, "to give birth to a cultural *world* within oneself and also to open up a cultural *horizon of globality* in

[36] NKC 4:336.

[37] NKC 4:345.

[38] NKC 4:422.

one's innermost depths."[39] The globality of culture is only possible through a "creative continuity with tradition."

SIMPLIFYING THE WELTANSCHAUUNG

"The Worldview of the New Japan" is in many ways the most fascinating and important essay in Nishitani's book. It delves deeply into several important issues—the relationship between the view of the world and the view of the nation, the foundations for a worldview, and the nature of the horizon of globality, particularly as a "transcendent openness"—from the standpoint of their connection with the shaping of a national ethos.

Nishitani opens his essay with the comment, "Frankly speaking, I am not in favor of using terms like *New Japan* at present." Part of the reason may have been the tendency at the time to associate the term with rather simple-minded ideas about the "Japanese spirit" and *yamato-damashii*, or to see it as a new form of ultranationalism. If "New Japan" means nothing more than this, the danger is that it would cut itself off from the real world and degenerate into a kind of self-deceptive abstraction. Nishitani's aim was rather to draw people's attention to the loss of the traditional Japanese ethos after the Meiji Restoration and the need for reestablishing continuity with it.[40]

Nishitani saw the living model of this ethos in the late-Edo and early-Meiji figures like Sakuma Shōzan 佐久間象山 (1811–1864), Yoshida Shōin 吉田松陰 (1830–1859), and Nanshū (南州: 西郷隆盛 Saigō Takamori, 1827–1877), who combined in their persons youthful passion and maturity of vision. For him the fundamental essence of this ethos lay in "the fusion of practice, Weltanschauung, and religious belief into one." What he means by *Weltanschauung* is not a logical, systematic worldview, but rather a kind of "direct, primitive intuition bound to practice, an existential *Orientierung* of the self within the world, not simply a personal opinion but an intuitive knowledge." In reference to the figures just mentioned, Nishitani speaks of the Weltanschauung being raised to the level of a "religious belief transcending life and death," which in turn "directly inspired their nation-building activities and, as part and parcel of their religious devotion to the emperor, was directly tied to love of country." Such intuition for Nishitani is

> tied to a religious faith that brings one spiritual peace in the midst of the world. On the one hand, it sows the seeds of a philosophy or worldview, and on the other, it is a motivating force for spiritual practice.[41]

[39] NKC 4:338.
[40] NKC 4:348.
[41] NKC 4:349–51.

Nishitani's point in focusing on the intuitional dimension (the *Anschau-ung*) of the Weltanschauung is to locate the source out of which a worldview arises, the fountainhead from which a philosophy flows. In this sense, his aim is actually to probe behind and beneath philosophy to the Weltanschauung that precedes it and grounds it, to reach a dimension that is not just "another dimension" but the native soil out of which both world and intuition emerge.

Nishitani discusses "three orientations" that govern the fundamental character and structure of this Weltanschauung: practice, philosophy, and religion.

Practice is the fundamental mark of Weltanschauung in the sense that one cannot speak here of practice and insight as separate. The idea is one deeply rooted in the traditions of the East, and Nishitani draws particularly on Japanese sources to argue that it represents "the Japanese character of a worldview." Indeed, he claims, "it is the most basic thing we have to con-tribute to the West, and to peoples in the world in search of a worldview."[42]

The orientation of *philosophy* shows up in the human need for rationality and learning ("science" in the broad sense), and as such runs in the opposite direction from the orientation to practice. The Western worldview's interest in logic as opposed to praxis (which is distinguished from practice by virtue of its divorce from primitive intuition) has the merits of an intellectual univer-sality and critical rationality, both of which help to exclude the subjective element and promote objective knowledge of the world. Nishitani concludes:

> The promotion of the Japanese spirit in the world at large is a task that can never be accomplished until this spirit has come to a standpoint of universality, of commonality between self and other—in other words, until this standpoint of rationality and science has become transparent to it. Even if it does not stand on the same foundations as Western science and the Western worldview, it must at least possess the capacity to engage in dialogue on such foundations.[43]

This is an issue vital to the formation of Japan's Weltanschauung. It repre-sents "the need for globality in the Japanese spirit." Openness to the future requires a loosening of its ties to the past.

The dilemma of the modern age, as Nishitani sees it, rests in the contra-diction between practice and reason. Not only does this drive a firm wedge between the past and the future, it also cuts the "Japanese" outlook off from the "world." If the orientation to overcoming this contradiction may be said to lie in *religion*, then the question becomes one of how religiosity can "in an

[42] NKC 4:351.
[43] NKC 4:352.

act of negation-in-affirmation pass through rationality and the scientific out-look." Nishitani writes:

> This can only be accomplished from the standpoint of a practice that can negate in turn the rationality that negates practice, and at the same time act autonomously to breathe new life into that rationality. This is both *a disassociation from our traditional spirit and a continuation of it*. It is, so to speak, *a creative continuation of tradition*.... The "religious belief" of such a standpoint, which we may rightly call a sublation of science in the broad sense by practice, must come to birth in the midst of the "pre-sent" where past and future negate each other.[44]

In this reconsideration of the meaning of religiosity and religious belief we see the "other dimension" of world and intuition that Nishitani spoke of open up. The worldview of the West, however solidly grounded in rationali-ty it may be, keeps the world before it as an object and looks at actual reality from the outside. In contrast to this way of seeing, the fundamental orienta-tion of the Eastern Weltanschauung, particularly as it developed in Japan, not only overcomes this *aporia* but takes a step further. Nishitani calls it "the sim-plification of the Weltanschauung and its ethos-shaping quality."[45] The pas-sage continues, and I cite at length:

> In general there is in our country a certain force working to bring to the outermost surface what lies at the innermost depths of all doctrines and systems. (This applies even to the case of Buddhist doctrines like *rijimuge* 理事無碍 and *jijimuge* 事事無碍, which speak of the radical inter-penetration of all phenomena.) It does so in terms of a practice that retains its interpretative character, but goes the further step to incorpo-rate into the practice what lies at the innermost depths. In this way, the apparently most shallow things—like *shikantaza* [只管打坐, the Zen of "just sitting"] and *shōmyō nenbutsu* [称名念仏, invoking the name of Amida Buddha]—become epiphanies of an unspeakable profundity. Such practices can be performed by anyone but exhausted by no one. They can be understood to perfection by anyone in an instant, yet con-tain within themselves unlimited potential for further insight....
>
> In addition to guiding the formation of ethos, this simplification of the Weltanschauung has another no less important quality. By melding into this shallowest and yet profoundest practice, the Weltanschauung is able to permeate body and mind, and become part of anyone's daily activities of moving, standing, sitting, and sleeping. Once it has made ties

[44] NKC 4:354. Emphasis added.
[45] NKC 4:356.

to everyday life, everyday life in turn comes to be shaped from within by practice, and an ethos, solidly rooted in what is most profound in the Weltanschauung, comes to birth through religious belief. This birth of ethos even surpasses the cultural achievements in the arts and scholarship that are the pride of other countries. It belongs not only to a cultural past that Japan can hold up proudly to the rest of the world, but to the *Kultur* of humanity as such.[46]

The influence of Zen in this "simplification of the Weltanschauung" is obvious. (One is reminded of the kōan, "What is the source of *mu?*", 無字の根源.) In the everydayness of practice there must be no trace of any source, and yet the profoundest depths must be expressed at the outermost surface. With Nishida we might call it "the self-expression of the world." In any case, this is where I believe we must place Nishitani on the question of nationalism. If, as he concludes, "the openness of reason is contained in the religiosity of the East with its transcendent openness as vast as the very sky,"[47] the proof can only come from the effort to restore that idea to the realm of personal practice. The question, as always, is how.

[TRANSLATED BY THOMAS KIRCHNER]

[46] NKC 4:357.
[46] NKC 4:365.

Questioning Nationalism Now and Then

A Critical Approach to Zen and the Kyoto School

John C. MARALDO

> The recent war must become a real question for us today. Otherwise we will not be able to think authentically about the present situation. In this sense, that past is a problem of the present.
>
> —Nishitani Keiji, "The Problem of Fascism"

W HEN CRITICS ACCUSE philosophers of the Kyoto school and certain Zen intellectuals of a "nationalistic" element in their thinking, and when supporters defend them against that charge, both sides are operating under the assumption that nationalism is something pernicious. The charge takes two forms that are often seen to reinforce one another: the nationalistic element lent support to Japan's wars of aggression in Asia, or it promoted a chauvinism that distorts the truth of one tradition and does injustice to others. Either way, the case for moral or intellectual censure hangs on proof that the suspected offensive element was indeed present.

Much of the current literature about twentieth-century nationalism works on a similar assumption. With each new report of the savagery of "ethnic cleansing" and other atrocities wrought in the name of a people's "right to self-determination," the iniquities of nationalism become more obvious and the tide of anti-nationalist literature swells. Political analysts and journalists of various persuasions, dismayed at current events, have come to the conclusion that nationalism, despite the occasional positive effect, is predominantly pernicious. In *The Wrath of Nations,* William Pfaff finds it "intrinsically absurd" that the accident of birth in a particular nation should impose loyalties that lead to conflict with those who, by similar accident, belong to another nation.[1] The British historian E. J. Hobsbawm finds that

---

[1] *The Wrath of Nations: Civilization and the Furies of Nationalism* (New York: Simon & Schuster, 1993), 17.

national identification is outdated and dangerous.[2] Michael Ignatieff argues that the sense of belonging defined by bloodline leads to needless bloodshed among both civilians and soldiers.[3] Even those we might expect to champion national self-determination condemn it instead. Polish activist Adam Michnik, writing in 1990 when Poland was thought to be fully justified in asserting its national identity, would have none of it:

> Nationalism always leads to egoism and self-deception. To egoism, because it allows one to ignore the injuries suffered by other nations and disregard other peoples' values and ways of seeing. To self-deception, because by focusing on one's own injuries, nursing the memory of those injuries, nationalism allows one to ignore the injuries one has also inflicted.[4]

Still, *nationalism* is an ambiguous term, and before going too far on the assumption that it is always and everywhere pernicious, we want to know what it is that we are censuring. In broad terms, we may define nationalism as the assertion of self-identity by a specific people made over against other peoples or states as a declaration of the right to preserve and advance its own identity in an international world. As Pfaff notes, such broad-termed definitions do not exist anywhere in their pure form. For him there is no "universality" in nationalism, only varieties of nationalisms—Serbian, German, American, and so forth.[5] Others catalogue nationalisms according to the object of loyalty—ethnic nationalism, cultural nationalism, state nationalism, and so on. Michael Ignatieff's *Blood and Belonging* distinguishes between civic nationalism, based on chosen citizenship and law, and ethnic nationalism, based on inherited common roots and leading to unnecessary divisiveness. Other scholars refer to "cultural nationalism," which emphasizes the perceived uniqueness, and sometimes superiority, of the values and achievements of a people by virtue of its common heritage.[6] Linguistic usage in Japan complicates matters by introducing its own terms—*kokuminshugi* (国民主義), *kokkashugi* (国家主義), *minzokushugi* (民族主義), *kokusuishugi*

[2] E. J. Hobsbawm, *Nations and Nationalism since 1780* (Cambridge: Cambridge University Press, 1990).

[3] Michael Ignatieff, *Blood and Belonging: Journeys into the New Nationalism* (New York: Farrar, Straus and Giroux, 1993).

[4] Adam Michnik, "Notes on the Revolution," *The New York Times Magazine* (11 March 1990), 44.

[5] *The Wrath of Nations*, 14.

[6] See Kosaka Yoshino, *Cultural Nationalism in Contemporary Japan* (London and New York: Routledge, 1992) for a sociological analysis of this phenomenon. In contrast to all these forms of nationalism, patriotism might designate a way of expressing national pride more inwardly than nationalism, among the people of a country rather than against surrounding peoples or states. Obviously the two reinforce one another.

(国粋主義), *kokkashijōshugi* (国家至上主義), to mention only the most common labels.

Catalogue the types as we may, none of our conventions quite captures the way in which nationalisms crystallize and organize feelings, motives, and actions that otherwise remain rudimentary and undirected and that evoke still other forces: patriotism, ethnocentrism, exclusivism, racism. The forces at work are simply too tangled to unsnarl with a single comb. In the end, we have no choice but to take our general assumption, that something pernicious is at work in nationalism, and apply it to concrete, specific cases.

In addition to the complexities of the subject matter, there are other, no less troublesome, complexities associated with the position of the critic. When making a case against the self-righteous assertion of nationalism in a concrete form, one should remain aware of the possibility of being infected with the same malady. Simply retreating to the high ground of supposedly disinterested analysis is no guarantee of immunity. The process of criticism must somehow remain present before the eye of the critic. The situation becomes even more complex when those being criticized as nationalists turn out to be critics of nationalism themselves. All these complications come together in the case of Zen and Kyoto-school thinkers. In order to sort them out as best I can, I would like to suggest three stages in the process of criticizing critiques, which I shall call location, dislocation, and relocation.

1. First, we identify someone's position as a criticism by locating the target of that criticism. Here the position appears along with its counterposition, whether the original author is that explicit or not. This *location* shows us whether the criticism occurs in a live exchange of give-and-take between, say, a ruling ideology and its challenger, or whether it sets up as a counterposition a dead target unable to respond. In any case, location alerts us to the fact that the position in question is defined not only by what it says but also by what is being spoken against.

2. Next, we expose another side of the position by dislocating it from its original context and target. The position then appears as a discourse, standing more or less on its own, but now subject to a new critique it did not anticipate. *Dislocation* reveals assumptions and consequences of the original position that may have been obscured when it was too wrapped up in its original circumstances.

3. Finally, we clarify the guiding interests of the new critique by relocating the suspect position in a wider context. Here the similarities as well as the differences between the position and the new critique come to light. *Relocation* reveals the interests, sensitivities, and prejudices of both the position and the new critique, and shows where answers to criticisms occasionally miss the point.

I will not occupy myself here with examples of what happens when one of these stages is skipped over, except to note that a good deal of skipping seems to be going on in the debate over nationalism in Zen and the Kyoto school. Rather, I would like to apply the pattern of location-dislocation-relocation to the positions of three figures in the debate: D.T. Suzuki, Abe Masao, and Nishitani Keiji.

D.T. SUZUKI'S SPIRITUAL NATIONALISM

The case of D. T. Suzuki (1870–1966) shows in a rather straightforward manner how criticism can be subject to the three stages of location, dislocation, and relocation. Although it is far from obvious today that Suzuki's war-period writings intended to criticize rather than to promote nationalism, a closer look will reveal another side. A brief sketch of Suzuki's wartime literary activity provides the necessary background to identify his work as criticism.

In December 1944 Suzuki Daisetsu published a book entitled *Japanese Spirituality* (日本的霊性), and soon followed it with three others: *The Construction of a Spiritual Japan* and *A Japanese Spiritual Awakening*, both in 1946, and *Spiritualizing Japan* in 1947. That Suzuki wrote all these books in Japanese and did not arrange for their translation is not a matter to be passed over lightly.

Since the World Parliament of Religions in 1893, he had been an indefatigable missionary of Zen Buddhism, both in the United States and in Japan. The year 1936 found him abroad once more, attending the World Congress of Faiths in London and lecturing in England and the United States on Zen. In 1938, he chose to write "Zen Buddhism and Its Influence on Japanese Culture" in English, and by 1946 he was again concerned to publish for foreign audiences.[7] He spent most of the last fifteen years of his life, from 1949 on, living and traveling outside Japan. The Pacific War did of course keep him in Japan and curtail his campaign to spread the gospel of Zen. Yet Suzuki directed his books on spirituality to his compatriots not because of wartime constraints but because his mission at that time was, in the view of one commentator, to remind his countrymen of "the spiritual awakening of Japan that continued to live eternally beyond war and defeat."[8]

---

[7] Together with R. H. Blyth, Suzuki edited *The Cultural East*, which appeared in only two issues, July 1946 and August 1947. That same year he translated his lectures to the Shōwa Emperor and published them in English as *The Essence of Buddhism* (Kyoto: Hōzōkan, 1948).

[8] 日本的霊性 [Japanese spirituality] (Tokyo: Iwanami Bunko, 1972), 274. This is the formulation of 篠田英雄 Shinoda Hideo in an explanatory note appended to this edition but not contained in the *Collected Works* (SDZ 8:1–223). There is an English translation by Norman Waddell, *Japanese Spirituality*, sponsored by the Japanese National Commission for UNESCO

Japanese Spirituality vs. Japanese Spirit

The motivation for Suzuki's *Japanese Spirituality*, according to Shinoda Hideo, was to promote Japan's contribution to the world's spiritual culture at a time when its image was anything but spiritual.[9] But to identify this writing specifically as a critique, we will need to locate its counterposition more clearly, a target that Suzuki aims at but never names. What he does name are two general categories that must not be confused. Before defining Japanese spirituality and specifying its historical manifestations, Suzuki takes pains to distinguish *reisei* (霊性) from *seishin* (精神). This latter term, covering a broad range of meanings relating to mind or spirit, became popular during the war in the expressions referring to the "Japanese spirit." But that usage, Suzuki insists, fails to connote the sense of will or willpower that *seishin* has in older expressions, or even the sense of the heart (*kokoro* 心), the soul, or the core of things. Nor is it the equivalent of *yamato-damashii* (大和魂),[10] the "soul of Japan" since ancient times.

At issue here is not the correctness of Suzuki's linguistic analysis, but rather his motive for doing it and for introducing a concept relatively new to his writings. Why is Suzuki so concerned at the very beginning of his essay to delineate the meanings of *seishin* and draw a strict distinction between them and the concept of *reisei*? Just what was he positioning himself against?

The term *seishin* had been co-opted by the government to designate the noble character and spiritual quality of the national agenda. A Center for National Spiritual Culture (国民精神文化研究所), for example, arose in the 1930s, and in 1937 the government sponsored its "national spiritual mobilization" (国民精神総動員) to marshal support for the war. Similarly, from the 1930s the related term *yamato-damashii* came to stand for the supposedly unique moral character of the Japanese and to suggest unfailing loyalty to the emperor and the nation. Suzuki's concern with the diverse meanings of *seishin* and their difference from *reisei* reflect his attempt to distance himself from militarist rhetoric. I think, therefore, that we may see in his belabored linguistic analysis a tacit criticism of current ideology, particularly of the nationalistic shibboleth *Nihon seishin* (日本精神). The ideology of the "Japanese spirit" is the position Suzuki is arguing against, though he does not—and under a repressive government *cannot*—name his counterposition. He avoids any discussion of the nationalistic overtones of *seishin*, but he is

---

and published by the Japan Society for the Promotion of Science and the Ministry of Education, 1972. Waddell notes that Suzuki wrote this essay between trips to the air-raid shelter during some of the heaviest bombing of the war, and directed it "to the Japanese at a time of growing uncertainty and despair...attempting to show them their true, unmilitary might" (viii).

[9] *Japanese Spirituality,* 274 (Iwanami Japanese edition).

[10] SDZ 8:17–21.

clearly not advocating the values of a nation asserting itself through warfare. His most important concern is to show that there is a forgotten kind of spirituality and that it is manifest in Japanese culture in a distinct way.

The spirituality that Suzuki has in mind is ostensibly a critique of values. Suzuki contends that *reisei* is beyond good and evil since it is nondiscriminating, whereas *seishin* is inherently dualistic. The dualism is most apparent where he opposes the concept of spirit to that of matter. But even the "spirit of Japan," *Nihon seishin,* is dualistic since it denotes the ideals of the Japanese people and since ideals are based on moralistic notions of good and evil. The spirit of Japan entails an ethic; [Japanese] spirituality transcends ethics.[11] Spirituality points to the unity that underlies all dualisms and oppositions. It is synonymous with religious consciousness, but only if we understand religion not in its institutionalized forms but as an "awakening to spirituality." This circular definition is reinforced when Suzuki implies that spirituality, as direct intuition that transcends the ego, is itself a way of understanding. This intuition is realized only through individual experience,[12] but can be communicated from individual to individual.

Spirituality in Suzuki's view transcends nationality, although it is "awakened" and transmitted only when a certain level of culture is achieved and appears in different forms in the spiritual life of a people. Hence we may speak of a Japanese spirituality, whose most pure manifestations, Suzuki says, are not primitive Shinto customs but rather Japanese Pure Land thought and Zen (especially since the Kamakura era). Again defining matters in circular fashion, Suzuki finds the spirituality of Zen not in its historical contingency as an imported form of Buddhism, but in the way that Zen took root deep within the spirit of *bushidō* and was a flowering of Japanese spirituality. Pure Land thought is likewise infused with Japanese *reisei,* and that is why a lay Buddhist movement like Shinshū and its teaching of *ōchō* (横超)[13] developed not in India or China, which had the same scriptures, but in Japan. Pure Land experience is the affective side of Japanese spirituality, and Zen (more precisely, "the Zenification of Japanese life") is the intellectual side.[14]

11 SDZ 8:22.

12 In fact, Suzuki's emphasis both on the individual and on experience may be post-Meiji characterizations of the Zen tradition.

13 SDZ 8:27. Norman Waddell's glossary at the end of his translation (216) defines *ōchō* as the "side-wise leap, the experience by which, according to Shinran, one's rebirth in the Pure Land is absolutely assured." Shinran uses this term, for example, near the end of the *Gyō* section of his work *Kyōgyōshinshō.*

14 SDZ 8:26–9.

Spirituality as Cultural Nationalism

Today we are in a position to criticize Suzuki's own tacit critique of state nationalism and celebration of Japanese spirituality from another angle. From where we stand, our critique dislocates Suzuki's position from the context of its original interchange, and sets it up as a target for objections that could not have occurred to him. What does this target look like, at least as far as *Japanese Spirituality* is concerned?

Readers of Suzuki will be familiar with his emphasis on nondiscriminating wisdom (無分別智), his appreciation of popular Shin (True Pure Land) Buddhism, and his way of giving "Zen experience" a privileged status. It comes as no surprise that he would identify Japanese spirituality with these forms. But his initial premise of spirituality (*reisei*) in general as nondiscriminating wisdom[15] belies a kind of nationalist slant that is not so obvious. Suzuki claims, on the one hand, that spirituality is spirituality, not confined to any particular race or people (*minzoku*, 民族). On the other hand, he defines spirituality quintessentially as nondiscrimination, as the central practice of Mahāyāna Prajñāpāramitā Buddhism that is realized in a special way in Japanese Zen. Suzuki takes his depiction of a particular tradition for something he claims is transnational and is at the root of every (genuine) religious tradition.

In effect Suzuki is saying that Japanese spirituality is the prototype of all spirituality. Writing for Japanese in 1944, he says that it is of far more value than Japan's military might and Asian leadership combined, both of which he recognized as already being in jeopardy at the time. In place of *state* nationalism, Suzuki advances a kind of *cultural* nationalism. More specifically, he promotes a "*spiritual* nationalism" that defines one nation's spirituality as the basis for all spirituality.[16]

Although I think this criticism is a valid one, the critical process should not stop here. It must go on to consider why this new criticism came to be possible. Relocating Suzuki's original criticism and projected alternative can bring to light the conditions of the contemporary critique that has, at least momentarily, displaced the original criticism, forgetting its opponent, but exposing its prejudices.

---

[15] SDZ 8:22.

[16] A similar criticism, which Suzuki could hardly have foreseen, is found in David A. Dilworth's statement that "the whole tenor of Suzuki's work [about Japanese spirituality] is religiously and culturally chauvinistic...." See the postscript in his translation, Nishida Kitarō, *Last Writings: Nothingness and the Religious Worldview* (Honolulu: University of Hawaii Press, 1987) 146. Robert H. Sharf argues that Suzuki's (and Nishida's) writings were the progenitors of *nihonjinron* theories that proclaim the uniqueness, and often the superiority, of Japanese cultural forms. See "The Zen of Japanese Nationalism," *History of Religions* 33/1 (1993): esp. 35.

We may now turn to the relocation. As we might expect, Suzuki's intended audience and the circumstances of his time help show his position to be somewhat different from the one we are aiming our criticisms against. Suzuki directed his work to a Japanese audience at a time when a direct criticism of state nationalism or expansionist policies would have been silenced immediately.[17] His criticism of wartime rhetoric was possible only because it was camouflaged. The denunciation of the slogan "Japanese spirit" is hidden among the layers of meanings of *seishin* that he uncovers. It is entailed by his shift to another kind of spirit, *reisei*, that in his eyes is far more worthy and expressive of what Japan has to offer the world. The extensive discourse on *reisei* is not a decoy to draw the attention of potential censors away from the implied denunciation; it is a sincere attempt to offer what was for Suzuki an alternative and much superior ideal to the Japanese people. Yet Suzuki directed his project not just to Japan, but to the West as well. In the belief that Japan was overcome by militarism, and the Western world by materialism, he proposed an idealized religiosity as a national and even global ideal.

This relocation of Suzuki's critique can now throw light on differences that both enable and qualify our contemporary critique. In comparison to Suzuki's times (especially the 1930s through the 1950s), not only have economic and cultural conditions allowed us more divergent views of the world, but academic interests have followed the diversification of knowledge. Today we tend to celebrate a plurality of spiritualities and discredit the attempt to find an exemplar for all. Any difference between an essentially Japanese spirituality and an ideological Japanese spirit is lost to us. We look for diversity and historical conditioning in religious expressions, not for a privileged experience that might be the unchanging core of a tradition. The attempt to express a core in "Western" as well as "Eastern" terms finds sympathy no longer. We question the centrality of singular voices of authority; we have no need to question an authoritarian Japan or a Western model of rationality. Finally, we labor to establish non-Japanese voices of authority on Japanese Buddhism, and our efforts there vie with the *Western* tradition of hearing in Suzuki a guru of the East.[18] These differences expose the unquestioned interests of present criticism as well as the agenda of past critics.

[17] It is not that dissent from or criticism of state policies did not occur in wartime Japan, but the reign of "thought control" by the Special Higher Police forced it underground. John W. Dower documents the amazing array of anonymous dissidence in "Sensational Rumors, Seditious Graffiti, and the Nightmares of the Thought Police," *Japan in War and Peace: Selected Essays* (New York: The New Press, 1993), but notes (110) that "no organized resistance or concerted protest was possible." Suspected individual critics were arrested and often tortured. See Hatanaka Shigeo, "Thought Criminal," in Haruko Taya Cook and Theodore F. Cook, *Japan at War: An Oral History* (New York: The New Press, 1992), 222–7.

[18] We should note that Suzuki Daisetsu has also had among his critics Japanese scholars of

ABE MASAO'S NATIONALISM–IN–ANTINATIONALISM

Suzuki's brand of spiritual nationalism is not, it seems, a relic of the past. We find a current version of it in the philosophy of Abe Masao (1915–), Suzuki's heir in promoting Zen in the West. The editor of the recent memorial volume, *A Zen Life: D.T. Suzuki Remembered*,[19] Abe has energetically carried on this one aspect of Suzuki's mission for more than two decades. Since 1980 he has held visiting positions at several American universities, has participated in numerous Buddhist-Christian dialogues, and has lectured widely in Europe as well as the United States. The elucidation of a Zen Buddhist perspective to Western audiences and its application to Western philosophical and theological problems are clearly Abe's central concerns. Less obvious is the undercurrent of spiritual nationalism in his work. He has not pursued the other part of Suzuki's mission, to reawaken Japanese people to their own spiritual heritage, although he was a teacher for a community of lay Zen practitioners in Japan. Abroad he is anything but an advocate for Japan's "national interests." Abe has deliberately presented himself as a spokesman for Buddhism, especially the Zen tradition, and he is accepted by Americans and Europeans as a Japanese Buddhist. That role hardly merits the label *nationalist,* spiritual or otherwise. Abe's spiritual nationalism is more subtle.

Conventional Absolutism

It is easy enough to identify criticisms of nationalism in his work. His target is obvious. The challenge is to dislocate his position in order to reveal its own tacit brand of nationalism. On the surface, the basic position that Abe takes would seem to preclude any such exclusivist nationalism. His favorite formula about the true Self expresses this position well enough. In representing his views, Abe does not, indeed *cannot,* say "I am a Japanese (offering my views on Buddhism, etc.)." His way of speaking requires an identity different from that of someone rooted in a particular people or culture. Rather, he must be someone who can say, "I am not I, and precisely therefore I am I"—or in its

---

Buddhism, not to mention the Chinese historian Hu Shih, who argued against Suzuki's ahistorical essentializing of Zen. The Japanese critics, however, tend to criticize Suzuki's method in the manner that Suzuki criticized state nationalism, that is, by proposing alternative views without explicitly naming the contested one. Such critiques are implied in the work of Yanagida Seizan, and in S. Watanabe's *Japanese Buddhism: A Critical Appraisal* (Tokyo: Kokusai Bunka Shinkōkai, 1970). Yanagida's researches represent an extensive if nonsystematic history of the Ch'an and Zen traditions, and the latter a realistic and detailed but nontechnical treatment of the characteristics of Japanese Buddhism.

[19] Tokyo & New York: Weatherhill, 1986.

expanded version, "I am not I because I am egoless, and thus negating the ego I am absolutely I because I am my true Self."[20]

On the one hand, this statement implies that the speaker is a realized self, an "I" that is ideally anyone and everyone. It is also, in a sense, no one—no "I" that is defined by a particular set of circumstances. On the other hand, this true Self is not an absolutized "I" that is abstracted from all circumstances, beyond all cultural and national conditioning. It is itself, rather, in its activity of negating every particular form that it assumes. The realized self is one who has awakened to this "egolessness or emptiness." Through this realization, Abe says, one overcomes ego-centeredness. He does not say that one overcomes one's "nationality," but his rhetoric distances him from the question of national identity. Obviously, neither the true Self nor the self "awakened" to its truth is an exclusively Japanese self.

In order to assume this position, Abe must be able to put himself in the place of the "I" in his statement, since it is a statement about everyone, including himself. But can he speak here *in propria persona*, that is, as a speaker who has realized its truth in himself? I think that Abe does claim the viewpoint of a realized self, in the sense of a self freed from any particular national identity. He does not say, "I, Abe, am a realized being," any more than he says, "I speak as a Japanese." But the definitive and repetitive character of his written and spoken statements suggest that he speaks and writes *as* one who knows. He might well explain that this knowledge is not a matter of a subject making claims about himself and others, but an absolute insight that speaks through him (perhaps in the way that one's culture and particular conditioning are revealed through one's speech). Perhaps he could say that he, Abe, negates himself (his particularly formed self), in making such statements, or that he makes them not as their originator but as their representative. Logically, he could claim to be a nonaligned speaker, one who speaks from a stance of nondiscrimination. In fact, however, the context of these statements makes it clear that he is speaking explicitly as a representative of Buddhism and a critic of modern European culture.

Abe means his statement about the true Self to represent a transcultural Buddhist position in distinction to the rationalist position of the West. My concern here, as in the case of Suzuki, is not whether Abe's representation of Buddhism is accurate, nor whether he is right to present it as a critique of the West. I want rather to elucidate the implications of this representation in order to dislocate his position and expose another side to it. Abe's basic for-

[20] The precise wording here is my own. One version of Abe's formula is "…in the realization of nirvana, I am not I because I am egoless, and yet I am absolutely I because I am my true Self." Cf. "Buddhist Nirvana: Its Significance in Contemporary Thought and Life," in Masao Abe, *Zen and Western Thought* (Honolulu: University of Hawaii Press, 1985), 213.

mula, "Self is not self, therefore it is self," is of course an example of the so-called logic of *soku-hi* (即非)—*is* and at the same time *is not*—that Suzuki popularized as the core of Mahāyāna thought.[21] This logic finds its locus classicus in the Chinese version of the *Diamond Sūtra*. It has Sanskrit analogues and appears elsewhere in the Chinese Zen (Ch'an) tradition, but it seems to be singled out as a core expression of the Buddhist way of thinking only in Japan, and then especially when Japanese Zen Buddhists needed to distinguish their way of thinking from that of foreigners.[22] In the sixteenth century, when Japanese first encountered Europeans and Jesuits questioned Zen monks as to their doctrines, a typical response was "The true Dharma [teaching] of the Dharma is no Dharma; this Dharma—no Dharma—is nonetheless Dharma..."[23] Probably no one, however, has employed the *soku-hi* formula more widely than Abe, who uses it even to suggest to Christian theologians the true meaning of God's incarnation in Christ.[24] Abe's appeal to the traditional formula to explain a central doctrine of another religion accentuates commitment to the superiority of his Buddhist logic. In effect, Abe is presenting one historically Japanese convention as a prototype that purports to represent not Buddhism per se, nor the historical form of any particular religion, but the standpoint from which all truths are to be viewed. Nothing could appear less nationalistic or freed from the conditions of a particular culture or people. Yet ironically, as if to exemplify the sense of *soku* , a "state in which two things that seem to be different outside are one inside,"[25] Abe's *absolutism* turns out to be a particular Japanese *convention*.

[21] One of Suzuki's English formulations of this "logic of prajñā-intuition" is: "A is not A and therefore A is A. A is A because it is non-A." Cf. D. T. Suzuki, *Studies in Zen* (New York: Delta, 1955), 119–20.

[22] My claim here is a hypothesis. I have not yet determined the extent of usage of the 即非 formula in China.

[23] According to the Japanese convert who took the name Fabian. Cf. Heinrich Dumoulin, *Zen Buddhism: A History*, vol. II: Japan (New York: Macmillan, 1990), 269; based on the translation of Pierre Humberclaude in *Monumenta Nipponica* 1(1938): 529.

[24] "The Son of God is not the Son of God (for he is essentially and fundamentally self-emptying); precisely because he is not the Son of God, he is truly the Son of God (for he originally and always works as Christ, the messiah, in his salvational function of self-emptying." "Self is not self (for the old self must be crucified with Christ); precisely because it is not self, it is truly self (for the new self resurrects with Christ)." "God is not God (for God is love and completely self-emptying); precisely because God is not a self-affirmative God, God is truly a God of love (for through complete self-abnegation God is totally identical with everything including sinful humans)." John B. Cobb, Jr. and Christopher Ives, eds., *The Emptying God: A Buddhist-Jewish-Christian Conversation* (Maryknoll: Orbis Books, 1990), 12, 16.

[25] *Japanese-English Buddhist Dictionary*, entry on *soku* (Tokyo: Daitō Shuppansha, 1965), 307.

343

Anti-State Nationalism as Cultural Nationalism

But can this absolutist stance be called nationalistic? To answer this question, I turn now to the part of Abe's position that seems explicitly to preclude nationalism: his view of the "true community" as opposed to the nation-state. Abe explicitly connects this position with that of the true Self; in fact, in the essay I have cited, he presents the realization of the true Self as a condition for achieving true community. He articulates his vision of that ideal in verses set at the beginning of another essay entitled "Sovereignty Rests with Mankind." I quote all but the first of these verses and italicize lines I wish to emphasize:

> *The present crisis* of the world arises
> From the ceaseless conflicts and disputes
> *Of sovereign nations which do not know self-negation.*
> What we must establish now
> Is not an international confederacy
> In the sense of a league of sovereign nations.
> Even less should it be a world empire
> Based on one great sovereign state
> Which has acquired hegemony as a result of a struggle.
> Rather, it must be a world of mankind
> Wherein sovereignty rests precisely with all mankind
> In the sense of one self-aware entity
> Which has become profoundly aware of itself
> As "mankind."
>
> It must be *a human community without nation-states,*
> Wherein the dignity and freedom of the individual are guaranteed
> And wherein the multi-colored flowers of races
> And cultures may bloom.
> *The age of nation-states* as the bearers of history
> *Must proclaim its end,*
> And the age of mankind must begin.
>
> We must not despair of the historical evil
> Which has transcended the power of the individual.
> We must realize that *national egoism is mankind's karma*
> Deeply rooted in the essential nature of human beings.
> We must place mankind within a new cosmology
> Which has extricated itself from anthropocentrism.
> Is not the boundless "expanse of Self-awakening,"
> Which gives life to both self and other

As it sets up the distinction between them—
Is not this precisely the foundation of a new human society?[26]

Taken at face value, these lines suggest a straightforward criticism of nationalism. Sovereign nations "which do not know self-negation" are the cause of a global crisis; "national egoism" is related to transindividual evil in the world; and so the true community of the future must be "without nation-states," with sovereignty resting in one self-aware mankind. Abe's essay, an exegesis of these verses, concludes with the proclamation,

> Until now, the nation-state was necessary. Now, however, the nation-state has been transformed into a demonic existence. The age of the nation-state must end.... We must build a cooperative society of mankind within the universe.[27]

Obviously, Abe's is no ordinary nationalist tract. It belongs to an age that has seen through the perils of promoting a state at the expense of its people. But, once again, dislocating his position from a context where the focus is on his target exposes a different side. Let us begin with a look at the means Abe proposes for realizing the true community.

> We each must awaken to the root of world evil and historical evil deeply within the self and—in the identical foundation of self, the world, and history—we must awaken to the original Self which has broken through the ego. We must take the cosmological "expanse of Self-awakening" which opens up therein as the new foundation of mankind...transcending peoples and national boundaries...[28]

In Abe's view, the Self-awakening of each and every individual leads to a new foundation for humankind. There are three aspects of this path that deserve notice. First is the step of identifying Self-awakening with breaking through the ego. Among others, D. T. Suzuki has proposed this as the timeless core of Zen. Abe's sense of Self-awakening relates indirectly to Suzuki's claims about the true nature of Sino-Japanese Zen. Second, this path begins with the individual, who "must break through his or her ego structure," and leads directly to a universal transformation.[29] Abe recognizes three levels of humankind—"individuals, peoples, and mankind"—but he bypasses the role of a national people in transforming the world and establishing "a single government." His scheme does not acknowledge national contributions,

[26] "Sovereignty Rests with Mankind," in *Zen and Western Thought*, 249–50.

[27] "Sovereignty," 260.

[28] "Sovereignty," 260.

[29] "Sovereignty," 251.

whether by Japan or other nations. Third, Abe's path is not one among many but the only viable one; it is foundational. ?

> The source of the sovereign authority for mankind lies not in law or justice but rather in true Self-awakening. At the same time that true Self-awakening as "mankind" is the most internal authority for a human society, it is also the most transcendent authority.[30]

The view that [Zen] Self-awakening is the foundation of a new global society is possible, of course, only in an international world. We can trace this view to Abe's teacher, Hisamatsu Shin'ichi (1889–1984), and also find variants of it in Suzuki and in some of the Kyoto-school philosophers. There is of course nothing new in relating Zen to government or in applying ethnic spiritual values abroad. Previously in Japan, Eisai (1141–1215) had presented Zen as a protector of the nation (more precisely, of the state), and Nichiren and others preached a religious nationalism; but neither of them offered his religion as the foundation of a global community. Outside of Japan, the spiritual values of people like Mahatma Gandhi have been used to promote transnational harmony, but Gandhi himself directed his philosophy of self-reliance (*swadeshi*) and self-rule (*swaraj*) to the formation of an independent Indian nation. Their cases are different from Abe's, where a recognizably conventional absolutism (Hisamatsu's and Abe's version of Japanese Zen awakening) is declared the sole basis for unifying the world.

The dislocation of Abe's position reveals it as another example of veiled cultural nationalism, a kind of nationalism that cannot, indeed *must not*, appear to be a nationalism. It cannot afford to advocate the identity, values, and ideals of a particular people or ethnic group, because it speaks in the name of all peoples. Indeed, in the cases of Suzuki and Abe, this veiled cultural nationalism occurs as a critique of state nationalism: Abe denounces the sovereignty of nation-states, and Suzuki insisted that spirituality was different from the nationalistic spirit of a people. Suzuki's notion of spirituality, which celebrated non-difference, posed also as a critique of values, which are based upon the distinction between good and bad. I find that these critiques done in the name of something universal are nevertheless nationalist in the sense that their authors identify them as a standpoint (of Zen awakening or nondiscrimination) that has been best realized historically among one people. Cultural nationalism designates a *Volksidee* in the guise of a global ideal. In the name of universality it absorbs the "other" into itself ("by transcending the relative differences of self and other") or else rejects the identity of others as undesirable ("national egoism is mankind's karma").

---

[30] "Sovereignty," 253.

The point of the criticism is not that Abe or Suzuki perpetrate some kind of sinister or underhanded crime. In fact they probably would not recognize the nationalist undertones of their rhetoric, and their ideology is not easily judged as pernicious. But this intriguing ideology is, I think, a doubly beguiling intrigue, a scheme that promotes one set of values (cultural nationalism) in the name of another (universal spirituality/community) and that is invisible perhaps even to its advocates. Once again, this revelation becomes possible only by dislocating the original criticisms from their intended targets and viewing them as detached discourses in a different universe of concerns. On the one hand, I will be the first to admit that the same interests that underlie the dislocation of Suzuki's position are at work in my attempt to expose Abe's cultural nationalism. Relocating Abe's position, on the other hand, can expose the slant of ideologies closer to home. His critique of nation-states reminds us that the promotion of particular national values as a universal norm is certainly not a habit peculiar to the Japanese. We need only evoke the popular image of American democracy as the prototype of all world governments to see an instance of one nation's value system presented as the global foundation of political values. We shall have occasion to be reminded of such similarity later.

NISHITANI KEIJI'S GLOBALIST NATIONALISM

Global foundations for a philosophy of the nation-state were once the focus of intensive efforts by Nishitani Keiji (1900–1990), a thinker better known today for finding new ways to understand religion. Historians, however, have not forgotten Nishitani's political involvement during the war and have gone so far as to condemn him as a nationalist. An assessment of Nishitani's position will require that we go through the process of location, dislocation, and relocation more than once, not necessarily in that order, but following Nishitani's own transition from political concerns to a deliberately apolitical philosophy of religion.

The Nation in Global Perspective

It is not difficult to identify the critique in Nishitani's early political writings. Nishitani defines a position he intends to be international and opposes it to a Western philosophical position. In his widely-read work of 1941, *View of the World, View of the Nation* (世界観と国家観), Nishitani argued that it is not enough to understand the state (*kokka* 国家) simply as a legal entity (法的主体) over against individuals and their rights; it is a living being (生命体) that arises, grows, and perishes, a subject that operates politically within international power relations. To expand classical liberalism's protection of the

JOHN C. MARALDO

individual to the protection of a nation under international law, he implies, is really just to continue an intra-national view that tends to reduce the state to society and does not recognize its autonomy as a subject in its own right, a subject interacting with others.[31] The nation-state comes about when "a people awakens as a community (共同体) and forms as it were an individual living, acting body (一個の生きた行動体) in the political world."[32] Nishitani's critique is aimed at the narrow view of a nation from within, a legalist conception of a nation as a legal standard, that is, an artificial construct. In its place he proposes a new and now globally necessary externalist view of the nation-state, a kind of organic conception of nations as autonomous but interacting beings. Nationhood for Nishitani is not something created by contractual agreement, but rather something achieved by the self-awakening (自覚) of a people to their international role.

In its own terms, Nishitani's text appeals to his fellow Japanese to take up this view of their nation "from the outside." His work aims not only at European liberalist views of the state but implicitly at narrow-minded xenophobia within Japan as well. Yet his implied target of Japanese attitudes is still framed within the larger target of the "internalist" constructs of European political philosophy. It is significant that his argument takes European theories and authors as its primary point of reference. He proposes his theory not as a Japanese view of the world but as a worldview that sees "the modern nation-state as a universal phenomenon."[33]

To substantiate his argument he invokes earlier twentieth-century writings by European political theorists such as Rudolf Kjéllen (1846–1927) and Friedrich Meinecke (1862–1954). His theoretical opponents are likewise European, though long dead, political philosophers. Although unnamed, they are easy to recognize: the classical liberalists, such as Locke and Rousseau, and Engels as the propounder of the view that the state will rightly wither away upon realization of a truly communist society. Nishitani alludes to Communism as the extreme form of liberalism in its tendency to dissolve the state into society. This move is not unlike that which takes fascism as an extreme form of Edmund Burke's conservatism in its sanctification of the state.

My point is not to align Nishitani with classical conservatism, which for him would be another internalist view of the state, but to suggest how his text presents him as an international—not a Japanese—philosopher. Although his audience is clearly Japanese, the terms of his argument let him

[31] NKC 4:265–6. I focus here especially on the title essay of Nishitani's book. See the article by Mori Tetsurō, pages 31–62 in this volume, for further elaboration of the entire book.

[32] NKC 4:271.

[33] NKC 4:277.

348

set himself alongside European theorists arguing against other Europeans. His vision of awakening to the stage and "standpoint of transnational freedom, of worldhood or universal humanity"[34] is meant as his own contribution. If it ends in self-betrayal to function as a particularlist view, that view cannot easily be identified as a Japanese nationalist one—at least not yet.

During and after the war, Nishitani's position was targeted for criticism from two sides, neither of which were the primary object of his original critique. In effect these two diametrically opposed critiques both dislocated Nishitani's position from its intended international context and from his specifically European target. On the one side were Japanese "rightists," who presumably read *View of the World, View of the Nation* as an internationalist (and thus antinationalist) treatise endorsing a "universal humanity." They considered him a turncoat (非国民), as he reports, and had him investigated by the Special Higher Police. On the other side were "leftists" and those who after the war recanted their complicity in the nation's war efforts. In what terms the real dissidents criticized his book at the time it was published I do not know. Presumably, under the conditions of an oppressive regime, their voices would have been muted if not totally censored. It is clear that, after the war at least, they read Nishitani's book—especially in light of his wartime dialogues—as endorsing an antidemocratic state acting as a world power. Nishitani was subject to the purge of the Allied Occupation Forces and forced to resign from Kyoto University from 1947 until 1952. Although the precise circumstances remain clouded in some mystery, the latter interpretation of Nishitani's work undoubtedly had something to do with his temporary expulsion.

What is more startling than this slap on the left cheek and slap on the right, as Nishitani puts it,[35] is the contrast between his sense of reality and that of his critics. *View of the World, View of the Nation* was, in Nishitani's view forty-four years later, "the first book which attempted to analyze, from a *philosophic* point of view, the historical *reality* of that time in terms of world politics (and of Japan as a country viewed from that same perspective)."[36] Postwar critics, in contrast, read in Nishitani's work an ultranationalist's support of a nation on the road to infamy. To more recent and more accommodating critics, the reality appears to be that his work propounded an idealist

---

[34] NKC 4:284.

[35] See his letter of May 1984 to Yusa Michiko, quoted in her reminiscence, "The Eternal is the Transient Is the Eternal" in *The Eastern Buddhist* 25, 1 (Spring 1992): 152.

[36] Quoted from the letter to Yusa. Nishitani says his is the first book, but an essentially similar approach may have already been taken in 高坂正顕 Kōsaka Masaaki, 歴史的世界 [The historical world] (Tokyo: Iwanami Shoten, 1937) and in 高山岩男 Kōyama Iwao, 世界史の理念 [The idea of world history], 思想 215 (1940): 1–20; 216 (1940): 1–52.

vision of universal humanity but in effect advanced the *Realpolitik* of an aggressive nation-state. Between his sense of historical reality and the reality felt by later critics, a radical shift of perspective has occurred. But to see how this happened, we will need to relocate Nishitani's position in a wider context that makes room for both.

I have suggested that although Nishitani's intended audience is Japanese, the terms of his worldview set him among European philosophers. In a wider context we can see him as speaking not so much to his fellow Japanese and their political leaders as to the philosophers with whom he is discoursing in a global forum. We can hear him basing what he has to say not so much on actual observations of conflict between or within nations, or even on dialogues with his own opponents, as on interpretations of political theories. Even the theoretical targets of his critique are narrower than their common names—classical liberal democratic theory and Communism—might suggest. Nishitani reproaches social-contract theory for its lack of international political and historical consciousness, but he does not criticize Western theoretical rationalizations of colonialism. He faults Communist theory for its view that the state is ultimately disposable, but does not examine communist justifications for a totalitarian state.

The changes in worldview that Nishitani advocates are changes in the way we should see things; they are contemplative changes in political theories. His argument is posed against anything that resembles social-scientific analysis or positivistic history. He is talking political theory from the heights, not the "real politics" of everyday life or international warfare. Although he does not write in the name of Japan, nor simply side with Japan, he argues in a way that positions him as a representative of one nation-state among others, even if this takes the form of posturing as one philosopher among other philosophers.

Was Nishitani's idealization of globality an effect in part of the limited and controlled news accessible to him and his countrymen? Was it his way of finding an alternative to an increasingly oppressive everyday existence in the Kyoto of 1941? These questions, of course, abandon a reading of the text in its own terms as an appeal to national and even global change of theory, and instead place the text in the range of more recent sensitivities to post-Marxist and post-Freudian critical theory. As I knew him forty years later, Nishitani was not favorably disposed toward any *Ideologiekritik* or reading of texts that cross-examines terms for their rhetorical effects or political conditioning. Was that because his text had long ago been read in a contradictory manner, as rhetoric that led to exploitation and was itself subject to exploitation?

The contradiction explicitly mentioned in Nishitani's text is that between the two principles of freedom and the power of authority, a contradiction that the nation-state (国民国家) is supposed to reconcile at its center point.

350

But Nishitani does not name Japan as that central point of encounter nor as an authoritative power in conflict with freedom.[37] Indeed, the relative paucity of direct references to Japan is striking in the title essay of *View of the World, View of the Nation*. The connection with Japan is made more explicit in the afterword that Nishitani appended in 1946 to restate his intention more explicitly.

The afterword is in effect Nishitani's own attempt to relocate his position. There he distances himself from nationalism and explains the rationale of his treatise:

> The basic point at which my thought broke with nationalism (国家主義) is that it regarded the global nature of the nation as a subjectivity of non-ego brought about through self-negation, and that [it proposed] this standpoint must somehow open up not only within Japan but within all nations.[38]

In other words, when the nation is conceived as a subject (主体), then, like the individual, it could be self-centered or self-denying. For Nishitani, nationalism is not only politically and psychologically self-engrossed; it is existentially deficient and does not do justice to the true vocation of the nation in the postmodern era. Nishitani claims his fundamental standpoint was a self-negation "necessary if the nation is to make the transition from modernity to a new mode of being," namely a national existence that integrates the universal or global element. Lest we mistake this conceptual incorporation for a de facto annexation of other nations, Nishitani reminds us that he "criticized the Nazi's idea of the state and proposed in place of its totalitarian standpoint a 'patriotism based on a moral of global self-awakening and universal humanity'."[39] He concludes his reflections by again identifying his work as a critique of nationalism that offered an alternative: "I tried...to open up a path in thought that might overcome from within the ideas of extreme nationalism that were taking control at the time."[40] It is only in view of certain published discussions between the time of the publication of Nishitani's treatise and its afterword that this rationale could come to appear as a gross rationalization.

Nationalism Exposed: The Chūōkōron Discussions

In November 1941, thirteen days before the attack on Pearl Harbor, Nishitani joined Kōsaka Masaaki, Kōyama Iwao, and Suzuki Shigetaka for the

[37] NKC 4:271.
[38] NKC 4:381.
[39] NKC 4:382. He refers himself to pages 275, 287, 291, and 295.
[40] NKC 4:384.

first of the now infamous round-table discussions published in *Chūōkōron*. The context of the discussions and the circumstances under which they arose are not my concern here.[41] Although any conclusive interpretation of the authors' *intended* meaning must take that context into account, I choose here to begin with the dislocation of Nishitani's position, precisely in order to give credence to later criticisms launched at him. I will select passages from Nishitani that have proven particularly offensive to postwar Japanese and Western critics. I am convinced that only then can we understand the reason for the outrage over Kyoto-school political philosophy. It would be possible to quote other passages in the discussions that probably would have provoked the ire of intellectuals to the right and occasioned the censure of the Special Higher Police. (In fact, the *Chūōkōron* journal itself came under repeated attack by these factions for the "liberal" articles it published, and was frequently censured and eventually shut down in July 1944.[42]) Such a selection might note that Nishitani advocates more education about European history in Japanese schools and gives absolutely no homage to the emperor. While quoting other passages might present a slight counterbalance to postwar condemnations of Kyoto-school political philosophy, it would not exonerate Nishitani in the eyes of the critics.

There are, I think, three more or less explicit claims in particular that disturb postwar critics:

1. It is Japan's unique mission to uphold and uplift the peoples of East Asia, enabling them to establish a new world order against Western colonialism and imperialism.

2. The oppressive colonialists and imperialists are Britain, America, and Holland, not Germany and Italy (not to speak of Japan).

3. The Japanese state's unique role and opportunity is justified by the relatively superior historical consciousness and achievement of the Japanese people or race.

Concomitantly, three assumptions underlie the umbrage taken at these claims: that Japan was an aggressor and perpetrated numerous atrocities against East Asian peoples, including Okinawans, Koreans, and others within their country; that Japan, Germany, and Italy were the imperialists in World

---

[41] See the essay by Horio Tsutomu, pages 289–315 in this volume, for a full explication. I deliberately avoid the question whether editors later whitewashed the discussions to make them acceptable to the authorities.

[42] See Hatanaka Shigeo, "Bringing the Liberals to Heel" and "Thought Criminal," in Cook and Cook, *Japan at War*, 64–8, 222–7.

War II; and that the rhetoric of a superior race and a new world order is no more than a thinly veiled rationalization of the oppression of other cultures.

In light of these assumptions, Nishitani's remarks are particularly startling in the second and third discussions that took place in March and November 1942 respectively. In these sessions we find Nishitani repeatedly condemning the "hypocrisy of Anglo-American democracy," that is, its economic exploitation of other peoples, for its own prosperity and satisfaction, in the name of advancing their self-determination and freedom. Japan's historically necessitated mission to elevate the Asian peoples to something befitting the races of a Greater East Asia, according to Nishitani, is a different case.[43] He stresses that Japan has a privileged role to play in the development of East Asian peoples and of a new world order for the entire globe. "This strikes me as something very singular," he asserts, referring to Japan's particular awareness of being a "world-historical race" (世界史的民族)—different from previous "world-historical" peoples like the Greeks, Romans, or Israelites by virtue of its awareness emerging out of constructive praxis and not merely historical necessity. Japan's "moral energy" enabled it, unlike other Asian countries, to digest European culture and technology voluntarily, in a very short time, without being either colonized or overcome culturally, and hence to prevent the colonization of China.[44]

At the same time that Nishitani elevates the Japanese people over other Asians, he is careful to distinguish Japan's motive from that of European states in a similar position: "In the case of Japan, Germany, and Italy, insuring one's own survival against the forces of other countries requires committing the nation to ground itself radically on racial unity." But Japan is not like the Nazis, who "have put forth a particular racial strain (人種)" and who "lack an intellectual position with a world-historical outlook." Germany's new world order is a repartitioning of colonies, "an idea greatly at odds with Japan's ideal of giving each country its due place."[45] Japan can do this by educating the Asian peoples, thus opening their eyes to racial or ethnic self-awareness and making them into something with the power to act autonomously. Yet Japan must maintain a leadership role. "The fundamental question is how to reconcile this contradiction."[46] A little further on, Nishitani notes that Japan's population is too small to construct the Greater East Asia Sphere by itself, and wonders whether it might be possible "to turn

[43] CK, 351.

[44] CK, 159–60.

[45] CK, 192, 198. This last remark implies that race was not biologically determined for Nishitani, for education, not intermarriage, is the way of incorporating other "races" into the Japanese race.

[46] CK, 205.

those races [of Asia] with superior qualities [but without a strong sense of their own history and culture] into a kind of 'half-Japanese...' in the sense of educating them until spiritually they are exactly the same as the Japanese."[47]

Nishitani's words, dislocated from their context and the opponent at whom they were directed, easily lend credence to the charge of outrageous nationalism. It will take some relocating to find any plausibility today in that nationalism. Much of what Nishitani says in these sessions indeed has the ring of the wartime government propaganda that identified the Japanese people with the state, solicited personal sacrifice for the sake of the war, and justified all-out war both as a self-defense and as the construction of an autonomous East Asia. The tone changes somewhat, however, when we vary the translation and substitute grammatical subjects. Replacing *Japan* with *America*, *spiritual development* with *economic development*, and *race* with *ethnicity*, what is at first shocking begins to sound much more familiar. After these substitutions, we are not so far from the popular sentiment that America is a superior nation incorporating various ethnic groups that, by virtue of its moral sense of justice and economic and military strength, has a duty to advance and protect its values globally. In one place[48] the text would read:

> On the one hand, we must open the eyes of the various ethnic groups to ethnic consciousness and empower them to participate actively and voluntarily; and on the other, the United States must continue to maintain its position of leadership.

We are not so remote from some official government policies, either, as we see in statements by two past American presidents. Harry Truman's inaugural address defined half the world as "underdeveloped areas" and proclaimed the path of their deliverance from suffering: "Greater production is the key to prosperity and peace."[49] The entire globe, and not merely the individual colonies claimed by particular nations, had become the arena of economic development and education.[50] It was in this global arena that President George Bush could pronounce, soon after the air attack that launched the Gulf War in response to Iraq's invasion of Kuwait:

[47] CK, 262–3.

[48] CK, 205.

[49] Cited in Wolfgang Sachs, "The Archeology of the Development Idea," *Interculture* 23/4 (Fall 1990): 3. Sachs notes that "the idea of defining the [whole] world as an economic arena was completely alien to colonialism." He also distinguishes the economic mandate predominant in Truman's policy from the colonialist mandate to elevate the "colored races."

[50] The school primers that were used to teach Filipinos to read English illustrate the bias of America's self-mandated education of a "Commonwealth." "*A* is for apple," the books began—but there were no apples in the Philippines.

We are Americans—part of something larger than ourselves.... What is at stake is more than one small country [Kuwait], it is a big idea—a new world order, where diverse nations are drawn together in common cause to achieve universal aspirations of mankind....[51]

The point of these substitutions is to let us hear the war-period Japanese rhetoric in a different way. It is not to excuse one crime by pointing a finger at the accuser, nor to evade the question of what kind of actions were rationalized by the rhetoric. We might also expect more of a philosopher like Nishitani than we would of an American president or a government bureaucrat when it comes to ethical judgments about war. Yet even with these caveats, the similarity in rhetoric, if not in the final justification of actions, is striking, and lets us see that wartime Japanese rationalizations have something in common with current American ideals.

Another dimension is added to this comparison when we recognize statements in the round-table discussions that remind us of recent critiques of Western cultural imperialism and Eurocentrism:

While to Europe Asia was seen as no more than a source of raw materials for its own activities, for us the problem was how to counter Europe's activism with our own. [Instead of a partner in dialogue] Europe's position was one of an exclusive 'I'.[52]

Of course, Japan's own history of colonialism, and the Japan-centrism at the heart of the discussions, prevent such statements from ever serving as a credible postcolonial critique. Nevertheless, the substitution of terms and contexts might unsettle the self-righteousness the contemporary critic feels in condemning the *Chūōkōron* discussions.

This relocation of Nishitani's remarks in the *Chūōkōron* round-table sessions still leaves the answers to crucial questions unanswered. These questions continue to cast a shadow over all his previous and following writings. Was Nishitani deceiving himself or others? Was he covering up his culpability? Was he sincere but mistaken? Or was he justified in claiming in the afterword of 1946 that *View of the World, View of the Nation* was a critique of nationalism? Answers will of course depend upon just what brand of nationalism we have in mind. I suggest that in the 1940s he did not set himself up as an advocate of state or ethnic nationalism, but of a globalism that seriously mistook his nation's capacity to negate itself and overcome self-centeredness. If this was a case of mistaken judgment on his part, however, he never admitted as much, not even when the Occupation forces had him suspended from his university

---

[51] From Bush's State of the Union Address on 29 January 1991.

[52] CK, 11–12.

post in the purge of intellectuals thought to have collaborated in the war. His few postwar political writings make this consistency clear.

Nishitani's Postwar or Suprahistorical View

In 1949 Nishitani published a brief but remarkable essay called "The Duty to Criticize and the Problem of Fascism."[53] The target of his analysis is soon apparent. Nishitani aimed his critique at unnamed, postwar critics of Japan's past and his own. But he turns the tables on them by dislocating their position from its target, Japanese ultranationalism, and placing it in a framework provided by Nietzsche. He begins by recalling Nietzsche's "Uses and Abuses of History for Life," a writing that finds a healthy use for forgetfulness and attacks the German esteem for history and Hegel's rationalization of it. "There is a limit [difficult to know], beyond which the past must be forgotten if it is not to be the gravedigger of the present."[54] Nishitani paraphrases this statement of Nietzsche to stress that a certain kind of preoccupation with the past will cripple a people's ability to act in the present and continue to create its life. There are, to be sure, different kinds of forgetfulness and different kinds of historical consciousness, he says, and reminds the reader of Nietzsche's "critical kind of history" and his qualification that "the unhistorical and the historical are equally necessary for the health of an individual, a people, and a culture."[55] The forgetfulness advocated does not call one to divert one's eyes from the past and then forget it, nor to see the past as a nightmare; rather the capacity to forget entails not being able to forget. It is a matter of "resigning" oneself to what has passed *as* something that has passed. It involves the creative ability of a man, people, or culture "to grow out of itself, transforming and assimilating everything past and alien, to heal wounds, replace what is lost and reshape broken forms out of itself" (once again Nishitani quotes Nietzsche.)[56] This, however, is not the kind of creative forgetfulness that Japan is engaged in after the war. Rather, it has fallen into its old habit of trying to forget. Critiques have become merely external, not arising out of real necessity; they are advanced by *Kritiker ohne Not*. Such critics ignore their own past and begin their critiques only postwar, after the fact. They colonize the spirit of a people or their "soul," that is, their "creative power to grow out of [themselves]."

[53] 批判の任務とファシズムの問題, NKC 4:452–63.

[54] *On the Advantage and Disadvantage of History for Life*, trans. by Peter Preuss (Indianapolis: Hackett Publishing Co., 1980), 10.

[55] NKC 4:453; Preuss, 10.

[56] NKC 4:454; Preuss, 10.

356

In contrast, Nishitani wrote, we should see the danger of fascism in its turning an originally transfactional (超党派的) standpoint, that of a transfactional life of a people, into the standpoint of a faction, turning the soul of a people (国民の魂) into an ideology. Fascism factionalizes the life of a national people by fixating on one form, thus stifling the power of creativity and depriving us of the search for new forms. But criticism, too, can play into the hands of fascism by optimistically taking it as a matter of past "imperialism" advanced by a power-hungry handful of people, instead of asking why fascism arises and whether the conditions and parameters of its emergence still exist. Unless the critique recognizes the possibility of fascism within itself and purifies its terms from within, it only targets others and misses the real danger.

Nishitani's critique has dislocated positions he thinks were not well anchored in the first place, because they never reflected on themselves. Some relocation of positions, his own as well as his critics, brings home the point of his exhortation to criticize, but also turns it against him. One hears in his essay the voice of a man arguing for unity and harmony, for a stance that would absorb the past and move on, that would, in its invocation of Nietzsche's "assimilation [of] everything past and alien," resist any distancing, critical or not, from past judgments, mistaken or not. In the statement that fascism factionalizes "the life and soul of a people," one hears echoes reverberating in the foreign idiom of today's historical critique that the wartime writings promoted particularism in the name of universalism.[57] But the message is not univocal, and one can also detect a credible if faint warning for present-day critics: the end of the war did bring on a rupture in the history of Japan, but the task is to begin with that rupture, not *after* it, not treating it as a discontinuity. The task is to tie critical thinking to that rupture, to "repeat" it and "sever the roots of oneself" as Nietzsche says, thereby planting new roots in history, activating creative power, and letting history be useful for life.[58] To overcome fascism, we must face it squarely and clarify the ambiguities of "democracy," "freedom," "fascism," and "totalitarianism." We must enter into the problem of fascism by questioning, now and then, the awakening of the soul of the people and its creative power. To look at fascism as a matter of the past, as other people's affairs, is to create a condition for its [re]emergence. That is factitious criticism, *Kritik ohne Not*. To draw oneself into the past really means to draw the past into oneself, for the

---

[57] This critique is most trenchantly advanced by Naoki Sakai in "Modernity and Its Critique," in Masao Miyoshi and H. D. Harootunian, eds., *Postmodernism and Japan* (Durham: Duke University Press, 1989), especially 109.

[58] NKC 4:461–2.

past is a problem of the present and is overcome only by confronting it as past, not simply letting it pass away.[59]

Ironically, this warning provides the basis for a contemporary criticism of Nishitani. He himself, it appears, neglected to confront his past involvement with Japanese expansionist policies. In "The Duty to Criticize," Nishitani seems to forget statements in Nietzsche's essay that would place his own direction in question. Nietzsche evaluates not only forgetfulness or the "unhistorical" that prevents historical consciousness from crippling creativity; he also names, toward the end of his essay, the "suprahistorical" (*das Über-historische*) as another antidote to this "historical sickness." "By 'suprahistorical' I mean the powers that divert one's view from becoming toward that which gives existence the character of the eternal and the equivalent—toward art and religion."[60] Nietzsche's own evaluation of the suprahistorical is ambivalent. In the first section of the essay, he parodies those who would "progress" and leave behind "the wisdom and nausea of the suprahistorical men [for whom] the past and the present are one and the same...a static structure of unchanged value and eternally the same meaning, [for whom] the world is complete and achieves its end at every single moment."[61] By the end, he finds hope in the youth, the "hopeful ones" who may someday "again be well enough to engage in studying history anew and to use history under the dominion of life."[62] Nishitani, for his part, had by this time quite definitely "progressed" to the suprahistorical. He soon abandoned attempts at political philosophy and devoted himself increasingly to the problem of religion in a scientific age.[63]

Earlier in 1949, during his banishment from Kyoto University, Nishitani gave a series of talks on a problem far more serious to him than fascism. Although that problem is not often conceived to be a political one, a location of the layers of Nishitani's target will reveal a political side to his new critique.

---

[59] NKC 4:459–61.

[60] "Vom Nutzen und Nachtheil der Historie für das Leben," in *Friedrich Nietzsche Sämtliche Werke: Kritische Studienausgabe I* (Munich: Deutscher Taschenbuch Verlag, 1980), 330. The translations by both Preuss and Adrian Collins have, mistakenly I think, *stable* for *gleichbedeutend*.

[61] Preuss, 13.

[62] Preuss, 63.

[63] After "The Duty to Criticize and the Problem of Fascism," Nishitani to my knowledge published only two short pieces devoted primarily to political concerns: 講和と自衛の在り方 [A way of peace and self-defense], 中央公論 (1 March 1952): 4–15; and 自衛についての再論 [Another argument on self-defense], 中央公論 (1 May 1952): 22–32, which was a reply to the response of 市川白弦 Ichikawa Hakugen, 「負わされた現実」の哲学 [The philosophy of "bearing the burden of actuality"], in the same issue. Reprinted in IHC 3:276–82.

On the surface the critique is explicitly aimed at "nihilism." Understood for the most part as a plight of modern European civilization that inflicts the individual soul, nihilism spread to Japan, in Nishitani's view, and thus affects a people nationally as well as the soul individually. Even in its own terms, therefore, a political reading of his book *Nihilism* is possible. This is especially true of the last chapter, "The Meaning of Nihilism for Japan."[64]

Nihilism came to Japan, Nishitani contends, at the time of the Meiji Restoration. Japan was then "cast on the stage of world politics" and underwent, from the perspective of "political history," the greatest change in its history. From that of "spiritual history," however, this great change precipitated a momentous crisis that was all the more critical because it went unnoticed. "Our spiritual core began to decay" after the Meiji Restoration, "until it is now a vast, gaping void in our ground."[65] Japan began to be severed from its spiritual traditions (Buddhism and Confucianism), which were the source of its ideas, ethics, and faith. To be sure, the Westernization of Japan was not simply forced upon it from the outside, but was "impelled by a powerful [national] will from within." Once underway, the vitality of a national (民族的) "moral energy" began to weaken and a split appeared in the subject pursuing its will. On the one side, Japanese intellectuals experienced (perhaps unconsciously?) a loss of spiritual self. On the other:

> National moral energy gradually metamorphosed into the violence of exclusionist and uncultured 'patriots' as a reaction against this loss of self. The self was clung to without consideration for others, or for the historical context...this, too, was a loss of ties to the historical ground."[66]

Nishitani's own context makes it clear that he is identifying the self (自己) here with "the culture" (文化).

Nihilism in Japan, then, is not the result of the war; quite the contrary, the statement about misguided patriots implies that the war is the consequence of nihilism. The aftermath of Westernization was not so much the emulation of Western imperialism and colonialism (which he does not mention) as the erosion of the tradition that had given the Meiji leaders their wisdom and moral energy. Nishitani invokes Nietzsche's call for a "return to the ancestors" in order to "redeem what is noble in the tradition" and "to face the future, [for] without a will toward the future, the confrontation with the

---

[64] The book has been republished as volume 8 of Nishitani's *Collected Writings*. The translation by Graham Parkes and Setsuko Aihara, *The Self-Overcoming of Nihilism* (Albany: SUNY Press, 1990), rearranges the order of the chapters. The quotations here are from this translation.

[65] *The Self-Overcoming of Nihilism*, 175.

[66] *The Self-Overcoming of Nihilism*, 177.

past cannot be properly executed." We [Japanese] are called to awaken to the crisis that has become *our historical reality.*[67]

At this point it has become evident that behind the name of nihilism is what we call the modernization of Japan. This forms the less visible layer of Nishitani's target. His critique in *The Self-Overcoming of Nihilism,* as the title has been translated, is a continuation of the debate on "overcoming modernity." But there is another side to the solution Nishitani proposes, as well. This side does not become apparent until we begin to dislocate his position from its own focus on the problem of modernity in Japan. Nishitani's own terms initiate the dislocation.

The way to overcome nihilism is to recover "our own tradition." But one does not have to go far to see that Nishitani's recovery is actually a step into the suprahistorical. In philosophical terms we might expect such a step, if nihilism means that history has no ground or reason and if nihilism is to be overcome. For Nishitani, tradition has been lost, and its recovery cannot mean pining after a bygone era. Rather the task is to rediscover tradition

> from the ultimate point where it is grasped in advance as "the end" (or eschaton) of our Westernization and of Western civilization itself...[it] must be appropriated from the direction in which we are heading, as a new possibility...the point is to recover the creativity that mediates the past to the future and the future to the past....[68]

Nishitani speaks in this context of problematizing the tradition, that of "Eastern culture" in general, and the Buddhist standpoint of "emptiness" and "nothingness" in particular. It soon becomes clear that to make Buddhism a problem means to view problems in its terms, that the Buddhist tradition is to be retrieved not as a historically conditioned phenomenon, but as the standpoint of the groundless ground of all phenomena. At the end of *Nihilism* Nishitani quotes Nāgārjuna: "By virtue of emptiness everything is able to arise, but without emptiness nothing whatsoever can arise."[69]

In subsequent works, especially *What Is Religion* published in 1961,[70] the "spiritual culture of the Orient"[71] to be recovered by the Japanese people has tacitly become the universal standpoint of emptiness [*śūnyatā*] to be personally realized by everyone. What is left of the perspective of political history is a muted echo of its difference from Nietzsche's suprahistorical equivalence:

---

[67] *The Self-Overcoming of Nihilism,* 177–8.

[68] *The Self-Overcoming of Nihilism,* 179.

[69] *The Self-Overcoming of Nihilism,* 180.

[70] Translated by Jan Van Bragt as *Religion and Nothingness.*

[71] *The Self-Overcoming of Nihilism,* 181.

Historicity is able to realize itself radically only on the standpoint of *śūnyatā* [emptiness], the standpoint of the bottomlessness of each moment. Each individual moment of unending time possesses the very same solemnity that is thought in Christianity to be possessed by the special moments of the creation, fall, redemption, and second coming. In bottomlessly embracing the endless past and endless future, we bring to fullness each and every moment of time.[72]

Each individual moment here is what Nishitani's teacher, Nishida, had called the "self-determination of the absolute present."

The nation too, in Nishida's view, was such a "self-determination of the absolute present," was itself a kind of subject (主体) that must not become too "subjective" or self-centered. By the time Nishitani himself published his opus on religion, however, the nation-subject of *View of the World* had bottomed out into a personal self that awakens to its selflessness. Nishitani had abandoned his political view, but after all, wasn't that *View of the Nation* also the object of later criticisms of him? At the same time, he did not need to abandon history, at least as historians research it, because he had never taken up such research in the first place. What Nishitani himself pursued was the project he had always had his sights set on: the task of providing religious foundations for our understanding of the world, the world to come as well as the world that was. Any fuller relocation of Nishitani's positions would have to take into account the wealth of critical discussions that have come out of his reinterpretations of Buddhism and Christianity. In the modest bounds of their own world, at least, these discussions continue to make history.

CONCLUSION

Criticisms of nationalism, even with the best of intentions, can display a nationalistic side of their own when considered in the context of the effects they produce. D. T. Suzuki indirectly criticized the national spirit from a position that today would count as cultural nationalism. Abe Masao condemns the nation-state in the name of a global awakening, which conceals the bias of cultural nationalism once again. Nishitani Keiji targeted liberal democratic views of the nation-state and Eurocentric views of the world, and seemed to promote Japanese expansionism. He later criticized fascism and its critics, dissociating himself from both, and so displayed an increasing lack of interest in the blunders of history that continue to vex our historical conscience.

---

[72] This translation of passages in 宗教とは何か (NKC 10:299) is an earlier rendition by Jan Van Bragt. See RN, 272, for another version.

In a wider context of effects, however, the critique of these criticisms wraps back upon *all* the critics involved. Cultural nationalism, as often as not, turns out to be the concern of cultures repenting of their former drive to hegemony. Historical consciousness becomes an increasing need for those aware of possible complicity, their own included, in historical mistakes. From our collective experience, we do want to render judgments where we perceive the mistakes of others: "He should have done this instead of that, said this instead of that; he should have strenuously objected, recanted, apologized...." We also know from experience that one day our verdicts will likely meet with criticism. And yet this knowledge can free us to be open to continued questioning. If there is no end to the process of critique, it is not because a final judgment is perpetually deferred, but because the goal is so close at hand: always to remember that the past is a problem of the present. Critique of nationalism is ultimately also self-critique.

Cumulative Index

Cumulative Index

Abe Hiroyoshi 安部博純, 175–6

Abe Masao 阿部正雄, vii, x, xiv, 43, 46, 160, 336, 341–7, 361

Abe Yoshishige 阿倍能成, 113, 120, 205

Absolute Nothingness, 26, 159–60, 163, 226, 245, 248, 275, 294–5; and Zen/Buddhism, 50–1, 233, 278–9, 284; and historical consciousness, 305, 322; and human rights, 252–4; and nationalism, 28, 166, 186, 257, 273, 281, 287, 303. *See also* Nothingness.

Action-intuition/active intuition, 23, 137, 140, 161–2

Aesthetics, 185, 205, 221, 223, 225, 233

Affirmation-in-negation, 276

Aggression, 32, 38, 51, 81–2, 85, 184, 189, 194, 255, 333

Aihara Setsuko 相原節子, 247, 359

Aihara Shinsaku 相原信作, 85–6, 268

Aizawa Saburō 相沢三郎, 22

Akashi Yōji 明石陽至, 272

Akazawa Shirō 赤沢史朗, 176

Akizawa Shūji 秋沢修二, 259

"All the world under one roof," 31, 39, 126–7, 169, 310. *See also* Hakkō ichiu.

All-out war, 240, 255, 262, 269–70, 274, 294, 311–12, 354

Amano Teiyū 天野貞祐, 120, 146

Amaterasu-ō-mikami, 141–2

America: Kyoto School and, vii, 233, 254; D. T. Suzuki and, 52, 55–6, 66–7, 72–3; and World War II, 77–8, 80–3, 85, 213, 303, 310

Americanism, 167, 177, 188–9, 210, 227–8, 291, 299–300, 30

Amida, 331

Analects, 58

Anarchism, 17, 26, 66, 203

Anthropocentrism, 138, 344

Arahitogami 現人神, 282

Arendt, Hannah, 50

Arima, Tatsuo, 36–7

Arisaka Yōko 有坂陽子, 151–2, 155–6

Aristocracy, 57, 78, 118

Aristotelian thought, 159–60, 281, 287

Army, Japanese: aggressions of, 82, 199, 255; and nationalism, 39, 176, 184, 186, 201; Nishida's relationship with, viii, 32, 37, 82, 90–1, 97, 122, 124; and Marxism, 203–4, 206; D. T. Suzuki and, 62, 64; Tanabe Hajime and, 269–70; and *Chūōkōron* discussions, 290–1, 300–3, 307, 310; Zen influence, 3–4, 8, 10

Arthavargīya Sūtra (義足経), 3

Asada Akira 浅田 彰, 152

Asano Akira 浅野 晃, 214

Asceticism, 211, 313

Ashida Hitoshi 芹田 均, 205

Ashikaga 足利 family, 126

Atheism, 164, 207

Atomic bomb, 81

Babylonian captivity, 98, 125, 172

Bakufu 幕府, 178, 191

Bankei Yōtaku 盤珪永琢, 59, 68

Baroni, Helen, 49

Bary, W. T. de, 154

Basho 場所, 160, 162, 164, 168, 171

Bashō. *See* Matsuo Bashō.

Bauer, Otto, 183

Beheiren ベ平連, 12

Being-in-the-one-world, 103

Bellah, Robert, 236–8, 241, 249, 251